RESURRECTION IN PAUL

EARLY CHRISTIANITY AND ITS LITERATURE

David G. Horrell, General Editor

Editorial Board:
Warren Carter
Amy-Jill Levine
Judith M. Lieu
Margaret Y. MacDonald
Dale B. Martin

Number 19

RESURRECTION IN PAUL

Cognition, Metaphor, and Transformation

Frederick S. Tappenden

 PRESS

Atlanta

Copyright © 2016 by SBL Press

All rights reserved. No part of this work may be reproduced or transmitted in any form or by any means, electronic or mechanical, including photocopying and recording, or by means of any information storage or retrieval system, except as may be expressly permitted by the 1976 Copyright Act or in writing from the publisher. Requests for permission should be addressed in writing to the Rights and Permissions Office, SBL Press, 825 Houston Mill Road, Atlanta, GA 30329 USA.

Library of Congress Cataloging-in-Publication Data

Names: Tappenden, Frederick S., author.
Title: Resurrection in Paul : cognition, metaphor, and transformation / by Frederick S. Tappenden.
Description: Atlanta : SBL Press, 2016. | Series: Early Christianity and its literature ; Number 19 | Includes bibliographical references and index.
Identifiers: LCCN 2015049192 (print) | LCCN 2015050113 (ebook) | ISBN 9780884141440 (pbk. : alk. paper) | ISBN 9780884141464 (hardcover : alk. paper) | ISBN 9780884141457 (ebook)
Subjects: LCSH: Bible. Epistles of Paul—Theology. | Resurrection—Biblical teaching.
Classification: LCC BS2655.R35 T37 2016 (print) | LCC BS2655.R35 (ebook) | DDC 236/.8092—dc23
LC record available at http://lccn.loc.gov/2015049192

Printed on acid-free paper.

For my parents,

Alan and Connie Tappenden

Contents

Preface and Acknowledgments ix
Tables and Figures xiii
Abbreviations xv

1. The Disembodiment of Resurrection: Literature Review,
   Problem Definition, and the Integration of Cognition and
   Culture 1
   1.1. Introduction   1
   1.2. On Cognicentrism and Mind-Body Dualism   3
   1.3. Literature Review and Problem Definition   7
   1.4. Theory and Method: Integrating Cognition and Culture   33
   1.5. Overview of the Study   40

2. Imaging Resurrection: Toward an Image-Schematic
   Understanding of Resurrection Belief in Paul and in
   Second Temple Judaism 43
   2.1. Second Temple Judaism and the RESURRECTION Gestalt   46
   2.2. Paul's Appropriation of the RESURRECTION Gestalt   72
   2.3. Conclusions   85

3. "We Will All Be Changed": On Dualism/Monism, Plants, and
   the Peculiarity of Wearing a House 87
   3.1. Concentric Circles of Cultural Embodiment   88
   3.2. Transformation and Resurrection   102
   3.3. Conclusions   132

4. Eschatological Somatology: Identifying the Already and the
   Not Yet in Paul 135
   4.1. Baptismal Death in Romans 6:1–11   137
   4.2. Anthropology and Ethics in Romans 7   146

4.3. Trajectories of Transformative Embodiment in
       Romans 8:9–11 — 155
  4.4. Paul's Eschatological Somatology — 164
  4.5. Conclusions — 171

5. Participating in Resurrection: UNION, Mutual Affectivity, and Ethnicity — 175
  5.1. Resurrection and UNION — 177
  5.2. Patterns of Embodiment 1: Life in Death — 190
  5.3. Patterns of Embodiment 2: Ecstasy, Ethnicity, and Resurrection — 207
  5.4. Conclusions — 225

6. Embodying Resurrection: Conclusions and Prospects — 229
  6.1. Major Conclusions — 230
  6.2. Scholarly Contribution and Areas of Further Research — 233
  6.3. Final Observations — 237

Bibliography — 239
Ancient Sources Index — 259
Modern Authors Index — 273
Subject Index — 276

Preface and Acknowledgments

Through the course of researching and writing this project, several people have contributed in ways both intellectual and personal. It is my pleasure to acknowledge this diverse community.

First and foremost, I am indebted to my doctoral supervisor, Todd Klutz, who guided this study from its inception and challenged and encouraged me at every turn. Todd's mentorship proved invaluable during my years at the University of Manchester. He tirelessly made himself available during my intensive research trips to England, and our mutual love for theory spurred in me many creative and challenging ideas. I also benefited greatly from regular meetings with George Brooke, Peter Oakes, and Maj-Britt Mosegaard Hansen. These exchanges deepened this study's theoretical apparatus and enriched my reading of the primary literature. On a more personal level, I am exceedingly grateful for Mark Coffey and Bob and Lynn Peck, who warmly opened their homes to me during my many research trips from Canada to England.

A very special thanks is due to the late Ellen Aitken of McGill University, who warmly welcomed me as a visiting research student at McGill (2010–2012) and later created a wonderful context for postdoctoral research (2012–2014). Ellen selflessly made herself available to me during my years as a visiting student, reading several chapters of this study and offering acute and insightful feedback. During my postdoctoral fellowship, Ellen oversaw the preparation of this manuscript and also encouraged me to pursue publication with SBL Press. I am grateful for the generous support of the Fonds de recherche du Québec—société et culture, which facilitated this postdoctoral fellowship. I am also grateful to my colleagues at McGill—Ian Henderson, Gerbern Oegema, and Patricia Kirkpatrick—who continue to foster an exceptional context in which to teach and research in biblical and religious studies.

In addition to those formally implicated in my studies, several people have read portions of this study and offered critical feedback: Wayne

Coppins, Troels Engberg-Pedersen, Risto Uro, Colleen Shantz, István Czachesz, Rikard Roitto, Bonnie Howe, Thomas Hatina, Geert Van Oyen, Tom Shepherd, Jeffrey Keiser, Meredith Warren, Kenneth Sheppard, Tamás Biró, Leszek Wysocki, and Alexey Somov. In various ways, these colleagues and friends have enriched this study, helping me refine my arguments, address shortcomings, and anticipate potential objections. Wayne Coppins deserves special note. In addition to reading and providing insightful feedback on an earlier version of chapter 4, Wayne also consulted with me regarding the translation of German scholarship into English. Beyond those who have provided written feedback, Ted Slingerland, Nathaniel Dykstra, Tom Troughton, Kipp Davis, Blair Major, Kenneth Sheppard, and Steve McAuley have all been wonderful conversation partners over the past several years. This study is richer for our exchanges.

Much thanks is due to Gail O'Day (former series editor of Early Christianity and Its Literature), who oversaw the peer-review process and accepted the manuscript for publication, and to David Horrell (current series editor), who carefully read my revisions and pressed several key points of clarity. Together, the editorial efforts of Gail and David were exemplary. I am also thankful to the anonymous reviewers who read this manuscript and offered astute and critical feedback. The team at SBL Press—especially Nicole Tilford and Heather McMurray—has been exceptional in guiding this manuscript through the publication process. I am grateful also to my brother Andrew Tappenden, who helped prepare the various figures in a format suitable for print, and to James Newman, who helped prepare the indices.

In 2011 an earlier iteration of chapter 2 was awarded the Founders Prize from the Canadian Society of Biblical Studies. I thank the anonymous review committee from that student essay competition, as well as Judith Newman for her insightful and encouraging words to me at that presentation. I am grateful for Carly Daniel-Hughes and André Gagné, who invited me to present portions of this research in their graduate seminars at Concordia University, thus allowing me to refine and (re)develop certain sections of this study. Additionally, several parts of this study benefited from presentation and scholarly critique at various conferences in the United Kingdom, Belgium, Canada, and the United States.

Certain portions of this monograph have already been published in print. Parts of chapters 1 and 3 appeared as "Embodiment, Folk Dualism, and the Convergence of Cosmology and Anthropology in Paul's Resurrection Ideals," *BibInt* 23 (2015): 428–55. These are reproduced here by permission of the journal editor, Tat-siong Benny Liew. Parts of chapters 1 and 5 appeared as "Luke and Paul in Dialogue: Ritual Meals and Risen Bodies as Instances of Conceptual Blending," in *Resurrection of the Dead: Biblical Traditions in Dialogue*, ed. Geert Van Oyen and Tom Shepherd, BETL 249 (Leuven: Peeters, 2012), 203–28. These are reproduced here by permission of the book's editors, Geert Van Oyen and Tom Shepherd, and Paul Peeters of Peeters Publishing.

Most important of all, I owe a great debt to my family for their unending love and support. I thank my loving wife Danielle, who has been a constant source of encouragement, and whose support and strength has seen this study through from beginning to end. Finally, I am forever grateful to my parents for their love, support, and encouragement in my scholarly pursuits. You are deeply appreciated, Mom and Dad, and it is my great pleasure to dedicate this book to you.

Frederick S. Tappenden
Montreal, QC
19 August 2015

Tables and Figures

Tables

1.1. Blending Map for the LIFE IS BEING AWAKE Metaphor	39
3.1. Blending Map for the EARTHLY BODY IS TENT Metaphor (ἡ ἐπίγειος ἡμῶν οἰκία τοῦ σκήνους, 2 Cor 5:1–2a)	125
3.2. Blending Map for the HEAVENLY BODY IS HOUSE Metaphor (οἰκοδομὴν ἐκ θεοῦ, 2 Cor 5:1–2a)	125

Figures

1.1. LIFE IS BEING AWAKE Metaphor	38
2.1. The VERTICALITY (or UP-DOWN) Schema	47
2.2. The PATH Schema	55
2.3. Integrated PATH and VERTICALITY Schematic Structure	59
2.4. Reciprocal Protagonist (TR-P) and Antagonist (TR-A) PATHS	59
2.5. The CONTAINER (or IN-OUT) Schema	62
2.6. The Micro-PATH (CHANGE) Gestalt	63
2.7. Integrated Micro-PATH Structure	63
2.8. Integrated PROXIMITY (NEAR-FAR) Structure	67
2.9. The RESURRECTION Gestalt	69
3.1. The CHANGE Gestalt	104
3.2. Foregrounding and Backgrounding the CHANGE Gestalt	107
3.3. The Plant Metaphor (1 Cor 15:36–38)	109
3.4. The Plant Metaphor (I_1 Restructured)	111
3.5. The Plant Metaphor (1 Cor 15:39–44)	113
3.6. The BODY IS HOUSE Metaphor (2 Cor 5:1–2a)	124
3.7. The BODY IS CLOTHING Metaphor (2 Cor 5:2b, 4)	127
3.8. Putting on a House (2 Cor 5:2b, 4)	128
4.1. Baptismal Death and Resurrection (Rom 6:4)	138
4.2. The Enspirited Earthly Body (Rom 8:9–11)	161

4.3. Scholarly Depictions of Paul's Modified Eschatological Schema   168
4.4. Paul's Appropriation of the RESURRECTION Gestalt   170
5.1. The UNION (CONTAINER-PROXIMITY) Gestalt   187
5.2. Paul's Appropriation of the RESURRECTION Gestalt   191
5.3. Resurrection and IN-OUT Affectivity (2 Cor 4:7–18)   202
5.4. Participation in/with Christ   219

Abbreviations

Primary Sources

1 En.	1 Enoch (Ethiopic Apocalypse)
1 Macc	1 Maccabees
2 Bar.	2 Baruch (Syriac Apocalypse)
2 En.	2 Enoch (Slavonic Apocalypse)
2 Macc	2 Maccabees
3 Bar.	3 Baruch (Greek Apocalypse)
A	MS BAN 45.13.4 of 2 Enoch. See *OTP* 1:92–94.
A.J.	Josephus, *Antiquitates judaicae*
Apoc. Ab.	Apocalypse of Abraham
Apoc. Zeph.	Apocalypse of Zephaniah
Barn.	Barnabas
B.J.	Josephus, *Bellum judaicum*
C. Ap.	Josephus, *Contra Apionem*
Deus.	Philo, *Quod Deus sit immutabilis*
Did.	Didache
Ezek. Trag.	Ezekiel the Tragedian
Her.	Philo, *Quis rerum divinarum heres sit*
Il.	Homer, *Iliad*
J	MS BAN 13.3.25 of 2 Enoch. See *OTP* 1:92–94.
Jos. Ascn.	Joseph and Aseneth
Jub.	Jubilees
LAB	Liber antiquitatum biblicarum (Pseudo-Philo)
LAE	Life of Adam and Eve
(Gk.)	Greek Recension (= Apocalypse of Moses)
(Lat.)	Latin Recension
Leg.	Philo, *Legum allegoriae*
Legat.	Philo, *Legatio ad Gaium*

LXX	Septuagint
Mand.	Shepherd of Hermas, Mandate(s)
Mos.	Philo, *De vita Mosis*
MT	Masoretic Text
Nat.	Seneca, *Naturales quaestiones*
OG	Old Greek
Opif.	Philo, *De opificio mundi*
Pss. Sol.	Psalms of Solomon
QE	Philo, *Quaestiones et solutiones in Exodum*
QG	Philo, *Quaestiones et solutiones in Genesin*
Resp.	Plato, *Respublica*
Sacr.	Philo, *De sacrificiis Abelis et Caini*
Sim.	Shephard of Hermas, Similitude(s)
Symp.	Xenophon, *Symposium*
T. Ab.	Testament of Abraham
T. Levi	Testament of Levi
T. Mos.	Testament of Moses
θ'	Theodotion
Trad. ap.	Hippolytus, *Traditio apostolica*
Virt.	Philo, *De virtutibus*
Virt. vit.	Plutarch, *De virtute et vitio*
Wis	Wisdom of Solomon

Secondary Sources

AB	Anchor Bible
ABD	*Anchor Bible Dictionary*. Edited by David Noel Freedman. 6 vols. New York: Doubleday, 1992
AGJU	Arbeiten zur Geschichte des antiken Judentums und des Urchristentums
ANRW	*Aufstieg und Niedergang der römischen Welt: Geschichte und Kultur Roms im Spiegel der neueren Forschung*. Part 2, *Principat*. Edited by Hildegard Temporini and Wolfgang Haase. Berlin: de Gruyter, 1972–
AR	*Archiv für Religionswissenschaft*
ASLL	Anglo-Saxon Language and Literature
BDAG	Frederick W. Danker, Walter Bauer, William F. Arndt, and F. Wilbur Gingrich. *Greek-English Lexicon of the New*

	Testament and Other Early Christian Literature. 3rd ed. Chicago: University of Chicago Press, 2000
BDB	Francis Brown, S. R. Driver, and Charles A. Briggs. *A Hebrew and English Lexicon of the Old Testament*. Oxford: Clarendon, 1907
BDF	Friedrich Blass and Albert Debrunner. *A Greek Grammar of the New Testament and Other Early Christian Literature*. Translated by Robert W. Funk. Chicago: University of Chicago Press, 1961
BETL	Bibliotheca Ephemeridum Theologicarum Lovaniensium
BHS	*Biblia Hebraica Stuttgartensia*. Edited by Karl Elliger and Wilhelm Rudolph. Stuttgart: Deutsche Bibelgesellschaft, 1983
BibInt	*Biblical Interpretation*
BibInt	Biblical Interpretation Series
BTB	*Biblical Theology Bulletin*
BZAW	Beihefte zur Zeitschrift für die alttestamentliche Wissenschaft
BZNW	Beiheft zur Zeitschrift für die neutestamentliche Wissenschaft
CEJL	Commentaries on Early Jewish Literature
CFJ	Flavius Josephus: Translation and Commentary. Edited by Steve Mason. Leiden: Brill, 1999–
CLR	Cognitive Linguistics Research
CogSci	*Cognitive Science*
ConBNT	Coniectanea Biblica: New Testament Series
Contr	Contraversions
CRINT	Compendia Rerum Iudaicarum ad Novum Testamentum
CTL	Cambridge Textbooks in Linguistics
CTSRR	College Theology Society Resources in Religion
CW	*Classical World*
DDD	*Dictionary of Deities and Demons in the Bible*. Edited by Karel van der Toorn, Bob Becking, and Pieter W. van der Horst. 2nd rev. ed. Leiden: Brill, 1999
DJD	Discoveries in the Judaean Desert
DSD	*Dead Sea Discoveries*
EBib	Études bibliques
ECL	Early Christianity and Its Literature
EDNT	*Exegetical Dictionary of the New Testament*. Edited by

	Horst Balz and Gerhard Schneider. ET. 3 vols. Grand Rapids: Eerdmans, 1990–1993
ESEC	Emory Studies in Early Christianity
ESV	English Standard Version
GSCC	Groningen Studies in Cultural Change
HALOT	Ludwig Koehler, Walter Baumgartner, and Johann J. Stamm. *The Hebrew and Aramaic Lexicon of the Old Testament.* Translated and edited under the supervision of Marvin E. J. Richardson. 5 vols. Leiden: Brill, 1994–2000
HTR	*Harvard Theological Review*
HTS	Harvard Theological Studies
HUT	Hermeneutische Untersuchungen zur Theologie
HvTSt	*Hervormde Teologiese Studies*
ICC	International Critical Commentary
JAAR	*Journal of the American Academy of Religion*
JAJSup	Journal of Ancient Judaism Supplements
JBL	*Journal of Biblical Literature*
JCC	*Journal of Cognition and Culture*
JCTCRS	Jewish and Christian Texts in Contexts and Related Studies
JJS	*Journal of Jewish Studies*
JLCRS	Jordan Lectures in Comparative Religion Series
JSJSup	Journal for the Study of Judaism Supplements
JSNT	*Journal for the Study of the New Testament*
JSNTSup	Journal for the Study of the New Testament Supplement Series
JSOTSup	Journal for the Study of the Old Testament Supplement Series
JSP	*Journal for the Study of the Pseudepigrapha*
JSPSup	Journal for the Study of the Pseudepigrapha Supplement Series
JTS	*Journal of Theological Studies*
KJV	King James (Authorized) Version
L&N	Johannes P. Louw and Eugene A. Nida, eds. *Greek-English Lexicon of the New Testament: Based on Semantic Domains.* 2nd ed. 2 vols. New York: United Bible Societies, 1989
LBS	Linguistic Biblical Studies
LCL	Loeb Classical Library

LEH	Johan Lust, Erik Eynikel, and Katrin Hauspie, eds. *Greek-English Lexicon of the Septuagint*. Rev. ed. Stuttgart: Deutsche Bibelgesellschaft, 2003
LeuB	*Leuvense Bijdragen*
LHR	Lectures on the History of Religions
LNTS	Library of New Testament Studies
LS	Henry George Liddell and Robert Scott. *A Greek-English Lexicon*. 8th ed. Oxford: Clarendon, 1901
LSJ	Henry George Liddell, Robert Scott, and Henry Stuart Jones. *A Greek-English Lexicon*. 9th ed. with revised supplement. Oxford: Clarendon, 1996
LSTS	Library of Second Temple Studies
NA^{28}	*Novum Testamentum Graece*. Edited by Eberhard Nestle and Kurt Aland. 28th ed. Stuttgart: Deutsche Bibelgesellschaft, 2012
NASB	New American Standard Bible
NHMS	Nag Hammadi and Manichaean Studies
NIGTC	New International Greek Testament Commentary
NIV	New International Version
NovT	*Novum Testamentum*
NovTSup	Supplements to Novum Testamentum
NRSV	New Revised Standard Version
NTL	New Testament Library
NTS	*New Testament Studies*
OTP	*Old Testament Pseudepigrapha*. Edited by James H. Charlesworth. 2 vols. New York: Doubleday, 1983–1985
PGL	*Patristic Greek Lexicon*. Edited by Geoffrey W. H. Lampe. Oxford: Clarendon, 1961
PhoSup	Phoenix: Supplementary Volume
PVTG	Pseudepigrapha Veteris Testamenti Graece
RBL	*Review of Biblical Literature*
RevQ	*Revue de Qumran*
SBLDS	Society of Biblical Literature Dissertation Series
SBLTT	Society of Biblical Literature Texts and Translations
SBT	Studies in Biblical Theology
SCS	Septuagint and Cognate Studies
SHR	Studies in the History of Religions
SJSHRZ	Studien zu den Jüdischen Schriften aus hellenistisch-römischer Zeit

SNTSMS	Society for New Testament Studies Monograph Series
SNTW	Studies of the New Testament and Its World
SPIB	Scripta Pontificii Instituti Biblici
SSU	Studia Semitica Upsaliensia
STDJ	Studies on the Texts of the Desert of Judah
StLit	*Studia Liturgica*
SVTG	Septuaginta: Vetus Testamentum Graecum. Auctoritate Academiae Scientiarum Gottingensis editum. Göttingen: Vandenhoeck & Ruprecht, 1931–
SVTP	Studia in Veteris Testamenti Pseudepigrapha
SymS	Symposium Series
TDNT	*Theological Dictionary of the New Testament*. Edited by Gerhard Kittel and Gerhard Friedrich. Translated by Geoffrey W. Bromiley. 10 vols. Grand Rapids: Eerdmans, 1964–1976
TENTS	Texts and Editions for New Testament Study
TS	*Theological Studies*
VT	*Vetus Testamentum*
VTSup	Supplements to Vetus Testamentum
WBC	Word Biblical Commentary
WUNT	Wissenschaftliche Untersuchungen zum Neuen Testament

1

The Disembodiment of Resurrection: Literature Review, Problem Definition, and the Integration of Cognition and Culture

1.1. Introduction

Paul's ideals are bodily ideals; his expectations are somatically oriented, his thinking corporally grounded. While the scope of σῶμα in Paul's letters is far reaching,[1] it is Paul's resurrection ideals that betray this somatic emphasis most acutely.[2] The apostle looks toward a future embodied existence that is patterned on and transformatively intertwined with Christ's risen body (Rom 8:23; 1 Cor 15:35–57; 2 Cor 5:1–5; Phil 3:21). The body

---

1. See, e.g., John Robinson's assertion that one can easily make a case for the concept of the body as the "keystone of Paul's theology" (1952, 9; see also 48); Robinson continues, "to trace the subtle links and interactions between the different senses of this word σῶμα is to grasp the thread that leads through the maze of Pauline thought." More recently, Troels Engberg-Pedersen (2010, 3) recounts a comment by Wayne Meeks: "I cannot think of anybody in antiquity who spoke so much about the body as Paul did."

2. In the present study, I prefer the term *ideals* (as in "Paul's resurrection ideals") to *theology* in that the latter can imply (though not always) a propositional and exceedingly a priori system of thought. The term *theology* often connotes, even presumes, a post-Cartesian understanding of human rationality that is not without problems (see §1.2). I adopt the term *ideals*, on the other hand, because it implies not only Paul's rational capabilities but also his hopes and expectations; it implies the whole of Paul's (inter)subjective disposition toward Christ. Though ideals might be a more fuzzy term, it points to a more holistic and integrative conception of Paul's thinking and perception. Of note, this use of ideals should not be confused with the various senses of philosophical idealism, which prioritize the noetic at the expense of the somatic, thus constituting a form of cognicentrism that is at odds with the theoretical commitments outlined below (again, see §1.2).

functions, for Paul, as the state or mode of postmortem existence, a feature that reflects the somatic focus of Paul's eschatology. In a much more immediate sense, however, one can also say that Paul's resurrection ideals are locatively somatic. This is particularly evident in the apostle's focus on transformation as part of the resurrection experience. In Paul's view, transformation is both a future and a present experience (compare 2 Cor 3:18 with 5:1–5). Believers are variously described as currently dying and (in some sense) rising with Christ (Rom 6:1–11; Phil 3:10–11; 2 Cor 4:7–18), and Paul locates this death and life pattern *in* believers' bodies. Thus 2 Cor 4:10 states, "[we are] always carrying the death of Jesus in the body so that the life of Jesus might also be revealed in our bodies."[3] Taking these two aspects together, Paul understands resurrection not only in an eschatological way that looks ahead to a future embodied existence, but also in a locative way that understands transformation as an experience that is currently happening in the body itself.

The somatic focus of Paul's resurrection ideals has not gone unnoticed in Pauline interpretation, though this balance between eschatological and locative foci is not always maintained. As early as the second and third centuries, the issue of bodily resurrection became an increasingly divisive topic among Christians, though focus shifted to the much more specific claim of a future resurrection of the flesh (see Lehtipuu 2009). From late antiquity through the Middle Ages, much theological discussion continued to stress the fleshly or material nature of resurrection vis-à-vis a more spiritual or immaterial understanding.[4] In modern scholarship, while it is widely acknowledged that the body functions as a more general category in Paul's thought (i.e., *bodily* does not necessarily imply *fleshly*), focus has remained largely on the futurist nature of resurrection (see §1.3.1 below). Accordingly, emphasis is given to the eschatological rather than locative nature of Paul's ideals, focusing specifically on resurrection as a literal, postmortem event. As we will see, such a temporal focus produces an understanding of resurrection as a theological proposition to which Paul ascribes rather than a somatic process in which Paul engages. By stressing the eschatological rather than locative importance of the body, modern

---

3. All translations of Greek, Hebrew, and Aramaic in this study are my own (unless otherwise stated).

4. For a helpful overview of the traditional view, see Dahl 1962, 37–58. For a more recent and sociohistorical discussion of resurrection from the patristic through medieval periods, see Bynum 1995.

1. THE DISEMBODIMENT OF RESURRECTION

treatments have produced an ironically disembodied view of resurrection in the Pauline letters.

In response to this tendency toward interpretive disembodiment, I explore in this study the various ways in which Paul's resurrection ideals are embodied. Seeking to move past the dubious opposition that is drawn between literal and metaphorical notions of resurrection, I draw on theories of cognitive linguistics to explore how human thought is grounded in and shaped by the body. Bringing these insights to bear on Paul, I argue two central theses. On the one hand, I will show that notions of resurrection are always metaphorical and necessarily comprehended with respect to more concrete experiences of human embodiment; on the other hand, I will demonstrate that Paul envisions Christ-devotees as currently caught up in an ongoing process of resurrection that is enacted on the human σῶμα. In both ways, the somatic foundations of Paul's thought preclude the imbalance of eschatological and locative foci noted above. As I will show, resurrection functions as a metaphor that Paul and his communities live by. For Paul, resurrection is embodied.

1.2. On Cognicentrism and Mind-Body Dualism

At the outset, it will prove helpful to introduce a concept that, when the relevant scholarly literature is viewed in its light, illuminates more clearly the problem at hand. The concept in question is *cognicentrism*, which (to my knowledge) was first employed by Michael Harner. For Harner (1990, xx), cognicentrism is analogous to ethnocentrism, the latter being concerned with the "narrowness of someone's *cultural* experience" and the former with the "narrowness of someone's *conscious* experience." At issue for Harner is the legitimization of nonscientific modes of knowing, specifically with respect to shamanic practices and altered states of consciousness.[5] In Pauline studies, Colleen Shantz (2009, esp. 26–33) has followed

---

5. Harner (1990, xix) distinguishes between what he calls an Ordinary State of Consciousness (OSC) and a Shamanic State of Consciousness (SSC), both of which must be recognized as really real to the participants in shamanic contexts. Thus Harner: "'Fantasy' can be said to be a term applied by a person in the OSC to what is experienced in the SSC. Conversely, a person in the SSC may perceive the experiences of the OSC to be illusory in SSC terms.… The myth of the SSC is ordinary reality; and the myth of the OSC is nonordinary reality" (xix–xx).

Harner's cognicentric critique in her assessment of religious experience in Paul. Shantz helpfully clarifies the term as follows:

> The bias of cognicentrism is rooted in the constructs of scientific enlightenment, especially the idea of objective truth as the product of critical thinking stripped of personal investment. A cognicentric stance purports to arbitrate what counts as acceptable knowledge as well as what counts as acceptable ways of coming to know. (26)

Taken in this direction, cognicentrism is not only about legitimating altered states of consciousness but more fundamentally about an epistemological stance that permeates sectors of the modern academy more broadly. Similar efforts to move past such a cognicentric bias can be found in Pieter Craffert's (2008, 3–34) call for ontological pluralism in historical methodology[6] or Troels Engberg-Pedersen's (2010, 1) recent insistence that much of Paul's theology be understood not metaphorically or cognitively (as he puts it) but rather as "non-metaphorical, concrete and basically physical."[7]

Moving in a similar direction as these scholars, I use the term *cognicentrism* to denote a deep-seated and persistent bias whereby theology (and indeed human cognition more generally) is understood as propositional in nature. In this tradition, theological concepts such as resurrection are understood as noetic abstractions; they are objective mental assents, and their truth claims exist independent of space, time, culture, and human agents. Put differently, cognicentrism refers to the preference given to the noetic at the expense of the somatic. The term cognicentrism, therefore, denotes the disembodiment of knowledge.

At the heart of this cognicentric bias is the Cartesian separation of mind and body whereby human cognition (i.e., rationality) is isolated

---

6. By "ontological pluralism," Craffert means the recognition of culturally conditioned determinations of what is *real*. The historian's task is to understand such realities. Thus Craffert (2008, 21), "what is 'culturally' real and historical is not necessarily 'comparatively' real and historical because of this comparative perspective." Craffert employs the term *ontological pluralism* in contrast to *ontological monism*, by which "whatever does not conform to the historian's *reality* catalogue cannot be historical" (4).

7. I agree with the overall thrust of Engberg-Pedersen's argument, though I am critical of the distinction he draws between literal and metaphorical (see §1.3.1).

from the physical matter of the natural world (i.e., the human body).[8] A common formulation of this anthropological dualism is the positing of objectivist and subjectivist epistemological binaries.[9] On the one side, *Truth* is propositional, absolute, literal, and fits the world as is; on the other, *truth* is contextual, relative, metaphorical, and socially constructed (see Lakoff and Johnson 1980, 186–89). The former assumes a ghost in the machine that can attain a God's-eye perspective, while the latter stresses the blank slate of human nature whereby human beings are helplessly socialized and inscribed by discourses (see Slingerland 2008a, 15).[10] For both camps, however, the isolation of mind from body is a central tenet, producing fantasies of epistemological objectivity (on the one side) and presuming an impotent connection between cognition and biological embeddedness (on the other).[11]

Parsing the history of Western thought into such caricatured categories is not without problems. While the objectivist/subjectivist binary admittedly highlights the strong expressions of these epistemological trends, much scholarly reflection on the mind-body problem cannot be so tidily encamped.[12] Important contributions have been made by theorists in various fields,

---

8. See esp. Damasio 1994.

9. See, e.g., Lakoff and Johnson 1980, 159–228; 1999. Despite the inherent difficulty in employing such sweeping—even essentialist—categories (as noted below), Lakoff and Johnson's alternative notion of "Embodied Realism" has proven formative for the present study.

10. Slingerland (2008a, 15) continues by noting that, in the blank slate view, it is taken as axiomatic that "language and/or culture [go] *all the way down.*"

11. On this latter point, while the subjectivist position asserts the formative nature of linguistic and cultural embeddedness, what is at issue in this critique is the assertion that human beings are only cultural and/or linguistic beings, thus presuming that the body plays no determinative role in the development of reason and consciousness. To cite Slingerland (2008a, 78) further, there is a pervasive scholarly presumption that the human experience is "mediated by language or culture *all the way down* … [thus asserting there is] nothing significant about the way in which we think or act [that] is a direct result of our biological endowment."

12. Phenomenology is an excellent example of a field that breaks these caricatured molds. Though often characterized within the camp of subjectivism/postmodern relativism, phenomenology (esp. the work of Maurice Merleau-Ponty [1945]) has proven formative for theories of embodied cognition (see further n. 94 below). Somewhat surprisingly, this is largely lost in Slingerland's (2008a) otherwise excellent study. Despite his astute and thorough engagement with an impressive range of interdisciplinary literature, Slingerland maps the history of the humanities within a

though it is the emergence of the cognitive sciences over the last half-century that have fostered an inter- and multidisciplinary arena in which to explore (among other things) questions such as how is human thought produced, how does meaning emerge from such thought, and how are such thoughts then reproduced.[13] One of the chief contributions of the cognitive sciences has been the integration of otherwise distinct—even disparate—disciplines. Slingerland (2008a, 2–8; 2008b, esp. 378–80) has succinctly articulated this theoretical and methodological program, arguing that the still prevalent divide in the modern university between the natural and human sciences has led to a disembodied conception of human culture. In response to this institutionalized Cartesian dualism, Slingerland contends:

> The manner in which we engage in the study of consciousness and its products—that is, the traditional domain of the humanities—should … be brought into coordination with the manner in which we study less complex (or differently complex) material structures, while never losing sight of the strange and wonderful emergent properties that consciousness brings with it. (2008a, 10–11)

Slingerland (9–28) advocates what he and others have called the vertical integration of cognition and culture. This theoretical agenda envisions a single explanatory chain (which ascends upward from the natural sciences to the humanities) whereby "different levels of explanation can, and must, coexist with one another" (2008b, 384). Central to this paradigm is the conviction of mind-body holism, an assertion that comes from, as Mark Johnson (2005, 16) notes, the "growing mountain of empirical evidence from the cognitive sciences that [suggests that] there can be no thought without a brain in a body in an environment." Although seemingly trivial,

---

similar objectivist vis-à-vis postmodernist binary (31–147). While he is aware of the problems that attend such sweeping generalizations (80) and further provides a clear rationale for his categorization (32–34, 77–79), Slingerland offers very little discussion of phenomenology and does not engage—either positively or negatively—the work of Merleau-Ponty.

13. Rather than speaking of cognitive science in the singular, it is better to speak of the cognitive sciences (plural) in that this academic category refers to "the interdisciplinary study of mind and intelligence, embracing philosophy, psychology, artificial intelligence, neuroscience, linguistics, and anthropology" (Thagard 1996, ix; see also J. Barrett 2011, 3–20).

this assertion stands in tension with the strong mind-body dualisms that dominate much of the Western philosophical tradition.[14]

It is this vertical integration of cognition and culture that serves as the theoretical apparatus for the present study. I take it as axiomatic that *cognition* (understood as a body-brain complex) and *culture* (understood to emerge from that body-brain complex) must be integrated with one another such that the two are studied in each other's light. In the present study I achieve this vertical integration by employing methodologies developed in cognitive linguistics. I will outline these methods in more detail below (§1.4). For now, however, I want to insist that the notion of cognicentrism outlined here is symptomatic of the separation of mind and body, which is a kind of disembodiment of the mind. With respect to Paul, cognicentrism results in the abstraction of the apostle's resurrection ideals as propositional and thus lacking concrete grounding within human experience and perception.

1.3. Literature Review and Problem Definition

With this broader theoretical framework in mind, we are now situated well to assess the relevant scholarly literature on Paul's resurrection ideals. Three specific issues are particularly germane to our topic: the problem of identifying resurrection (§1.3.1), the nature of dualism and monism in Paul's thought (§1.3.2), and the relationship between Paul's participationist and resurrection ideals (§1.3.3). As we will see, scholarly conclusions on these issues tend to gravitate toward interpretations that reflect the problem of cognicentrism just outlined.

---

14. Though the integration of cognition and culture may seem reductive to some, I follow Slingerland (2008a, 2008b) in insisting on the importance of different (though integrated) levels of explanation. While the cognitive sciences may enable explanation at *some* levels, they do not enable explanation at *all* levels. Accordingly, specialist studies within individual disciplines offer descriptive and explanatory depth that can complement and test the more general work of cognitive scientists. Herein lies the value of the vertical integration paradigm. By studying human culture in light of both cognitive and sociocultural processes, a rightly elaborate and heuristic theoretical foundation is envisaged. In recognizing that all description/analysis requires some form of reductionism, my goal is "productive, explanatory reductionism [and not] crudely eliminative reductionism" (Slingerland 2008b, 387).

1.3.1. The Problem of Identifying Resurrection

A methodological problem in any study of resurrection belief in both Paul and Second Temple Judaism (more generally) is that, in many instances, it is not entirely clear what constitutes the concept of *resurrection*. To be sure, certain passages stand as prime examples (e.g., Dan 12:1-3; 1 Thess 4:13-18; 1 Cor 15), though beyond these one can point to several pericopes that may or may not refer to resurrection (e.g., various passages in the Qumran sectarian literature; Rom 6:1-11). We will have occasion to explore this issue in depth in chapter 2. For now, it will suffice to show that at the heart of these concerns stands the question: how does one identify the idea or concept of resurrection within a given text?

Aside from those who limit notions of resurrection to specific terms such as ἐγείρω and ἀνίστημι,[15] the most common approach is to reduce the richness of resurrection traditions to uniformity at the literary level. One way this has been achieved is by distinguishing that which is literally resurrection from that which is metaphorically resurrection. Consider N. T. Wright's (2003, 127, emphasis added) statement: "YHWH's answer to his people's exile would be, *metaphorically*, life from the dead (Isaiah 26, Ezekiel 37); YHWH's answer to his people's martyrdom would be, literally, life from the dead (Daniel 12)." Though Wright suggests that a hard distinction should not be made between differing thematic contexts (116) and further nuances his use of metaphorical and literal (201-3),[16] the parsing of the period literature into such categories creates a distinction between

---

15. John Sawyer (1973), for example, identifies five terms in Hebrew literature (חיה, "to live"; קום, "to stand"; הקיץ [or קיץ], "to wake"; שוב, "to come back"; and ציץ, "to sprout"), while Jerzy Chmiel (1979) examines LXX translation equivalents and proposes a reduction of Sawyer's five Hebrew terms to the two Greek terms ἐγείρω and ἀνίστημι. In Pauline studies, Alexander Wedderburn (1987, 164-232) defines resurrection based on the usage of ἀνάστασις, ἐγείρω, and their cognates, while Joost Holleman (1996, 86) similarly focuses on "agreement in terminology and concepts." James Charlesworth (2006a, 238) criticizes this approach, rightly noting, "the concept of resurrection … can be detected only by examining exegetically a cluster of words in a particular context." That is, the identification of resurrection has much to do with literary contexts and the frames employed in rendering such lexemes meaningful. Notions of resurrection depend not merely on specific lexical signs but also on the discursive contexts in which those signs convey and acquire meaning.

16. Wright (2003, 116) makes this point in addressing what he refers to as the fallacious either/or distinction between individual resurrection and national restoration.

1. THE DISEMBODIMENT OF RESURRECTION

first- and second-order notions of resurrection, that is, between that which really is resurrection and that which is not. Most commonly, resurrection is mapped within a trajectory that runs from earlier metaphorical notions to later literal notions.[17] On this reading, literal resurrection is reduced to assertions of postmortem corporeality, thus adding a layer of somatic concreteness that is absent from the metaphorical side.[18]

The problem becomes acute when one considers Paul's resurrection ideals. Wright insists, for example, that Paul understood resurrection as both a future literal event and a present metaphorical event such that the literal event metaphorically "coloured and gave shape to present Christian living" (2003, 210); later, he states that present resurrection is a "worldview which Paul developed and did his best both to teach and to embody" (371; see also 373). On these points, Wright stands as a representative of much Pauline scholarship.[19] As the present study will demonstrate, such parsing of

---

17. Wright (2003, 201–3), for instance, suggests a movement within ancient Judaism from metaphorical, political notions of resurrection (evinced in Ezek 37 and Isa 26) to literal, somatic expressions (evinced in 2 Maccabees). John Collins (1993, 391–92) suggests that Ezek 37 and Hos 6:2 speak metaphorically of resurrection while Dan 12 refers to "actual resurrection." He goes on to draw a distinction between passages that were (likely) "originally metaphorical" but that eventually facilitated a "more literal" afterlife belief (395). Similarly, Cavallin (1974, 26) characterizes Dan 12 as describing "real resurrection," while Day (1996, 240) sees it as reflecting "a literal belief in bodily resurrection after death."

18. Wright (2003, 202) is quick to insist that the "metaphorical meaning of 'resurrection' … retained a concrete referent … [namely], the literal and concrete return from exile." On this point Wright surely is correct, though his vision of development from metaphor to literalness within ancient Jewish thought seems overdetermined and overly prioritized toward the literal. As I will show in §1.4, literal and metaphorical interlace each other in ways that render difficult the objectification of either within such cultural development. It is not enough to see a simple trajectory from metaphor to literalness—indeed, in important respects, certain kinds of literalness must be prioritized (see §1.4)—but rather more important to explore how the two interlace and inform one another in the ongoing construction of meaning. What Wright categorizes as literal resurrection is actually metaphorical in many crucial respects.

19. For example, Wedderburn (1987, 231) argues for an "obstinate corporeality and physicality about the language of resurrection … which only gradually and under considerable pressure yielded to attempts to introduce a figurative, non-corporeal and non-physical sense" (see also 164–232 generally). Cognicentric tendencies are explicit here, as Wedderburn asserts that only under later "intellectual and spiritual" pressures did resurrection come to be used metaphorically (84). Similarly, Holleman (1996, 198) insists the "metaphor" of presently dying and rising with Christ (e.g., through baptism

literal and metaphorical is both theoretically problematic and theologically imprecise. By holding literal and metaphorical in opposition to one another, the notion of a present metaphorical resurrection stands as a disembodied (or cognicentric) concept. While Wright clearly stresses the physicalist, actual nature of Paul's resurrection ideals,[20] this real (or literal) experience of resurrection is always in waiting and only propositionally grasped as a metaphor in the present. As I will demonstrate (see esp. §1.4), more is lost than gained when literal and metaphorical are pitted against one another. Indeed, I hope to show that, for Paul, the perception that resurrection has already begun is as important as the claim that resurrection will happen in the future; and further, that both present and future expressions of resurrection are metaphorical in important respects.

In response to overly metaphorical readings of Paul, Engberg-Pedersen (2010) has stressed the concrete and physicalist nature of Paul's language. Engberg-Pedersen's main interest is Pauline pneumatology, though with respect to resurrection he makes striking statements such as "Christ-believers' bodies of flesh and blood *literally* die—or atrophy—while they are living here on earth to become fit for the final transformation" (speaking of 2 Cor 4:16); and later he offers the following translation of Rom 8:17: "we [literally] co-suffer (with him) *in order that* we may also become [literally] co-glorified (with him)."[21] Engberg-Pedersen understands Paul's worldview as "materialistic, concrete, and tangible" rather than "idealistic" (19), and to this end I think Engberg-Pedersen is moving in the right direction. His analysis seems overly burdened, however, by a consistent pitting of literal and metaphorical against one another, thus implying that metaphor has no place in a concrete, tangible, or physicalist understanding of Paul.[22] Given that the literal versus metaphorical dichotomy functions as Engberg-Pedersen's methodological departure point,[23] one cannot

---

and suffering) "should be distinguished from ... the eschatological resurrection" (see also 188–98 generally).

20. For Wright (2003, 372–73), the physicalist nature of resurrection is firmly located in the eschatological, somatic expectation.

21. These citations are from Engberg-Pedersen 2010; the first is from p. 45 (emphasis added), the second is from p. 53 (reproduced exactly as is; all emphases and parenthetical remarks are original).

22. This dichotomy pervades Engberg-Pedersen 2010, even being introduced in the first several pages as the primary topic at issue (see, e.g., 1–2, 51–55, 82–83, 147–53, 173–75).

23. Thus Engberg-Pedersen (2010, 83) admits that he "always start[s] out from

help but wonder if such linguistic woodenness is required. Must Paul be taken literally in order to take his materialism seriously? Is there no room for metaphor within Pauline materialism?

A fruitful way forward can be found in the theory of conceptual metaphor that has been developed primarily in the work of George Lakoff and Mark Johnson, and that I will employ in this study (see esp. §1.4).[24] It is a striking feature of human language that metaphor pervades discourse, but even more striking that language users are, as Steven Pinker (2007, 248) notes, able to "effortlessly transcend the metaphors implicit in their language." Pinker continues,

> This implies that speakers have the means to entertain the underlying concepts: the abstract idea of an approach to a climax, not the concrete idea of the head of a pimple [as in "coming to a head"]; the abstract idea of a profusion of problems, not the concrete idea of a can of worms.[25]

For Lakoff and Johnson, metaphor is not a poetic device that can be reduced to literal expressions, nor is it a linguistic phenomenon that underscores the disconnect of language and reality;[26] rather, metaphor is a central aspect of human cognition. Lakoff and Johnson focus on what they call *conceptual metaphors*, which are grounded in patterns of human

---

the literal interpretation," to which he further insists, it is "generally advisable as a methodological principle to adopt this line of interpretation since our own intuitive penchant for the metaphorical reading makes us less susceptible to finding traces of the literal one that may point to Paul's own understanding." Accordingly, the language of *literal*, *concrete*, and *tangible* pervades his analysis (e.g., 41, 44, 51–52, 69, 93, and 150).

24. See esp. Lakoff and Johnson 1980, 1999; Lakoff and Turner 1989; and Johnson 1987.

25. Pinker is not a cognitive linguist, and it is worth noting that the section quoted here is offered in criticism of the lengths to which Lakoff and Johnson press conceptual metaphor theory (see Pinker 2007, 247–51).

26. This binary is formulated within Lakoff and Johnson's (1980, 159–228) objectivist vs. subjectivist caricature. Slingerland (2008a, 161) has recently renewed this line of framing, noting that objectivists view metaphor as essentially superfluous and not easily accounted for within a theoretical model wherein language fits the world as is, while postmodern relativists (= subjectivists) rightly identify the pervasive nature of metaphor in human thought/communication, though they fail to recognize metaphor's embodied grounding, instead attributing metaphor "to the free movement of the hermeneutic *Geist* or *Dasein*" (161).

embodiment and are structured in relation to recurrent image schemata. We will have occasion to return to these (and other) theoretical concepts below (§1.4); for now it will suffice to note that within the theory of metaphor advanced here, descriptors such as *literal* and *metaphorical* undergo revised definition to suggest that the vast majority of human language is metaphorical in nature. While this does not preclude literal linguistic descriptions, metaphor functions as the norm.[27] When viewed in this way, the contributions of Wright and Engberg-Pedersen represent opposing views that betray symptoms of the aforementioned problem of cognicentrism. The former (implicitly) presumes language and experience are disconnected, while the latter strenuously asserts that the real must be literal and cannot be metaphorical.[28]

Returning to the question at hand, namely, the problem of identifying resurrection, the parsing of resurrection into both literal and metaphorical descriptions problematically presumes the existence of a singular and unified concept (i.e., the identification of what is literally resurrection). Ultimately, such treatments sacrifice cultural nuance at the altar of homogeneity. While some work has been done to redress this narrowing (Charlesworth 2006a, 2006b), such approaches often fragment resurrection into several different (even disparate) categories without defining the framework by which variety is unified.[29] Accordingly, there is an acute

---

27. In delineating literal and metaphorical, Lakoff (1993, 205) suggests: "there is nonetheless an extensive range of nonmetaphorical. Thus, a sentence like 'The balloon went up' is not metaphorical, nor is the old philosopher's favorite 'The cat is on the mat.' But as soon as one gets away from concrete physical experiences and starts talking about abstractions or emotions, metaphorical understanding is the norm."

28. Of note, Wright does not engage with contemporary advancements in metaphor theory, and while Engberg-Pedersen (2008, 153 n. 26) is aware of Lakoff and Johnson, his cursory reference to their work suggests a misperception.

29. Charlesworth (2006a), for example, sets out a preliminary taxonomy of sixteen categories that classify concepts of resurrection within literature spanning the late Second Temple through the early rabbinic periods. While rightly stressing cultural and motific variety, Charlesworth offers no framework by which to tie such variety together. For instance, several of his categories concern motifs of *redemption* and *vindication*, but what have these to do with other categories such as *spiritual awakening* or *the raising of an apocalyptist to heaven*? The closest Charlesworth comes to offering such a unifying framework can be found at the conclusion of his article, where he suggests: "the varieties and differing taxonomies of resurrection beliefs represent not a system but an expression of *the common human hope that God will have the last word and the future of the righteous will be blessed*" (261, emphasis added). This unifying

1. THE DISEMBODIMENT OF RESURRECTION   13

need to assess the strictures by which notions of resurrection are identified and interpreted within the period literature. Such will be the focus of chapter 2, where I apply cognitive linguistic analyses to a selection of Second Temple Jewish and Pauline texts.[30] As I will show, resurrection is categorically an abstract domain of human thought, one that is necessarily metaphorical and structured in relation to more concrete and familiar human experiences.

1.3.2. The Nature of Dualism and Monism in Paul's Thought

Paul understands resurrection as a distinctly bodily affair. He looks toward the future "redemption of [believers'] bodies" (Rom 8:23), to a time when the earthly "body of humiliation" (Phil 3:21) will be "clothed over with [the] dwelling from heaven" (2 Cor 5:2). At the same time, however, Paul couples these somatic descriptions with notions of cosmological transformation. He models his understanding of risen bodies on that of celestial glory-bodies (Rom 8:17–18; 1 Cor 15:40–41) and even insists that believers will one day share in Christ's own risen "body of glory" (Phil 3:21; see also 1 Cor 2:8; 2 Cor 3:18; 4:4–6; and Rom 8:29). Taken together, Paul's resurrection ideals stand at the intersection of his anthropology and cosmology such that metaphors of somatic alteration and cosmological transposition interlace one another. While this interconnectivity is generally acknowledged, there exists a deep incongruence between scholarly treatments of Paul's cosmology and anthropology. Many read Paul within an apocalyptic context characterized by opposition (e.g., heaven vs. earth; now vs. then), thus advocating a strong degree of cosmological dualism between the earthly and the heavenly. At the same time, however, Paul's anthropology is usually understood within the context of an assumed Jewish monism, expressly rejecting any whiff of what generally is regarded (and often dubiously constructed) as Greek

---

thread is unfortunately more reflective than critical, offering little to our understanding of what actually constitutes a resurrection text.

30. Throughout this study, the terms *Judean* and *Jewish* are used largely interchangeably with no hard distinction between the two. That being said, "Judean" is used often with an outlook toward issues of ethnicity and kinship, whereas "Jewish" denotes *broader traditions and ideas*. For a recent scholarly discussion on the appropriateness of such terms (particularly with respect to translations of Ἰουδαῖος), see Law and Halton 2014.

dualism. What emerges, then, is a confused discussion of both dualism and monism in which Paul's understanding of resurrection is sometimes understood monistically and sometimes dualistically. This is not because the concept of resurrection is understood dualistically/monistically (per se), but rather because resurrection is indelibly wrapped up with cosmology and anthropology, both of which are hotbeds of scholarly debate regarding dualism and monism.

It will be helpful first to identify more clearly what one means by *dualism* and *monism*. While some prefer to distinguish dualism from duality,[31] there is a growing body of literature in the cognitive sciences that suggests dualistic modes of thought universally pervade human cultures. For some, this natural inclination is understood in a strong, Cartesian sense; so Paul Bloom (2006, 211): "people universally think of human consciousness as *separate* from the physical realm" (emphasis added).[32] More preferable is the recent work of Edward Slingerland and Maciej Chudek (2011; see also Slingerland 2013), who advocate a *weak* rather than *strong* folk dualism thesis that accounts for the reality that most cultures in history do not advance a simple either/or binary of mind and body. Instead, weak folk dualism allows for shades of cultural variety whereby certain capacities (thought, emotion, personhood, physiology, etc.) tend to cluster together and gravitate toward certain poles (such as in/out, mind/body).[33] What

---

31. In this view, dualism is narrowly defined as a radical and ontological break between opposing concepts/forces, whereas duality is understood as a weaker and more attenuated term whereby a broad range of distinctions stand in varying degrees of opposition (see Wright 1992, 252–56). I understand *dualism* in a more general sense to denote a conceptual framework involving two (perhaps more) different values that stand in relation to one another, and where that relationship is characterized either by opposition or interrelation (or some mixture thereof). Two points are worth unpacking in detail. First, while dualism proper is a system of two distinct values (e.g., body and soul), Paul and other ancient writers often work not with neat pairs but rather overlapping multiples (e.g., body, soul, and spirit/mind). What counts for my analysis, then, is not the individual values but rather the character of the relationship between those values. This leads to a second point, which is the importance I place upon allowing room for opposition and interrelation as part of the dualistic relationship, for this enables both strong and weak expressions of dualism without need for the category of duality.

32. Elsewhere, Bloom (2004, 191) insists that people are dualists "who have two ways of looking at the world: in terms of bodies and in terms of souls. A direct consequesnce of this dualism is the idea that bodies and souls are separate."

33. Accordingly, weak folk dualism allows for the recognition that "mind-stuff and

is at issue, then, is not the formal—or strong—dualisms of the West, but rather a more commonsensical—or weak—dualism as a characteristic aspect of human cognition across cultures.[34] The term *folk dualism* refers to this latter, commonsensical notion, even though stronger expressions are themselves built up from the weaker default.[35]

By *folk dualism*, I mean notions of dualism that are intuitive and not necessarily wrapped up—or worked out—in any formal, systematic way. To say these notions are intuitive is to insist that they emerge as a result of embodied human existence in the world (including both cognitive processing and somatic functioning; we will have occasion to explore many of these embodied foundations throughout this study [esp. §1.4]).[36] Folk dualism points toward embodied patterns of human thought that, though variously understood, are cross-culturally recurrent. Given the seeming naturalness (as it were) of such weak folk dualisms, it is likely—indeed, inevitable—that Paul functions with some set of dualistic assumptions.[37] The question is not whether Paul is best read as a dualist or monist; rather, it is better to inquire as to what kinds of dualistic and monistic tendencies are present in his cosmology and anthropology.

With notions of folk dualism firmly in view, I turn to Paul's cosmology, which is indelibly wrapped up in Jewish apocalypticism. Of particular note is the influential work of Ernst Käsemann, who understood Paul's apocalypticism to be essentially eschatological and characterized by a strongly

---

body-stuff [can] overlap and interact ... [even if] human cognition will tend to cluster person-concepts around [certain] attractors" (Slingerland and Chudek 2011, 998).

34. To this end, Slingerland (2008a, 3) insists, "when the 'dualistic West' is contrasted with other, presumably more holistic, cultures, what is really being picked out is the singular intensity with which mind-body dualism has been articulated [in the West]."

35. For more on weak dualism, see chs. 3 and 4 (esp. §§3.2.3 and 4.2.)

36. That is, notions of folk dualism emerge because of the kinds of brains and bodies human beings possess and the ways that humans function and interact in their habitual environments. Related to this is the growing body of evidence that posits the naturalness of "theory of mind" (i.e., folk understandings that cause human beings from a very early age to distinguish between animate and inanimate things), thus suggesting that humans are "born to be dualists" (Slingerland 2008a, 26).

37. It is worth stressing that, although in the present study I eschew dualistic notions of the human self (as noted in §1.2), such theoretical commitments do not preclude the possibility that Paul may or may not function with a particular set of dualistic assumptions.

demarcated set of dualistic propositions. Käsemann (1971c) insists that humanity always exists within a cosmos, which is to say that human beings stand in relation to one of two opposing cosmic powers (either Christ or Sin).[38] Central to Käsemann's thesis is the positing of a fundamental eschatological break between two aeonic spheres of human existence: one that is earthly, conditioned by σάρξ and characterized by disobedience; the other that is heavenly, conditioned by πνεῦμα and characterized by obedience.[39] Within this framework, human existence is essentially passive and always understood vis-à-vis external cosmic lordship. Käsemann (1980, 204, 208, and 205, respectively) speaks, for example, of the fleshly person as "demonically enslaved" and under "alien rule" to the cosmic power of Sin, which is the "opponent" of God.[40] Käsemann's apocalyptic dualism is strong here, and while he (rightly) understands the human body as inextricably tied to the cosmos, such dualistic commitments fight against and ultimately preclude such one-world ideals.[41] Indeed, for Käsemann, it is the radical break between old and new that stands as the hallmark of Paul's resurrection ideals; hence, "discontinuity is the mark of both existence and history" (1971c, 9).[42] In all of these ways, for Käsemann the cosmos has less to do with physics and more to do with intersubjective spheres of hegemony and influence; cosmology refers to a world of opposing suprahuman forces in which humanity finds itself and to which human beings declare allegiance.

---

38. That is, "there is no such thing as man without his particular and respective world" (Käsemann 1971c, 27). Käsemann is here responding to Bultmann's existential analysis whereby the individual believer stands in relation to him- or herself.

39. For example, the key eschatological distinction for Käsemann is the realm in which humanity exists. Thus Käsemann (1964, 133): the human being "is qualified by [its] present Lord, by [its] present allegiance, because the power of the cosmos in the σάρξ and the power of Christ in the πνεῦμα are fighting over [the human] body."

40. In all these quotations, Käsemann is speaking with reference to Rom 7:14–25.

41. Thus Käsemann (1980, 176), "corporeality is standing in a world for which different forces contend and in whose conflict each individual is caught up, belonging to one lord or the other and representing this lord both actively and passively.... It is clear that we are never autonomous, but always participate in a definite world and stand under lordship."

42. Käsemann (1971c, 9) goes on to insist that continuity between the earthly and risen states "only results from the divine faithfulness." For his discussion of the radical break between the old and the new, see 1971c, 8–9.

1. THE DISEMBODIMENT OF RESURRECTION

The influence that Käsemann has exerted on scholarship pertaining to Paul's resurrection ideals cannot be overemphasized.[43] Martinus de Boer (1988), for instance, presumes Käsemann's dualistic portrayal and even intensifies it.[44] Dualistic language abounds throughout Boer's study, as *opposition* is understood as the taken-for-granted axiom of Paul's apocalyptic ideals.[45] Similarly, despite Edward Adams's (2000) astute insistence that cosmology is constructed differently depending on the social contexts of Paul's writings, he nevertheless takes dualism as the default starting point for the apocalyptically informed cosmology of 1 Corinthians.[46]

It should be noted that both Boer and Adams rightly recognize that apocalyptic eschatology is, as Boer (1988, 7) says, a "construct of scholars." Crispin Fletcher-Louis (2011, 2008) has offered a critique of this scholarly construct, specifically pointing to the German tradition as the strongest articulation of such dualistic tendencies. Philipp Vielhauer and Georg Strecker (1991, 549), for example, argue that dualism is "the essential feature of Apocalyptic."[47] Such emphases are less pronounced in the Anglo-American tradition, though they do persist. J. Louis Martyn (1997, 87–88,

---

43. See esp. Tannehill 1967. As noted in his preface, Tannehill studied briefly with Käsemann in Tübingen prior to the completion of his *Dying and Rising with Christ*.

44. For example, Boer (1988, 139; see also 21–23) argues that Paul presents death as a "hypostatize[d] ... quasi-angelic ... power" and further that death "marks 'this age' as radically discontinuous from 'the age to come'" (88). Boer continues by arguing that Death has been brought under the cosmic lordship of Christ in as much as "the gospel ... has unmasked the fact that behind the universal human reality of physical dying there is an inimical, cosmological power at work, a power of 'this age' that as such is doomed for destruction" (138).

45. See, for example, the strikingly dualistic language of Boer's conclusion, which includes the strong oppositions of the two ages, descriptions of division between the "human world and God," and the description of the present age as "the all embracing epoch or sphere of death, viz., the epoch or sphere in which human beings are separated or excluded from the divine presence and life" (1988, 181).

46. On dualism and Jewish apocalyptic in 1 Corinthians, see Adams 2000, 105–7; on the implications of this perspective for Paul's resurrection ideals (esp. 1 Cor 15), see 145–46. Adams rightly removes the presumption of strong dualism generally in Paul's cosmology, though such freeing is due to Paul's forming a social rhetoric in Romans that is not dependent upon the apocalyptic frame-structure. In 1 Corinthians and even Galatians, by contrast, Paul is seen as "forc[ed] ... into a narrow apocalyptic social and spatio-temporal dualism" (193).

47. Vielhauer and Strecker (1991, 549) continue by insisting that "dualism ... dominates [the] thought-world" of the apocalypses.

111–23), for instance, presumes dualism to be the touchstone by which to identify the presence of apocalyptic thought in Paul's otherwise unapocalyptic Epistle to the Galatians.[48] More subtle is John Collins (1979, 9), who stresses the revelatory nature of the apocalyptic genre as being concerned with a "*transcendent* reality which is both temporal, insofar as it envisages *eschatological* salvation, and spatial insofar as it involves another, *supernatural world*" (emphasis added). Though Collins prefers the language of *transcendence* to *dualism*, such an emphasis is not counterbalanced by any significant treatment of imminence, thus retaining a dualistic quality (so noted by Fletcher-Louis 2011, 1586). By way of contrast, the work of Christopher Rowland stresses both vertical and horizontal axes within a more integrated system.[49] For Rowland (1982, 70), the key feature of apocalyptic is the "revelation of the divine mysteries through a vision or some other form of immediate disclosure." By placing revelation rather than eschatology at the center of Jewish apocalyptic, one no longer sees dualism as *the* essential feature, even if many apocalypses stress concepts or contain language that lean in such directions.[50] To this end, Boer's narrowly defined scholarly construct is problematized, thus displacing many

---

48. The thrust of Martyn's (1997) argument presumes a certain Hegelian dialectic in Paul's thought in that cosmic pairs are jointly set aside—a true negation of the negation (see esp. 115). Martyn identifies this disappearance of the old antinomies as an "apocalyptic event" precisely because the old cosmos has now been replaced by the new creation (118–19). While Martyn's description of the new creation's "*unity* in Christ" (119) is compelling, his assertion that opposition stands as the hallmark of apocalypticism betrays the tendency to see dualism at the heart of Jewish apocalyptic thought. Indeed, Martyn's own concession that Paul's "new creation" also consists of new pairs of antinomies (120–22) suggests the emphasis should perhaps shift from an oppositional dualism to a more integrative dualism.

49. That is, Rowland (1982, 73–189) understands the apocalypses as concerning eschatology and history (thus the horizontal axis), on the one hand, and the transcendent heavenly realm and the purposes of God here on earth (thus the vertical axis), on the other.

50. To insist that dualism is not *the* central element of apocalyptic literature does not deny the important role that opposition plays in these texts (or in the employment of apocalyptic modes of thinking). One cannot escape the reality that apocalyptic includes descriptions of "this age" and "the age to come," the contrasting of the forces of God and the forces of Evil, and the elaboration of all that such contrasting is normally taken to involve. Indeed, one need look no further than 1 Cor 15:20–28 for just such an example. The key point to stress is that, though opposition is a pronounced feature of apocalyptic, it should not be taken as the determinative point of definition;

1. THE DISEMBODIMENT OF RESURRECTION

of the traditional dualisms that Käsemann (and others) take for granted.[51] There is, accordingly, a renewed need to assess Paul's resurrection ideals within the context of a nondualistic—or less oppositionally dualistic—apocalyptic framework; I will address this issue in chapters 3–4.

As already noted, Käsemann understands cosmology and anthropology as inextricable,[52] and while he views the former dualistically, his anthropological commitments are much more monistic. That is, for Käsemann (1971c, 26), Paul envisions the "whole man" rather than any kind of partitive anthropology, and on this point Käsemann is in general agreement with the scholarly consensus of his day.[53] Käsemann's *Doktorvater* Rudolf Bultmann also argued for anthropological holism in Paul, though his understanding of such a concept differed from Käsemann significantly.[54] Bultmann (1951–1955, 1:209) upholds the human being as a "living unity" that exists in a constant state of introspective tension.[55] Central here is Paul's use of σῶμα, a term that Bultmann understands as referring to the whole person rather than an individual part of the human composition. Indeed, for Bultmann's Paul, "man does not *have* a soma; he *is* soma" (1:194),[56] which is to say that the individual subject exists as a unified being in relationship to him- or herself and thus able to distinguish self

---

apocalyptic has a far more holistic vision, and oppositional motifs ultimately work in the service of this integrative end.

51. To suggest that Käsemann and others take cosmological dualism for granted is to question the extent to which apocalypticism functions as a so-called worldview, distinct and different from other worldviews of the first century CE. In this study, I seek to recognize the multivalent nature of Paul's apocalyptic language, which was certainly employed throughout Paul's letters but is broadly integrated into issues of empire (1 Thess 4:13–5:11), ethnicity and covenant inclusion (Gal 4:1–7), ethics (Rom 6–8), and popular philosophy (1 Cor 15; see also 1 Cor 1–4). While Paul certainly works with and draws upon the categories of Jewish apocalyptic, his worldview is more broadly elaborated and not limited to apocalyptic alone.

52. So Käsemann (1971c, 27): "anthropology is cosmology *in concreto.*"

53. For example, J. Robinson (1952, 11) stresses the (then) scholarly consensus that "in his anthropology [Paul is] fundamentally … a Hebrew of the Hebrews."

54. Indeed, a significant debate ensued between the two; for a convenient summary, see Wasserman 2007, 795–800.

55. On body-soul dualism, see Bultmann 1951–1955, 1:201.

56. Bultmann (1951–1955, 1:198) later insists that Paul's "capacity for abstract thinking is not … developed," thus resulting in the apostle's inability to "distinguish terminologically between *soma* in the basic sense of that which characterises human existence and *soma* as the phenomenon of the material body."

(the I) from not-self (the not-I).[57] As a neutral category, Paul uses σῶμα to refer either to the "the self under the rule of *sarx*" (as in Rom 6:12; 7:24) or the self under the rule of the πνεῦμα, the latter being the "Spirit-ruled soma" (1:200–201). Bultmann's real distinction, however, is not between two *soma*-ruling powers but rather the introspective tension between "I" and "not-I."[58] Somewhat ironically, though Bultmann rejects a so-called gnostic/Greek body-soul dualism, he nonetheless advocates an implicit (and ontologically stark) Cartesian dualism of knowing subject (I) and known object (not-I).[59] Bultmann here stands within the Augustinian-Lutheran tradition,[60] and his insistence upon anthropological monism is undermined by his own dualistic presumptions.

Bultmann's hegemonic relationship of self to not-self vis-à-vis the power of God has exerted lasting impact on interpretations of the phrase σῶμα πνευματικόν (1 Cor 15:44). Though Bultmann (1951–1955, 1:198–99) concedes that πνεῦμα is the substance of the risen body in Paul's thought, he insists that the apostle's "real intention" is not "a body formed of an ethereal substance, but [rather] that the self is determined by the power of God." The risen body, then, is not a body per se, but rather a mode of existence in which the Spirit of God is infused. Though often critical of Bultmann, many subsequent exegetes have taken up this sense of the Spirit-ruled self. Murdoch Dahl (1962, 81), for instance, argues, "the human totality … begins as a body-animate [that is, a body animated by ψυχή] … [but] ends as a body-spiritual [that is, a body animated by the divine πνεῦμα]."[61] More recently, James Dunn (1998b), Anthony Thiselton

---

57. See, e.g., Bultmann 1951–1955, 1:199 and 227.

58. For Bultmann this is specifically evident in Rom 7:7–25. Here Bultmann's Paul personifies sin and the flesh as a way of asserting that "self and self are at war with each other; i.e. to be innerly divided, or not to be at one with one's self, is the essence of human existence under sin" (1951–1955, 1:245). With respect to Rom 7:22, however, Paul's description of the "inner person" is understood as a reference to the "real self who can distinguish himself from his *soma*-self.… The 'inner' is man's real self in contrast to the self that has come under the sway of sin" (1:203).

59. So noted by Wasserman 2008, 52–53.

60. See, famously, Krister Stendahl (1976, 88), who characterizes Bultmann's Paul as the most "drastic" and "far-reaching" extreme of the Augustinian-Lutheran tradition that dominates Western understandings of the self.

61. By "human totality," Dahl envisions something like the notion that human beings do not possess bodies but rather *are* bodies. Accordingly, to be a "body-spiritual"—Dahl's rendering of σῶμα πνευματικόν—implies a certain kind of Hebraic

(2000), and Wright (2003) have all made similar claims.⁶² We will have occasion to explore these positions in more detail in chapter 3 (§3.2.2). For now, it can be noted that, despite the monistic veneer, all these exegetes implicitly ascribe to at least a folk dualism that distinguishes between body (on the one hand) and soul/spirit (on the other).

There is, to be certain, nothing wrong with this kind of dualistic conception, and I will explore how such folk understandings result from recurring patterns of human embodiment. Where such scholarship is found wanting, however, is in two key respects. First is the issue of inconsistency that comes from simultaneously presuming certain folk dualisms while at the same time asserting the strenuous scholarly construct of Jewish monism. Second is that Jewish monism is often defined vis-à-vis a particularly narrow view of partitive Greek dualism. This is, as it were, a certain kind of cultural dualism that is methodologically problematic though ubiquitous in Pauline scholarship. The standard scholarly position is presented as an either/or choice between Jewish monism and Greek dualism, and preference is overwhelmingly given to the former (e.g., J. Robinson 1952, 11–16; Betz 2000, 316; Schnelle 1996, 55–60; A. Segal 1998, 412). To a large degree, this kind of cultural dualism is doomed from the start; it constructs an idealized monistic view that stands in contradistinction to what is essentially a dualistic straw man (see Aune 1995).⁶³

To a large extent, then, scholarly overgeneralizations regarding Paul's anthropology reflect ahistorical caricatures that are falsely held as dichotomous; such views cannot be critically held. As I hope to show, once the

---

monism that nevertheless retains the idea of innate animating substances. Hence for Dahl, the "body-spiritual" is "a totality taken up into the life of the Spirit himself, so that the whole totality is so controlled and possessed by the Spirit that it shares his life-giving powers" (1962, 81–82).

62. Both Dunn (1998b, 60) and Wright (2003, 347–56) distinguish between two different bodies, one that embodies the soul and the other that embodies the spirit. In a similar way, Thiselton (2000, 1277) argues that Paul envisions a body that is "more than physical but not less [than the earthly body]" and further that σῶμα πνευματικόν refers to a "mode or pattern of intersubjective life directed by the Holy Spirit."

63. On the Jewish side, we can rightly ask what traditions/writers are to be taken as normative; and even if we could identify these, we are still left with the problem that anthropological presuppositions are often only tacit within the surviving traditions. On the Greek side, the most dominant philosophical school in Paul's day (namely, Stoicism) was thoroughly monistic, and even Plato's body-soul dualism was often characterized by body-soul interaction rather than opposition (as we will see in chs. 3 and 4).

straw men of both Jewish monism and Greek dualism are dispersed and we instead turn our attention toward ancient conceptions of the embodied soul, it becomes less problematic to see Paul holding a view of the human being as a whole composed of parts. Put differently, Paul is able to simultaneously hold a partitive view of the human constitution while at the same time affirm the overall unity of the human subject. Gerd Theissen (2007, 78) has articulated this very point, insisting of Paul's anthropology: "It is both holistic and dualistic.... Instead of denying such contradictions, one should acknowledge them."[64] Theissen continues,[65]

> In my opinion, with soul, reason, conscience, body, and flesh Paul always thinks of constituent parts of the human being. These are (in contrast to the exegetical consensus) not always synonyms for the whole person, even though it is correct that body and flesh at times are replaced by a personal pronoun and then stand for the whole person.... For Paul, the human being retains its architecture from parts, layers, and aspects, even though at times a part can stand for the whole.[66] (80–81)

---

64. My translation; German original: "Es ist sowohl ganzheitlich als auch dualistisch.... Anstatt solche Widersprüche zu leugnen, sollte man sie anerkennen."

65. Theissen (2007, 76–95) identifies two tendencies in Paul's anthropology: both view the human subject as a whole consisting of parts, though one stresses holism and ethical responsibility ("Das ganzheitliche Menschenbild") while the other stresses the transformation of the partitive ethical agent ("Das dualistische [transformative] Menschenbild," 78). He argues (76–78) that, though these two pictures find expression elsewhere in the early Christian movement (notably in the Gospels of Matthew and John, respectively), in Paul they are synthesized into a single worldview. Though Paul's anthropology does, at times, lend itself to a view of the human subject as able to act morally in and of themselves (the holistic view), Paul's emphasis falls on the transformation of the human subject, which Paul conceptualizes and articulates through a partitive view of the human constitution. As I will demonstrate, the synthesis of ethical responsibility and transformative potentiality that Theissen highlights is grounded, for Paul, in his resurrection ideals (see §4.2 below). On this point, I go beyond Theissen's treatment.

66. My translation; German original: "Paulus denkt bei Seele, Vernunft, Gewissen, Leib und Fleisch m. E. immer an Bestandteile des Menschen. Es handelt sich (anders als es ein exegetischer Konsens meint) nicht immer um Synonyme für die ganze Person, auch wenn es richtig ist, dass Leib und Fleisch hin und wieder durch ein Personalpronomen ersetzt werden und dann für den ganzen Menschen stehen.... Der Mensch behält bei Paulus seine Architektur aus Teilen, Schichten und Aspekten, auch wenn hin und wieder ein Teil für das Ganze stehen kann."

Working in a similar vein, and following the recent work of Emma Wasserman (2008) and George van Kooten (2008), my analysis locates Paul's anthropological descriptions within a broader, more integrative cultural matrix of both Judean and Greek traditions. As I will demonstrate, this has implications for the apostle's resurrection ideals precisely because such ideals are cosmo-somatic in nature.

In summary, then, we have seen a peculiar mixture of dualistic and monistic tendencies in Pauline scholarship. On the one hand, there is a general tendency toward understanding Jewish apocalyptic as being exceedingly dualistic, while on the other hand, there is an assertion that Paul's anthropology is essentially monistic. In both cases, claims to dualism/monism are overextended. Bearing this in mind, there is a pressing need to delineate more clearly dualism and monism in Paul's writings, a task that I take up in chapter 3 and that will have implications for how we understand somatic (dis)continuity across terrestrial and celestial somatic states (see chs. 3 and 4) and the somatic effect of resurrection for Christ-devotees (see chs. 4 and 5). As we will see, cognitive linguistics provides a set of methodological tools (see §1.4) that are particularly apt for mapping and analyzing the creative blending of cosmology and anthropology in Paul's letters.

1.3.3. Paul's Participationist and Resurrection Ideals

As with so many aspects of the undisputed epistles, participation in/with Christ permeates Paul's resurrection ideals, and this extends to both sides of the soteriological equation. On the one hand, in Rom 6:4–8 Paul insists believers have been "crucified with" (ὁ παλαιὸς ἡμῶν ἄνθρωπος συνεσταυρώθη), have been "buried with" (συνετάφημεν), and thus have "died with Christ" (ἀπεθάνομεν σὺν Χριστῷ). For Paul, believers are "deeply enmeshed" or "intertwined" (σύμφυτος) in the likeness of Christ's death. On the other hand, the "deep enmeshing" (σύμφυτος) in Christ's death is balanced by an anticipated future enmeshing in Christ's resurrection (Rom 6:5),[67] what Paul later refers to as "living with" (συζήσομεν) and being "glorified with" (συνδοξασθῶμεν) Christ (Rom 6:8 and 8:17, respectively). More striking still are those instances where Paul describes believers as

---

67. Thus following most commentators in supplying σύμφυτος in the apodosis of 6:5 (e.g., Dunn 1988, 1:318).

"morphed together with" (σύμμορφος) Christ's risen existence (Rom 8:29 and Phil 3:21; see also Phil 3:10). In all of these instances, Paul's resurrection ideals are premised upon notions of participation in which distinct entities are brought together into a singular, organic whole.

Despite this motif within the undisputed epistles, no scholarly consensus exists on the participatory dimension of Paul's resurrection ideals. In the following discussion, I map four interpretive tendencies within contemporary scholarship. Returning again to the category of cognicentrism, we will see that many of the dualistic presumptions outlined above (§§1.2 and 1.3.2) yield disembodied understandings of participation and/or resurrection. As I will show, participation is most commonly viewed as a mental awareness that exists at the expense (or even rejection) of any meaningful description of somatic union. Given that Paul consistently maps resurrection and participation to the human body, such a prioritizing of the noetic at the expense of the somatic unhelpfully disembodies Paul's ideals.

The first tendency is the characterization of participation in Christ's death and resurrection as an experience in which Christ-devotees passively partake. Though this interpretive stream is ubiquitous in Pauline studies, in many ways it is a product of scholarly reactionism. In the late nineteenth/early twentieth century, it was not uncommon to identify notions of an already realized resurrection in Paul's thought. For example, Albert Schweitzer (1968, 75 and 96, respectively) understood "redemption [to be] realising itself in the present" precisely because believers had already "mysterious[ly] ... shar[ed] the dying and rising again of Christ."[68] The earlier *religionsgeschichtliche Schule* (of which Schweitzer was critical) made similar assertions, proposing that Paul's baptismal theology had been influenced by the cultic drama of the Hellenistic mystery religions.[69] Accordingly, Paul was understood either to promote a cult patterned on the initiate's dying and rising with the deity

---

68. Though critical of Schweitzer, Davies (1962, 317–18) similarly sees in Paul an assertion that believers have "died and risen with Christ and [thus are] already being transformed."

69. For a sympathetic overview of the "mysteries," see Lohse 1976, 232–43. Though many have problematized the mystery religions comparison (e.g., Wedderburn 1987), the history of scholarly discussion is fraught with ideological anachronism (on this point, see famously Smith 1990).

in baptism⁷⁰ or to confront certain baptismal developments that had arisen through (in)direct cultic influence.⁷¹ By the mid-twentieth century, Käsemann had incorporated the latter into his apocalyptic reading of Paul, suggesting that the apostle opposes a pre-Pauline eschatological enthusiasm within the Greek churches. Thus Käsemann, speaking with respect to Rom 6:4–8, insists:

> [Paul] builds in a remarkable caveat in the shape of an eschatological reservation. Participation in the Resurrection is spoken of not in the perfect tense, but in the future. Baptism equips for it, calls to it, but does not itself convey this gift.... Further than this Paul ... is not prepared to go. (1969, 132–33)

The attention Käsemann draws to Paul's temporal description is important. Any assessment of present participation in Christ's resurrection must account for the nuances of Paul's language in Rom 6:4–8. Among modern scholars, it has become axiomatic to stress this temporal distinction.⁷² Alexander Wedderburn (1987, 232), for instance, argues that Rom 6:4–8 advocate a fundamental "asymmetry" that stresses participation in Christ's death without a corresponding participation in resurrection.⁷³ For Wedderburn, the literal and physical nature of resurrection precludes Christ-devotees from presently participating in resurrection (395; see also 160–232). Slightly preferable to Wedderburn is the earlier work of Robert

---

70. Wilhelm Bousset (1970, 188–200), for instance, understood Paul's mystical and cultic participation with the risen Christ as having been patterned on the mysteries.

71. For example, Lohse 1976, 241–43.

72. A prime example is Bart Ehrman's (2008, 386–92) widely used introductory text, where Paul's eschatological reservation is taken as a scholarly commonplace and one of the concrete points of difference between the undisputed and disputed Pauline letters. Among commentators on Rom 6:1–11, Dunn (1988, 1:314) argues that baptism "is linked only with Christ's death ... [and Paul] refus[es] to extend the association to resurrection." More recently, Frank Matera (2010, 150) insists that "[baptism] into death ... is the central notion Paul is trying to communicate." While there are many excellent reasons to see the six disputed letters as secondary to Paul—including reasons that relate to claims of a realized resurrection—I hope to show that it is too simplistic simply to read Paul as rejecting any sense of a present, already realized resurrection experience.

73. Thus Wedderburn (1987, 395): Paul is unable to "bring himself to speak of resurrection in the present." For a critical engagement with Wedderburn on this point, see §4.1 below.

Tannehill (1967), who remains open to some form of present risen life.[74] For Tannehill, however, this is more mental assent than participation in/with Christ. For example, concerning Paul's insistence that believers have died with Christ, Tannehill argues:

> [Paul] is speaking of the destruction of the dominion of sin, of which all believers were a part.... [Such destruction] is an inclusive event, for the existence of men was bound up with this old aeon, and what puts an end to it also puts an end to them as men of the old aeon. (1967, 30)

Tannehill here objectifies the soteriological event, abstracting it as a "theological foundation" (81).[75] The logic runs from abstract theological principle to ethical activity. Everything is contingent on an objectified view of Christ's death that is once removed from believers such that life is mediated through opposing aeons. In this way, apocalyptic dualism has unduly colored and disembodied participation in Christ's death and resurrection. Believers participate not so much in/with Christ but rather in the conditions that Christ enables.

This reading of Tannehill leads us into a second interpretive tendency within Pauline scholarship, one that downplays—even rejects—the experiential dimension in Paul's writings in favor of a more subjective—certainly cerebral—articulation of theology and faith. Bultmann stands as a prime example. Indebted both to his existentialist analysis and the primacy given to the justification by faith metaphor, he understands participation with Christ primarily as acknowledgment:

---

74. So Tannehill (1967, 12): "The believer participates in the new life in the present, but Paul is careful to make clear that it does not become the believer's possession. It is realized through a continual surrender of one's present activity to God, a walking in newness of life, and at the same time it remains God's gift for the future."

75. For Tannehill (1967, 77; see also 127), ongoing participation with Christ's sufferings is a pastoral issue: "This continuing participation in death ... prevent[s] the believer from trusting in himself and so falling back into the old life." The more Tannehill stresses the absolute and definitive nature of Christ's past death/resurrection, the more obscure Paul's insistence on ongoing participation becomes. This is because, in Tannehill's view, sharing Christ's sufferings is about remaining cognizant and aware of the decisive break rather than actually participating in such sufferings (see esp. 127).

1. THE DISEMBODIMENT OF RESURRECTION

> *Recognition* takes place only as *acknowledgment*. This is the decision-question which the "word of the cross" thrusts upon the hearer: whether he will *acknowledge* that God has made a crucified one Lord, whether he will thereby *acknowledge* the demand to take up the cross by the surrender of his previous understanding of himself, making the cross the determining power of his life, *letting himself be crucified with Christ*. (1951–1955, 1:303, emphasis added)[76]

For Bultmann, Paul's participationist language constitutes a mental assent. One does not so much die and rise with Christ as acknowledge the theological proposition of the crucified one's lordship. A similar move is made by Joost Holleman (1996, 130), who understands Paul as "systematizing" early Christian eschatology and further insists that participation in Christ's death and resurrection is an "idea" that Paul develops and that carries a certain amount of rational force.[77] Holleman presents Paul's resurrection ideals as a history of ideas. While his study makes important contributions to the traditio-historical background of Paul's thought, it strenuously assumes an unbalanced picture of human cognition in which notions of resurrection are devoid of somatic grounding (both conceptually and experientially).

Whereas Bultmann and Holleman steer away from the language of experience, Schweitzer was quite comfortable to describe Paul's participationist ideals within experiential categories. Identifying what he labeled as the "mystical doctrine of the dying and rising again with Christ," Schweitzer (1968, 97) sought to place mystical Christ-participation at the center of Pauline theology.[78] Despite this insistence, whereby Paul's mysticism is not "merely metaphorical … but a simple reality" (15), the great irony of

---

76. In the same volume Bultmann (1951–1955, 1:302) also says, "the union of believers into one *soma* with Christ now has its basis … in the fact that in the word of proclamation Christ's death-and-resurrection becomes a possibility of existence in regard to which a decision must be made." That Bultmann speaks in these passages more as theologian than biblical scholar may perhaps excuse him from the criticism just offered, not because his reading of Pauline participation is any less cognicentric in a theological context, but rather because Bultmann's chief aim in such a context is demythologization rather than historical description.

77. Thus Holleman (1996, 206, emphasis added): "If one *accepts* that Jesus has been raised, and *believes* that Christians are united with Christ, then *one can and must also believe* that all Christians will be raised at the end of time."

78. For Schweitzer (1968, 225) this was an either/or choice between juristic and participationist language. Thus he famously insisted, "The doctrine of righteousness

Schweitzer's work is that mysticism is understood purely from an intellectual standpoint (so noted by Ashton 2000, 143–44).[79] For Schweitzer (1968, 98), Paul's mysticism is coherent to those who "think consistently," because it is a "logical inference"; and later, "[Paul] is a logical thinker and his mysticism is a complete system" (139). Schweitzer therefore does not posit Paul the mystic so much as Paul the rational theologian. Experience itself is understood as a noetic activity, and Paul's understanding of Christ-believer participation is configured as a disembodied mysticism. Here, as with Tannehill (1967), experience is limited to thought and rationality.

Schweitzer was, of course, working with many of the categories used by his contemporaries, categories that to this day are perennially employed though often found on the margins of mainline scholarship. Herein lies a third approach to Paul's *in/with Christ* ideals, which is the tendency to locate Paul's participatory language in the context of the exceedingly fuzzy categories of *mysticism* and/or *religious experience*. Alongside Schweitzer, we can also place the work of Wilhelm Bousset (1970) and Adolf Deissmann (1957), both of whom stressed (at least conceptually) a more experientialist understanding of Paul's theology.[80] Dunn (1998b, 393) remarks that such trends waned in the mid-twentieth century. Pushing the category of mysticism to the side, much twentieth-century scholarship implicitly bracketed out the category of *experience* as analytically unhelpful. Indeed, many understood experience as a rather shaky foundation upon which to construct Paul's theology.[81] In recent decades, however, discussions of religious experience in Paul's writings have undergone resurgence (e.g., Shantz 2009; DeConick 2006a), especially with respect to Paul's resurrection ideals. For some, this is an issue of visionary experience, thus focusing not on participation but rather on the historical nature of the resurrection

---

by faith is therefore a subsidiary crater, which has formed within the rim of the main crater—the mystical doctrine of redemption through the being-in-Christ."

79. For Schweitzer (1968, 97), the eschatological disjunction of Christ's past resurrection, on the one hand, and the anticipated existence of believers in the messianic kingdom, on the other, is a presumed theological problem that leads "Paul as a thinker to his Mysticism."

80. Bousset (1970, 156) focused on Paul's cultic experience, while Deissmann (1957) stressed Paul's individual mystical experiences.

81. So Käsemann (1971a, 73): "The Pauline doctrine of justification is a protection not only against nomism but also against enthusiasm and mysticism." Elsewhere Käsemann (1971b, 82) contrasts proper expressions of faith with those in which "faith must be rescued from the dimension of recurrent religious experience."

1. THE DISEMBODIMENT OF RESURRECTION

claim (Lüdemann 1994). More to this study's interests is the work of Alan Segal (1998; 2008), who has argued compellingly that Paul's understanding of resurrection is patterned not merely on an encounter with the risen Christ but more particularly on a temporary "experience of the resurrected body" (2008, 19). Here the participatory and somatic dimensions of Paul's resurrection ideals are brought into coordination.

Central to Segal's treatment is the locating of Paul the Judean within an emerging tradition of apocalyptic mystical praxis (see 2004, 322–50, 399–440; 1990, 34–71). The present study follows Segal down this path. Nevertheless, though Segal rightly points to heavenly ascent as the experiential and traditional context in which Paul's resurrection ideals are framed, he fails to give full attention to the rhetorical nuance that characterizes the apostle's writings. Indeed, while traditions of heavenly ascent speak to cosmological transposition (going up and down), they do not speak as readily to somatic union (being in and out). For this latter register, which is characteristic of Paul's participation language, Segal (2004, 322–50; 2006) appeals to neurobiological studies and comparative traditions of mystical oneness (or *unio mystica*). While much is gained in this line of inquiry,[82] ecstatic experience alone remains unconvincing as the contextual frame for Paul's participationist ideals.[83] In sum, then, though Segal rightly points to the inextricable nature of Paul's participationist, resurrection, and heavenly ascent ideals, descriptions of oneness between Christ and believers requires more than an appeal to ecstatic experience.

A fourth (and final) way in which Paul's participationist ideals are commonly understood relates to notions of corporate or representational figures. According to this line of research, Christ and other ancestral personages (Adam, Abraham, Moses, etc.) are perceived as collective personalities. The individual stands for the whole such that Christ (or Adam, etc.) represents all those who come after him and share some perceived affinity or likeness with him. The term *corporate personality* was first used by H. Wheeler Robinson (1936) to refer to ideas of corporate responsibility (in

---

82. Particularly compelling is Shantz (2009, esp. 93–108 and 110–44), as well as the growing body of historical comparatives being brought to light (Morray-Jones 1992; 1993a; 1993b; 2006; and Rowland and Morray-Jones 2009).

83. Indeed, language of Christ-believer union pervades the apostle's letters, being simultaneously found in passages where Paul (likely) reflects on ecstatic experiences (e.g., 2 Cor 3:7–4:6; 12:1–10) and others where he uses the phrase ἐν Χριστῷ in a more common, identity-forming way (e.g., Gal 1:22; Rom 9:1; 16:9–10; Phil 1:1; 4:21).

Hebrew law contexts) and transindividual identity, the latter denoting a "primitive" psychological state in which it was impossible to "distinguish between the individual and his group in the way that we [moderns] do" (Rogerson 1970, 5).

Robinson's understanding of corporate personality has subsequently been problematized (J. Porter 1965; Rogerson 1970), though related notions continue to persist in New Testament scholarship.[84] Wedderburn (1985, 91), for instance, understands Christ, Abraham, and other traditional persons as *"representative figures* through whom God acts towards the human race; he acts towards them 'in' those figures and they are caught up 'with' them in that divine initiative of grace" (emphasis added).[85] In line with many of the interpretations noted above, this understanding of Paul's *in/with Christ* language suggests a cognicentric (and deritualized) bias that sets the body aside;[86] Christ-devotees do not participate in/with Christ so much as they acknowledge their "solidarity" with Christ.[87]

More promising is the work of Caroline Johnson Hodge (2007), who, like Wedderburn,[88] refocuses our understanding of corporate personality.[89] Drawing on ancient theories of patrilineal genetics, Johnson

---

84. In addition to Wedderburn (1985) and Johnson Hodge (2007), who are discussed in detail, see also Kister (2007).

85. See also Wedderburn 1987, 342–59.

86. Indeed, Wedderburn (1985, 89–91) rejects any sense in which Paul's language might actually denote being located in either Christ or Abraham, opting instead for a reading of Gal 3 whereby the Galatians are to "imitate" Abraham's faith and "profoundly identify" with Christ's suffering and death. For Wedderburn, Christ stands as a "prototype and example of the saved," and baptism into/with Christ's death and life is but a mere *"remind[er]* ... that [the baptisand] had already been caught up in, involved in, Christ's past death and resurrection" (358, emphasis added).

87. So Wedderburn (1987, 349–50), speaking of Rom 6: "God has also associated us with Christ, not this time as co-recipients of the pronouncement of a blessing [as with Abraham in Gal 3], but as co-recipients of his verdict upon human sin. They receive that verdict together with their representative and in his person; ... [Paul's *with* language] arises out of this idea of the solidarity of the race with its representative."

88. Wedderburn (1987, 351–56) intentionally distinguishes his understanding of representational figures from Robinson's notion of corporate personality; of the latter, Wedderburn is "thoroughly appreciative of the idea expressed by it as long as exaggerated claims are not made from it" (352).

89. Johnson Hodge prefers to speak of a "corporate identity for descendants" (2007, 97), one in which "the ancestor represents all his descendants, and the descendants collectively represent the ancestor" (98). She is careful to distinguish her under-

1. THE DISEMBODIMENT OF RESURRECTION 31

Hodge stresses what she calls a "containment theory of descent" (94). In this framework, emphasis is placed on material kinship connections such that descendants are thought to exist in their progenitor's seed and subsequently emerge out of that same ancestral figure: "in the seed of [the progenitor] is the 'stuff' of all future descendants" (109).[90] While Johnson Hodge's work provides a promising way beyond the cognicentrism inherent in many of the aforementioned interpretations, she does not attend to issues of resurrection and the extent to which Paul's resurrection and participationist ideals interlace one another. This is particularly important because, as A. Segal (2008, 19) has noted, there are good reasons to see much of Paul's participationist ideals as grounded in and spurred by Paul's temporary "experience of the resurrected body." In the chapters that follow (esp. §5.3), I will explore this dimension in detail, suggesting solutions to some of the interpretive problems that Johnson Hodge raises but is unable to address.

As the preceding discussion has demonstrated, much hinges on the context in which Paul's participationist ideals are located. Should *being in Christ* be understood as a passive experience of dualistically opposed aeonic spheres (so Käsemann and Tannehill), abstracted as a noetic act of recognition (so Bultmann, Holleman, and even Schweitzer), experientially universalized as a *unio mystica* (so A. Segal), or framed within the context of corporate persons (Wedderburn) and patrilineal genetics (Johnson Hodge)?[91] As I have demonstrated, none of these contexts is wholly convincing, and most presume participation in Christ's death and resurrection to be a noetic affair that is tied less to the body and more to a proper theological outlook. It was, in part, this lack of a precise context that forced E. P. Sanders (1977, 522) famously to concede that the modern

---

standing of patrilineal descent from Robinson's corporate personality (193 n. 41). On the one hand, she shows that notions of being contained within one's ancestors are not particular to ancient Hebrew thought but rather pervade ancient thinking more generally (see 94–96). On the other hand, she rightly points to the ambiguity of the term *corporate personality* and more importantly takes issue with Robinson's implicit assumption that (so-called) "primitive" societies are less developed than their more evolved modern counterparts (see 193 n. 41).

90. Johnson Hodge earlier cites S. Williams (1988, 717) along the same line: "offspring are incorporated in the ancestor, and the ancestor is later present in his offspring."

91. This list is not exhaustive; beyond many of the interpretive contexts listed here, Richard Hays (2008) adds the following frame-structures: political and/or military solidarity, ecclesial participation, and narratological participation.

scholar "lack[s] a category of 'reality' [by which to understand] real participation in Christ."[92] In the chapters that follow, I will not suggest such a category but rather refocus our theoretical orientation (see esp. §1.4) so as to explore the interpretive creativity and categorical hybridity of Paul's language and thought.[93] This will be done largely with respect to issues of cosmology and anthropology (see chs. 3 and 4), though it will also call for a reassessment of Paul's eschatology (ch. 4) and a direct discussion of the relationship between the apostle's participationist and resurrection ideals (ch. 5).

1.3.4. Problem Definition

Although the preceding literature review has pointed to several problems in the current state of scholarship, three specific issues have come to the fore. First, there is a pressing need to demarcate more clearly a conceptual framework within which resurrection texts can be identified and interpreted. As we have seen, the current scholarly tendency to bifurcate resurrection into literal and metaphorical expressions is theoretically problematic and hermeneutically imprecise. Second, we have seen that, with respect to treatments of Jewish apocalyptic and Paul's anthropology, constructions of dualism and monism are overdrawn and often implicitly premised on modern assumptions. Given the centrality of these topics to Paul's resurrection ideals, there is an acute need to delineate more clearly the nature of dualism and monism in Paul's thinking. Finally, I have identified several ways in which the relationship between Paul's resurrection and participationist ideals is construed. Most commonly, Paul's ideals are abstracted into a noetic act of faith and/or interpersonal solidarity that is often contextualized within dualistic aeonic spheres or disjointed temporal referents. In light of Paul's own descriptions, which speak of an organic morphing together with Christ's death and resurrection, there is a profound need for a less abstract, more embodied account of Paul's resurrection and participationist ideals.

---

92. Sanders (1977) tries to navigate a course that lies between Käsemann and Bultmann. As we have seen, modern dualisms permeate both views, and the unmasking of such dualisms may actually provide a better hermeneutical way forward.

93. That is, the problem is found not so much in the need for a new category of reality, but rather a better and more acute theoretical orientation that enables appreciation of Paul's categories of reality.

At the heart of these issues, however, is a pervasive tendency toward understanding resurrection as a propositional, cognicentric category. This trend is premised on the traditional Cartesian opposition of body and mind that, when projected onto Paul, produces a disembodied view of resurrection. In light of this general tendency, a renewed examination of Paul's resurrection ideals is in order, one that takes seriously the integration of body and mind and that examines more clearly the extent to which Paul's understanding of resurrection is somatically grounded.

1.4. Theory and Method: Integrating Cognition and Culture

In the chapters that follow I employ theories of cognitive linguistics and embodied cognition so as to reenvision Paul's resurrection ideals. By grounding both language and human thought within recurrent patterns of human embodiment, cognitive linguistics provides, as Slingerland (2008a, 218) notes, "a clear way out of the postmodern prison house of language without committing us to a rightly discredited form of Enlightenment realism." Seen against the backdrop of the above literature review, cognitive linguistics thus enables a move past the otherwise ubiquitous problem of cognicentrism. My analysis draws heavily on the work of Lakoff, Johnson, Gilles Fauconnier, and Mark Turner.[94] Rather than focusing on traditional

---

94. See esp. Lakoff and Johnson 1980; 1999; Johnson 1987; Lakoff and Turner 1989; and Fauconnier and Turner 2002. The intellectual roots of these theorists' works are somewhat opaque, which is perhaps an unfortunate by-product of the so-called "second generation" of cognitive science, from which cognitive linguistics emerged. In direct response to the first generation, which assumed many of the tenets of traditional Anglo-American philosophy, this second generation necessarily eschewed prefigured assertions and thus prioritized philosophical reflection that began from empirical data (see Lakoff and Johnson 1999, 75–78). But theory cannot develop in a vacuum, and data is never theory-neutral; the prioritized empiricism of this second generation flirts with the potential perils that come from uncritical self-reflection. To my knowledge a full intellectual history of the cognitive linguistic project has not been written, though some have offered cursory reflections (see, e.g., Wolf 1994, 38–41). Lakoff and Johnson (1999, 97–98) briefly trace their project back to the work of phenomenologists such as John Dewey and Maurice Merleau-Ponty, though their discussion at this point is quite general and offers no detailed or thorough engagement. One of the richer assessments, even if it is not focused on cognitive linguistics specifically, is the work of Varela, Thompson, and Rosch (1991, 15–33), which engages both Western and Eastern philosophical and scientific traditions so as to explore embodied cognition.

linguistic issues such as grammar, syntax, and semantics,[95] I am interested in how the products of human imagination and creativity are not only grounded in but also arise organically from recurrent patterns of human embodiment. Three theoretical concepts are particularly important—image schemata, conceptual metaphors, and blending theory—each of which I will briefly introduce and illuminate with respect to 1 Cor 15:3-4.

There is a growing consensus among cognitive scientists that human thought is primarily image-based and derived from patterns of sensory-motor experience (Slingerland 2008a, 56). While there is good empirical evidence to support this claim (Slingerland 2008a, 56-59 and 162-63), Johnson (1987) has explored its philosophical dimensions in significant detail. Johnson points specifically to the image schema as the basic unit of human meaning creation. Image schemata are conceptual structures that are skeletal in nature (i.e., they have not rich but rather schematic content) and that arise experientially as a result of the kinds of bodies we have functioning in the kind of world in which we live.[96] Such schemata exist at the conceptual level and are what Johnson refers to as gestalt in nature—that is, they function as recurrent, organized, and unified wholes (44). One example of an image schema is the VERTICALITY schema, to which we will return throughout this study.[97] The concept of VERTICALITY is something we learn with our bodies through both perception (for example, looking up at the sky and down at the ground) and general somatic movement (for example, standing up, lying down). Accordingly, VERTICALITY is not an abstract proposition but rather a concept that is somatically obtained. It is a concept that emerges organically from patterns of human embodiment.

I have already introduced conceptual metaphor above (§1.3.1), so my comments at this point will be more focused and precise. Conceptual metaphor is rooted in the assertion that human thought is metaphorical in nature. To again cite Johnson,

---

95. For a cognitive linguistic overview of these issues, see Croft and Cruse 2004.

96. For an excellent and succinct introduction to image schemata, see Evans and Green 2006, 176-205.

97. Following the convention outlined in Lakoff and Johnson (1980), I will designate image-schematic concepts by the use of small caps. This allows for the distinction between lexical signs and the concepts they represent (e.g., verticality is a lexical sign; VERTICALITY denotes the concept behind the sign).

1. THE DISEMBODIMENT OF RESURRECTION 35

> Metaphor is not merely a linguistic mode of expression; rather, it is one of the chief cognitive structures by which we are able to have coherent, ordered experiences that we can reason about and make sense of. Through metaphor, we make use of patterns that obtain in our physical experience to organize our more abstract understanding. (1987, xv)

Conceptual metaphors arise when one, often more abstract, conceptual domain is understood in relation to another, often more concrete, conceptual domain. These more concrete domains are the image schemata noted above, which serve as conceptual templates by which more abstract domains are understood and whereby conceptual metaphors emerge. Though conceptual metaphors are reflected in linguistic constructions, it is important to note that they are conceptual in nature and thus capable of multimodal, nonverbal expression (Gibbs 2008, 447–524; Lakoff and Johnson 1999, 57). For cognitive linguists, metaphor is a general cognitive principle operative within the minds of all human beings. As such, conceptual metaphors are expressed not only through human language and verbal communication (for example, narrative, speech, poetry), but also in gestures, art, music, pictures, and even ritual.[98] An example of a conceptual metaphor is the RESURRECTION IS BEING AWAKE metaphor, whereby the concept RESURRECTION is understood with respect to experiences of waking and sleeping.[99] Before we can sufficiently appreciate this metaphor, however, it will be beneficial to introduce blending theory.

Whereas Lakoff and Johnson envision a process of unidirectional projection from concrete source domain to abstract target domain, Fauconnier and Turner (2002) describe a more general mental operation of

---

98. Conceptual metaphors have been demonstrated to undergird various languages, including English, French, Japanese, and Chinese (Slingerland 2008a, 171). Beyond linguistics, conceptual metaphors have been demonstrated in political ideology, poetry, religious discourse, and even mathematics (respectively, see Lakoff 1996; Lakoff and Turner 1989; Slingerland 2004; Lakoff and Núñez 2000). For uses of conceptual metaphor theory in New Testament studies, see Howe 2006; Lundhaug 2010; Stovell 2012; McNeel 2014; Howe and Green 2014.

99. Again following Lakoff and Johnson (1980), I articulate conceptual metaphors via the small-caps formula A IS B (or A AS B), where A and B refer to the conceptual domains being cross-mapped. This stylistic notation should be understood not as a statement in its own right (e.g., resurrection is being awake), but rather as a symbolic description of cross-domain mappings: the target domain (RESURRECTION) is mapped to the source domain (BEING AWAKE), with the mapping represented by the copula (IS). See further Lakoff and Johnson 1999, 58.

conceptual integration wherein conceptual domains are simultaneously blended with one another to produce emergent meaning not found in either domain. This process is called *conceptual blending*, and it has been demonstrated as "a general, basic mental operation ... [that is] fundamental to all activities of the human mind" (37–38).[100] Blending happens through the organization of conceptual networks that always consist of at least two input spaces (i.e., the domains being blended), one generic space (which establishes cross-space correlations), and one blended space (where emergent structure is created).[101] Drawing on image schemata and conceptual metaphors, blending happens on the fly as human communication unfolds. Mental spaces are created from working memory, cross-mapped with one another through vital relations, and blended to create emergent meaning. Though much of this process happens unconsciously, emergent meaning is said to achieve human scale when it becomes intelligible and consciously perceived, that is, recognized in a moment or "flash of comprehension" (44).

By way of demonstrating this methodological matrix, a brief examination of a very common resurrection metaphor will suffice (see fig. 1.1 on p. 38). In 1 Cor 15:3–4, Paul recounts an early Christian traditional unit wherein Jesus is described as having "died" (ἀπέθανεν) and been "woken" (ἐγήγερται) on the third day. Though the metaphor in this case is entirely conventional and predates Paul by several centuries (e.g., Dan 12:2), the underlying conceptual network is no less relevant.[102] The metaphor reflects

---

100. Like conceptual metaphor, blending undergirds not only linguistic discourse but understanding more generally. For examples of conceptual blending at work in numerous aspects of human life, see Fauconnier and Turner 2002 throughout, esp. 17–73. Applications of blending theory in New Testament studies include Howe 2006; Lundhaug 2007; 2010; Tappenden 2010; 2012; Thaden 2012.

101. Conceptual networks are typically structured according to certain patterns—namely, simplex networks, mirror networks, single-scope networks, or double-scope networks (Fauconnier and Turner 2002, 119–35; see also 337–45).

102. Lakoff and Johnson (1999, 125) note that so-called dead metaphors are (in most cases) linguistic expressions in which the "conceptual metaphorical mapping is still alive, but the term has ceased to be a linguistic expression of that mapping.... Conventional metaphors are relatively fixed, unconscious, automatic, and so alive that they are used regularly without awareness or noticeable effort." The key distinction between a dead or living metaphor, then, is not whether the author of a text is consciously speaking metaphorically, but rather whether the unconscious mapping is still utilized in conveying meaning. Alternatively, dead metaphors are limited to those

the blending of the more concrete experience of waking and sleeping (I_1) with the more abstract notions of life and death (I_2).[103] Through the construction of general correspondence in the generic space (G), vital relations are drawn between the two inputs, thus linking paired counterparts between I_1 and I_2 (for example, linking death with sleep).[104]

As demonstrated in figure 1.1 and table 1.1, the perceptual connections are quite robust but generally mapped according to the VERTICALITY schema.[105] Once these links are established, various elements from the inputs can be selectively projected to the blended space. What emerges in the blend are the conceptual metaphors LIFE IS BEING AWAKE and DEATH IS SLEEP, which, when framed with respect to the afterlife, entail the actual "waking up" (ἐγείρω) of the physical corpse that had died and was buried. In this way, the blend contains an emergent structure not found in either of the inputs—for example, though actually being dead is not the same as being asleep, in the blended space death *is* sleep. What results is the structuring of the concept RESURRECTION in relation to the basic human experience of waking from sleep, hence the conceptual metaphor, RESURRECTION IS BEING AWAKE. As I will show, this (and other) metaphor(s)

---

instances where the metaphorical mapping has been completely severed. For example, Lakoff and Johnson note the English term *pedigree* is derived from the French *ped de gris* ("a grouse's foot"), which originally functioned as an idiom for a "family-tree diagram," though such cultural concepts cease to convey meaning in English (124).

103. Each of these input spaces (I_1 and I_2), as well as the blended and the generic spaces, are what Fauconnier and Turner (2002, 102–6) refer to as mental spaces. Mental spaces are "small conceptual packets constructed as we think and talk, for purposes of local understanding and action. They are very partial assemblies containing elements, structured by frames and cognitive models" (102). On a physiological level, Fauconnier and Turner contend that the elements within each mental space correspond to activated neuronal assemblies that operate within working memory.

104. These cross-spaces correlations are called vital relations (Fauconnier and Turner 2002, 92–102). Physiologically speaking, vital relations link mental spaces through neurobiological binding (e.g., coactivation [102]). Such relations are not random connections, but rather are characterized by specific types of correspondence (e.g., Identity, Time, Role-Value, Analogy).

105. For the sake of brevity, not all the elements of table 1.1 have been diagrammed in the generic space in fig. 1.1. Instead, fig. 1.1 has been drawn to include the VERTICALITY schema and the corresponding contents for I_1 and I_2. The reader should note that all contents listed in table 1.1 (and perhaps more) should also be included in the corresponding spaces. Earlier versions of this table and figure are published in Tappenden 2012.

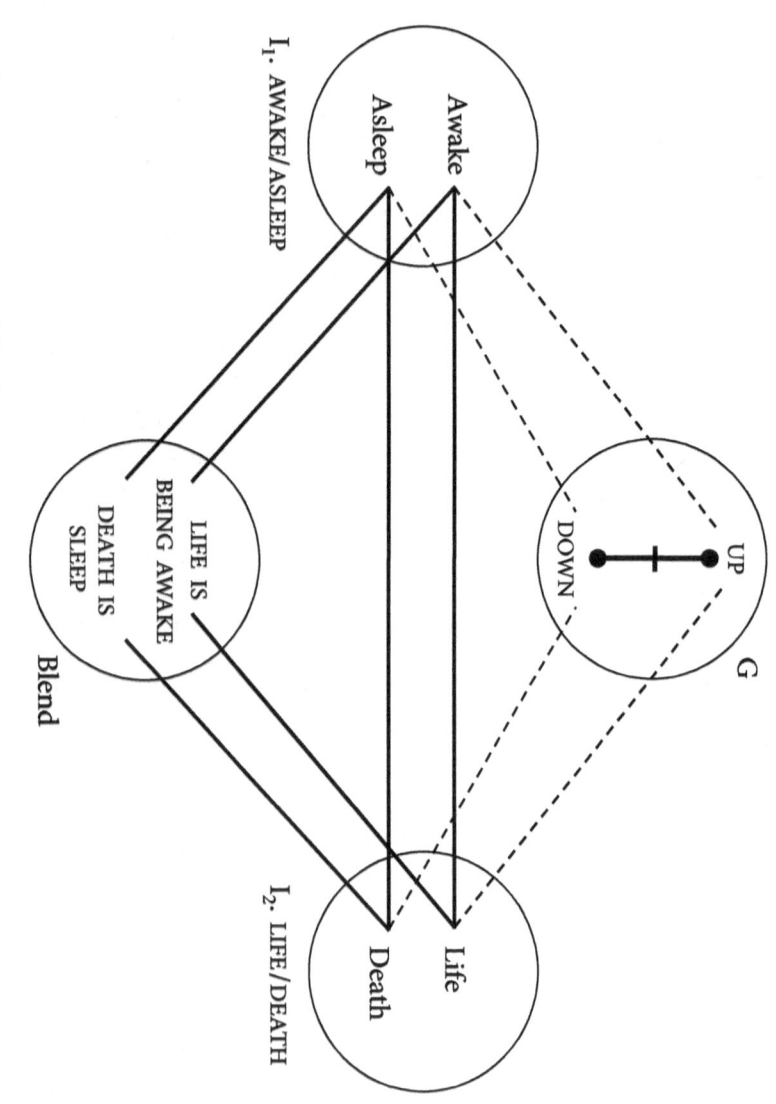

Figure 1.1. LIFE IS BEING AWAKE Metaphor

Table 1.1. Blending Map for the LIFE IS BEING AWAKE Metaphor. Reprinted from Tappenden 2012. Used with permission.

I$_1$. AWAKE/ASLEEP	Generic Space	I$_2$. LIFE/DEATH
Bed	Resting Place	Grave/tomb
Physical body	Body	Physical body
UP: Erect and able to act when awake DOWN: Lying down and still when asleep	Somatic/ Kinetic State	UP: Erect and able to act when alive DOWN: Lying down and still when dead
UP: Able to perceive and communicate when awake DOWN: Unable to perceive or communicate when asleep	Cognizant State	UP: Able to perceive and communicate when alive DOWN: Unable to perceive or communicate when dead
UP: Waking up DOWN: Going to sleep	Transition	UP: Birth DOWN: Dying

enable Paul and other ancient writers to reason about the abstract idea of resurrection—in this case, the activity of waking from sleep characterizes, or gives definition to, the resurrection process.

This brief cognitive linguistic analysis of 1 Cor 15:3–4 demonstrates the robust nature of the methodological tools employed in this study. While Lakoff and Johnson's embodied mind (i.e., image schemata and conceptual metaphors) provides anchor points by which to ground human cognition, Fauconnier and Turner's blending theory supplies an analytical tool by which to examine such metaphors and their emergence at human scale. When applied to Paul, this methodological triad enables the grounding of the apostle's resurrection ideals within patterns of human embodiment while still accounting for the fundamental role and importance of cultural and historical analyses. In this way, cognitive linguistics enables the integration of cognition and culture in a productive and illuminative way.

1.5. Overview of the Study

In the chapters that follow, I argue for a nonpropositional, embodied understanding of Paul's resurrection ideals. My analysis is directed toward the undisputed Pauline epistles, though examination will also extend to a number of Jewish and broader Hellenistic traditions. While preference will be given to epistle-specific analyses, I will also consider the undisputed letters as a whole, seeking to offer a holistic reading that understands the apostle as a consistent though not systematic thinker.[106] The parameters of analysis are the seven undisputed Pauline epistles—Romans, 1 and 2 Corinthians, Galatians, Philippians, 1 Thessalonians, and Philemon. The deutero-Paulines are all considered secondary, despite the fact that some may contain elements that stem from Paul himself.[107] In terms of epistolary integrity, I consider the canonical forms of 2 Corinthians and perhaps Philippians and Romans to be composite texts. Analyses of the relevant passages within these letters will commence accordingly.[108]

---

106. So following Sanders's (1977, 433) characterization. One of the advantages of this study's methodological apparatus is that it enables the identification of recurrent conceptual structures that lend themselves to differing—even contradictory—manifestations at human scale. In this way, it is possible to explore how consistency, in the absence of systematicity, might be found across Paul's writings.

107. I take Colossians, Ephesians, 2 Thessalonians, and the Pastoral Epistles as secondary to Paul. Colossians may well retain portions or a nucleus that is original to the apostle, though in its present form it seems to reflect an author/redactor who has shaped the material to a post-Pauline context. Accordingly, I have not included Colossians, nor the other deutero-Paulines and the Pastorals as part of this analysis.

108. With the majority of New Testament scholars, I take 2 Corinthians as a composite letter, likely consisting of fragments from five different Pauline correspondences and one later pseudepigraphical interpolation. Though not crucial to my study, I hold to the following partitions: (1) 1:1–2:13; 7:5–16; and 13:11–13; (2) 2:14–6:13 and 7:2–4; (3) ch. 8; (4) ch. 9; (5) 10:1–13:10; and the likely pseudepigraphical (6) 6:14–7:1 (so following Mitchell 2005). Determining the precise chronology of these correspondences is debatable. For the purposes of this study, I assume the following chronological ordering of the fragments: 3, 2, 5, 1, and 4 (with the one caveat that fragment 3 might be better located between fragments 1 and 4). Philippians too seems composite, consisting primarily of three distinct fragments: (1) 1:1–3:1a; (2) 3:1b–4:1; (3) 4:10–20; and a handful of other units that are likely original to Paul: (4) 4:2–3, 4–7, 8–9, and 21–23; so following Koester 2000, 2:53–54. Romans is a more difficult matter for two main reasons: first, we have documentary and manuscript evidence for no less than fifteen different forms of Romans (for a detailed discussion, see Jewett 2007, 4–18); and second, it is possible that ch. 16 originally was a separate letter written to

The study will unfold as follows. In chapter 2, I identify a framework by which resurrection texts can be identified and interpreted. Rather than focusing on Paul specifically, I direct attention toward a selection of Second Temple Judean texts so as to uncover broader patterns of resurrection thinking. As we will see, Paul fits squarely within this cultural context. In chapter 3, I examine the cosmo-somatic categories that Paul works with, specifically with an eye toward the transformation metaphors of 1 Cor 15:35–50 and 2 Cor 5:1–5. Here again Paul will be contextualized in his historical world, which is understood as a matrix of both Judean and Hellenistic traditions. In this chapter, I will address specifically issues of dualism and monism and further examine the extent to which Paul envisions (dis)continuity across earthly and risen somatic states. In chapter 4, I will further develop the issue of transsomatic (dis)continuity. Turning attention to Paul's descriptions of dying (and rising) with Christ in baptism (Rom 6–8), I will demonstrate that clarifying the nature of (dis)continuity also clarifies the extent to which Paul understands resurrection as a present experience. Such a task requires, however, a critical reassessment of Paul's eschatology, which I argue is thoroughly somatic in nature. Continuing with the theme of resurrection as a present experience, I examine in chapter 5 the relationship between Paul's *in/with Christ* language and his resurrection ideals. As I will demonstrate, resurrection is understood as a participatory experience precisely because Paul perceives it to be enacted on the human body; that is, believers are currently in the process of being resurrected, continually dying on the somatic exterior such that life is continually manifested on the somatic interior. Finally, in chapter 6, I conclude with a summary of this study's main points and scholarly contributions, as well as suggestions for subsequent research.

---

commend Phoebe, not to the believers in Rome but most likely to Ephesus (see esp. 16:5, and cf. 16:3 with 1 Cor 16:9 [Koester 2000, 2:52–53]). In recent decades, there has been a general movement toward viewing ch. 16 as originally addressed to Rome (e.g., Jewett 2007, 8–9), though the sheer number of people that Paul greets in a community to which he is primarily introducing himself remains puzzling. In any event, the relation of ch. 16 to the rest of the epistle has little bearing on this study.

2

Imaging Resurrection:
Toward an Image-Schematic Understanding
of Resurrection Belief in Paul and in
Second Temple Judaism

A methodological issue that must be overcome when studying resurrection beliefs in Paul and Second Temple Judaism more broadly is the problem of demarcating the topic or concept of resurrection within the literature of the period. While certain passages stand as prime examples of resurrection ideals (e.g., Dan 12:1–3; 1 Thess 4:13–18; 1 Cor 15), several pericopes are disputed. Within broader Second Temple Judaism, the sectarian literature at Qumran is a prime example. Despite Émile Puech's (1993) encyclopedic treatment in favor of resurrection belief at Qumran, others such as John Collins (1994; 2009, esp. 307–10) consistently insist there are no clear references to resurrection within the sectarian literature. At a more specific level, what are we to make of a tradition like Jub. 23:29–31, which affirms postmortem existence but is variously interpreted as referring either to immortality of the soul or to resurrection proper?[1] The Enochic Book of Watchers poses a similar problem in that most scholars uphold the work as early evidence for Jewish resurrection belief, despite

---

1. Many understand Jub. 23:29–31 to propose something closer to the idea of immortality of the soul rather than resurrection (e.g., Cavallin 1974, 38). The immediate context of 23:22–32, however, does not mention a final judgment or historical break (though see 5:13–16; 10:7; 23:11), thus causing some to de-eschatologize the passage and instead to see it as anticipating future judgment (Wright 2003, 143–44). Alan Segal (2004, 355) takes a middle ground, arguing "a sort of resurrection is blended with a sort of immortality of the soul, though neither one of them is a typical example of that belief."

the fact that no explicit reference to resurrection can be found therein.[2] Concerning the substance of resurrection discourse, though many texts speak of resurrection in relation to notions of life and death, how are we to account for those that speak of ethnogeographic motifs of land and exile or religio-political motifs of recompense and persecution/injustice? The interrelation of these differing descriptions under the one topic of *resurrection* surely is part of the problem, and any account of resurrection belief in broader Second Temple Judaism (including Paul) must accommodate such flexibility.

The problem is evident also in the epistles of Paul. While some passages certainly do look ahead to a future resurrection event (e.g., 1 Cor 15), in many instances the apostle speaks of death as a present event that seems to imply some form of present resurrection (Rom 6:1–11; 2 Cor 4:7–18). Indeed, in one instance, Paul's resurrection ideals are so strongly oriented toward the present that the apostle feels compelled immediately and emphatically to insist on the not-yet nature of risen existence (Phil 3:10–14).

In the present chapter, I will address this issue of how one identifies the concept of resurrection, specifically answering the question: what enables a particular text to be interpreted as referring to resurrection? My analysis seeks not to define *what a resurrection text is*, but rather to illuminate *what enables recognition of resurrection* within various discursive contexts. Put differently, this chapter seeks to explain interpretive flexibility rather than taxonomic classification. I suggest that any such examination must meet three criteria. First, we must identify recurrent patterns that are general enough to be found across the texts being studied, but also specific enough to warrant distinction and cogency. Second, we must demonstrate how such patterns are able to cut across discursive and topical contexts (addressing issues of death, persecution/martyrdom, social injustice, ethnogeographic exile, etc.). Finally, this analysis must also demonstrate how

---

2. The reference in 1 En. 22:13 to the inhabitants of the fourth hollow not rising seems to imply that the inhabitants of the other three hollows will rise. This description, coupled with the recognition that resurrection likely necessitates some kind of postmortem intermediary state for the dead, causes many exegetes to see the Book of Watchers as presuming resurrection (Cavallin 1974, 41–42; Nickelsburg 2006, 169–70; A. Segal 2004, 279; Wright 2003, 157). Nevertheless, it is worth noting that the Book of Watchers does not explicitly mention resurrection, even in the description of the great judgment in chs. 1–5.

such patterns can give rise to differing (even contrary) understandings of resurrection while still retaining an overarching degree of cogency and systematicity.

In light of the three analytical criteria just outlined, the following analysis will proceed in two steps. First, I draw on cognitive linguistics to illuminate the image schemata and conceptual metaphors that structure, even constitute, the concept of RESURRECTION within Second Temple Judaism (§2.1). This analysis will be textual in nature and will focus on those passages that stand as prime examples of resurrection beliefs within the pre-70 CE period literature—namely, Dan 12, 2 Maccabees (esp. ch. 7), the Epistle of Enoch, the Similitudes of Enoch, Enoch's Dream Visions, T. Mos. 10, and Pss. Sol. 3.[3] Where needed, my analysis also will examine a number of scriptural traditions so as to identify the traditional and conceptual worlds from which such notions draw.[4] As I will show, the traditions examined here evince a recurrent constellation of concepts and image schemata that, when taken collectively as a gestalt, constitute the concept of RESURRECTION. In §2.2 I turn to Paul specifically so as to examine the extent to which this constellation of image-schematic patterns can be seen also to constitute the apostle's resurrection ideals. By focusing on recurrent conceptual structures that work in concert with one another, I hope to demonstrate how and why one reader's expectation of postmortem recompense can also be another's hope of ethnogeographic restoration.

---

3. Accordingly, I will not examine the Qumran sectarian documents (which are contested on the issue of resurrection), texts that refer to nonresurrection postmortem existence (e.g., Wisdom of Solomon), or Puech's (1990) reconstructed Hebrew Sirach fragment. Other notable exclusions include the Testaments of the Twelve Patriarchs (which in its present form is a Christian text that dates from the second century CE) and the Enochic Book of Watchers (which perhaps refers to resurrection but not explicitly enough to warrant examination here; see above, n. 2).

4. I use the term *scriptural traditions* (or just *Scriptures*) to refer to texts that emerged within Hebrew culture and that were read as authoritative within Judean communities of the Second Temple period. I intentionally do not use the terms *Hebrew Bible* and *Old Testament*, to avoid anachronism, though much of what is referred to as *scriptural* overlaps with what was eventually included in those canons (namely, the Torah and Deuteronomistic History, the Prophets, the Psalms, and most of the wisdom literature). A good portion of this literature predates, in one way or another, Alexander's conquest in the late fourth century BCE, though in some cases the literature dates to the Hellenistic period (e.g., Daniel, Ecclesiastes, Sirach).

2.1. Second Temple Judaism and the RESURRECTION Gestalt

2.1.1. RESURRECTION IS UP: The VERTICALITY Schema

Perhaps the place to begin is with the framing of resurrection in relation to conceptualizations of LIFE and DEATH. We are justified in starting here for the simple fact that, while resurrection can be identified in relation to notions of social injustice or ethnogeographic exile (for example), such descriptions are frequently expressed in the language of life and death. Accordingly, these notions provide entry points into the network of interlocking concepts that structure RESURRECTION. Because human experiences of life and death are so pervasive, several metaphors are required to make sense of such experiences.[5] The following will focus on Hebrew traditions that conceptualize LIFE/DEATH via the VERTICALITY schema. Later in this chapter (§2.1.3), I will also examine related descriptions that are premised on the PROXIMITY schema.

One of the most pervasive image schemata that Lakoff and Johnson (1980, 1999) identify is the VERTICALITY schema (also referred to as the UP-DOWN schema; see fig. 2.1), of which Johnson (1987, xiv) provides the following description:

> We grasp this structure of verticality repeatedly in thousands of perceptions and activities we experience every day, such as perceiving a tree, our felt sense of standing upright, the activity of climbing stairs, forming a mental image of a flagpole, measuring our children's heights, and experiencing the level of water rising in the bathtub. The VERTICALITY schema is the abstract structure of these VERTICALITY experiences, images, and perceptions.

Lakoff and Johnson (1980, 14–21) examine a handful of ways that the UP-DOWN image-schema structures human thought. Of particular note are the metaphors LIFE IS UP and CONSCIOUSNESS IS UP, along with their

---

5. Thus Lakoff and Turner (1989, 2), "life and death are such all-encompassing matters that there can be no single conceptual metaphor that will enable us to comprehend them." In their study of poetic metaphors in the Western literary tradition, Lakoff and Turner note at least nineteen conceptual metaphors for LIFE/LIFETIME and fourteen for DEATH (221–23). Their list is not meant to be exhaustive, and it likely includes some metaphors that are exclusive to Western literature and others that are found in several cultures.

corresponding opposites DEATH IS DOWN and UNCONSCIOUSNESS IS DOWN. Both of these metaphors share an interrelated experiential grounding. Humans experience life through active, erect agency in the world. To be a living human being is to be able to stand up and walk around, while death conversely forces the otherwise erect and active body to fall down and lay limp, thus ceasing active agency. Correlated with this is the human experience of CONSCIOUSNESS, which Lakoff and Johnson understand generally as the experience of being able to exercise agency and perceptual awareness in the world (e.g., being asleep or in a coma are experiences of unconsciousness).[6] The CONSCIOUSNESS IS UP metaphor is rendered meaningful precisely because it reflects the correlation in embodied experience between erect agency and the state of being awake and able to perceive. (The same is true of the obverse metaphor UNCONSCIOUSNESS IS DOWN, where conscious perception ceases when one physically lies down and sleeps.) In these ways, the conceptual metaphors LIFE IS UP and CONSCIOUSNESS IS UP arise because of the type of physical bodies that human beings possess, functioning in the kinds of environmental and habitual contexts in which human beings live.

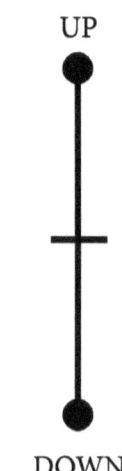

Figure 2.1. The VERTICALITY (or UP-DOWN) Schema

The conceptual correlation of LIFE/DEATH with UP/DOWN can be demonstrated nicely in Hebrew tradition already in many scriptural texts. Death, for instance, is repeatedly conceptualized in relation to downward directionality.[7] It is described as something people dig for (Job 3:21; see

---

6. I must stress that this is a pragmatic or functional understanding of (un)consciousness and thus should not be understood either as a technical definition of consciousness or as a limitation to the scope of what constitutes conscious experiences (e.g., I do not intend to preclude the existence of conscious states while one sleeps, nor altered/alternative states of consciousness).

7. It should be noted that death is described variously in the Hebrew Scriptures (for a full catalog of descriptions, see Johnston 2002, 23–46). For example, in some passages death is described as terminal (Ps 39:13; Job 7:21), while in others the dead have some kind of continued existence in the earth (e.g., Ps 22:30, taking the *BHS* editors' suggested reading). Other examples include the portrayal of Yahweh's power

also Amos 9:2), and the psalmist characterizes death as "downward movement into the pit" (ברדתי אל שחת, Ps 30:10).[8] In Job, death is described as lying down (שכב) and compared to rivers and lakes that dry up (14:10–12);[9] just as the water level is *high* when rivers and lakes are full, so too humans are characteristically *up and erect* when they are alive.[10] Likewise, the dried-up water body leaves only the parched ground, as the deceased leave only the dust of the earth. Thus Gen 3:19, "from [the ground] you were taken; you are dust, and to dust you will return" (see also Job 34:15; Ps 22:30).[11] Cosmologically speaking,[12] Sheol exists at the lower strata of the world (Job 11:8; Ps 139:8; Amos 9:2[13]) and thus is *downward* in relation to the plane of human existence.[14] Like death, accessing Sheol requires

---

over and presence within Sheol (e.g., compare Ps 88:5–6 with Amos 9:2), as well as the portrayal of death as both (in Johnston's terminology) a friend (Job 3:13) and an enemy (Ps 55:4).

8. The verb ירד, which generally denotes downward movement, is used specifically of the dead in reference to going to Sheol (e.g., Gen 37:35; Num 16:30, 33; Ezek 31:15–17; 32:27; Ps 55:16; Job 7:9), to the Pit (with בור, see Isa 14:19 and 38:18; with שחת, see Ps 30:10; Job 33:24), to death (e.g., Prov 5:5), and to the dust (e.g., Ps 22:30).

9. Though the date of Job is disputed, I do not see this text as affirming any kind of postmortem rising of the dead. Job 19:25–27 should thus be read against the backdrop of Job's broader attitude toward death (including the immediate passage) and therefore does not refer to resurrection (Wright 2003, 105).

10. A similar image is found in 2 Sam 14:14, where human futility is likened to water that is poured on the ground and that cannot be gathered up again. The image here is a blending of both downward movement (that which is "poured" [הנגרים]) and displacement (in the futility of being able to gather again).

11. The same life cycle referred to in Gen 3:19 is described also in Job 14:1–2, where the course of human life is likened to a flower that grows and then withers. This blend clearly correlates and contrasts life/vitality/erectness with death/inaction/lowness via the same UP-DOWN image schema.

12. Following Oden (1992, 1167–68), the "great majority of biblical texts assume the three-storied universe so clearly assumed in other, ancient traditions." Generally speaking, this three-tiered cosmology included the heavens (where the gods dwelt), the earth (where living humanity dwelt), and the netherworld (where the dead and various chthonic deities dwelt). Notable exceptions may include Job 11:8–9 and Ps 139:8–9, which perhaps betray a four-tier universe.

13. To this we should also add Isa 7:11.

14. In addition to Sheol, the related underworld term אבדון occurs six times in the Hebrew Scriptures (Prov 15:11; 27:20 [*qere*]; Job 26:6; 28:22; 31:12; Ps 88:12), thrice paralleled with Sheol (Job 26:6; Prov 15:11; 27:20 [*qere*]) and specifically having a downward orientation in Ps 88:12 and Job 31:12. Additionally, several synonyms

that one *descend* into the earth (Gen 37:35; Ps 55:16; Prov 9:18; Isa 14:15),[15] while escape requires *ascent* (Ps 30:4; see further Ps 40:3).[16] It is not surprising that the inhabitants of Sheol, the shades, are consistently described within the context of vertical orientation—either as being located *downward* or (un)able to *rise up*.[17]

The correlation of death with downward movement in scriptural tradition is expressed also in relation to language of sleeping and waking,[18]

---

for Sheol betray the same downward orientation. Most significant are בור (e.g., Pss 30:4; 88:5, 7; Isa 38:18) and שחת (e.g., Ps 16:10; Job 17:14; Isa 38:17). In various contexts, the former can refer to a "cistern" and the latter to a "grave," though elsewhere they both refer to a "pit" and even to the netherworld. To these we can also add באר, which often is translated "pit" or "well" (e.g., Gen 14:10; 21:19; Prov 5:15; Song 4:15) but is used twice to refer to the underworld (Pss 55:24; 69:16). Finally, ארץ is also used to denote the lower levels of the earth, often in conjunction with the modifier תחתיות to emphasize downward directionality (e.g., Isa 44:23; Ps 139:15). In Ezek 26:20; 31:14, 16, 18; and 32:18, 24, this pairing refers specifically to the underworld, even being linked to בור (except in 31:18) and שאול (only 31:16). For similar usages, see Exod 15:12; Ps 63:10; Jer 17:13. For a full discussion of these terms, see Johnston 2002, 83–85.

15. Compare also the description that, should the ground open up, one would be *swallowed* (בלע) *down* (ירד, Num 16:29–33). The personification of Sheol along consumptive lines is relatively common (Prov 1:12; Isa 5:14; Hab 2:5; see further Prov 27:20; 30:16) and may reflect Canaanite mythological personification, though this has been questioned (Barstad 1999).

16. This is particularly expressed in passages where the cosmological mapping is blended with experiences of pain/suffering, such that Sheol and its various synonyms stand for despair or trouble, from which Yahweh will *raise up* the afflicted (e.g., Ps 40:3).

17. See Isa 14:9; 26:14, 19; Ps 88:10; Job 26:5; Prov 2:18; 9:18; 21:16.

18. In the Hebrew Scriptures, several contexts that use sleep-related language likewise have correlations with death. The verb שכב, "to lie down," is used elsewhere in reference to the dead/death (e.g., Isa 14:8; 43:17; Ezek 31:18; 32:21, 27, 30; Job 3:13; 14:12), to lying in a grave (e.g., Ps 88:6), and to lying down in the dust (e.g., Job 7:21; 20:11; 21:26). Similarly, ישן, which is used elsewhere in reference to natural sleep (e.g., Gen 41:5; 1 Kgs 19:5; Ps 3:6; Isa 5:27; Ezek 34:25), is used by Jeremiah to refer to "a perpetual [or everlasting] sleep" (Jer 51:39, 57; see also Job 3:13; Ps 13:4) and also by the psalmist to refer to "all who sleep in the earth" (Ps 22:30, following the *BHS* editors' suggestion to read ישני rather than דשני). The cognate שנה, "sleep," is used in Job 14:12 (see also Jer 51:39 and 57) to refer to the sleep from which mortals neither "wake" (קיץ) nor "rouse" (רוע). The verb קיץ, "to wake," is used elsewhere to denote the impossibility of waking from the dead (Jer 51:39, 57), though its usage in Isa 26:19 suggests the opposite.

which reflects the conceptual metaphors LIFE IS BEING AWAKE /DEATH IS SLEEP introduced in the previous chapter (recall fig. 1.1). In scriptural tradition, these metaphors are expressed in discursive units where the dead are said to "sleep with their fathers," an idiom used to describe the death of ancestral leaders in the Torah and historical books.[19] By extension, this conceptual structure enables subsequent reasoning about postmortem life—namely, that one is able to wake from death. Neither insignificantly nor surprisingly, the conceptual metaphor LIFE IS BEING AWAKE is pervasive in resurrection discourses. One of our earliest texts to evince this is Dan 12:2, which looks ahead to a time when "many of the sleepers in the dust of the earth" (רבים מישני אדמת עפר)[20] will "wake up" (יקיצו).[21] The same metaphor is also found in 2 Macc 12:44–45 and perhaps 1 En. 92:3, and related conceptions can be seen in 1 En. 100:5–6 and Pss. Sol. 3:1–2.[22]

The gestalt nature of the UP-DOWN image schema requires that one identify not only the elements associated with UP but also those associated with DOWN. In turn, this requires that we must identify both the activity of rising/falling and the contexts that occasion such movement (what cogni-

---

19. For example, Jacob (Gen 47:30), Moses (Deut 31:16), David (e.g., 2 Sam 7:12; 1 Kgs 2:10), Solomon (1 Kgs 11:43 // 2 Chr 9:31), and several other monarchs. The related idiom "gathered to his people" is found in the Torah and is used of all the patriarchs when they die (Gen 25:8, 17; 35:29; 49:33), as well as of Moses (Num 27:13; 31:2; Deut 32:50) and Aaron (Num 20:24; Deut 32:50). The phrase also has some parallels in the historical books (Judg 2:10; 2 Kgs 22:20 // 2 Chr 34:28).

20. Both the OG and θ' use the same inflected verb to refer to "the ones who sleep" (τῶν καθευδόντων).

21. OG "they will rise up" (ἀναστήσονται); θ' "they will wake up" (ἐξεγερθήσονται).

22. In addition to other UP-DOWN language in 2 Macc 12:44–45, those who have died are described as "the ones who have fallen asleep" (τοῖς κοιμωμένοις, 12:45). In 1 En. 93:2, the description of the righteous one waking and walking in the way of righteousness may be a collective singular speaking of resurrection, though this is disputed (cf. Stuckenbruck 2007, 227–29). In 1 En. 100:5–6, the focus seems to be upon those righteous who have already died and are now awaiting a future judgment; this passage reflects the DEATH IS SLEEP metaphor, though it does not mention a correlated future waking (see Nickelsburg 2001, 501; Stuckenbruck 2007, 442–43). In Pss. Sol. 3, the language of sleeping and waking frames the entire passage. Though it is not used to describe resurrection specifically, emphasis throughout the psalm is placed upon being awake (3:1–2) and upon the value of life (3:9–12). Further, the description of the Lord as "awake" (γρηγόρησιν, 3:2) coheres well with the psalm's focus on life, light, and other UP-oriented images. Beyond these traditions, see also Matt 9:24–25 // Mark 5:39–42 // Luke 8:52–55; Matt 27:52; and John 11:11–14 (also 11:23–24; 12:1, 17); see also Acts 7:60.

tive linguists identify as the profile-frame relationship; Croft and Cruse 2004, 7–39). Within the literature of the period, we can point to several different frames wherein resurrection is emphasized. Some texts employ the SOCIAL INJUSTICE frame (e.g., Epistle of Enoch) while others cast resurrection in the light of the PERSECUTION frame (e.g., 2 Maccabees). Depending on the frame employed, the roles of protagonist(s) and antagonist(s) take on differing values. For example, texts framed by SOCIAL INJUSTICE fill such roles with the values poor and rich (respectively), while the PERSECUTION frame provides values like martyr(s) and wicked ruler(s).[23] Each frame provides the skeletal gestalt structure with a richer set of contextual nuances, thus enabling the concept of RESURRECTION to have varying and distinct nuances across discursive settings.

For example, the PERSECUTION frame, which is employed in 2 Maccabees, frames resurrection in relation to a series of grotesque martyrdoms, thus looking ahead to the regaining of corporeal bodies (7:10–11; 14:43–46). This focus on corporeality demonstrates the extent to which conceptual metaphors such as LIFE IS BEING AWAKE/DEATH IS SLEEP enable emergent meanings not otherwise possible.[24] In scriptural tradition, the correlation of SLEEP with DEATH was initially in the service of describing death vis-à-vis sleep,[25] though this conceptual metaphor now is extended to enable postmortem speculation concerning renewed life. When elaborated in this way, the DEATH IS SLEEP/UNCONSCIOUSNESS

---

23. Such frames and their values are, of course, culture-specific and thus demonstrate variance. I have proposed here typical values (e.g., the poor and the rich). In actuality, we see at times many synonymous values existing within a single frame. For example, the Epistle of Enoch, which exhibits to a great extent the SOCIAL INJUSTICE frame, refers to the protagonists and antagonists variously (e.g., protagonists: righteous, wise, suffering ones, etc.; vis-à-vis antagonists: sinners, foolish, rich).

24. One should not, of course, make too much of this presumed postmortem corporeality. Corporeal resurrection is envisaged in 2 Maccabees as a response to the horrible and gruesome deaths that are described and thus is tied to the martyriological situation. As such, postmortem corporeality cannot be disconnected from the narratological world and thus should not be essentialized as central to notions of resurrection.

25. Though perhaps this correlation was minimally focused on the afterlife, given the presumed existence of the shades. On this, Wright (2003, 90) astutely notes: "The minimal sort of 'life' that the shades had in Sheol, or in the grave, approximated more to sleep than to anything else known by the living.… They were not completely nonexistent, but to all intents and purposes they were, so to speak, next to nothing."

blend entails the conceptual metaphor RESURRECTION IS CONSCIOUSNESS, where the experience of conscious human agency in the world provides a set of conceptual mappings that inform one's understandings of resurrection. The RESURRECTION IS CONSCIOUSNESS metaphor enables interpreters to conceptualize resurrection variously, including (but not limited to) the resurrected state (i.e., awake, standing up, even being embodied, etc.), the resurrection event itself (e.g., waking up), or even certain characteristic activities (risen beings are active agents, they can perform certain actions, etc.). There is much interpretive play here, as the conceptual metaphor allows for variance in meaning depending on how certain readers use it.

Another context that frames Judean notions of resurrection is that of (CELESTIAL) LUMINOSITY, which expresses a more general trend toward the clustering of UP-structured concepts with a given frame's protagonists and DOWN-structured concepts with the antagonists. A prime example is the association of light/darkness with such protagonists/antagonists. From an embodied perspective, light is most commonly experienced during the day and darkness at night, both of which naturally cohere with the LIFE IS BEING AWAKE and DEATH IS SLEEP metaphors. Similarly, light is perceived as coming primarily from the sun and moon (which are orientationally upward), while darkness is found in caves and places that are hidden from the sun/moon (i.e., in the earth, which is down). Within the literature of the period, the highest resurrection ideal in Dan 12:3 is that the wise are elevated to shine as celestial bodies/beings. Similar postjudgment luminous elevation is also found in passages that either characterize the protagonists with light terminology or simply speak of them as standing in the light of the Lord, often in contrast to the antagonists (e.g., 1 En. 58:2–6; 62:15–16; 104:2; Pss. Sol. 3:12; T. Mos. 10:9; see further 1 En. 39:7). The conceptual metaphor at work in such passages reflects the more general RESURRECTION IS UP metaphor, here understood via the specific frames LUMINOSITY or even CELESTIAL LUMINOSITY.

One final frame that structures conceptualizations of RESURRECTION via the UP-DOWN image schema is that of ETHNOGEOGRAPHIC RESTORATION, which correlates LIFE/DEATH with LAND/EXILE. Though the concept of LAND is not readily associated with notions of VERTICALITY, the correlation of land with life, which stretches back into the Hebrew Scriptures, enables metaphors such as LAND IS LIFE (UP) and EXILE IS DEATH (DOWN). The Deuteronomist, for instances, correlates "life," "land," and "torah" such that obeying the Lord's commands will bring life and blessing in the land

(Deut 30:11–20).²⁶ In the prophets, Ezek 37:1–14 envisions postexilic restoration as an instance of dry bones "standing" (יעמדו, 37:10) such that all God's people will come "up" (העליתי) from the grave and thus return "to the land of Israel" (אל אדמת ישראל, 37:12).²⁷ Similarly, Isa 26:19 refers to the dead coming to "life" (יחיו), "rising" (יקומו), and "waking" (הקיצו). Within the Isaianic context such references are most likely concerned with ethnogeographic restoration,²⁸ though in light of the LAND IS LIFE metaphor it is perhaps not surprising that many interpreters—ancient and modern²⁹—see this passage as referring to resurrection.³⁰

---

26. While Deut 30:16 correlates "life," "land," and "torah," the converse is upheld in 30:17–18, where disobedience and the worship of other gods is said to lead to death and a truncated stay in the land. Moses continues by paralleling life/blessing and death/curse (30:19), and he explicitly connects "land" with "life" in 30:20. Unlike the LIFE IS BEING AWAKE metaphor discussed above, here the UP-DOWN image schema does not tie the various conceptual domains together (i.e., LIFE/DEATH and LAND/EXILE) but rather is projected from one domain (LIFE) onto the other (LAND). This is what Fauconnier and Turner (2002, 126–31) refer to as a single scope blend.

27. Israel is also described in 37:12 as "being raised/led up" (העליתי) from the grave.

28. Donald Polaski (2001, 214) has argued that this verse not only is consonant with the broader chapter (and therefore not a later interpolation), but that the focus of the passage is squarely upon the restoration of Israel: "the most telling piece of evidence … is the focus of ch. 26 on corporate bodies, including 'national' groupings [26:2, 9, 10, 11, 15, 16–18, and 20–21]." Several other exegetes concur with Polaski's assessment (e.g., Doyle 2000, 304–5; J. Collins 1998, 25).

29. In the LXX tradition of Isa 26:19, for instance, the focus is more explicitly upon the act of rising (note the renderings ἀναστήσονται and ἐγερθήσονται for MT יחיו and יקומון, respectively). Wright (2003, 116–18) suggests that during the Hellenistic period this passage was understood as referring to resurrection. Alternatively, the MT's third reference to those who will live again ("awake and sing for joy, O dwellers of the dust" [הקיצו ורננו שכני עפר]) is translated, "and those in the earth/land will rejoice" (καὶ εὐφρανθήσονται οἱ ἐν τῇ γῇ). Given this shift away from the actual description of "rising," at least one modern commentator has argued that the Greek text looks ahead to those who will survive the judgment in the land (Cavallin 1974, 106–7). Among modern interpreters, Nickelsburg (2006, 31–32) sees in Isa 24–27 the simultaneous affirmation of Israel's restoration and the resurrection of those Israelites who are deceased (though the resurrection of the wicked is not affirmed).

30. Such a tendency is compounded by the presence of other motifs and themes that are representative of later resurrection descriptions (e.g., the affirmation of cosmic catastrophic destruction [Isa 24], the promise that Yahweh will destroy death [Isa 25:8]), which in turn betray other image schemata that structure resurrection conceptualizations (as argued in this chapter).

Within subsequent Jewish tradition, just as postexilic restoration is possible for LAND, so too is postmortem restoration possible for LIFE. When framed in relation to Israel's ethnogeographic identity, the concept of RESURRECTION is expressed via the metaphor RESURRECTION IS RESTORATION TO THE LAND. Enoch's Dream Visions, for example, describe the postjudgment reuniting of many who were dispersed and destroyed (1 En. 90:33). Similarly, in several other texts the recipients of resurrection are the members of Israel itself vis-à-vis foreign rulers/oppressors (e.g., Dan 12:1–3;[31] 2 Maccabees; T. Mos. 10:7–10).[32] In these texts, both eschatological resurrection and ethnogeographic restoration are structured by the same UP-DOWN schema, which allows these ideas not only to signify each other but also enables later interpreters to find one in the other.

The foregoing has demonstrated that the VERTICALITY image schema is pervasive within Second Temple Jewish notions of resurrection. All the metaphors examined thus far express the very general conceptual metaphor RESURRECTION IS UP, a conceptual mapping that has little meaning on its own. However, when framed in relation to differing aspects of Judean experience (erect human agency [CONSCIOUSNESS], heavenly light [CELESTIAL LUMINOSITY], ethnogeographic restoration [LAND], etc.), the metaphor can be specified so as to find distinct meanings across discursive contexts.

2.1.2. RESURRECTION IS GOAL: The PATH Schema

Another image-schematic structure, which functions at both macro- and microlevels in structuring notions of resurrection, is the PATH schema (or SOURCE-PATH-GOAL schema). At times both the PATH and VERTICALITY schemata work in correlation with one another (e.g., the linking of UP with GOAL, as we will see). In an important respect, however, the PATH schema supplements its VERTICALITY counterpart so as to enable a conceptual structure not made possible by the latter. As with UP-DOWN, the SOURCE-PATH-GOAL schema functions as a gestalt structure—that is, the schema has a basic set of interdependent elements that all work in concert with one

---

31. Thus following those who read Dan 12 as a resurrection of some of the righteous and the wicked, which then results in contrasting fates of these two groups (see J. Collins 1993, 393). For an alternative view, see Puech 2006, 252–55.

32. The references within many texts to a postjudgment restoration and inheritance of the earth might also fall within this category as well (e.g., 1 En. 51:5b), though this is broader than a strict understanding of exilic return.

Figure 2.2. The PATH Schema.³³

another (a SOURCE, a TRAJECTOR, a PATH, etc.; see fig. 2.2).³⁴ Like all image schemata, the PATH schema is pervasive in human experience. Thus Johnson (1987, 113):

> Our lives are filled with paths that connect up our spatial world.... Some of these paths involve an actually physical surface that you traverse, such as the path from your house to the store. Others involve a projected path, such as the path of a bullet shot into the air. And certain paths exist, at present, only in your imagination, such as the path from the Earth to the nearest star outside our solar system.

Though no one in the ancient Mediterranean would ever conceive the path a bullet would travel, they would certainly perceive the path of an archer's arrow or of a thrown stone. Johnson here is illuminating an image-schematic structure that is commonly shared by the human animal across cultural contexts.

2.1.2.1. The Macro-PATH Structure

At the macrolevel, the PATH schema provides the concept of RESURRECTION with a more robust structure than the VERTICALITY schema alone permits. This robustness is akin to the difference between a one- and two-dimensional object. Where the VERTICALITY schema enabled conceptions along a single axis (orientated vertically), the PATH structure creates a second, horizontal axis. The most common expression of the PATH schema

---

33. According to Lakoff and Johnson (1999, 33), the "Source-Path-Goal" schema, as they call it, contains the following elements: (1) "a trajector that moves"; (2) "a source location"; (3) "a goal, that is, an intended destination of the trajector"; (4) "a route from the source to the goal"; (5) "the actual trajectory of motion"; (6) "the position of the trajector at a given time"; (7) "the direction of the trajector at that time"; and (8) "the actual final location of the trajector, which may or may not be the intended destination."

34. For an overview of the PATH schema, see Lakoff and Johnson 1999, 32–34.

is via the structuring of time as progressing toward a looming divine visitation.³⁵ For example, Dan 11:40 looks ahead to "the time of the end" (ובעת קץ)³⁶ in which a great judgment will take place (12:1–3). Several other texts likewise point to similar teleological judgments, which reflects the same schematic structuring (e.g., Enoch's Dream Visions, esp. 1 En. 90:20–27; the Epistle of Enoch, esp. 1 En. 99:11–102:3; the Enochic Book of Similitudes, esp. 1 En. 51 and 62; Pss. Sol. 3:11–12; T. Mos. 10).

In some instances, the SOURCE and GOAL elements of the PATH structure are characterized by values such as present conflict and judgment (respectively). Other texts, however, scale the PATH structure to a much larger degree, thus identifying the present distress as a single event on the path toward the end. Such is the case in 2 Maccabees; the martyrdom of the seven brothers and their mother in chapter 7 is particularly worth noting. In 7:23, the mother asserts that the creator of the world, who has "formed" humankind, "will give breath and life back to you again." Of note is the mother's focus upon God as the "creator" who restores life in the

---

35. Other expressions of this schema can also be demonstrated, such as the use of Two Ways theology in the midst of resurrection contexts. While Nickelsburg (2006, 214–15) suggests that the blending of Two Ways theology with resurrection was only possible once the idea of resurrection became a topos and thereby eschewed its initial associations with suffering/persecution, one implication of the present analysis is that such blending was possible because the PATH structure inherent in notions of RESURRECTION easily lends itself to Two Ways (or Two Paths) descriptions.

36. J. Collins (1993, 389) rightly sees this as referring primarily to the anticipated end of the present crisis (i.e., the conflict with Antiochus) but also as drawing upon a "mythic pattern," attested within Hebrew tradition, which is concerned with the destruction and restoration of Israel. Perhaps not surprisingly, such a *mythic pattern* is littered with tight correlations between UP-DOWN and SOURCE-PATH-GOAL image-schematic structures. An excellent example is Isa 14:1–20, which speaks of Judah's return from exile. The passage stresses the abasement (e.g., ירד and נפל, 14:11–12, 15) of the king of Babylon, a kind of setting right of the social order such that those exiled who were once under foreign rule will one day return from exile and themselves be rulers (14:2). The entire passage is premised on an UP-DOWN interplay where the downfall of the king of Babylon is juxtaposed with the elevation of Israel to a place of political autonomy. This restoration manifests the HAVING CONTROL IS UP/BEING SUBJECT TO CONTROL IS DOWN metaphors (see Lakoff and Johnson 1980, 15), articulated here in relation to the metaphor (RETURN TO THE) LAND IS UP (14:1). This entire UP-DOWN drama is envisioned as a promised future event (GOAL), and thus is yet to come (14:1). Though Isa 14 is not explicitly identifiable within Dan 12:1–3, the coupling of the UP-DOWN and SOURCE-PATH-GOAL image schemata constitute the shared mythic ideal of future redemption in the face of current calamity.

end (GOAL) on account of his creative impetus in the beginning (SOURCE). The hope of these martyrs is premised on the assertion that history has an inevitable outcome, a teleological drive that flows from SOURCE to GOAL, and which thus diminishes physical death in light of anticipated resurrection (7:9).[37] Such a teleological feature further demonstrates the inherent sense of purpose that accompanies conceptualizations of RESURRECTION, which is doubtless tied to the presence of the PATH schema.[38]

Beyond the mere structuring of time, the interrelation of the PATH and VERTICALITY schemata creates tight correlations between the constituent elements. This is expressed in two ways: (1) through the correlation of DOWN-structured concepts with the SOURCE element (e.g., death, exile, injustice), and (2) the correlation of UP-structured concepts with the GOAL element (e.g., renewed life, ethnogeographic restoration, just recompense). What results is a PATH structure that is, conceptually speaking, vertically inclined so as to denote sequential movement from DOWN (SOURCE) to UP (GOAL) via PATH (see fig. 2.3 on p. 59). As noted above, the roles of protagonist(s) and antagonist(s) are filled with either UP- or DOWN-structured values, respectively. With this in mind, the gradient structure that we have just outlined is, of course, described from the point of view of the protagonist(s), and an obverse path is also projected for the antagonist(s). The resultant structure is vertical sequential movement

---

37. Though the youngest brother's comments in 7:36 may imply the immediacy of these martyrs' resurrection, on the whole 2 Maccabees understands resurrection as an eschatological event (see 12:43–45). Moreover, the martyrs of ch. 7 speak of both resurrection and the judgment of their oppressors as a future event (7:9, 19, 36). Though the temporal period is not specified, a broader teleological focus is likely in mind (see further Wright 2003, 150–52).

38. Lakoff and Johnson (1999, 52–53) note that one of the primary metaphors that humans use to conceptualize purposes is the PURPOSES ARE DESTINATIONS metaphor, which is built upon the PATH schema. The primary experiences from which this metaphor arises are, as Lakoff and Johnson suggest, embodied experiences such as "reaching destinations throughout everyday life and thereby achieving purposes (e.g., if you want a drink, you have to go to the water cooler)" (53). In 2 Maccabees, and other literature of the period too, martyrdom is seen as an acceptable end precisely because natural death is not an end in and of itself. Rather, natural death is only one step along the temporal path (i.e., PATH) toward resurrection (i.e., GOAL). The same idea is found in other literature of the period too; for example, J. Collins (1993, 403) rightly notes that "Daniel 10–12 … provides a *rationale* for martyrdom.… The hope for salvation is beyond death" (emphasis added).

wherein opposing role-value figures traverse reciprocal paths, one toward GOAL (UP), the other toward GOAL (DOWN). (This is sketched in fig. 2.4.)

The reciprocal nature of this gradient structural interrelation facilitates the concept of REVERSAL, expressed via the conceptual metaphor RESURRECTION IS REVERSAL and thus enabling the elevation of the protagonists vis-à-vis the abasement of the antagonists. The structure is readily apparent in the Epistle of Enoch (esp. 1 En. 99:11–102:3), where the righteous enjoy postmortem recompense/reward, including luminous existence (104:2), while the unrighteous/sinners go down to Hades into darkness and great judgment (103:7–8). Similarly, Dan 12:1–3 holds that some will be raised to "everlasting life" (חיי עולם)[39] and others "to shame and everlasting disgrace" (לחרפות לדראון עולם, 12:2).[40]

The foregoing demonstrates a tight connection between the PATH and VERTICALITY schemata in structuring conceptualizations of RESURRECTION. These tight correlations enable a variety of frames, which are themselves rooted in different kinds of Judean experiences, to produce a variety of expressions of resurrection—for example, death/martyrdom (RESTORED LIFE IS GOAL), ethnogeographic restoration (RESTORATION TO THE LAND IS GOAL), or even social injustice (JUST RECOMPENSE IS GOAL). All are reflective of the more general RESURRECTION IS GOAL metaphor.

2.1.2.2. The Micro-PATH (CHANGE) Structure

In addition to offering an overarching framework (at the macrolevel) whereby UP- and DOWN-structured concepts can be organized, the SOURCE-PATH-GOAL schema is also used to structure a specific subset of resurrection ideals: the idea of postmortem transformation. In this regard, the PATH schema is employed twice in constructing the concept of RESURRECTION—once at the macrolevel to provide an overarching framework and again at the microlevel to enable the concept of CHANGE in relation to postmortem form.

As already noted, texts such as Dan 12:3, 1 En. 104:2, and T. Mos. 10:9–10 frame their resurrection ideals with celestial categories. In Dan 12, celestial association is reserved only for the wise, whereas in 1 En. 104

---

39. Both OG and θ' read "everlasting life" (ζωὴν αἰώνιον).

40. OG: "to disgrace, and others to dispersion [and shame] everlasting" (εἰς ὀνειδισμόν, οἱ δὲ εἰς διασποράν [καὶ αἰσχύνην] αἰώνιον); θ': "to disgrace and everlasting shame" (εἰς ὀνειδισμὸν καὶ εἰς αἰσχύνην αἰώνιον).

2. IMAGING RESURRECTION

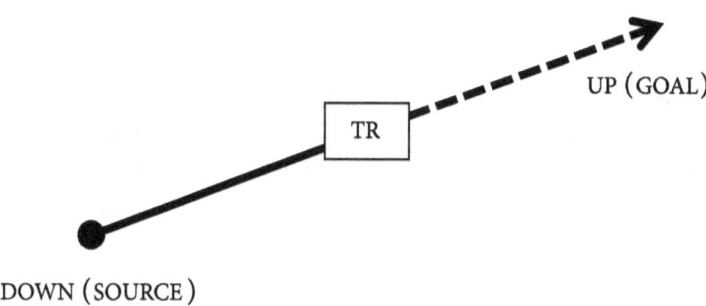

Figure 2.3. Integrated PATH and VERTICALITY Schematic Structure

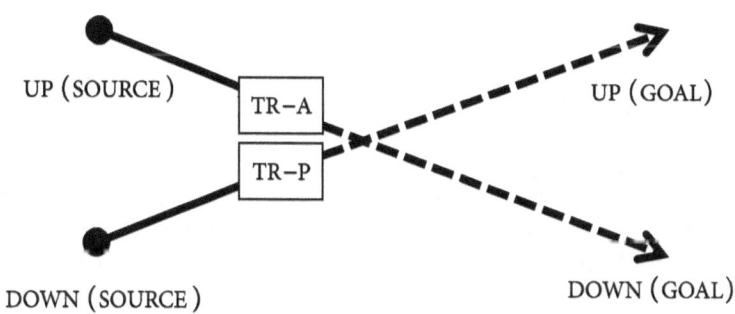

Figure 2.4. Reciprocal Protagonist (TR-P) and Antagonist (TR-A) PATHS

it is for the righteous and in T. Mos. 10 it is an ethnogeographic hope. In Dan 12:3, the comparison is made with the stars and luminous heavens and is specifically characterized by temporal length (i.e., shining forever).[41] Because angels are at times described with such luminous imagery (e.g., Job 38:7; 1 En. 86:1, 3; 90:21), this comparison may be understood in terms of angelic likeness and even angelomorphic transformation.[42] Very similar language is used in 1 En. 104:2, where the comparison is directly correlated with heavenly beings in the Ethiopic text (see also 104:4, 6).[43] By contrast, in T. Mos. 10:9, God will raise his people and fix them in the "heaven of the stars," a celestial elevation that is specifically contrasted with Israel's enemies on earth (10:10).

The introduction of CELESTIAL LUMINOSITY to resurrection conceptualizations results in the metaphor RESURRECTION IS CELESTIAL LUMINOSITY, which differs significantly from the aforementioned RESURRECTION IS CONSCIOUSNESS metaphor. That said, both metaphors have strong elements of VERTICALITY built into them (as noted above), and they also presuppose the concept of (POSTMORTEM) CHANGE. In the CELESTIAL LUMINOSITY metaphor, the envisaged change is more imaginative and radical in that, though premortem human bodies neither shine like stars nor exist in the heavens, their postmortem counterparts take on these qualities. Alternatively, the CONSCIOUSNESS metaphor leans in the direction of the reconstituted human body, which requires the changing of the decomposed corpse (back) into a corporeal state. Thus, while the CELESTIAL LUMINOS-

---

41. In Dan 12:3, the wise will "shine like the brightness of the sky, ... like the stars" (יזהרו כזהר הרקיע ... ככוכבים). While כ here certainly is comparative (Waltke and O'Connor 1990, §11.2.9; R. Williams 1976, §256), Waltke and O'Connor (1990, §11.2.9.b.3) note, "the logical outcome of comparison is correspondence or identity." Accordingly, Dan 12:3 could also be read in a stronger way as indicating the identification of the wise with the stars (though assertions of identity are often marked by the double use of כ [i.e., כX כY]). The Greek translations of Dan 12:3 retain the same comparative quality: the OG uses ὡς (12:3a) and ὡσεί (12:3b); θ' only uses ὡς (12:3a, b).

42. See also Matt 22:30 // Mark 12:25 // Luke 20:35–36, where Jesus's understanding of resurrection leans toward angelomorphic transformation.

43. Similar to Daniel, in the Epistle the righteous are said to shine and appear "like" (ὡσεί) the stars of heaven (104:2) and are later called "companions" of the angels of heaven (104:6, Ethiopic text only). Though the references to angels in 104:4 and 6 are found only in the Ethiopic text, Stuckenbruck (2007, 567) suggests they were originally in the Greek *Vorlage* (even offering a reconstruction of that *Vorlage*). (N.B. in the above I use the translation of Nickelsburg and VanderKam 2004.)

ITY and CONSCIOUSNESS metaphors result in very different resurrected states, both presuppose postmortem transformation.

From an embodied perspective, experiences of change are ubiquitous within human life patterns. The human body experiences change in mundane tasks such as sitting up (change of position) and walking across the room (change of location). Throughout the course of life, the process of human maturation is marked by many changes that are both physical (growth, fitness conditioning, puberty, etc.) and social (shifting social circles, relationships, marriage, work, etc.); for example, the process of growing from a baby into an adult is both immediately experienced and observed in others. One of the most common and basic experiences of change is that of using force to manipulate an object from one shape into another, such as a potter moulding clay into a bowl.[44]

Given both the ubiquitous and complex nature of such experiences, several different metaphors are used by the human animal to conceptualize change.[45] One of the most basic is the CHANGE IS MOVEMENT metaphor, which is premised on the PATH image schema, thus enabling CHANGE to be conceptualized as movement from one location to another. In addition to this, however, one must also account for differences between both pre- and postchange states. Such states are commonly conceptualized via the CONTAINER schema (see fig. 2.5), which is oriented along a simple IN-BOUNDARY-OUT axis.[46] When constructed in this way, both locations and states are conceptualized as containers that can be either

---

44. Lakoff and Johnson (1999, 208–9) highlight this experience, providing examples such as changing a log into a canoe, or lead into gold.

45. For example, CHANGE can be understood in terms of directionality (TURNING), substitution (REPLACEMENT), and forceful alteration (MAKING) (see esp. Lakoff and Johnson 1999, 206–11). On ancient philosophical reflection regarding the complexity of change, see Songe-Møller 2009, 110–12.

46. Like the other schemata examined here, the CONTAINER schema arises from human embodiment; thus Johnson (1987, 21): "Our encounter with containment and boundedness is one of the most pervasive features of our bodily experience.... From the beginning, we experience constant physical containment in our surroundings (those things that envelop us). We move in and out of rooms, clothes, vehicles, and numerous kinds of bounded spaces. We manipulate objects, placing them in containers (cups, boxes, cans, bags, etc.). In each of these cases there are repeatable spatial and temporal organizations. In other words, there are typical schemata for physical containment."

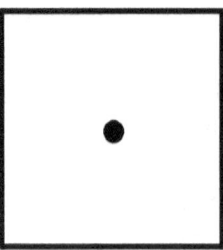

The CONTAINER schema contains the following elements (or "roles"):
An interior (IN)
A boundary for the interior
An exterior (OUT)

Figure 2.5. The CONTAINER (or IN-OUT) Schema. For a discussion of the logic behind this schema, see Lakoff and Johnson 1999, 32.

moved *into* or *out of*.[47] With respect to CHANGE, both the PATH and CONTAINER schemata work interdependently with each other so as to form a CHANGE gestalt (see fig. 2.6). Here the SOURCE and GOAL roles of the PATH schema are characterized by contrasting CONTAINERS. These CONTAINERS represent differing states/locations (i.e., A and B), and the TRAJECTOR represents the subject undergoing the change in question. What results is a conceptual structure that facilitates the movement of a TRAJECTOR from one CONTAINER (state/location A) to another (differing) CONTAINER (state/location B).[48]

---

47. This builds upon Lakoff and Johnson's (1999, 180) STATES ARE LOCATIONS metaphor, where they define "locations" as "bounded regions in space. Each bounded region has an interior, an exterior, and a boundary." Earlier in the same work, Lakoff and Johnson explicitly define the container schema as denoting "a bounded region in space" (31). In the present analysis, I am stressing the CONTAINER image-schematic structure of the STATES ARE LOCATIONS metaphor.

48. This coheres with Lakoff and Johnson (1999, 183–84) who, in describing the CHANGE IS MOVEMENT metaphor, speak of "a change of state as a movement from one bounded region in space to another."

2. IMAGING RESURRECTION

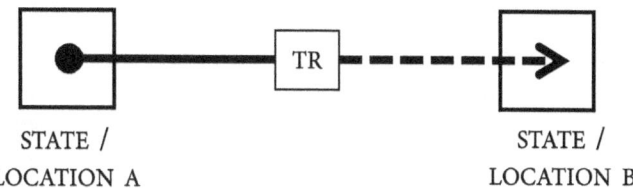

Figure 2.6. The Micro-PATH (CHANGE) Gestalt

Returning to conceptions of RESURRECTION, we see that the CHANGE IS MOVEMENT metaphor functions at a microlevel in that it structures the GOAL element of the larger SOURCE-PATH-GOAL schema (see fig. 2.7). As such, the CHANGE IS MOVEMENT metaphor characterizes the protagonist's UP-structured associations in two significant ways, both of which can be demonstrated nicely with respect to the CELESTIAL LUMINOSITY frame. On the one hand, the CHANGE IS MOVEMENT metaphor expresses a change of location such that the elevated protagonists are no longer on earth but in the heavens (e.g., Dan 12:3; 1 En. 104:2 [see also 104:6]; T. Mos. 10:9–

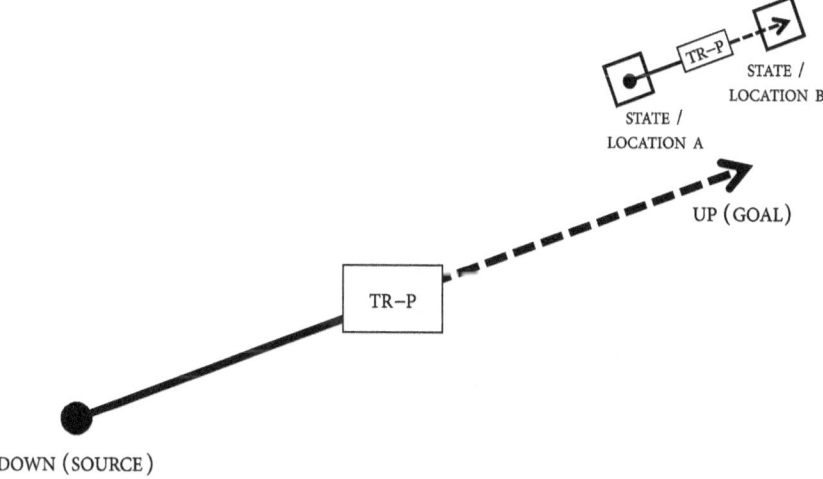

Figure 2.7. Integrated Micro-PATH Structure

10). In this regard, the change in question is locative and is characterized by movement (i.e., a trajector moving along the PATH toward the GOAL of celestial elevation). In a more categorical way, however, the same metaphor can also be extended to refer to stative or transformative change. Conceptually speaking, this CHANGE is both locative (i.e., point A *to* point B) and stative (i.e., state A *into* state B), thus producing descriptions of both celestial ascent and celestial transformation.

Similar change dynamics can also be demonstrated for the RESURRECTION IS CONSCIOUSNESS metaphor, though the meaning that arises from the CONSCIOUSNESS frame vis-à-vis the CELESTIAL LUMINOSITY frame differs. On the one hand, the CONSCIOUSNESS frame produces the idea of restorative transformation (e.g., restoration of the natural body in 2 Macc 7:10–11; 14:43–46), which gives rise to understandings of resurrection such as redemption and a kind of setting right that which has gone awry. On the other hand, the CELESTIAL LUMINOSITY frame produces the idea of categorical transformation, which is usually seen as transformation into a more desirable state and thus produces notions of an improved and even beatific future. Both notions are central to resurrection modes of thought.

2.1.2.3. Summary: The PATH Schema

The preceding examination has demonstrated that the PATH schema structures many aspects of resurrection belief in Second Temple Judaism. This schema functions at both macro- and microlevels, the former constructing notions of time and purpose while the latter concerns conceptions of transformation. I have also demonstrated that the PATH schema works interdependently with its VERTICALITY counterpart, thus resulting in notions of reversal as well as opposing protagonist/antagonist TRAJECTOR movements.

2.1.3. RESURRECTION IS NEAR: The PROXIMITY Schema

In §2.1.1, I demonstrated that the VERTICALITY schema is utilized in structuring notions of life and death. Because experiences of life and death concern all aspects of human existence, several conceptual metaphors are required to make sense of these experiences. An important counterpart to these VERTICALITY metaphors is the structuring of LIFE/DEATH by the PROXIMITY (or NEAR-FAR) schema. Within this metaphor system, LIFE and DEATH are conceptualized as opposing proximity values rather than verticality values; life is understood as being near to something (LIFE IS NEAR)

2. IMAGING RESURRECTION

while death is marked by a certain degree of separation and distance (DEATH IS FAR). Such PROXIMITY metaphors find expression in scriptural and Second Temple Jewish traditions, each of which I will analyze in turn.

John Collins (1993, 394–98) identifies two "strands of thought" in the Hebrew Scriptures that were "conducive" to Second Temple Jewish resurrection ideals: (1) the emphasis on union and enjoyment of God within God's presence and (2) the restoration of the people. I have already examined the latter above (§2.1.1); I now turn attention to the former. The LIFE IS NEAR/DEATH IS FAR metaphors emerge from Israel's rich textual traditions, especially the Psalter. In Ps 73:27–28, for instance, the psalmist insists, "those far from you will perish ... but for me, nearness to God is good" (רחקיך יאבדו ... ואני קרבת אלהים לי טוב). This same psalmist earlier speaks of entering the sanctuary of Yahweh (73:17), confesses his desire for Yahweh (73:25–26), and even speaks of Yahweh holding the psalmist's hand and guiding him such that they are always together (73:23–25). In all these instances, the PROXIMITY schema is employed as a way of structuring both divine-human relations and notions of life and death—death is explicitly correlated with distance (DEATH IS DISTANCE FROM YAHWEH, 73:27), while the corresponding opposite is implied (LIFE IS BEING NEAR TO YAHWEH).[49] The same metaphors are also at work in Ps 91:1, where the psalmist addresses those who "dwell in the shelter of the Most High, who lodge in the shadow of the Almighty" (ישב בסתר עליון בצל שדי יתלונן). This very intimate expression of divine-human proximity results in both the protection and sustained life of the protagonist vis-à-vis the antagonist (91:3–6, 7–8, 14–16).[50]

Like other image schemata, PROXIMITY is rooted in recurrent patterns of human embodiment. It emerges from experiences such as walking toward an object such that one's location is measured relative to that object (e.g., walking toward a tree is movement from FAR to NEAR relative

---

49. Psalm 73 also stresses motifs that we have already encountered: for example, the contrasting of protagonists (i.e., the upright, 73:1) with antagonists (i.e., the wicked, 73:3, 12), each of which is characterized either by life or death, respectively. Given the prevalence of these image schemata and motifs, it perhaps is not surprising that many scholars have found in Ps 73:23–24 a possible allusion to resurrection (e.g., Wright 2003, 105–6).

50. The passage characterizes nearness in terms of cohabitation in the same space, thus also containing notions of CONTAINMENT (i.e., one actually abides *in* the same space as Yahweh, 91:9; see also Ps 84).

to that tree). As embodied social beings, one of the primary ways humans experience PROXIMITY is within relationships. Those we are intimate with are close to us (spatially speaking); likewise, those whom we do not wish to associate with are (ideally) kept at a distance. As Joseph Grady (1997, 23) highlights, this recurring social phenomenon constitutes a correlation between affection and physical proximity, which itself gives rise to a number of conceptual metaphors (e.g., EMOTIONAL INTIMACY IS PROXIMITY). In the passages examined here, these experiences of human intimacy are projected onto the divine figure itself and blended with notions of life and death, thus resulting in the LIFE IS BEING NEAR TO YAHWEH metaphor.

One of the most striking features of the Hebrew Scriptures is the way the PROXIMITY, VERTICALITY, and PATH schemata are already correlated with one another. In Amos 5, for instance, the prophet instructs the house of Israel to "seek Yahweh and live" (דרשו את יהוה וחיו, 5:6; see also 5:14), specifically contrasting this imperative with warnings of death/destruction expressed through the language of exile (see also 5:6, 11, 16–20, and 27). Here we see the PATH and PROXIMITY schemata working interdependently such that movement toward Yahweh (i.e., a TRAJECTOR on a PATH) denotes the achievement of life (i.e., LIFE IS NEAR/GOAL).[51] We also see a similar correlation of the PROXIMITY and VERTICALITY schemata in scriptural traditions that stress the absence of Yahweh from Sheol (Ps 88:5–7; Isa 38:18; see further Ps 16:10).[52] In these contexts, the understanding of Yahweh as UP and Sheol as DOWN (cosmologically speaking) lends itself to assertions that those in Sheol are FAR from Yahweh. Generally speaking, then, in these scriptural traditions, we already see a correlation of UP/NEAR/GOAL with LIFE and DOWN/FAR/SOURCE with DEATH, all of which create a conceptual web wherein schematic patterns lend themselves to later resurrection descriptions.

Turning to the Second Temple literature, we again see that metaphors for premortem life (i.e., LIFE IS NEARNESS TO YAHWEH) are projected onto postmortem existence (i.e., RESURRECTION IS NEARNESS TO YAHWEH). In 2 Macc 7:33, the seventh brother anticipates the postmortem "reconciliation" (καταλλαγήσεται) of the Lord with his servants (see also 7:16). Simi-

---

51. See further Ezek 18, where this early account of individual retribution is framed in relation to paths that lead to death and/or life.

52. Contra Ps 139:8, Job 26:6, and Prov 15:11, all of which hold to Yahweh's presence or power in/over Sheol.

larly, the Book of Similitudes anticipates a time when the chosen will "eat" with "the Son of Man," and where the "Lord of Spirits will abide over them" and their garments of glory "will not fade *in [his] presence*" (1 En. 62:14, 16; emphasis added). We can also point to texts that speak of postmortem luminous existence not as celestial transformation but rather as the protagonists abiding in the presence of Yahweh (Pss. Sol. 3:12). Additionally, texts that speak of postmortem upward celestial movement (Dan 12:3; 1 En. 104:2, 6) denote an anticipated closeness between Yahweh and his people, where the latter are transformed so as to dwell with the Lord in the heavens. As we can see, then, the PROXIMITY schema is conceptually integrated with the VERTICALITY and PATH schemata, further enriching the concept of RESURRECTION in Judean thought (see fig. 2.8). By orienting the entire macro-PATH structure on the fixed point of Yahweh's presence (signified by θ), the macro-GOAL of the protagonist's PATH is characterized by divine-human propinquity while all other role-value locations are characterized by distance.

In sum, then, the PROXIMITY schema works interdependently with its PATH and VERTICALITY counterparts. In this light, notions of resurrection are seen to have a very robust schematic grounding, one that is thoroughly metaphorical and premised upon recurrent patterns of human embodiment.

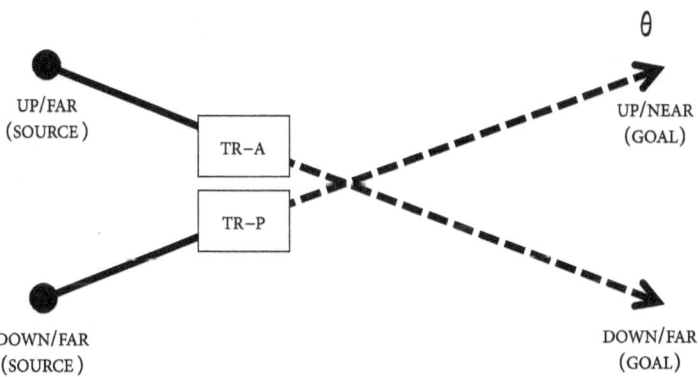

Figure 2.8. Integrated PROXIMITY (NEAR-FAR) Structure

2.1.4. Summary: The RESURRECTION Gestalt

I have argued in the foregoing that a network of recurrent and interdependent image schemata and conceptual metaphors undergirds various expressions of resurrection beliefs in Second Temple Judaism. This network is specifically structured by the VERTICALITY, PATH, and PROXIMITY schemata, all of which contribute differing structural elements to the gestalt. The VERTICALITY schema provides notions of spatial movement/orientation (UP, DOWN) and opposition (UP versus DOWN) as well as experiential links with concepts such as LIFE/DEATH, LIGHT/DARK, and HEAVENS/EARTH. The PROXIMITY schema likewise provides notions of spatial movement/orientation (FAR, NEAR) and opposition (FAR versus NEAR) while also introducing relational elements such as divine-human propinquity. Finally, the PATH schema introduces elements of sequence (movement from SOURCE to GOAL), purpose (achievement of GOAL), change (from state/location A *into* state/location B), and reversal (switching of UP and DOWN, NEAR and FAR; this is achieved through combination with VERTICALITY and PROXIMITY). The interrelation of these schemata is not a simple matter of overlay but rather a dynamic blending, resulting in a gradient conceptual structure that enables sequential vertical movement for either protagonist (upward movement) or antagonist (downward movement) TRAJECTORS.

The overall structure is sketched in figure 2.9.[53] As is apparent, the structure itself is quite general, even abstract. In this way, I have identified a recurrent cluster or network of concepts that is (1) coherent in and of itself and that (2) displays certain internal interrelations that give rise to different components of meaning while still being (3) general enough as not to be tied to or dependent on any one set of resurrection motifs and/or themes. Contextual specificity is achieved through differing cultural frames (e.g., PERSECUTION, SOCIAL INJUSTICE), which are metaphorically elaborated so as to flesh out such skeletal structures with richer and more robust sets of information.

---

53. The schematic structure mapped here should not be taken as a definitive articulation of what constitutes Second Temple Jewish resurrection ideals. Rather, this gestalt functions as a recurrent schematic system that underpins many—perhaps most—understandings of resurrection within the period literature. The analytical emphasis should fall not on the gestalt's ability to define resurrection, but rather on its functionality in identifying notions of resurrection.

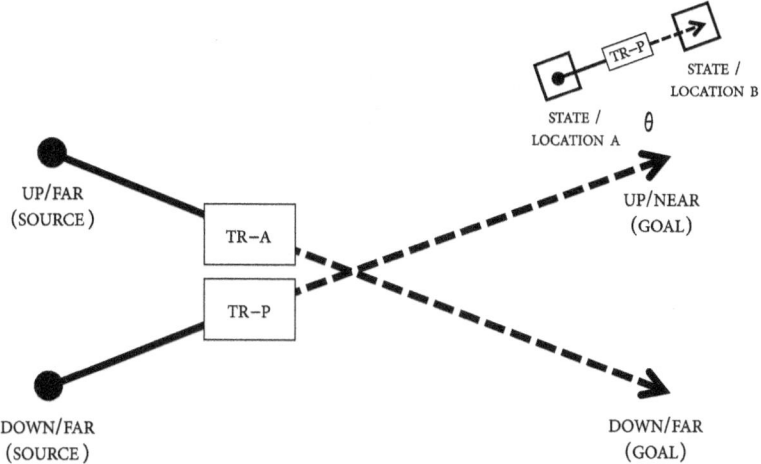

Figure 2.9. The RESURRECTION Gestalt

To demonstrate this point, we can examine the conceptual metaphor RESURRECTION IS UP. As noted above, this metaphor is very general and has little meaning on its own. When framed in relation to UP-structured concepts, however, the metaphor gives rise to varying and even divergent conceptualizations. The focus in 2 Maccabees on corporeality, for instance, is doubtless an expression of the RESURRECTION IS CONSCIOUSNESS metaphor, which projects elements of the one domain NATURAL LIFE (including elements such as walking, talking, earthly body, etc.) onto the other domain RISEN LIFE such that risen bodies are understood as reconstituted earthly bodies. Conversely, the focus on celestial ascent in the Epistle of Enoch reflects the RESURRECTION IS CELESTIAL LUMINOSITY metaphor and thus envisions postmortem life vis-à-vis astral (even angelic) categories. Despite the fact that these two metaphors reflect the general RESUR-

RECTION IS UP metaphor (by virtue of shared conceptions of VERTICALITY), they nonetheless give rise to differing resurrection descriptions.

We can also note that some texts are able to trigger several different, even divergent, metaphors simultaneously, thus resulting in differing interpretations of the same text. Daniel 12:1–3 is a prime example. Many scholars find in 12:2 the affirmation of bodily resurrection, a point that is made on the grounds of intertextual associations with Deutero- and Trito-Isaiah.[54] Verse 2, however, does not address the issue of risen form and instead only speaks of sleepers waking (see J. Collins 1993, 392). Here we have the concept of RESURRECTION being framed via the DEATH IS SLEEP metaphor, and while readers can use the LIFE IS CONSCIOUSNESS metaphor to infer corporeality in Dan 12:2, such an interpretation is not explicitly warranted. Indeed, the very next verse upholds celestial ascent as the highest postmortem ideal.[55] The assertion that the wise will be granted heavenly luminosity calls forth the RESURRECTION IS CELESTIAL LUMINOSITY metaphor and thus projects astral (even angelic) categories onto the envisioned risen form. That the language of this text is able to trigger both conceptual metaphors betrays not only the richness of the literary unit (intertextual echoes and all), but also exposes the degree to which differing readers are able to frame a text like Dan 12:1–3 via differing (though related) conceptual metaphors.

To extend our analysis beyond the dossier of texts just examined, further support for the RESURRECTION gestalt can be found in comparison

---

54. The association centers primarily on the use of the word *abhorrence* (דראון), which in the Hebrew Scriptures occurs only in Dan 12:2 and Isa 66:24. In its Isaianic context, the focus is specifically upon dead corpses, which cues exegetes to see in Dan 12:2 an intertextual reference to corporeal resurrection (e.g., Cavallin 1974, 27). Others stress intertextual connectivity with Isa 26:19, which speaks of dead bodies rising (e.g., Nickelsburg 2006, 38). We should not forget, however, that intertextual connections are not fixed but rather are constructed always within reading communities. If one removes the comparison with Isa 26:19, such corporeal conclusions cannot be sustained. Despite this, others who find corporeality in Dan 12:2 without explicitly relying on Isaianic traditions include Wright (2003, 109), who strongly asserts, "There is little doubt that [Dan 12:2–3] refers to concrete, bodily resurrection." See also Day 1996.

55. The argument could of course be made that Dan 12:3 deals more with the concept of exaltation rather than resurrection; and while this may indeed be the case, we perhaps should not make too firm of a distinction between the two (see below, §3.1.1).

with so-called nonresurrection traditions. The presumption of the immortality of the righteous in Wisdom of Solomon is an excellent example. Here ideas of TRAJECTOR reversal (between the righteous [protagonists] and unrighteous [antagonists], Wis 5:1–14) and of divine-human propinquity (PROXIMITY, 5:15) permeate the text's afterlife beliefs. Beyond this, however, there is very little conceptual correlation with the RESURRECTION gestalt. Notions of an eschatological judgment are obscured in favor of a much more immediate realization of death and life (cf. 1:12, 15, 16), thus muting (perhaps omitting) the macro-PATH.[56] At the same time, while there are a few references to the transformation of the righteous,[57] these lack teleological correlation (i.e., the micro-PATH is not connected with the macro-GOAL) and further are premised not on transformation (per se) but rather on the idea of sameness and consistency; that is, the righteous only "seem to die" (ἔδοξαν ... τεθνάναι, 3:1–3); they "will live forever" (εἰς τὸν αἰῶνα ζῶσιν, 5:15; see also 1:15), and their hope is "full immortality" (ἀθανασίας πλήρης, 3:4; see also 4:14).[58] While some of the elements of the RESURRECTION gestalt are present in the Wisdom of Solomon, certain key schematic constellations are missing.

Beyond Wisdom of Solomon, it is also worth examining a few of the traditions that scholars contest on issues of resurrection.[59] The Enochic Book of Watchers is a famous example. Here we find clear references to the separation of the righteous from sinners (hence, contrasting TRAJECTORS, 22:9–14) and the assertion of a future judgment (hence, the macro-PATH, 1 En. 22:4, 11). The latter is correlated with a brief note that some will "rise" (22:13), a reference that seems best understood with respect to

---

56. Nickelsburg (2006, 113–14) notes that, though the Wisdom of Solomon clearly presumes a day of judgment (3:13, 18; 4:6; 4:20–5:14), the exact timing of that day is not clear (perhaps it is a singular eschatological event, or perhaps individual judgments at the end of each one's life). Thus Nickelsburg, speaking of the eschatological timetable in the Wisdom of Solomon: "[our author] has no interest in such a timetable, because he radicalized eschatological categories. And since immortality is already the possession of the righteous man, his death is viewed as his assumption" (114).

57. See, e.g., Wis 3:6–7, and specifically the transposition of the righteous to the presence of God (5:15).

58. On this point, even if one grants a teleology to the Wisdom of Solomon's time frame, Nickelsburg (2006, 115) rightly notes that the key emphasis falls on "identity, or at least continuity between death and exaltation"; that is, notions of transformation are downplayed in the Wisdom of Solomon.

59. For scholarly discussion of Jub. 23:29–31 and 1 En. 22:13, see nn. 1–2 above.

the righteous. No details are provided here; both divine-human propinquity (PROXIMITY) and transformation (micro-PATH [CHANGE]) seem to function as implicit assumptions in 22:9–14, though they are not given specific articulation.[60] A second contested text is Jub. 23:29–31, which contains elements of progression toward a GOAL (23:26–29), contrasting protagonists and antagonists (23:22–31), and perhaps also indications of divine-human propinquity at the goal (see 23:29). Notions of transformation are also explicit (23:26–29), though Jubilees scales the micro-PATH (CHANGE) structure so as to reflect a more gradual transformation.[61] The protagonists do not die but rather find that "their days ... begin to increase and grow longer ... until their days approach a thousand years" (23:27), at which point "their bones will rest in the earth" (23:31). There perhaps are thematic shades of Wisdom of Solomon here in that death is supplanted and there is a greater emphasis on continuity vis-à-vis discontinuity; nevertheless, all the elements of the RESURRECTION gestalt are present, even if they are realized at human scale in ways that seem contrary to other, more typical, *resurrection* texts. Taking 1 Enoch and Jubilees together, scholarly debate of these passages is not without merit, for there is a great deal of conceptual coherence and ambiguity with respect to the RESURRECTION gestalt. That being said, it is perhaps wrong to ask if resurrection is present in these texts; rather, it is better to recognize that passages such as these contain certain conceptual constellations that, when taken together, enable readers to identify resurrection therein.

2.2. Paul's Appropriation of the RESURRECTION Gestalt

The preceding analysis has identified a conceptual structure—the RESURRECTION gestalt—that undergirds a wide variety of resurrection ideals within Second Temple Jewish literature. In what remains of this chapter, I want to explore the extent to which Paul appropriates this gestalt into his own understanding of resurrection. My focus in doing so will be global in nature. While I will focus the microscope much more acutely on epistolary

---

60. On both points, the stress in 22:13 on the togetherness-of-sinners vis-à-vis those who rise suggests (1) a level of divine-human propinquity for the risen ones (PROXIMITY) and (2) some kind of transformation—at least spatial transposition—for the risen ones (micro-PATH [CHANGE]).

61. Notably, the transformation of our protagonists (23:26–29) takes place before the time at which they "will rise up" (23:30).

specifics in the chapters that follow, I attempt here a view of Paul that spans the whole of the undisputed corpus. Such a move is justified for the simple fact that resurrection has, as Wright (2003, 309) correctly notes, "woven its way into the very fabric of Paul's thinking, so that it emerges all over the place not as one topic among others ... but as part of the structure of everything else." With this more global perspective in mind, attention will be given to the frame, TRAJECTOR, macro-PATH, and micro-PATH elements of Paul's resurrection ideals, all of which will be finally anchored in 1 Thess 4:13–18. Through the course of doing so, I will illuminate not only the broader patterns of Paul's resurrection ideals but also anticipate a number of specific concerns to which we will return in the chapters that follow.

2.2.1. Frame-Structure

While one could point to several different frame-structures at work in Paul's resurrection ideals,[62] one overarching concept gives structure to the whole. This concept centers on the figure of Christ, who stands at the fore of Paul's thought and determines the values that Paul assigns to schematic roles. Throughout this study, I will refer to this frame-structure as the CHRIST frame. While such an identification may seem overly vague—even ambiguous—it is appropriately so in that Paul understands Christ as the fulfillment of all God's promises (see 2 Cor 1:19–20). Given this global, all-encompassing aspect of Paul's worldview, the CHRIST frame evinces a certain plasticity that serves to enable the tying together of several different cultural frames under the single rubric of CHRIST.

As noted above, frames arise within contexts (e.g., martyrdom occasions the PERSECUTION frame). To speak of Paul's CHRIST frame is to say that the risen Christ stands at the center of the apostle's experience. As Dunn (1998b, 400) has aptly noted: "in some sense [Paul] experienced Christ as the context of all his being and doing." In a related way, Sanders (1977, 434–47) is surely correct that Paul's theology develops not from an

---

62. For example, in addition to notions of CELESTIAL LUMINOSITY (e.g., 1 Cor 15:35–57; 2 Cor 5:1–10; see also 2 Cor 12:1–10) and RECONSTITUTED LIFE (e.g., 1 Thess 4:13–18), one can point to issues of SOCIAL STRUCTURE (e.g., the reversal of social hierarchy in the Corinthian correspondence) and even ETHNOGEOGRAPHIC RESTORATION (as is evident in Romans and even Galatians; thus Boyarin [1994, 112] holds that the central message of Paul's gospel is the "constitution of all the Peoples of the world as the new Israel").

experience of introspective restlessness but rather proceeds from solution to plight.[63] But this raises, of course, the issue of identifying the kind(s) of experience(s) from which this CHRIST frame emerges. Such experiences will be explored throughout this study (esp. in §5.3), though any working list must include Paul's adoption of early traditions regarding Jesus's resurrection (1 Cor 15:3–5), communal rituals and worship (Rom 6:3–5; 1 Cor 10:16–17; 11–14), (ecstatic) experiences of having *seen* the risen Christ (Gal 1:11–16; 1 Cor 9:1; 15:8; 2 Cor 12:1–4), somatic perceptions of the indwelling Christ/πνεῦμα (Rom 8:9–11), anticipation that Christ will be glorified in the earthly body (Phil 1:20; also 2 Cor 4:10–11), as well as the ecclesial experience of the collective as the body of Christ (1 Cor 12:12–27). Though giving precise definition to many of these experiences is difficult, the ubiquity of Paul's experience of Christ is clear.

2.2.2. TRAJECTOR Role-Values

Within the CHRIST frame, Paul describes protagonists and antagonists with respect to the risen Christ; that is, Paul distinguishes the TRAJECTOR values on the basis of each TRAJECTOR's relation to Christ. Depending on the epistolary context, the apostle uses several different role designations, though distinction is consistently drawn with respect to issues of faith: protagonists are "believers," antagonists are "unbelievers."[64]

It is particularly noteworthy that Paul does not contrast protagonists and antagonists along ethnoreligious lines but rather insists that Judeans

---

63. I here touch (albeit briefly) upon the challenge of identifying the so-called center of Paul's thought, which is traditionally (though problematically) construed as an either/or choice between juristic and participationist foci. If one can identify such a center (and this by no means is certain), in the present study I follow Sanders's (1977) insistence that the juristic and participationist need not be opposed, even though the latter leads much more naturally into a wider array of Paul's thought.

64. The sheer variety of terminology underscores the plasticity of the CHRIST frame. In Romans alone, protagonists are "believers" (1:16), "saints/holy ones" (1:7), "righteous ones" (5:19), those "in Christ" (8:1), "a great family" (8:29), and even "all those who call upon [the Lord]" (10:12–14). Conversely, antagonists are "unbelievers" (15:31), "sinners" (5:19), "the ungodly" (5:6), and "enemies" (5:10). (Note: neither this list nor its citations are exhaustive.) Outside Romans, see also the contrasts that Paul draws between opposites in 1 Cor 1:18–2:16, as well as the familial metaphor that characterizes believers as "sons of the light and sons of the day" rather than of "night or darkness" (1 Thess 5:5; cf. Gal 1:2; 6:10; Rom 8:14–23, 29).

and gentiles stand equally before the Lord (Rom 1:18–3:31). The apostle's thinking is framed according to an ethnically inclusive description of those who have faith in Christ.[65] In a most curious manner, however, Paul does draw a dividing line according to an in-out somatic distinction. This is especially seen in Rom 2, where the soteriological problem and solution are understood to lie *in* the human being, not on the surface; the one who is justified before God is so on internal rather than external grounds (2:25–29).[66] This in-out somatic characterization highlights the apostle's distinction between protagonist and antagonist—that is, one is rightly related to the divine when they are such inwardly, not outwardly. This is not to oppose interior to exterior, nor to set the two in an overly schematic binary, but rather to highlight that the boundary between protagonist and antagonist is drawn somatically. As I will discuss in chapters 4 and 5, this has important implications for Paul's resurrection ideals.

2.2.3. The Macro-PATH

Another way that Paul articulates protagonist and antagonist role-values is through the identification of such TRAJECTORS with Christ and Adam, respectively. The analogy of the two figures is found in only two Pauline texts (Rom 5:12–21 and 1 Cor 15:21–22, 45–49), though the nuances of each differs.[67] In Rom 5, the Adam-Christ typology is articulated with

---

65. Thus Boyarin (1994, 94–95), speaking with respect to Rom 2, "'true Jewishness' ends up having nothing to do with family connections (descent from Abraham according to the flesh), history (having the Law), or maintaining the cultural/religious practices of the historical Jewish community (circumcision), but paradoxically consists of participating in a universalism, an allegory that dissolves those essences and meanings entirely."

66. In Rom 2, Paul constructs a conceptual mapping that favors inner to outer. In 2:12–16, he elevates those gentiles who, apart from the law, do what is written "in their hearts" on account of their "conscience" (2:15). By contrast, earlier in the same passage he describes a "hard and unrepentant heart" (2:5) as a precursor to eschatological wrath. Thus Paul insists that one is a Judean not "outwardly" (φανερός, i.e., "visible, known, or plain," 2:28) but rather "inwardly" (κρυπτός, i.e., "hidden or secret," 2:29). Accordingly, eschatological judgment is executed not according to an external signifier but rather according to the "secret [thoughts] of [all] people" (2:16). Much of Paul's address here is directed to a rhetorical interlocutor, the identity of whom is disputed; see recently Thiessen 2014.

67. Despite the relative infrequency of Paul's references to the primordial patri-

respect to the macro-PATH, while in 1 Cor 15 it is used with respect to the micro-PATH. I examine the former here (and the latter below, in §2.2.4).

It is important to recognize that, in many respects, the relationship between Adam and Christ is antithetical; Adam represents sin/trespass, death, and condemnation, while Christ represents righteousness, grace, life, and justification (Rom 5:12–21). Ole Davidsen (1995, esp. 252) stresses the "structural typology" of the Adam-Christ correlation, specifically noting that Adam represents a movement from provisional life to definitive death, while Christ represents the opposite movement, from provisional death to definitive life. The two are each other's obverse in that they cross-map opposing VERTICALITY role-values. With respect to the RESURRECTION gestalt, the Adam-Christ typology reflects the conceptual metaphors ADAM IS DEATH [DOWN] and CHRIST IS LIFE [UP] (Rom 5:12, 17–19).

Within the logic of this gestalt, Adam and Christ stand metonymically for opposing TRAJECTORS (ADAM FOR UNBELIEVERS/CHRIST FOR BELIEVERS).[68] Adam as the metonymic value for the antagonists represents a movement from SOURCE [UP] to GOAL [DOWN] via declined PATH, while Christ stands metonymically for the protagonists' obverse movement from SOURCE [DOWN] to GOAL [UP] via inclined PATH. In this way, the Adam-Christ typology is premised on the macro-PATH symmetry of the RESURRECTION gestalt. This schematic structuring has important implications for how we understand Adam and Christ as corporate referents. While these metonymic correlations are best understood within the context of a representational figure theory that stresses patrilineal genetics,[69] the common scholarly parlance of *spheres of influence* seems strained. As we

---

arch, many scholars suggest the Adam-Christ typology is generally pervasive in Paul's thought (e.g., C. Barrett 1962, 6).

68. I use the term *metonymy* to denote the substitution of X for Y, where X and Y are understood to be in some way related to each other. Accordingly, references to Adam and Christ can be understood as references to unbelievers and believers, respectively, via the conceptual metonymies ADAM FOR UNBELIEVERS and CHRIST FOR BELIEVERS. What is envisioned in these Adam/Christ metonymies is a PART FOR WHOLE relationship. In line with ancient ideologies of patrilineal genetics, Adam is understood to be part of the whole group to which he is connected (on patrilineal genetics, see Johnson Hodge 2007, esp. 93–107). On metonymy as a conceptual structure, see Lakoff and Johnson 1980, 35–40.

69. See, e.g., Wedderburn 1987, 342–56; and more recently, Kister 2007. Neither Wedderburn nor Kister explores the patrilineal dimension. While Johnson Hodge

can see, what are typically understood as spheres are better identified as contrasting PATH structures that set their TRAJECTORS on obverse routes. It is in this way that Adam and Christ determinatively impact those for whom they metonymically stand; each figure's referents traverse opposing paths, one toward death (DOWN), the other toward life (UP).[70]

2.2.4. The Micro-PATH (CHANGE)

One of the most striking features of Paul's resurrection ideals is the emphasis placed on (postmortem) transformation. This is particularly seen in 1 Cor 15:35–57 and 2 Cor 5:1–5 (also Phil 3:21; Rom 8:29) and perhaps implicit in 1 Thess 4:13–18 (esp. 4:17; see §2.2.6). While some have suggested that Paul's emphasis on transformation is a mutation of the Jewish worldview,[71] and others see it as evidence for a development in Paul's thought,[72] my analysis suggests instead that such transformative ideals are consistent with the broader resurrection expectations of the period. As we have seen above, notions of change are inherent in the RESURRECTION gestalt. In this way, though Paul stresses postmortem transformation, one goes too far to insist that he has altered *the* Jewish view (if such a thing ever

---

(2007) offers the most detailed treatment of patrilineal genetics in Paul's letters, she does not explore the Adam-Christ typology.

70. Given that Paul evinces a strong degree of permeability between these two PATHs, it would be erroneous to understand their obverse nature as a soteriological dualism. That is, Paul envisions a system wherein the lines between protagonist and antagonist are permeable and thus not ontologically drawn. This is especially true for the possibility of coming to faith in Christ, and Rom 11:21 suggests such permeability runs both ways.

71. So Wright 2003, 372; similarly, Asher (2000, 205) argues that Paul introduces Greek philosophical notions of transformation into his Judean ideals.

72. For an overview of the relevant scholarship and critical assessment of developments in Paul's resurrection ideals, see Meyer 1986 and Longenecker 1998. Such developments are usually identified as movement from a Jewish (1 Thess 4:13–18) to a more hellenized anthropology/cosmology (2 Cor 5:1–5), with 1 Cor 15 standing as an intermediate point. To a large extent, the positing of such a development rests on two problematic assumptions: (1) that Judean and Greek modes of thought stand in isolation and thus contradistinction from one another and (2) that Paul's resurrection descriptions are not (or cannot be) shaped by individual epistolary contexts. On this latter point, the diversity of Pauline expression should first be explored at the level of individual epistolary addresses.

existed). Indeed, Paul is better seen as exploiting a conceptual structure already inherent within the RESURRECTION gestalt.

Paul develops his transformation ideals in relation to the Adam-Christ typology. In 1 Cor 15:21 the apostle speaks in a way similar to Rom 5:12–21; the typological contrast centers on the death and life that Adam and Christ, respectively, impart. Paul's focus shifts in 15:22, however, as he now insists that those associated with Adam die "not only *because* of Adam's sin, but 'in Adam'" (Kister 2007, 685). This terminological modification is accompanied by a universalizing tendency (note the use of πᾶς) and a corresponding reference to Christ—just as all die "in Adam" (ἐν τῷ Ἀδάμ), so all will be made alive "in Christ" (ἐν τῷ Χριστῷ).

Here the language of influential spheres seems more apt (i.e., being *in* the sphere of X or Y), though this is perhaps best understood not in an abstract theological way but rather in a patrilineal genetic way. Though notions of kinship are absent from 1 Cor 15, the descriptions of being *in Adam* and *in Christ* echo the language of patrilineal genetics at work in Paul's participationist ideals more generally (for more, see §§1.3.3 and 5.3.1).[73] In this way, Adam and Christ function as progenitorial ancestors who share the same "stuff" as those with whom they are associated (see further, Johnson Hodge 2007, 109). This is particularly pertinent when we consider the locative nature of this modification, which is clearer in 15:45–49. Here Paul again contrasts Adam and Christ, not as differing TRAJECTORS (as in Rom 5:12–21 and 1 Cor 15:21) but rather as differing somatic states that are cosmologically drawn. Adam is described as being "from the earth" and thus the "image of dust," while Christ is both "from heaven" and the "image of heaven" (15:47, 49). Again the ADAM IS DOWN/CHRIST IS UP metaphors persist, though they are applied so as to denote earthly (DOWN) and heavenly (UP) somatic states. Given that the focus of 15:35–57 is on postmortem transformation, Paul here understands

---

73. Whereas Paul's *in Abraham* language serves the ideological purpose of constructing a fictive kinship for gentiles in Christ (see §5.3.1; see Johnson Hodge 2007, 93–107), his *in Adam* language differs in that more general, universal claims are made concerning humanity as a whole. Such universal claims also serve an ideological end, one that is more negative than positive in that it articulates both plight (as in Rom 5:12–21 and 1 Cor 15:21) and the σῶμα ψυχικόν (as in 1 Cor 15:22, 45–49). Accordingly, the language of being *in Adam* seems to trade on the logic of patrilineal descent while at the same time expressing something more general (and more negative) than Paul's *in Abraham* descriptions.

the Adam-Christ typology not with respect to the macro- but rather the micro-PATH structure. More precisely, the figures of Adam and Christ are mapped onto the SOURCE and GOAL elements of the transformation/change PATH, thus standing as opposing CONTAINER states in the CHANGE structure. Paul conceptualizes this PATH as transformational movement from Adam (EARTHLY BODY [DOWN]) to Christ (HEAVENLY BODY [UP]). Accordingly, to die in Adam is to die in the earthly body, whereas to live in Christ refers (in this context) to being made alive in the heavenly, risen body (15:22).[74] While this interpretation differs significantly from that found in Rom 5:12–21 (and 1 Cor 15:21), the ADAM IS DOWN/CHRIST IS UP metaphors are consistent. In this way, we see conceptual coherence in Paul's thought despite a lack of human-scale systematicity across epistolary contexts.

Much of the following chapters will examine Paul's transformation language in greater detail. For now, it will suffice to note that Paul conceptualizes pre- and posttransformation states in various ways, including (but not limited to) opposing Adamic and Christic bodies. In such instances, however, Paul's emphasis on transformation exploits an inherent aspect of the RESURRECTION gestalt.

2.2.5. Paul and His Pharisaic Background

Before looking at a specific Pauline text in detail, I want to take a brief detour to examine the little of what can be reconstructed of first-century Pharisaism.[75] Paul is, as A. Segal (1990, xi) reminds us, the only first-century Pharisee—albeit a former Pharisee—from whom we have writings. Accordingly, exploring how Paul's resurrection ideals cohere with what we know of Pharisaism seems not only appropriate but also potentially enriching to our vision of the apostle's resurrection ideals. On this brief detour away from the undisputed letters, I draw attention to three passages from the Gospels, Josephus, and Acts.

---

74. In this view, Adam stands metaphorically for the "likeness of an image of [that which is] mortal" (Rom 1:23), the "body of humiliation" (Phil 3:21), or the "form, … likeness, … and appearance of humanity" (Phil 2:7).

75. Here my analysis turns to select passages from the Gospels, Acts, and Josephus, all of which date to 70 CE and later. Nevertheless, there are good reasons to find in these sources traditional information that takes us closer to the time of Paul.

In the challenge-riposte exchange of Mark 12:18–27 (and parr.), the Sadducees challenge Jesus regarding the question of marriage in the resurrection. As part of his response, Jesus insists to his Sadducean interlocutors that transformation—specifically in the direction of angelomorphism—is the nature of postmortem existence.[76] The Pharisees are not present in this episode, and the evangelists place this transformational ideal on the lips of Jesus. Nevertheless, Sanders (1977, 150–51) notes that contexts of scriptural interpretation regarding resurrection suggest influence from Pharisaic circles.[77] At the very least, then, Jesus shares a stance with his Pharisaic counterparts,[78] and elements of this stance are found also in Paul. Notably, the inclination toward angelomorphism, as we will see in chapters 3 and 4 of this study, is very much at home in Paul's writings. With respect to the RESURRECTION gestalt, this inclination toward angelomorphism suggests the micro-PATH (CHANGE) structure that we have discussed above. Though this evidence for Pharisaism is roundabout, it nevertheless finds resonance with aspects of Paul's writings (specifically) and the RESURRECTION gestalt (generally).

More important are Josephus's descriptions of what the Pharisees believed concerning the soul and afterlife:

> Although every soul [ψυχήν] is imperishable, only that of the good passes over to a different body [εἰς ἕτερον σῶμα], whereas those of the vile are punished by eternal retribution. (*B.J.* 2.163, trans. Mason 2008, 133)

And elsewhere:

---

76. Matt 22:30: ὡς ἄγγελοι ἐν τῷ οὐρανῷ εἰσιν // Mark 12:25: ἀλλ' εἰσὶν ὡς ἄγγελοι ἐν τοῖς οὐρανοῖς // Luke 20:36: ἰσάγγελοι γάρ εἰσιν. Mark and Matthew retain a comparative quality (ὡς ἄγγελοι) that is similar to what we saw in Dan 12:3. Luke uses the much rarer ἰσάγγελος (from ἴσος + ἄγγελος), which perhaps conveys a sense of "sameness," "equality," "equivalen[ce] in ... size, quality" (BDAG s.v. ἴσος; LSJ s.v. ἴσος), thus intensifying the angelomorphic ideal. As we will see in §3.1, there are excellent reasons for seeing angels as embodied beings and for viewing the angelomorphic nature of resurrection belief as an acquisition of such angelic glory-bodies.

77. See also Mason (1991, 156), who notes that Josephus presents the Pharisees in direct contrast with the Sadducees on issues of the soul and postmortem existence.

78. See Davies and Allison (2004, 379), who rightly note that Jesus's riposte is formulated on grounds consistent with the Sadducees' hermeneutical outlook; that is, Jesus cites Exod 3:6 rather than something like Dan 12:1–3 as proof of the resurrection (see Matt 22:32).

[The Pharisees] believe that souls [ταῖς ψυχαῖς] have power to survive death and that there are rewards and punishments under the earth for those who have led lives of virtue or vice: eternal imprisonment is the lot of evil souls, while the good souls receive an easy passage to a new life [ἀναβιοῦν]. (*A.J.* 18.14, trans. Thackeray 1926–1965)[79]

Much of Josephus's presentation of the Pharisees is shaped by his literary aims and presumed readership (see Mason 2003, 193–209; see also Sanders 1985, 195–96);[80] nevertheless, his descriptions in these passages evince several points of correlation with both the RESURRECTION gestalt and Paul's appropriation of that gestalt: (1) the presence of transformation (in this case, transposition from one body into another); (2) the presence of contrasting PATH structures; (3) the presence of both protagonist and antagonist TRAJECTORS, each progressing toward a particular end; and (4) the association of somatic transformation with ethical uprightness (a theme that we will explore in ch. 4 with respect to Paul).[81] On all four points, the afterlife beliefs of Josephus's Pharisees demonstrate both schematic and thematic coherence with Paul's resurrection ideals.

The first point is worth discussing in detail; scholars have long noted that Josephus uses the language of reincarnation to describe both his and the Pharisees' views, though Mason (1991, 169) notes that such language is "peculiar" and that "the form of reincarnation attributed to the Pharisees … bears many similarities to what we should call resurrection."[82] Central to Mason's judgment is the recognition that a soul's reembodiment is neither a punishment nor a discontinuity of identity; rather, Josephus emphasizes "the holiness and singularity of the new body [and] its nature

---

79. See also *B.J.* 3.374 and *C. Ap.* 2.218, which relay Josephus's views on souls and the afterlife. For a full discussion, see Mason 1991, 156–70, 297–300.

80. Noteworthy here is the portrayal of the Pharisees, Sadducees, and Essenes as "philosophical schools" (e.g., *A.J.* 18.11; *B.J.* 2.119), a description that no doubt serves Josephus's tendency to present Judaism as a "high philosophical culture, comparable to that of the Greeks, with its parallel spectrum of philosophical opinion" (Mason 2003, 194).

81. For Josephus, however, ethical uprightness is tied to the keeping of torah (see *C. Ap.* 2.218), whereas for Paul it is tied to somatic participation in Christ's death and resurrection (see below, §§4.1–2).

82. See also Mason (2008, 133). Josephus's use of ἀναβιόω is perhaps compared with 2 Macc 7:9, where the noun ἀναβίωσις is used with respect to resurrection (specifically somatic reconstitution).

as *reward*" (Mason 2008, 133). Importantly, from the perspective of this study, the continuity of identity that Josephus stresses means that his language of reincarnation coheres nicely with the micro-PATH (CHANGE) structure; what is asserted is movement of a ψυχή from one container into another (i.e., from one body into another body; see below, §§3.2.2–3 and 4.2–3). Within the analytical categories we have explored, Josephus's Pharisees utilize the RESURRECTION gestalt so as to make meaningful sense of death, the afterlife, and the intermediary state between. As I will show in chapters 4 and 5, Paul too exploits the micro-PATH (CHANGE) structure, though with a much more terrestrial focus. In all of these ways, though important differences between Paul and Josephus's Pharisees exist at the descriptive level (i.e., at human scale), at the schematic level there is much coherence.

A final text, which adds further nuance to our vision of Paul vis-à-vis Pharisaism, is Acts 23:6–10. Here the Lukan author echoes the challenge-riposte of Jesus with the Sadducees (Luke 20:27–40), though now the Pharisees come to the fore. Luke's Paul, here identifying as a Pharisee (23:6), exploits the theological differences between these groups. In the process, the Lukan narrator informs the reader: "the Sadducees say there is no resurrection, neither angel nor spirit, but the Pharisees acknowledge all" (23:8). Knowing exactly what to make of this comment—specifically how the categories of resurrection, angels, and πνεῦμα fit together—is difficult to assess.[83] Without overreaching too much, we can note that this triad of themes is central to Paul's ideals (namely, the centrality of πνεῦμα in the resurrection process, and the presumption that transformation is directed toward an angelomorphic state). All of this is premised, as I will show in chapters 3–5, upon Paul's specific appropriation of the RESURRECTION gestalt.

---

83. Pervo (2009, 575) simply notes that "exegetes have labored hard to explain [the reference to angel and spirit], which conflicts with the Torah, an authority accepted by the Sadducees." Fitzmyer (1998, 719) reads the verse appositionally, whereby Luke denotes "two modes of resurrection, as angel or as spirit." Conversely, Wright (2003, 132–33) finds in this verse a reference to the intermediary state between death and reembodiment. Parsons (2008, 315–16) agrees with Wright on the understanding of "spirit," though for "angel" he proposes a concern for divine providence (in line with Josephus, *A.J.* 13.171–173; 18.13; *B.J.* 2.162–165). Further interpretive options can be found in Pervo 2009, 575 n. 38.

2. IMAGING RESURRECTION

In each of these texts, both Paul and the Pharisees are seen to share a number of resurrection ideals. At times, these are shared thematic ideals, but more pervasively there is a shared schematic appropriation of the RESURRECTION gestalt. Most notably, this includes convictions about contrasting PATH structures and somatic transformation, though there are also important parallels with respect to categories of πνεῦμα, angels, and ethics.

2.2.6. The RESURRECTION Gestalt and 1 Thessalonians 4:13–18

With the exception of 1 Cor 15 and a selection of non-Pauline pericopes, the preceding overview has focused on Pauline texts that are not primarily concerned with resurrection. Such analysis demonstrates the ubiquity of the RESURRECTION gestalt in Paul's thought more globally. Turning to 1 Thess 4:13–18, I now examine Paul's earliest (surviving) discussion of the topic of resurrection. As we will see, the RESURRECTION gestalt functions as the conceptual structure upon which the apostle's resurrection ideals are premised.

Much of what scholars typically identify as "resurrection" is really concerned with the macro-GOAL element of the RESURRECTION gestalt.[84] This is particularly evident in 1 Thess 4, where Paul's address is occasioned by a concern for the fates of those who have died prior to the parousia (4:13).[85] Paul formulates his response by focusing his readers' attention on the macro-GOAL element, which is here characterized by an eschatological drama that includes events such as the parousia (4:15–17), the dead coming back to life (4:16), and the heavenly transposition

---

84. This is not surprising, as resurrection is often conceptualized via the RESURRECTION IS GOAL metaphor.

85. Given that 1 Thess 4:13–18 centers on the question of whether the dead will miss the parousia, some argue that Paul's initial proclamation to the Thessalonians concerned only Christ's resurrection and future coming, thus omitting references to eschatology and/or a future, general resurrection (Nickelsburg 2006, 234–35; cf. Holleman 1996, 123–30). Given the immediacy of Paul's eschatological expectations, such an assertion should not be dismissed out of hand. However, if Paul's initial teaching did downplay—even omit—the future, general resurrection, this de-emphasis perhaps reflects the apostle's heavenly ascent expectations more than it betrays an early stage in Paul's theological thinking. That is, Paul may have initially omitted futurist expectations precisely because he expected Christ-devotees to rise/ascend at any minute. Accordingly, we need not presume developments in Paul's thought, as though he had an underdeveloped understanding of future resurrection.

of the living (4:17).⁸⁶ The sequential nature of this drama (note πρῶτον and ἔπειτα, 4:16–17) coupled with Paul's fostering of hopeful expectations (4:13, 18) underscores the PATH structure inherent in Paul's thinking on resurrection.⁸⁷

Paul also draws heavily on the VERTICALITY and PROXIMITY schemata. For example, the DEATH IS DOWN/LIFE IS UP metaphors permeate Paul's address, here framed by notions of sleeping (4:13–15) and standing (4:14, 16). More pressing, the entire eschatological drama is characterized by vertically structured movement (esp. 4:16–17). Paul contends that the Lord will "descend from heaven," at which point the dead will be "raised" and the living will be "snatched [up]" (ἁρπαγησόμεθα) into the "clouds/air." Though ἁρπάζω does not typically imply verticality,⁸⁸ in both Paul and contemporary Jewish traditions it is used to denote transposition to the heavenly realms.⁸⁹ Accordingly, believers are elevated from the ground *up* into the sky to meet the Lord. Such an anticipated divine-human propinquity betrays Paul's use of the PROXIMITY schema. Paul insists that the

---

86. We perhaps could include future judgment here as well (see 1 Thess 1:10; 5:2–4), though Paul does not explicitly incorporate it into the present narrative (see elsewhere, 1 Cor 15:24; 2 Cor 5:10; and Rom 2:1–16). It should be noted that Paul offers no systematic account of eschatological events, and any attempt to construct a coherent narrative from Paul's various descriptions should be cautioned against.

87. As noted in §2.1.2.1, notions of hope are commonly conceptualized via a PATH schema in which achievement of the GOAL is assured.

88. The verb ἁρπάζω is commonly glossed as "snatch away, carry off" (LSJ, LEH, BDAG, PGL), "to seize hastily" (LSJ, LEH), "overpower" (LSJ, PGL), and even "steal, carry off" (LEH, BDAG). In both Septuagintal and non-Pauline New Testament usage, it can have any of these senses. The verb can carry violent overtones such that something is forcibly (re)moved (Trilling 1990), and in several instances it is used to denote involuntary movement under divine impetus (e.g., Acts 8:39; Rev 12:5; Jos. Asen. 12:8, 11; LAE [Gk.] 37:3).

89. In Paul, see 2 Cor 12:2–4. In Jewish literature, see esp. Wis 4:11 (and perhaps also Philo, QG 1.86), where Enoch is characterized as being "snatched away" (ἡρπάγη) by God. Though the Wisdom of Solomon lacks explicit vertical reference, Christopher Rowland (1982, 385–86) rightly notes that, within the context of contemporary Enochic traditions, it is very likely ascent overtones are intimated. For example, the Hebrew of Sirach describes Enoch as having been taken into God's presence (הוא נלקח פנים, MS B, 19 recto, line 4 [= 49:14]; cf. MS B, 13 verso, line 18 [= 44:16]), and the Greek tradition includes an explicit vertical orientation (αὐτὸς ἀνελήμφθη ἀπὸ τῆς γῆς, 49:14). The notion of ascent is explicit here, and it is complemented by many pre- and post-Sirach traditions that describe Enoch as a heavenly ascender (e.g., 1 En. 14–16; 39:3; 70–71; 2 En. 1:8; 3:1).

Lord will bring the dead "with him" (4:14) and later stresses that both the dead and the living will be "with the Lord forever" (4:17).

Finally, though notions of transformation (the micro-PATH) are muted in 1 Thess 4, I suggest they are implicit in Paul's description. The key reference here is ἁρπάζω (4:17), which Paul presents as the parallel experience of the living vis-à-vis the ἀνίστημι of the dead (4:16). As I will show in chapter 3 (§3.1.1), heavenly ascent often presumes some form of somatic transformation. Accordingly, though Paul does not use metaphors of CHANGE in 1 Thess 4, such may well be presumed in his characterization of the living being "snatched [up]" to the heavens.

To summarize, then, the entire RESURRECTION gestalt undergirds Paul's resurrection (indeed, his eschatological) ideals in 1 Thess 4. All the constituent elements of the RESURRECTION gestalt are found in Paul's thought; though most are explicit, some are more implicit and are only teased out through comparative work. Nevertheless, it is clear that Paul thinks of resurrection much like his Second Temple Judean counterparts—resurrection is conceptualized via a constellation of interlocking concepts that all work in concert with one another so as to convey meaning.

2.3. Conclusions

In the present chapter, I outlined several factors that enable the recognition of resurrection within a variety of Second Temple Jewish texts. In doing so, I have identified a recurrent gestalt structure—the RESURRECTION gestalt—that is constructed through the dynamic interplay of various image schemata and grounded in recurrent patterns of human embodiment. Though this gestalt is schematically fixed and quite abstract, it can be variously elaborated within a number of different frame-structures so as to yield a wide variety of resurrection expressions. We have also seen that Paul appropriates this gestalt in its entirety, using it to construct not only his resurrection ideals but also many of the general contours of his epistolary addresses. While I will examine with more precision Paul's use of the gestalt in the following chapters, the analysis here justifies my placement of Paul within this tradition.

As we have seen, notions of resurrection are thoroughly contextual, conceptual, and metaphorical, all of which promises a way beyond the limitations of the scholarly approaches examined in chapter 1 (§1.3.1). On the one hand, identification of resurrection is not reducible to mere lexical signs (such as ἐγείρω or ἀνίστημι), for discursive contexts—both literary and social—are formative and determinative for the comprehension of such signs. On the other hand, any attempt to distinguish between literal and metaphorical notions of resurrection is theoretically problematic. Resurrection is an imaginative category; it is constructed by and reflective of the poetic or figurative nature of human cognition (Gibbs 1994). Accordingly, resurrection always is metaphorically elaborated in relation to more basic, common somatic experiences. One strength of the foregoing analysis is the identification of a recurrent constellation of concepts and image schemata that are grounded in patterns of human embodiment and that then are extended metaphorically to various frames and/or domains of Judean experience (e.g., ethnogeographic restoration, postmortem life). It is this process of metaphorical elaboration that accounts for the plurality of resurrection ideals in the period literature, thus offering a rationale for the clustering of these disparate notions under one category, *resurrection*. Taken together, the foregoing all points to an understanding of resurrection as a nonpropositional, embodied concept.

3
"WE WILL ALL BE CHANGED":
ON DUALISM/MONISM, PLANTS, AND THE
PECULIARITY OF WEARING A HOUSE

Paul's resurrection ideals are transformation ideals. Scattered throughout the undisputed epistles are references to somatic change whereby the earthly body will (or is) undergo(ing) alteration into a heavenly somatic state (Rom 8:29; 1 Cor 15:35–54; 2 Cor 3:18; 5:1–5; Phil 3:21; perhaps also 1 Thess 4:17). For Paul, transformation is the central process by which resurrection is achieved. Indeed, though some believers will escape death at the parousia, Paul confidently insists that "we will all be changed" (1 Cor 15:51). Central to Paul's transformation ideals, however, are certain built-in assumptions regarding both cosmology and anthropology. For Paul, eschatological transformation concerns not only the body but also the body's location within the cosmos. In this way, the apostle's resurrection ideals are premised on his cosmo-somatic outlook.

At the intersection of cosmology and anthropology lie issues of both dualism and monism. As already noted in chapter 1 (§1.3.2), much Pauline scholarship incongruently conflates Paul's dualism and monism. In many modern treatments, Paul is read within the context of an apocalypticism characterized by opposition (e.g., heaven vs. earth; now vs. then), thus advocating a strong degree of contradistinction between earthly and heavenly somatic states. At the same time, however, Paul's anthropology is usually understood within the context of an assumed Jewish monism. While proponents of this view expressly reject certain forms of Greek dualism, modern dualistic tendencies are often implicitly imported. As I have demonstrated, both views are problematic, and there is a need to demarcate more clearly the nature and character of Paul's dualism/monism, especially as it relates to his cosmo-somatic presuppositions.

In the present chapter, I will address this issue. In an attempt to better appreciate the categories of reality with which Paul himself works,[1] my aim will be the contextualization of Paul within a broader cultural matrix while also identifying the particulars of Paul's own worldview. The chapter is broken into two halves. In §3.1, I focus on what are identified as concentric circles of cultural embodiment, specifically identifying the character of dualism and monism in many Jewish and Hellenistic traditions. Attention will be directed to issues of cosmology and anthropology so as to identify broader cosmo-somatic presuppositions in Greco-Roman antiquity. With these in view, I turn in §3.2 toward the transformation metaphors of 1 Cor 15:35–50 and 2 Cor 5:1–5, specifically examining the nature of Paul's cosmo-somatic presuppositions and the extent to which continuity and discontinuity characterize such transformations. To anticipate my conclusions, I will argue that Paul's cosmology and anthropology are characterized not by opposition but rather interrelation, which is to say that Paul distinguishes between *parts* while stressing their overall integration within the *whole*. In this way, overly drawn descriptions of both dualism and monism are set aside in favor of a more nuanced and integrative approach.

3.1. Concentric Circles of Cultural Embodiment

To insist that all human meaning is embodied is not to deny the impact of culture but rather to recognize the formative and fundamental role culture plays in the meaning-making process. To again cite Johnson (2005, 16), "there can be no thought without a brain in a body in an environment." It is this environmental embodiment, which has as much to do with culture as it does with physiology, that I now examine. The following will illuminate the cultural environments within which Paul is embodied. I suggest that Paul is best located within many interlocking contexts (e.g., within both Jewish and Greek traditions). This is not to deny that certain traditions are more prevalent in Paul than others, nor to unhelpfully con-

---

1. I here echo Sanders (1977, 522), who concludes his treatment of Paul with the insistence that scholars "lack a category of 'reality' [by which to understand] real participation in Christ." In this chapter and the arguments that follow in chs. 4–5, I explore the extent to which Paul's participationist language is rooted in certain cosmo-somatic presuppositions, all of which exist at the creative intersection of Jewish and Greek ideas.

flate differing cultural streams with one another. Rather, it is to recognize that Paul is able to draw on several differing backgrounds in constructing meaning. The following analysis will travel from the inside out through three concentric circles of cultural embodiment: Jewish apocalyptic (the inner circle), Second Temple and early Judaism generally (the broader circle), and Hellenistic philosophy (the broadest circle). As we will see, in each of these circles, issues of cosmology and anthropology are premised upon a one-world model that is often characterized by integration rather than opposition.

3.1.1. The Inner Cultural Circle: Jewish Apocalyptic

Though Paul draws on several cultural contexts in constructing his resurrection ideals, it is Jewish apocalyptic that constitutes (arguably) the formulaic core of his thought. Of particular interest for this study are traditions of heavenly ascent, which are important for two reasons. First, we have already seen in 1 Thess 4:13–18 (§2.2.6) that Paul understands resurrection and heavenly ascent as analogous experiences, thus suggesting Paul's resurrection ideals are correlated (at least in part) with ascent ideals. Second, ascent traditions reveal much about the dualistic nature of Jewish apocalyptic, specifically with respect to issues of cosmo-somatology. As I will demonstrate, heavenly ascent traditions presume a one-world model premised upon cosmological permeability rather than separation.

An overview of the relevant period literature reveals a cosmological model wherein heaven and earth are vertically aligned such that heavenly ascent requires upward spatial movement. The Enochic Book of Watchers stands as an early witness to these traditions (1 En. 14:8–9),[2] and the later Similitudes recount two heavenly ascents (1 En. 39:3; 70–71), the latter of which may presume a storied heavenly structure.[3] The existence of multiple heavenly layers is common in the broader period literature, with descriptions of one, three, five, or even seven layers all denoting a vertical structure that extends upward toward a cosmic pinnacle.[4] Such layers

---

2. Note the use of ἐπαίρω/עלא to describe heavenly ascent (1 En. 14:8–9; Aramaic from 4Q204 1 VI, 21).

3. Though the Similitudes generally envision a single heaven, the reference in 1 En. 71:5 to the "heaven of heavens" may envision a multiplicity of heavenly layers (Himmelfarb 1993, 59–61).

4. See, e.g., the Book of Watchers (one heaven), 2 Cor 12 and the Testament of

are explicit in Paul (see 2 Cor 12:1–10), and they are variously articulated in ascent apocalypses that postdate the turn of the eras. For example, the post-Pauline Apocalypse of Abraham envisions seven heavenly layers and describes an ascent (15:4–7; see also 12:10) whereby Abraham is directed in chapter 20 to look down at the stars beneath him (a cosmological reversal of Gen 15:5). Though alternative understandings of heaven-earth spatial relations existed,[5] what is of importance here is the construction of heaven and earth as vertically distinct locales that are mutually permeable.

Many of these traditions correlate heavenly transposition with some form of transformation, specifically in the direction of angelomorphism. The so-called Self-Glorification Hymn from Qumran stands as a striking (though extreme) example.[6] The hymn's speaker repeatedly insists that he shares in angelic "glory" (כבוד, lines 13–15, 18), that his desires are not according to the flesh (line 14), and that he is reckoned with the "angels/gods" (אלים, lines 12, 14–15, 18).[7] The language is unequivocally strong,[8] and it seems to point to the angelic transformation of a human figure.[9] While other traditions use more graphic images such as flesh melting off the ascender's body (1 En. 71:11), the most common metaphor is that of clothing exchange.[10] This is particularly evident in the post-Pauline com-

---

Levi (three heavens), 3 Baruch (five heavens), and 2 Enoch and the Apocalypse of Abraham (seven heavens). For an overview, see A. Collins 1995, 59–93.

5. Philip Alexander (2006, 118–19), for instance, draws attention to (what he calls) a "more sophisticated" understanding of heaven and earth as parallel universes, not *on top* of each other but rather *beside* or even *within* one another. Alexander is correct to draw attention to this aspect of broader Jewish thought, though even these descriptions are often correlated with notions of verticality (e.g., T. Levi 5:1–3). See also Alexander 2011.

6. Though this fragmentary hymn does not have an explicit reference to heavenly ascent, such may well be implied. The hymn is likely sectarian and the surviving manuscripts date to the turn of the eras (Angel 2010, esp. 585–88).

7. All references correspond to Recension B (4Q491 11 I).

8. Davila (1999, 475), for instance, rightly notes the similarities between the hymn and the much later 3 Enoch on the issue of heavenly transformation.

9. Though initially titled "Cantique de Michel" (Baillet 1982, 26–29), the majority of subsequent scholarship has strongly suggested this text presumes a human figure that undergoes angelomorphism (even apotheosis).

10. We cannot overlook the priestly nature of these ascents. Heaven is conceptualized as a celestial temple in which the angels and the ascender function as priests, and the endowment of a heavenly, priestly garment (= transformation) enables priestly service before the Great Glory (see Himmelfarb 1993, 9–46).

parative literature. In 2 Enoch, for instance, the patriarch is "extract[ed] ... from [his] earthly clothing" and "put ... into the clothes of glory," a process that results in "no observable difference" between Enoch and the angels (A 22:8–10; J is similar). We can also point to several traditions (both pre- and post-Pauline) wherein the righteous dead are said to acquire a heavenly garment.[11] Though transformation is not presumed in all ascent traditions,[12] in those where it is, the ascender's proximity to the divine is a key feature. The closer the visionary comes to the divine, the greater the need for transformation.[13] Taken together, these texts correlate both locative change (earth to heaven) and somatic transformation (earthly body to heavenly body) within a one-world model of cosmo-somatic interrelation.

Given the texts just examined, we can now see there are important image-schematic parallels between heavenly ascent and resurrection traditions.[14] In addition to cosmological transposition (VERTICALITY), divine-human propinquity (PROXIMITY), and celestial transformation (CHANGE gestalt), both rapture and resurrection are premised upon the PATH schema—that is, the movement of an ascender (TRAJECTOR) from earth (SOURCE) to heaven (GOAL). This is not to say that these traditions are identical,[15] but rather to demonstrate a shared conceptual structure

---

11. See, e.g., Apoc. Zeph. 8:3–4 (Achmimic text); 1 En. 62:15–16; and Apoc. Ab. 13:14.

12. For example, the Apocalypse of Abraham attributes no transformation to Abraham during his ascent, though it looks ahead in 13:14 to a future time when Abraham will be clothed with Azazel's heavenly garment (and Azazel with Abraham's corruptibility).

13. This theme comes to full articulation in the much later *hekhalot* literature, though its roots are found already in Jewish apocalyptic (Morray-Jones 1992).

14. The relationship between resurrection and rapture has long been noticed by New Testament scholars (e.g., Bousset 1901). Alan Segal (1980) has offered a structuralist account of this correspondence, positing an underlying and pervasive "mythical structure" of ascent/descent that finds expression in numerous ancient cultures. Segal focuses on culture as a generative matrix, thus arguing that myth is always created in relation to external stimuli (not vice versa). While his analysis is illuminating, by pitting culture against any kind of transcultural grounding, Segal rejects a broader foundation upon which such a "mythic structure" could stand. In short, Segal offers no explanation for (1) why the structure exists and (2) what causes the structure to find widespread, cross-cultural appeal. In contrast, this study deepens Segal's analysis in that the conceptual correlations between rapture and resurrection become more robust and somatically grounded.

15. In Jewish tradition, ascents are (typically) understood to happen in the pres-

that enables blending with one another. It is for this reason that Paul is able to describe both eschatological transposition and present heavenly ascent with the same descriptor, ἁρπάζω (1 Thess 4:17; 2 Cor 12:2–4). The two are understood as correlated precisely because Paul understands his experience of heavenly ascent as an experience (or foretaste) of resurrection.[16]

The traditions examined here point toward a worldview in which heaven and earth stand as vertically configured spatial locales that are mutually accessible via the process of heavenly ascent. Such traditions take for granted the permeability of the cosmos. For Martha Himmelfarb (1993, 71), far from denoting any kind of radical or oppositional dualism, the ascent apocalypses claim the "possibility of transcendence":

> The descent of a divine figure expresses the certainty that God cares enough for the righteous to send them help. But the ascent apocalypses make greater claims for the nature of humanity: human beings ... have the potential to become like the angels, or even greater than the angels.

Within this world, heaven is not ontologically other but rather interconnected with the earth. Heaven lies just beyond the scope of human perception (hence the need for "uncovering" or "revealing" [ἀποκαλύπτω]). In this way, then, Jewish apocalyptic points to a gradient cosmological dualism that is characterized by integration rather than opposition.

3.1.2. The Broader Cultural Circle: Second Temple/Early Judaism

Extending my analysis beyond Jewish apocalyptic, broader scriptural and pseudepigraphical traditions further presume this dualistically integrated one-world system. Here the lines between earthly and heavenly somatic states are not ontologically drawn, which is to say that permeability extends to somatology as much as cosmology.

In the period just after Paul, a number of traditions describe Adam's prelapsarian existence as a state of angelomorphic glory.[17] Some texts insist

---

ent, while resurrection is relegated to the future. Such temporal variance results not from schematic differences but rather different PATH-structure scaling. In resurrection the PATH schema is both temporally and spatially elaborated, while in ascent it only is spatially elaborated. Accordingly, resurrection and rapture exist as distinctly different expressions that share a strong degree of image schematic structure.

16. So argued most strongly by A. Segal (1998).

17. Attention is given to Adamic traditions for the simple fact that Paul himself

that Adam was created as "a second angel" (2 En. J 30:11), while others assert that the angels were directed to worship the prelapsarian couple (LAE [Lat.] 13–15).[18] Related descriptions can be found in LAE (Gk.) 20:1–2 and 3 Bar. 4:16, both of which characterize the lapsarian event as the loss of a garment of glory (note the clothing metaphor). These descriptions all betray a strikingly high view of Adam (and Eve), one in which the prelapsarian couple are perceived as being created in a state of divine/angelic "glory."[19] That such descriptions likely have a broader anthropological referent is suggested in the Enochic Similitudes (for example), which insist "humans were not created to be different from the angels" (1 En. 69:11).

The evidence from Qumran is also informative. It is well known that the Qumranites perceived their communal worship in concert with the angels,[20] a feature that may reflect an ideal angelomorphic human form. Fletcher-Louis (2002) has argued this point. Focusing on the intersection of the liturgical genre and the Qumran cultus, he insists that through the liturgy of the Songs of the Sabbath Sacrifice the Qumran community, specifically its priesthood, is seen as embodying the Great Glory of the Lord. In this way, the cult restores humanity to its prelapsarian divine/angelic glory.[21] Though Fletcher-Louis's treatment has not gone uncriticized,[22] it is complemented by exegetical work that examines the aforementioned

---

stresses Christ as the "last Adam" (1 Cor 15:45). For other commemorative figures who similarly are described angelomorphically, see n. 25 below.

18. See additionally LAE (Lat.) 4:1–2; 47 (// ch. 39 [Gk.]).

19. Indeed, Fletcher-Louis (1997, 142) notes, with respect to LAE (Lat.): "not only is Adam angelomorphic in this text, he is also unequivocally set over the angels."

20. This aspect of the Qumranite self-identity has garnered much scholarly debate. Fletcher-Louis's (2002) emphasis on the experience of angelomorphism represents a maximalist position. Others such as Björn Frennesson (1999) argue that the concept of liturgical communion pervaded the sectarian literature but found concrete expression in only a few liturgical texts. At the other end, Devorah Dimant (1996) sees the Qumranites' worship as analogous with the angels.

21. See esp. Fletcher-Louis 2002, 356–94, where he argues: "[there is] an analogous identification of the prelapsarian Adam with the Glory of God,… [a connection that is] likely made because of the belief that the high priest recapitulates the Adamic identity and the notion that the cult is a restored Eden or prelapsarian world" (382).

22. As several reviewers have noted, the maximalist nature of Fletcher-Louis's analysis results in a "keen [interest to] read several ambiguous texts in such a way as to support his thesis" (Brooke 2005, 163), a feature that comes across as "heavy handed" (Goff 2005, n.p.).

Self-Glorification Hymn together with the attached Canticle of the Righteous (Recension B). Joseph Angel (2010) explores correlations between the singular and plural referents of the hymn and the canticle, respectively. He argues that the speaker and the community inseparably mirror each other such that they share in a number of experiences, including exalted heavenly status (598).[23] In this way, the hymn's transformative ideal has a communal focus, one that moves in the direction of angelomorphism.

I highlight these Adamic traditions not to stress a unitary picture of Adam's prelapsarian glory[24] but rather to demonstrate the blurred boundaries between angels/divinity and humanity in many streams of Jewish thought. Accordingly, this enables an idyllic human form premised on angelomorphic descriptions.[25] Heavenly and earthly somatic forms may be distinct, but they are not strongly disconnected, and many streams of tradition affirm the possibility of transformation from one into the other.

Josephus's descriptions of both the Pharisees and his own afterlife beliefs are also interesting on these points. As I discussed in chapter 2 (§2.2.5), there are indications from the Gospels and Acts that the Pharisees held to some form of angelomorphic postmortem ideal (see Mark 12:25 parr.; Acts 23:8). This is complemented to some extent by the picture of the Pharisees presented by Josephus. Here the Pharisees are said to believe that the souls of the good pass over "into a different body" (εἰς ἕτερον σῶμα, B.J. 2.163; see also A.J. 18.14). Josephus unfortunately tells us nothing about the character of these "different bod[ies]"; nevertheless, when betraying his own thinking on such matters (which Mason [1991, 168–69] concludes is similar to that of the Pharisees), Josephus does look ahead to "pure bodies" (ἁγνοῖς ... σώμασιν, B.J. 3.374; see Mason 1991, 167). Angelomorphism is not explicitly noted here, though somatic transposition in the direction of a different and better bodily state beyond the terrestrial clearly is presumed. So Mason (1991, 167): "Josephus's references to the new body seem to suggest that it is more than simply

---

23. Philip Alexander (2006, 86) advances a more tentative conclusion, while Michael Wise (2000, 216–19) suggests that through liturgical performance each individual member of the community spoke of themselves as ascended to heaven.

24. John Levison (1987) has rightly cautioned against such an approach.

25. That similar angelomorphic descriptions are ascribed to a number of commemorative figures (e.g., Abel, Enoch, Noah, Jacob/Israel, Moses, Elijah, and the high priest) underscores this cosmo-somatic permeability. On the angelomorphic motif, see Charlesworth 1980.

another human or animal form.... Josephus is talking about a holy or sacred body that will bring a better life." Though Josephus's perspective is perhaps stronger than many of the broader traditions we have explored,[26] the general thrust of his ideas are the same: different bodies exist for different modes of existence.

Within a conceptual world where humanity can be described angelomorphically, it is perhaps not surprising that angels and other divine beings are often described anthropomorphically. A prime example is the angelic figure of Dan 7, whose identification as בר אנש may not be titular but rather connotative of a "humanlike form" (A. Segal 1990, 53; contra Nickelsburg 1999, 800). Similarly, it is not uncommon to find references to angels as men (Dan 9:21; see also 10:5–6, 16–18), to the Enochic Watchers as being able to lay and procreate with women (1 En. 6–7), and to angels being able to speak (19:1), look (9:1), stand (39:12–13), and exist in a perpetual state of wakefulness (39:12–13; 61:12; 71:7). Indeed, in several instances angels are indistinguishable from humans,[27] thus denoting an anthropomorphic angelic form.[28]

Related to angelic anthropomorphisms are the descriptions of God via somatic categories. Already in the Hebrew Scriptures, references to the Glory of Yahweh/the Lord (כבוד יהוה/δόξαν κυρίου) came to acquire the near technical meaning of God's human appearance.[29] Carey Newman (1992, 1997) has offered a detailed treatment of this glory language, arguing the phrase "Glory of the Lord" is not attributive but rather denotes "*the*

---

26. For Josephus, the granting of this new body occurs ἐκ περιτροπῆς αἰώνων (*B.J.* 3.374), a phrase that Mason (1991, 167–68) suggests is best understood as "in/at the succession (or change) of the ages." Accordingly, while there is continuity of ψυχή, Josephus more clearly emphasizes distinction between somatic states.

27. For example, see in the Hebrew Scriptures: Gen 19:1–29 and 32:25–31; in the New Testament: Heb 13:2; and in the Pseudepigrapha: Jos. Asen. 14:3(4).

28. Not all held to such somatically oriented understandings of angels; see, e.g., the descriptions of angels as *bodiless* (ἀσώματος) in Philo, *Sacr.* 5; T. Ab. A 3:6; 4:9; 9:2; 11:9; 15:4–6; and 16:2. However, even here we find a peculiar mix of somatic and a-somatic language; for example: "Abraham ... fell at the feet of the bodiless one" (Ἀβραάμ ... προσέπεσεν τοῖς ποσὶν τοῦ ἀσωμάτου, T. Ab. A 9:2; also 3:6; 15:4). (N.B. numbering for Testament of Abraham follows Sanders 1983.)

29. For example, see Exod 33:12–34:9, especially the anthropomorphisms of 33:17–23 and 34:5–6. In addition to anthropomorphism, the glory of Yahweh is associated with clouds and fire such that the presence of Yahweh is understood as having appeared in both (Exod 16:7 and 10 [see also 13:21–22]; 40:34–38).

visible, movable divine presence. To see or experience Yahweh's Glory is to see or experience Yahweh" (1997, 62, emphasis original). Such anthropomorphized glory language is associated with eschatological promise (i.e., GOAL = NEARness to YAHWEH),[30] and it also becomes a key motif in early Jewish throne-chariot and later *merkabah* mystical traditions (see A. Segal 1990, 34–71). Ezekiel stands as an early text in this tradition, where the prophet describes the Glory of Yahweh as an enthroned, humanlike figure with a luminous, fiery body (1:26–28).[31] Within postscriptural tradition, this Glory figure is increasingly identified as the heavenly agent encountered at the pinnacle of ascent (e.g., 1 En. 14:18–21), and the enthroned figure is often characterized as a luminous human form or glory-body (Ezek. Trag. lines 68–72). In such cases, the anthropomorphic descriptions used of Yahweh lean toward hypostatization, and this embodied glory functions as the material or visible expression of the divine.

The importance of these cultural traditions for our understanding of Paul's resurrection ideals cannot be understated. On the one hand, Paul characterizes resurrection via the category of "glory" (Rom 8:17–18; 1 Cor 15:40–41), and even insists that the risen Christ has a "body of glory" (Phil 3:21; see also 1 Cor 2:8; 2 Cor 3:18; 4:4–6; Rom 8:29). For Paul, then, Christ is the Great Glory, but he is also described as the "last Adam" (1 Cor 15:45). While many scholars would like to find in Paul the assertion that Adam's forfeited prelapsarian glory is regained in Christ, such conclusions cannot be extended to the whole of Paul's letters.[32] Indeed, in 1 Cor 15:45–49, Paul contrasts the prelapsarian Adam with the risen Christ,[33]

---

30. In the Hebrew Scriptures, glory language is associated not only with a future GOAL (e.g., Isa 40:5; 58:5; 60:1–3), but also with divine judgment (e.g., Isa 59:19; Ezek 39:13, 21; see Newman 1997, 64–70).

31. The Hebrew of Ezek 1:26 reads, דמות כמראה אדם, "[something] like the appearance of a human"; the Greek, ὁμοίωμα ὡς εἶδος ἀνθρώπου, "a likeness as the image of a human." Though a body is not explicitly identified, the description presumes a somatic form and is premised on the idea of anthropomorphic analogy. The same anthropomorphic Glory appears again in Ezek 8:2, 9:3–4, and 10:4, and there seems to be no distinction between this luminous body of Glory and Yahweh (esp. in 9:3–4; see Fossum 1999, 349).

32. The point is often made with respect to Romans; see Hooker 1959–1960; Wedderburn 1980.

33. Paul cites Gen 2:7 LXX in 15:45, taking from it the phrase ψυχὴν ζῶσαν, "natural-living being," which he thus maps as both DOWN and in need of transformation. Similarly, Paul's use of χοϊκός, which only occurs four times in the New Testament (all

and he does so without recourse to notions of initial Adamic glory.³⁴ The passage has important Philonic parallels (see below, §3.1.3), though Paul's description of Christ as the "last Adam" does not cohere with those parallels and is best understood within this broader trend toward an idyllic Adamic state. In this way, Paul focuses on an eschatological Adamic form premised on Christ's risen glory-body.³⁵ Paul's resurrection descriptions presume both human angelomorphism and divine anthropomorphism. The two are interrelated, and they cohere in the resurrected Christ and those who share in his risen existence.

In summary, if the descriptions of human beings via angelic or divine categories serve to elevate the human form, then the related expressions that anthropomorphize the divine stand as the former's obverse. The majority of traditions examined here demonstrate worldviews that do not distinguish sharply between heavenly and earthly realms. Two worlds exist, yes, but their relation to one another is constructed not via an oppositional dualism but rather characterized by permeability. The possibility of vertical transformation exists; human beings can become angelic and thus possess anthropomorphised glory-bodies.

3.1.3. The Broadest Cultural Circle: Hellenistic Philosophy

Expanding this analysis further, I turn now toward Hellenistic philosophical traditions so as to understand the nature of dualism and monism in Paul's broadest cultural context. I can begin by noting that the integrated, one-world model that I have thus far described has an important correlate in broader first-century Mediterranean thinking. Focusing on popular

---

within 1 Cor 15:47–49) and is rare outside the New Testament, may be derived from χοῦς (dust) and was perhaps coined in relation to the Greek text of Gen 2:7 (Balz 1993).

34. Paul never explicitly describes primordial Adamic glory, nor does he contrast Christ's risen state with Adam's prelapsarian state. Indeed, while Paul frequently speaks of Christ as the "image" or "form" of God (Rom 8:29; 2 Cor 3:18; 4:4; Phil 2:6), he never speaks of the prelapsarian Adam with such language and only once speaks of humanity currently bearing that image (1 Cor 11:7). Kooten's (2008, 304) suggestion that Paul "forgets about the temporary and very brief period in which … man did effectively posses *pneuma*" is unpersuasive.

35. On this point, Wright (2003, 355) is certainly correct in asserting, "the *pneumatikos* state is not simply an original idea in the mind of the creator, from which the human race fell sadly away; this model of humanity is the future reality, the reality which will swallow up and replace merely *psychikos* life."

Hellenistic philosophy, Dale Martin (1995, 4–37, esp. 29–37) illuminates a cosmo-somatic mapping wherein the body, like the universe and society, is conceptualized as a hierarchical spectrum. At the bottom end of the spectrum are those things that are less desirable—thick, heavy, weak, passive, ugly, and feminine (which include bodily traits such as being cold, moist, and soft). By contrast, the upper end constitutes the more desirable—fine, thin, strong, active, beauty, and masculine (which includes bodily traits such as warmth, dryness, and hardness). Within this mapping, earthly and heavenly are understood as both spatially and qualitatively different, though not ontologically opposed; thus Martin insists, "a 'one world' model is much closer to the ancient conception, and, instead of an ontological dualism, we should think of a hierarchy of essence" (15).[36]

The most dominant philosophical tradition at the turn of the eras—Stoicism—held to this one-world model,[37] and Stanley Stowers (2003, 527) has noted that the first century CE was largely dominated by philosophical monism: "All of the other [non-Platonic] schools of philosophy were so-called materialists or physicalists. Everything in the universe, including God or the gods, is one part of the 'natural' or physical order and can in principle be investigated by humans." To a similar end, Edward Adams (2000, 65) insists that notions of order and unity pervade the range of lexical senses for κόσμος: "the word κόσμος connotes the idea of an ordering of distinctive parts into a *cohesive* unit. Insofar as the universe is a κόσμος, it is conceived as a unity, with its varied and constituent elements ... integrated into a perfect whole" (emphasis original).

Within this ordered, physicalist worldview, concepts that we moderns take as immaterial or incorporeal were not understood as such. Heinrich von Staden (2000, 79), for instance, has demonstrated that Hellenistic philosophers and physicians generally considered the ψυχή to be a material substance in a way similar to the σῶμα: "all *psychē* is *sōma* but not all *sōma* is *psychē*." Similarly, the Stoics understood πνεῦμα as the all-encompassing material substance that permeates and holds the cosmos together (see Engberg-Pedersen 2010, 20), and Martin (1995, 21–25) has shown

---

36. Martin (1995, 15) here takes specific aim at Cartesian dualism, of which he rightly stresses, "*all* the Cartesian oppositions—matter versus nonmatter, physical versus spiritual, corporeal (or physical) versus psychological, nature versus supernature—are misleading when retrojected into ancient language."

37. See, e.g., Engberg-Pedersen (2010), who stresses the Stoic material πνεῦμα as the all-encompassing substance that permeates the world.

that pneumatic materiality was generally accepted in broader Hellenistic thought.[38] Within this worldview, *incorporeal* does not necessarily denote *immaterial*, which means that πνεῦμα can be perceived as both a material and incorporeal substance at the same time. Though many treatments of Paul understand πνεῦμα as the immaterial aspect of the human composition (a truly Cartesian dualism),[39] Engberg-Pedersen (2010) has compellingly argued that, throughout the epistles, Paul's pneumatology is thoroughly materialistic.[40] This is, as we have seen, consistent with the broader one-world model that I have been characterizing.

To insist on such a unitary worldview is not to eschew but rather to refocus our understanding of dualism. It is well known that Plato advocated an anthropological dualism drawn primarily along sense-thought lines, though Thomas Robinson (2000) rightly points to developments in Plato's thought from the strong body-soul opposition in the *Phaedo* to the more nuanced inner tension of the trichotomous soul in *Respublica* and *Timaeus*.[41] In this way, he who is often upheld as the staunchest proponent of dualism in antiquity is seen to hold a much more attenuated view. Standing in the Platonic tradition is Philo of Alexandria, whose exegesis of Gen 1–2 is commonly identified as the closest historical parallel to

---

38. Martin (1995, 22) notes that πνεῦμα was linked with the air/wind (though not exclusively) and was commonly understood as "the life-giving material for the members of the body." Πνεῦμα was a substance both inherent within and external to human beings; as an entity within the human body, πνεῦμα was particularly linked to the optical system, though it was tied also to motion, reason, and life itself.

39. A few examples will suffice. Despite his insistence that πνεῦμα does not stand in contrast to either body or nature, Bultmann (1951–1955, 1:153) nonetheless defines πνεῦμα as the "miraculous divine power that stands in absolute contrast to all that is human." Similarly, though Robert Gundry (1976, 48–49) is critical of Bultmann, he also asserts that πνεῦμα is ontologically distinct from σῶμα, thus arguing (with respect to 1 Cor 10:10) that "*sōma* retains its purely physical connotation over against *pneuma*" and later that "the contrast with *pneuma* makes *sōma* exclusively physical." Dunn (1998a, 3) insists that "*pneuma* denotes that power which humanity experiences as relating it to the spiritual realm, the realm of reality which lies beyond ordinary observation and human control."

40. See specifically Engberg-Pedersen 2010, 8–74.

41. T. Robinson (2000, 47) notes that Plato's description of the soul in the *Timaeus* advocates a tripartite division wherein the highest part of the soul (i.e., Reason) is understood as immortal and material. This is, as Robinson notes, a development from the earlier *Phaedo* and *Respublica* (which held a more immaterial view), and it evinces the degree to which the one-world system pervades even Plato's descriptions.

the ideologies Paul confronts at Corinth (see Pearson 1973; Horsley 1976; Sterling 1995). While there are several points of connection between Philo and Paul,[42] the key issue is the Philonic distinction between the heavenly person (who was created in Gen 1:26–27) and the earthly composite person (who was created in Gen 2:7).[43] For Philo, the former is the imperishable, incorporeal heavenly ideal that was created according to the divine image and is only perceived by the mind (*Opif.* 134). By contrast, the latter is a composite being who, as both body and soul, is mortal, formed of the dust, and perceived by the senses (*Opif.* 134).

Philo envisions the relation between these two persons in various ways. In some cases, the two are contrasted according to a Platonic Form-Image distinction, thus denoting the heavenly archetype vis-à-vis the earthly and visible expression of that Form (*Opif.* 24–25, 35–36).[44] In other places, however, Philo speaks of these two figures being somatically interrelated.[45] In *Quis rerum divinarum heres sit*, for instance, Philo insists that the inbreathing of the divine breath at creation (Gen 2:7) causes the earthly person to be formed "after the image" (*Her.* 56), a phrase that Philo elsewhere and much more ubiquitously reserves for the heavenly person (e.g., *Opif.* 134).[46] Here the two persons come into closer somatic correlation. Philo understands the earthly person as a trichotomous mind/spirit-soul-body,[47] and he correlates the heavenly person with the earthly

---

42. With respect to resurrection, the key connections are fourfold: (1) Paul's use of Gen 2:7 in 1 Cor 15:45; (2) the contrasting of the heavenly and earthly persons (compare 1 Cor 15:47–49 with Philo, *Leg.* 1.31–32; *Opif.* 134); (3) the description of Adam as the "first person" (compare 1 Cor 15:45, 47 with Philo, *Opif.* 136–150); and (4) the description of the heavenly person as the divine/life-giving spirit (compare 1 Cor 15:45 with Philo, *Her.* 56–57).

43. I have opted for the translation of ἄνθρωπος as "person" rather than the more traditional "man" so as to denote the gender generality of ἄνθρωπος. I do so with full consciousness that, at least in the case of Philo, the gender of the "earthly ἄνθρωπος" may indeed be exegetically important (see, e.g., *Opif.* 136–150).

44. Thus Levison (1987, 85), speaking of *QG* 2.56, notes that the "Platonic distinction between noetic pattern and sense copy" is unequivocally present.

45. Here following Kooten 2008, 64–66.

46. Noted by Pearson 1973, 19.

47. It was more common in the Hellenistic world to draw a trichotomous distinction between mind-soul-body (νοῦς-ψυχή-σῶμα), and indeed Philo himself employs this construction very frequently. Nonetheless, at several points Philo correlates mind (νοῦς) with spirit (πνεῦμα), which has led some to argue for a specifically Jewish interpretation of the Platonic trichotomy: not mind-soul-body but spirit-soul-body. Berger

person's mind/spirit.⁴⁸ Though Philo certainly retains a strong sense of differentiation between the two persons, the key distinction in this text is less about body-soul opposition and more about proper body-soul alignment. That is, Philo's blurring of the earthly and heavenly persons has less to do with cosmology and more to do with ethical reflection.

Philo continues in *Her.* 57 by stressing two opposing human "forms" (or "races," *Leg.* 1.31): one is the earthly person who lives according to "blood and the pleasure of the flesh" (αἵματι καὶ σαρκὸς ἡδονῇ [= ψυχή, *Her.* 55–56]),⁴⁹ the other is the heavenly person who lives according to the "divine spirit-reason" (θείῳ πνεύματι λογισμῷ [= νοῦς, *Her.* 56]). Philo does not have a Form-Image opposition in mind but rather contrasting modes of ethical behavior understood as the trichotomous mind-soul-body being submitted to the divine breath. Though Philo, on the whole, is otherwise a stricter dualist than many, at times his cosmo-somatology is much more integrative than oppositional (especially with respect to ethical ideals).

Taking the above traditions together, we see a general trend wherein cosmology and anthropology are understood within a one-world model. In most traditions, this is understood as a thoroughly materialist construction premised on a hierarchical scale of cosmo-somatic qualities. In other traditions that are Platonically influenced, while a stronger Form-Image dualism is maintained, we nonetheless see that anthropology is often characterized by body-soul interrelation rather than opposition.

Pearson (1973, 17–21) argued this in his influential Harvard dissertation, and while Richard Horsley (1976, 270–75) sought to problematize it, Kooten (2008, 279–80) has recently revived the idea.

48. So Kooten (2008, 64 and 65, respectively): "[when] Philo focuses on the spirit-part of [the] second man, he is in fact speaking of the first type of man.... The overlapping area consists of the uppermost part of the second type, in which he has been inbreathed by God's Spirit," and later, in commenting on a similar blurring in *Leg.* 1.42, "in Philo's view, the Spirit which is inbreathed into the highest part of (the individual, earthly) man is virtually identical with the image of God after which (the heavenly) man is created."

49. In *Her.* 56–57, Philo uses "blood and pleasures of the flesh" (αἵματι καὶ σαρκὸς ἡδονῇ) rather than ψυχή to speak of the lower soul. Nonetheless, Philo draws on Lev 17:11 to insist that αἷμα correlates with the soul (ψυχή) generally (i.e., the lower soul), while πνεῦμα correlates with the dominant part of the soul (the upper soul, *Her.* 55–56).

3.1.4. Summary: Concentric Circles of Cultural Embodiment

The preceding excursion through these concentric cultural circles has demonstrated a widespread one-world model characterized less by opposition and more by integration. The Jewish traditions we have examined demonstrate this in two ways. On the one hand, heaven and earth are upheld as distinct spatial locales that each requires its own somatic state. On the other hand, these locations are characterized by a high degree of permeability. Travel between them is possible, and transformation from one somatic state into another (more idealized) state is expressly articulated. Accordingly, the obverse possibilities of human angelomorphism and divine anthropomorphism demonstrate that, though distinctions between celestial and terrestrial exist, they are not sharply delineated. Within broader Hellenistic thought, the philosophical milieu of the first century CE was dominated by one-world, monistic conceptions. Even those who held a more radical dualism of sense-thought perception nonetheless advocated the interdependency of mind-soul-body.

I employ the term *polarity* to characterize the dynamic interrelations that exist within the one-world model just described. Polarity is adopted not in the sense of opposition or antitheses (e.g., "polar opposites") but rather in the sense of an integrated system; it implies a unified whole wherein opposing forces exist in interdependent tension.[50] This tension is interdependent because the individual parts of the system are understood as inextricable within the whole. This kind of interconnectivity is essential, I argue, to understanding Paul's resurrection ideals. Paul does not oppose earth to heaven (*down* to *up*) or body to soul (*out* to *in*) but functions with a strong sense of interconnectivity between distinct elements. Accordingly, the apostle perceives contrasting categories as systemically characterized by integrative polarity rather than determinative opposition.

3.2. Transformation and Resurrection

As noted at the outset of this chapter, transformation is a central component of Paul's resurrection ideals. With the foregoing cultural contexts firmly in view, I now turn attention to Paul's transformation metaphors in

---

50. In this way, the present study differs from Jeffrey Asher (2000), who employs the term *polarity* as a synonym for *opposition*.

1 Cor 15 and 2 Cor 5, both of which express the apostle's cosmo-somatic presuppositions. In chapter 2, I examined the overall role-value relations of the RESURRECTION gestalt in Paul's thinking. In what follows, I want to focus more acutely on the micro-PATH (CHANGE) structure of the RESURRECTION gestalt, as it is this element that enables Paul to articulate postmortem transformation from the earthly body into the idyllic or angelomorphic heavenly body. My examination of 1 Cor 15:35–50 and 2 Cor 5:1–5 will use conceptual blending analysis, though before turning to these passages it will be helpful to explicate more clearly the micro-PATH (CHANGE) structure (or simply, CHANGE gestalt) in greater detail.

3.2.1. The CHANGE Gestalt Refocused

Though experiences of change are ubiquitous in human existence—one can hardly escape the realities of physiological maturation or societal alteration or locative transposition, to name only a few—articulating exactly what change is and how change occurs has intellectual roots that stretch back at least as far as the beginnings of Greek philosophy.[51] In differing ways, thinkers such as Parmenides, Plato, and Aristotle wrestle with the inherent paradox at work in change; namely, "change presupposes its own opposite: 'no-change,' or sameness" (Songe-Møller 2009, 110). The problem of continuity amid alteration, then, is central to how cultures make sense of these altogether common and everyday occurrences. Pragmatically, this means that human beings utilize several different conceptual structures to make sense of experiences of change. One of the primary conceptual structures to this end is the CHANGE IS MOVEMENT conceptual metaphor, which I have already discussed in some detail (§2.1.2.2). This metaphor is schematically structured by opposing CONTAINERS that are correlated with the SOURCE and GOAL elements of a PATH schema (see fig. 3.1 [= fig. 2.6]). The TRAJECTOR that moves between these poles is understood as the one changed, and each CONTAINER represents different locations and/or states. Depending on the discursive context, the CHANGE IS MOVEMENT metaphor can denote either locative change (point A *to* point B) or stative change (*out of* container A *into* container B). Both are central to Paul's resurrection ideals.

---

51. See esp. Songe-Møller 2009; Asher 2000, 172–205.

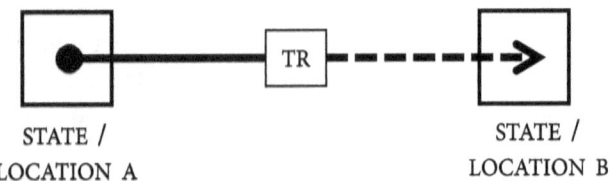

STATE /   STATE /
LOCATION A   LOCATION B

Figure 3.1. The CHANGE Gestalt

In an effort to substantiate more fully this CHANGE gestalt, in the following analysis I examine the extent to which the CHANGE IS MOVEMENT metaphor undergirds various descriptions of change/transformation in the period literature. Consider the following examples, all of which have been drawn from the New Testament:

1. χωρισθεὶς ἐκ τῶν Ἀθηνῶν ἦλθεν εἰς Κόρινθον
He [Paul] departed *from* [or *out of*] Athens and went *to* [or *into*] Corinth (Acts 18:1)

2. ἐγένετο εἰς δένδρον
It [the mustard seed] became a tree [lit. *into a tree*] (Luke 13:19)

3. ἡμεῖς δὲ πάντες ... μεταμορφούμεθα ἀπὸ δόξης εἰς δόξαν
But all of us ... are being transformed from one degree of glory to another [lit. *from/out of glory into glory*] (2 Cor 3:18)

4. ὃς ἐρρύσατο ἡμᾶς ἐκ τῆς ἐξουσίας τοῦ σκότους καὶ μετέστησεν εἰς τὴν βασιλείαν τοῦ υἱοῦ τῆς ἀγάπης αὐτοῦ
He [God] rescued us *from* the power of darkness and *transferred* us *into* the kingdom of his beloved son (Col 1:13)

5. ὁ γέλως ὑμῶν εἰς πένθος μετατραπήτω καὶ ἡ χαρὰ εἰς κατήφειαν
Let your laughter *be turned into* mourning, and your joy *into* gloom (Jas 4:9)

Number 1 is an example of the kinds of somatic experiences upon which the CHANGE IS MOVEMENT metaphor is premised, here denoting the TRAJECTOR (Paul) leaving and entering into the physical containers of

3. "WE WILL ALL BE CHANGED"

Athens and Corinth.[52] In number 2, such change is metaphorically projected so as to allow movement *into* (εἰς) another state.[53] Johannes Louw and Eugene Nida (L&N §13.62) note that εἰς commonly is used to denote the state *into* which something is changed.[54] This is particularly evident in ἀπό ... εἰς (no. 3)[55] and ἐκ ... εἰς constructions (no. 4),[56] both of which denote movement *from/out* of one place (understood as a CONTAINER) *into* another. In number 3, for example, differing types of δόξα are conceptualized as bounded regions (containers) that one departs *from* (ἀπό) and then enters *into* (εἰς). Accordingly, categorical change is conceptualized as transposition from one container into another; this is evident in examples 2, 4, 5, and several other examples too.[57]

As we can see in these examples, not every element of the gestalt structure is utilized in every case. At times the entire structure is accounted for (see example 4 in fig. 3.2), whereas at other times certain elements

---

52. Many cities in the ancient Mediterranean were enclosed by fortified walls, thus demarcating the city as a contained space into and out of which people moved.

53. While no verb of movement is made explicit, it is perhaps implicit. Compare further with Matt 19:5 // Mark 10:8; 1 Cor 6:16; Eph 5:31; and Luke 3:5, which all use "to be" verbs with εἰς so as to denote change. Given that many of these passages include scriptural citations (Matt 19:5 // Mark 10:8; 1 Cor 6:16; and Eph 5:31 = Gen 2:24 LXX; Luke 3:5 = Isa 40:4 LXX), we may be dealing with a conceptual structure that is shared by both Semitic and Greek cultures. On this point, however, further study is required.

54. In addition to no. 2, see John 5:24; Acts 2:20; 26:24; 1 Pet 1:3; 1 John 3:14; and Jude 4.

55. For example, Gal 1:6 and Rom 8:21.

56. For example, Mark 1:29; Luke 10:7; John 5:24; Acts 13:34; 1 Pet 2:9; and 1 John 3:14.

57. A few examples will suffice: (1) The verb ἀναγεννάω denotes the birthing image of movement from one container (the womb) into another metaphorical container (the world), and this container structure is explicit in 1 Pet 1:3: God has given believers "new birth *into* a living hope" (ἀναγεννήσας ... εἰς ἐλπίδα ζῶσαν). (2) The verb μετατίθημι occurs six times in the New Testament, most commonly with the meaning of movement or transference from one location to another (e.g., Acts 7:16; Heb 11:5). In both Gal 1:6 and Jude 4, this movement is metaphorically projected onto more abstract categories, though it still retains the sense of movement *into* something (i.e., μετατίθημι ... εἰς). (3) Though μεταστρέφω only occurs twice in the New Testament (Acts 2:20; Gal 1:7), in both instances it has the sense of radical alteration or change (note the use of εἰς in Acts 2:20). (4) The verb περιτρέπω is commonly glossed "to turn and bring around, to turn upside down" (LSJ). The verb occurs only in Acts 26:24, where Festus says to Paul: your learning is "driving you insane [or, turning *into* insanity]" (σε ... εἰς μανίαν περιτρέπει).

are foregrounded and others backgrounded (in example 3 the SOURCE/ CONTAINER element is backgrounded [fig. 3.2]). In still other instances, the same PATH-CONTAINER gestalt is utilized in a slightly different way. In example 5, for instance, a TRAJECTOR is envisioned whose projected PATH is altered (or turned), thus resulting in an alternative LOCATION (fig. 3.2).[58] In each case, even though certain elements are explicit and others muted, the same gestalt is at work—that is, CHANGE is conceptualized as movement between differing containers.[59]

Though the five examples cited above should not be taken as a definitive representation of broader Greek usage, we nonetheless see conceptual consistency across several lexical signs. These examples point to a recurrent and common gestalt that undergirds notions of change within the conceptual milieu of the early Christian movement. With this gestalt in mind, we can now examine the ways in which Paul employs the CHANGE IS MOVEMENT metaphor in the construction of eschatological transformation.

3.2.2. "Sown *in* X, Raised *in* Y": The Plant Metaphor of 1 Corinthians 15:35–50

Within the broader cultural contexts sketched earlier in this chapter, Paul's use of the plant metaphor in 1 Cor 15:35–50 is extremely robust and culturally nuanced. Here the apostle utilizes the horticultural metaphor in response to the rhetorical question of how the dead will be raised, specifically addressing the nature of risen bodies themselves (15:35).[60] Paul

---

58. In this case, both the SOURCE and INTENDED GOAL are understood as identical container states (i.e., STATE A), and the UNINTENDED GOAL is STATE B. Nonetheless, the same gestalt structure is at work in this description.

59. It should not surprise us that verbs of movement denote change, as the CHANGE gestalt emerges from somatic experiences of locative movement (among others). Of the twelve New Testament occurrences of μεταβαίνω, for instance, ten denote spatial movement while the remaining two project this somatic experience onto more abstract categories (e.g., John 5:24, the one who hears and believes in Jesus's words has "*passed from* [or *out of*] death *into* life" [μεταβέβηκεν ἐκ τοῦ θανάτου εἰς τὴν ζωήν]; see also 1 John 3:14). Other verbs of movement evince similar trends (e.g., στρέφω, προκόπτω, φέρω, πίπτω, and ἐκπίπτω).

60. Demarcating the precise meaning of the resurrection denial by some at Corinth (see 1 Cor 15:12, 35) has garnered much scholarly discussion. The three most dominant theories are that (1) Paul is addressing a certain kind of realized eschatology at Corinth; (2) Paul is confronting a particular kind of Hellenistic Jewish wisdom

3. "WE WILL ALL BE CHANGED" 107

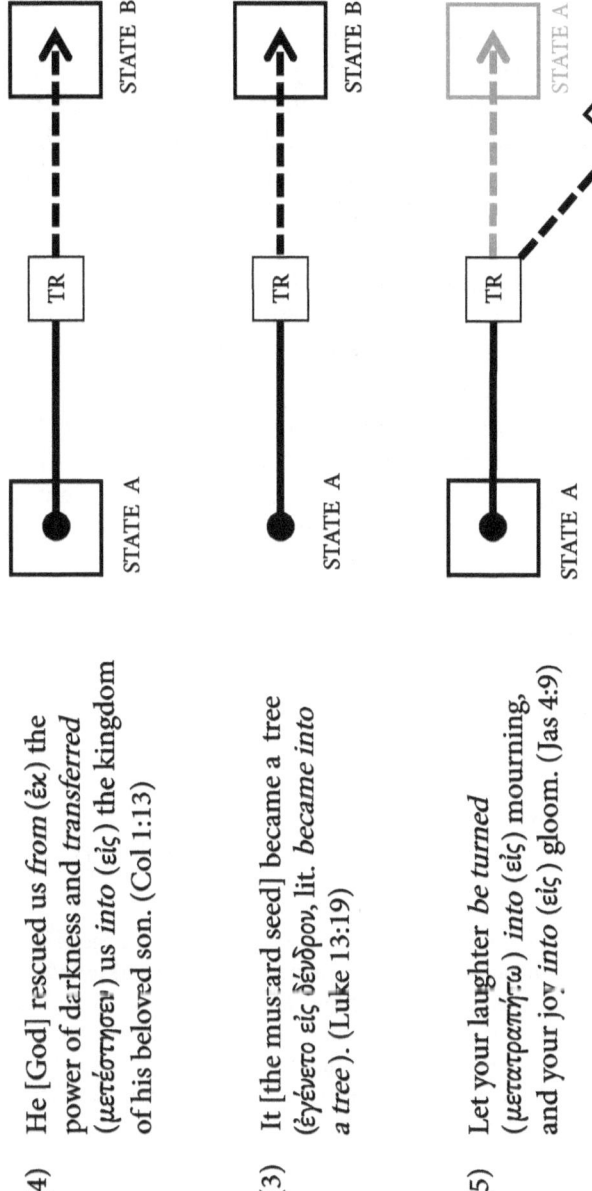

(4) He [God] rescued us *from* (ἐκ) the power of darkness and *transferred* (μετέστησεν) us *into* (εἰς) the kingdom of his beloved son. (Col 1:13)

(3) It [the mustard seed] became a tree (ἐγένετο εἰς δένδρον, lit. *became into a tree*). (Luke 13:19)

(5) Let your laughter *be turned* (μετατραπήτω) *into* (εἰς) mourning, and your joy *into* (εἰς) gloom. (Jas 4:9)

Figure 3.2. Foregrounding and Backgrounding the CHANGE Gestalt

asserts (15:42–44) that the higher, more desirable σῶμα πνευματικόν is characterized by "imperishability," "glory," and "power" (ἀφθαρσία, δόξα, and δύναμις), while the lower, less desirable σῶμα ψυχικόν is characterized by "perishability," "dishonor," and "weakness" (φθορά, ἀτιμία, and ἀσθένεια). This language is multivalent. Jewish apocalypticism and Greco-Roman popular philosophy coalesce in this passage in such a way that Paul locates apocalyptic notions of heavenly glory-bodies within an overarching cosmo-somatic status hierarchy.[61] I will demonstrate this by conducting a blending analysis of 1 Cor 15:35–50, specifically highlighting Paul's creative use of the plant metaphor so as to stress somatic differentiation configured along vertically drawn cosmological lines. Because several mental spaces are constructed through the course of 15:35–50, it will be helpful to describe each in turn before assessing the blended spaces themselves (for a mapping of the blend, see fig. 3.3).

The first input (I_1) is cued in 15:35 and consists of differing kinds of bodies. The space includes elements such as the present σῶμα (signified by [x] in fig. 3.3), the risen σῶμα (signified in fig. 3.3 by [?], for the identity of this body is in question), and some degree of continuity between the two (z and z). The space is not (yet) structured by any kind of gestalt relation (such as the VERTICALITY gestalt, or the CHANGE gestalt), because Paul has thus far only raised the question of how these two bodies relate to one another, hence the ambiguity of (x) and (?).

In 15:36–38 Paul introduces the second input space (I_2), which is initially triggered by the reference to "sowing" (σπείρεις, 15:36) and thus is structured by the PLANT GROWTH frame. This input space includes several different elements: the seed that is sown in one form (signified by [x]),[62] the plant that eventually grows in another form (signified by [y]),[63] the

---

philosophy from Alexandria that is particularly indebted to Philo's exegesis of Gen 1–2; and (3) some in Corinth had a problem not so much with the afterlife, but rather with resurrection of the body. I lean in the direction of Philonic influence while recognizing the likelihood that these views are not mutually exclusive. Indeed, apocalypticism and philosophical reflection need not be differentiated categorically from one another, and a philosophically informed anthropology of πνευματικός vs. ψυχικός need not exclude certain overtones of eschatological realization.

61. On the blending of Jewish and Greek ideas in 1 Corinthians, see also Tronier 2001.

62. Paul refers generally to κόκκος/σπέρμα, "seed" (15:37–38), though κόκκος can refer to a *kernel* of various plants (e.g., mustard, wheat, etc. [BDAG]).

63. The example Paul gives is σῖτος, "wheat" (15:37).

3. "WE WILL ALL BE CHANGED"   109

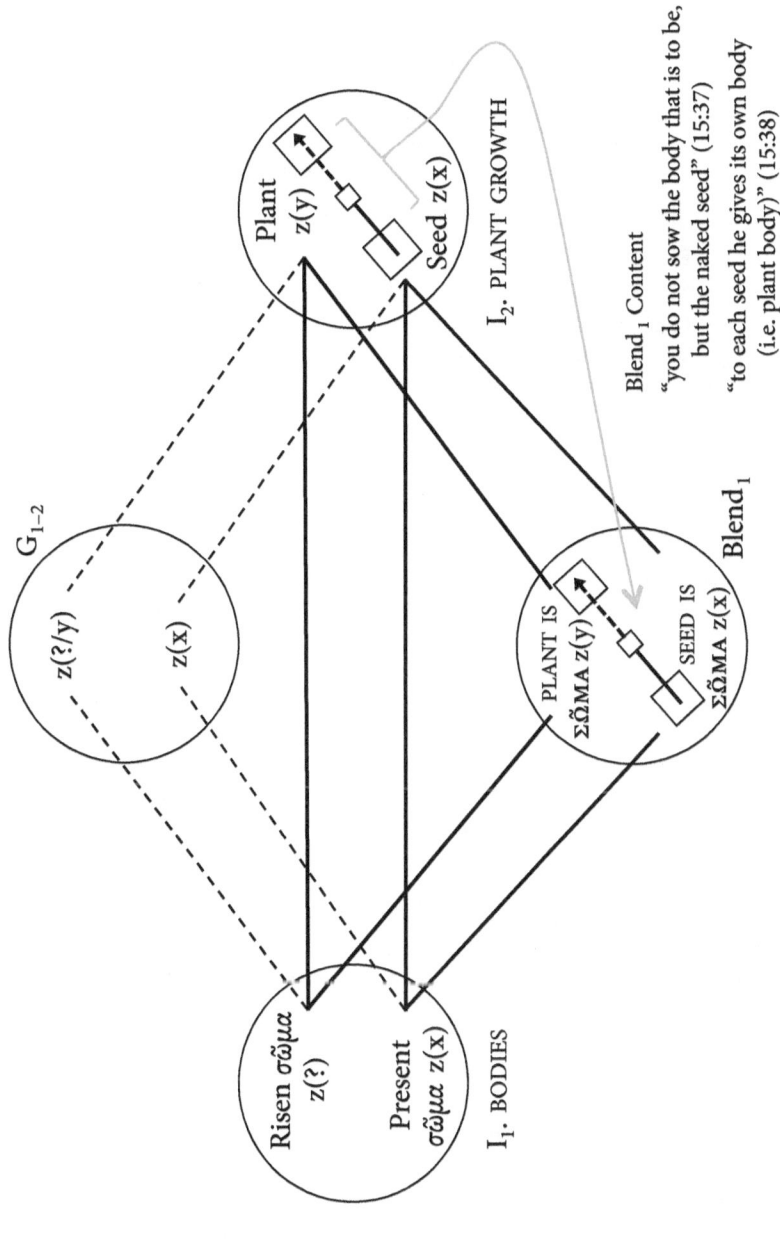

Figure 3.3. The Plant Metaphor (1 Cor 15:36–38)

process of CHANGE between the two (hence the CHANGE gestalt, which here is inclined so as to signify vertical plant growth), and some measure of continuity between the two (z and z).

As one can see, both I_1 and I_2 share general content, which constitutes the generic space (G_{1-2}).[64] The blend itself is elaborated in 15:36–38; it is structured by the CHANGE gestalt from I_2 (indicated by the curved gray line) and includes several emergent elements.[65] The cross-space mapping of "seed" with "earthly body" and "plant" with "risen body" enables the recognition of two bodies that are at once different and yet continuous with one another. Once the blend is elaborated, it projects back onto I_1 a clearer understanding of the risen body as (dis)continuous with the earthly body (i.e., z[?] becomes z[y]), while also characterizing the relationship between the two as that of CHANGE (see fig. 3.4, where I_1 now is revised, and the back-projection from Blend$_1$ to I_1 is represented by the

---

64. The generic space consists of distinct role-values, which map a single value z that is differentiated as "form [x]" and "form [?/y]." In addition to what I have mapped in fig. 3.3, the generic space might also include (1) the idea that seeds/bodies must die before they can be changed (15:36; see also John 12:24; though it is worth noting that Paul does not presume death as a necessary precursor to resurrection [1 Cor 15:51–52; 1 Thess 4.17]); and (2) the notion of being "made alive" (ζωοποιεῖται, 15:36; ζωοποιέω certainly is at home in the RESURRECTION TRANSFORMATION frame [15:22, 45; Rom 4:17], though it is used [also in the middle voice] already in the fourth century BCE to refer to the growth of plants [Bultmann 1964]).

65. For instance, the reference in 15:37 to *sowing the body* is a projection of both the "sown seed" element of I_2 and the "body" element of I_1. Though σῶμα can be used to refer to the form/body of a plant, this usage is less common than when σῶμα refers to a human or animal body (LSJ lists only 1 Cor 15:38 as an instance of σῶμα referring to a plant, whereas BDAG has a handful of examples). Xenophon (*Symp.* 2.25) may be the earliest documented usage of σῶμα for plants that survives in Greek literature. In the Apocrypha and Pseudepigrapha, σῶμα is only used to denote human or animal bodies, never to refer to a plant (Schweizer and Baumgärtel 1971). Nonetheless, the metaphorical nature of Paul's description can be seen within the blended space where the earthly σῶμα (I_1) is cross-mapped with the sown seed (I_2): "you do not *sow* the body that will be, but the naked *seed*" (οὐ τὸ σῶμα τὸ γενησόμενον σπείρεις ἀλλὰ γυμνὸν κόκκον, 15:37). This cross-space characterization of the sown seed as a σῶμα is further articulated by the description of that seed as "naked" (γυμνός). While Fitzmyer (2008, 588) rightly notes that some seeds, prior to being sown, must be stripped of their natural coverings, it is surely more natural and congruent to read the reference to the "naked seed" as referring not to a botany procedure but rather to the human body that the seed is cross-mapped with. This presumes the clothing metaphor in 15:49, 53–54 (see discussion below in §3.2.3).

3. "WE WILL ALL BE CHANGED" 111

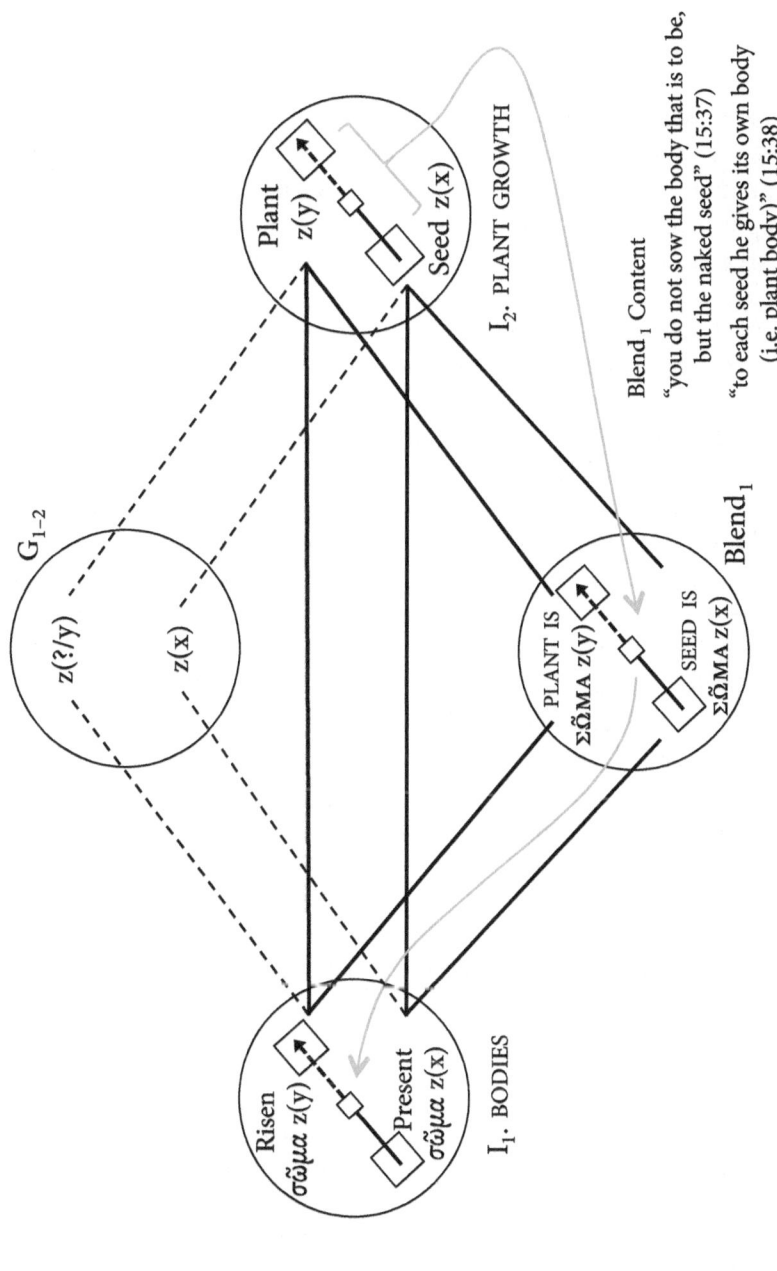

Figure 3.4. The Plant Metaphor (I₁ Restructured)

curved gray arrow). In light of the above cultural contexts, this conceptual mapping aligns with broader trends in ancient Judaism that posit both earthly and heavenly somatic existences characterized by transformation.

How these two somatic forms are continuous with one another does not concern Paul in the present text. He simply asserts that just as a wheat seed is linked to a wheat stalk, an earthly body will be raised a heavenly body. In 15:39, Paul turns his attention toward more clearly delineating somatic differentiation. The blend that I have just elaborated now is blended with a third input space (I_3) to create a megablend (see fig. 3.5). This third input is constructed in 15:39–41 and is framed by a cosmo-somatic mapping that contrasts lower and higher body types. Consistent with the findings above, Paul holds to a one-world model wherein qualitative differences (rather than ontological opposition) are mapped along a vertically drawn cosmological spectrum. In this respect, the conceptual mapping denotes transformation *within* the material world (i.e., seed to wheat; earthly to heavenly). This is further elaborated with respect to Paul's Adam-Christ typology, which we have already seen is vertically configured (i.e., ADAM IS DOWN/CHRIST IS UP; see §2.2.4). When framed cosmologically, Adam stands metonymically for the earthly, natural body, while Christ stands for the celestial, risen body.[66] This is borne out in 15:39–41, where Paul asserts that different types of "flesh" (σάρξ) exist on earth (that of humans, animals, birds, and fish, 15:39), while different types of "glory" (δόξα) exist in the heavens (the sun, moon, and stars, 15:41).[67]

The key concept, however, that ties these contrasting states together is that of the "body" (σῶμα, 15:40). For Paul, the various fleshes-of-earth and glories-of-heaven are differing somatic types (i.e., a body of *flesh* vs. a body of *glory*), which are conceptually perceived as DOWN and UP and thus correlated with Adam and Christ. Paul is doubtless drawing on the matrix of Jewish traditions that speak of divine and human glory-bodies (e.g., the "Great Glory," angelomorphic human forms).[68] The apostle perceives all

---

66. So argued above (§2.2.4).

67. Paul is here drawing a cosmological mapping that gives rise to the contrasting metaphors FLESH IS DOWN/GLORY IS UP. These correspond with the aforementioned Adam/Christ mapping, thus linking earthly Adamic existence with flesh and heavenly Christic existence with glory.

68. The language is reminiscent (for instance) of the Self-Glorification Hymn from Qumran. As already noted, the glorified figure is said to share in incomparable angelic "glory" (כבוד, 4Q491 11 I, 13–15, 18), and their desires are expressly not of the

3. "WE WILL ALL BE CHANGED" 113

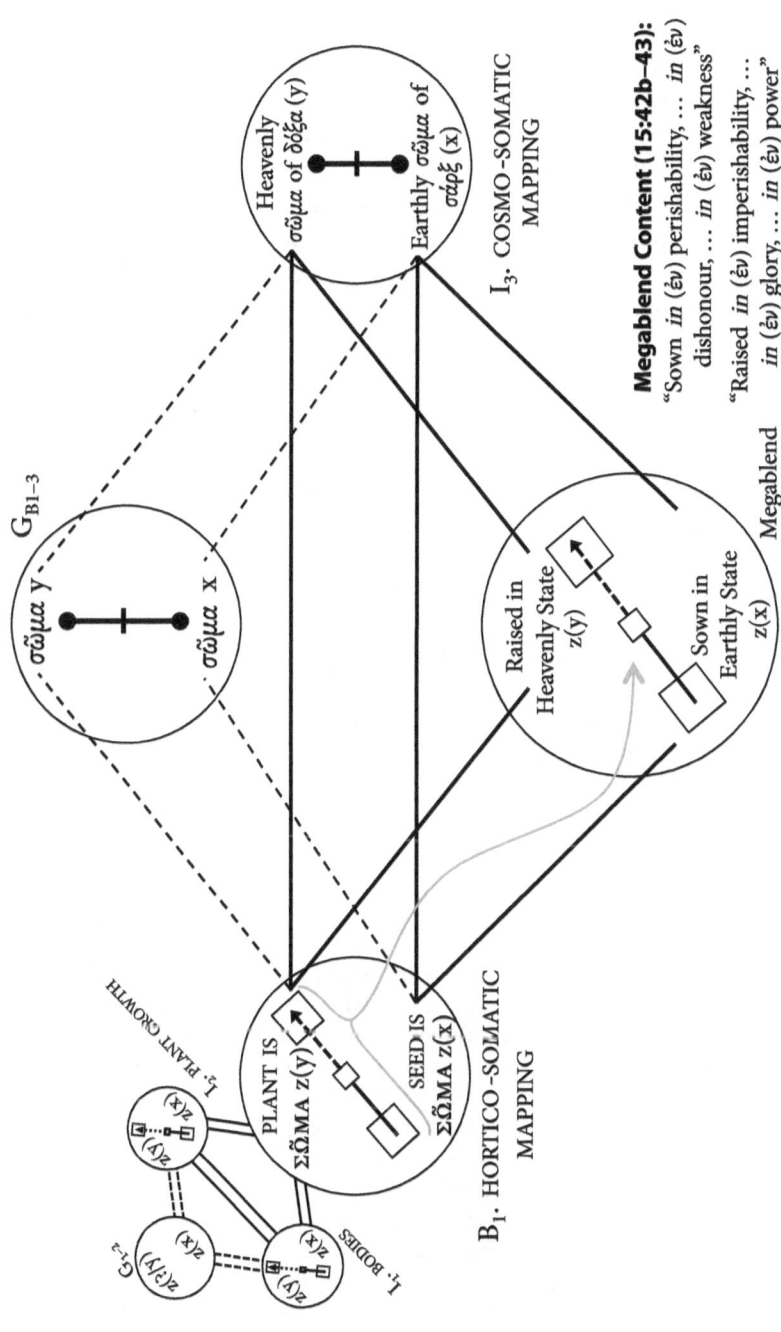

Figure 3.5. The Plant Metaphor (1 Cor 15:39–44)

celestial bodies within this matrix, though each one differs in glory from the others (a reference that perhaps preserves the highest glory-body for Christ, the Glory of the Lord).[69] This coheres with the findings in §2.1, where we identified CELESTIAL LUMINOSITY as a common frame-structure for understanding resurrection. Here CELESTIAL LUMINOSITY denotes the angelomorphic human form.

In light of this cosmological distinction, the schematic structure of I_3 consists of a simple VERTICALITY schema that opposes DOWN (i.e., Adamic, earthly, flesh-bodies) and UP (i.e., Christic, heavenly, glory-bodies), thus highlighting differentiation (i.e., [x] vis-à-vis [y]). Despite this structural difference, both B_1 and I_3 are blended together on account of a shared schematic structure and general correspondence in the generic space (G_{B1-3}).[70] The emergent blend—the megablend—is realized at human scale in 15:42b–43. Here Paul contrasts what is "sown *in* x" but "raised *in* y," and he thrice repeats the formula, each time denoting the contrast between opposing container states.

σπείρεται ἐν φθορᾷ, ἐγείρεται ἐν ἀφθαρσίᾳ·
σπείρεται ἐν ἀτιμίᾳ, ἐγείρεται ἐν δόξῃ·
σπείρεται ἐν ἀσθενείᾳ, ἐγείρεται ἐν δυνάμει·

It is sown in perishability, it is raised in imperishability;
It is sown in dishonor, it is raised in glory;
It is sown in weakness, it is raised in power. (1 Cor 15:42b–43)

"flesh" (בשר, 4Q491 11 I, 14). On earthly flesh being incompatible with an angelomorphic state, see further 1 En. 71:11.

69. Though the contrast drawn in 15:40 suggests a measure of "glory" can be ascribed to the earthly body, the passage clearly insists that the glory of the heavenly is greater (i.e., *higher*) than the earthly. It should not be overlooked that Paul elsewhere insists that the risen image/form of believers will be the same as that of Christ's (e.g., Phil 3:21; Rom 8:17, 29), who is the "divine glory." Within this context of cosmic glory-bodies (which is drawn from broader Jewish traditions), Martin's (1995, 129) claim that Paul is "redefining *sōma*" seems overstated (though even he notes instances in which σῶμα is used in reference to celestial entities [117–20]).

70. For example, the generic space includes the VERTICALITY schema as well as shared references to more concrete ideas such as the earth (e.g., the seed/body is associated with the earth [B_1]; Paul speaks of "earthly" bodies in I_3) and also differentiation between oppositions (e.g., seed/body vs. plant/body in B_1; earthly vs. heavenly bodies in I_3).

As the mapping demonstrates, these references to being "sown" and "risen" can be traced back to I_2 and I_1, respectively. Of particular note is the attribution of container structure to these various states (note the use of ἐν), a description that arises from the CHANGE gestalt projected from B_1. What emerges in the megablend is a single entity that has two forms (i.e., movement from SOWN $z[x]$ to RAISED $z[y]$ via inclined CHANGE structure), and thus resurrection is understood as transformation from an earthly to heavenly somatic existence. Paul's resurrection ideals are framed via the RESURRECTION IS CELESTIAL LUMINOSITY metaphor, which here points toward an angelomorphic glory-body that differs from its earthy counterpart. In light of the one-world model articulated above, though these bodies are distinct, they are not ontologically opposite. In this way, Paul foregrounds discontinuity of the external somatic state, despite the fact that both continuity and discontinuity are implicit in the megablend (i.e., $z[x]$ and $z[y]$).

In 15:44a, however, Paul appears (at first glance) to alter the conceptual structures he uses to describe the earthly and risen bodies; the text reads as follows:

σπείρεται σῶμα ψυχικόν, ἐγείρεται σῶμα πνευματικόν
It is sown an ensouled body, it is raised an enspirited body.[71]

---

71. Translations of σῶμα ψυχικόν and σῶμα πνευματικόν are notoriously difficult and perhaps reveal more about the translator's implicit assumptions than the meaning of these adjectival constructions. Certainly "natural body" vis-à-vis "supernatural body" are imprecise translations, for they import a Cartesian matter/nonmatter dualism into the text. In a similar vein, even the conventional "natural/physical body" and "spiritual body" (NRSV, NIV, NASB, ESV, KJV) seems to imply—at least to modern readers—this same set of assumptions, thus obscuring rather than illuminating the passage. One caveat might be the suggestion of some older commentators who interpret σῶμα ψυχικόν as "animal body" (so noted in Thiselton 2000, 267). This is perhaps closer to the *cosmological* presuppositions at work in the passage (namely, the hierarchical cosmological scale). Still others have pointed to the function of the adjectival form. For example, Thiselton (2000, 1276–77) notes the difference between adjectival formations ending in -ικος (which usually denote modes of being or characteristics) and those ending in -ινος (which usually denote composition). For Thiselton, Paul's use of the former makes it unlikely that he has a compositional substance in mind, and this lends support to his understanding of the σῶμα πνευματικόν as a "mode or pattern of intersubjective life directed by the Holy Spirit" (1277). We should perhaps not make too much of this adjectival argument, however. Wright (2003, 351–52) correctly cautions against conclusions based on generalized Koine usages. Even Paul uses -ικος

The previous descriptions of 15:42b–43 have stressed CONTAINER (ἐν) language. As I have shown, the plant metaphor of 15:35–50 is oriented toward contrasting container structures (i.e., sown *in* x, raised *in* y) as a way of differentiating the exterior (i.e., earthly σῶμα vis-à-vis heavenly σῶμα). This decidedly external focus is interrupted, however, in 15:44a; rather than contrasting differing states into which believers are raised, Paul now draws a distinction between internal referents (ψυχή and πνεῦμα, articulated in 15.44a by the cognate adjectives, ψυχικόν and πνευματικόν). To describe this shift in crude spatial terms, Paul transitions from a description of the container itself (i.e., the body, which is external and can contain certain things) to a contrast between the contents of the container (namely, ψυχή and πνεῦμα, which are inside the body).

This shift is both sudden and stark, and while it has not gone unnoticed by modern exegetes, three common scholarly interpretations can briefly be problematized. First, given the one-world model outlined above, we can put aside claims that the phrase σῶμα πνευματικόν is oxymoronic.[72] As we have seen, *incorporeal* does not necessarily denote *immaterial*, and thus there is no compelling reason to understand the adjective πνευματικός as ontologically opposed to σῶμα (or even σάρξ, for that matter, for both πνεῦμα and σάρξ consist of differing kinds of stuff). Second, many have argued that the phrase σῶμα πνευματικόν denotes the material composition of the risen believer (i.e., a body composed of πνεῦμα).[73] While this view

---

and -ινος adjectives in tandem (e.g., 1 Cor 3:1), thus suggesting that no major exegetical difference should be found in the contrasting of these forms. Nonetheless, there may be something to Thiselton's line of reasoning. For Paul, as we will see, the ethical and compositional interlace each other, which is to say that one's somatic composition either enables or hinders their ethical aptitude (see further §§4.1–2). Accordingly, this blending of various domains—ethics, cosmology, and somatic composition—complicates translations of σῶμα ψυχικόν and σῶμα πνευματικόν. In an effort to highlight the *anthropological* dimensions of Paul's address—which include both IN-OUT somatic mappings and cosmo-ethical convictions—I here render these phrases as "ensouled body" and "enspirited body" (respectively). The full import of these terms will be unpacked throughout this study.

72. For example, A. Segal (1998, 418) insists that σῶμα πνευματικόν "is a complete contradiction in terms for anyone in a Platonic system."

73. Martin (1995, 126–27) is a proponent of this view. He argues that, for Paul, a resurrected body is "composed only of pneuma" and further that risen bodies represent a kind of refinement such that resurrection is akin to the heavy material of σάρξ being "sloughed off" so as to leave only the light material of πνεῦμα (126). Against this position, it is worth noting that Paul posits a heavenly *container* that stands in contrast

coheres with the one-world model that I have posited, it fails to address the parallel description of the σῶμα ψυχικόν (which is not a body composed of ψυχή).[74] The third scholarly position, already introduced in chapter 1 (§1.3.2), suggests that σῶμα πνευματικόν denotes a body that is under the rule of the Spirit. While this view is dominant in Pauline scholarship, it presumes an anthropological dualism that is often uncritically recognized and that places the emphasis of transformation on the somatic interior (ψύχη versus πνεῦμα) rather than exterior (σῶμα). This is problematic for the simple reason that, as the blending analysis demonstrates, Paul's focus throughout 15:35–50 is squarely on the somatic exterior. Taken together, then, none of these views is wholly convincing.

Paul's address in 1 Cor 15:45–49 is particularly indebted to some form of Philonic exegesis of Gen 1–2. Although the apostle confronts this exegesis (see 15:46), in one important respect he is aligned with it. As I discussed earlier in this chapter (§3.1.3), in certain instances Philo stresses the interrelation of the earthly and heavenly persons; that is, the earthly person lives *as* the heavenly person when their actions are informed by the higher soul, which is the inbreathed πνεῦμα (= νοῦς). On this point, Paul seems in agreement with Philo, and he uses it to his rhetorical advantage. In 1 Cor 2:14–3:3, Paul similarly contrasts the "ensouled person" (ψυχικὸς

---

to the earthly *container* (i.e., body vis-à-vis body [15:44] or garment vis-à-vis garment [15:49, 53–54]). Moreover, elsewhere Paul rejects any notion of an eschatological stripping or "sloughing off," to use Martin's term (see 2 Cor 5:1–5). Accordingly, it seems pertinent to explore how Paul envisions heavenly reembodiment—a new container, as it were—that also makes sense within the process of somatic refinement that Martin so helpfully illuminates. Interestingly, while Troels Engberg-Pedersen (2009, 126) rightly recognizes the need not to read Paul in terms of somatic "shed[ding]," he nevertheless posits the σῶμα πνευματικόν as "a body made up of pneuma."

74. It is important to note that the σῶμα ψυχικόν that Paul has in mind certainly does presume a particular kind of compositional character—not a body composed of ψυχή (though this would not be wholly inconceivable in the Hellenistic period; see Staden 2000), but rather a body composed of σάρξ καὶ αἷμα (1 Cor 15:50). At issue is the parallel logic between scholarly treatments of the σῶμα ψυχικόν vis-à-vis the σῶμα πνευματικόν; that is, it is not entirely obvious why πνεῦμα should be seen as the compositional material of the container (i.e., σῶμα πνευματικόν as a body composed of πνεῦμα) if the same logic is not extended to σῶμα ψυχικόν (which Paul understands as a container [= body] composed of σάρξ καὶ αἷμα rather than ψυχή). Given Paul's explicit compositional insistence in 1 Cor 15:50, we can concede that a σῶμα πνευματικόν need not be composed of πνεῦμα and further note that the particular kind of resurrection body Paul has in mind is a celestial glory-body (see further n. 81 below).

... ἄνθρωπος) with the "enspirited [person]" (πνευματικός), with respect not to the future but rather to the present. The "enspirited [person]" is specifically said to have the "mind of Christ" (νοῦν Χριστοῦ), while the "ensouled person" is correlated with the flesh. Thus Paul's characterization of the Corinthians as "fleshly" (both σαρκίνοις and σαρκικοί, 3:1–3) serves as a criticism that cuts to the core of their pneumatic identity. Paul is insisting that they are in fact dominated by the lower, earthly part of the soul rather than the higher, heavenly part. The rhetorical thrust of Paul's address, then, is his insistence that the Corinthians are not submitting to the upper soul (πνεῦμα or νοῦν Χριστοῦ).

It is important to note what Paul and his interlocutors take as implicit; namely, because the upper soul is presently embodied, there exists an inherent tension between the πνεῦμα/νοῦς and the ψυχή/σάρξ. Indeed, this tension seems to underscore the presumption of some Corinthians that body will one day be disposed of (see 15:35). But for Paul the problem is not one of embodiment, but rather the kind of body in which the πνεῦμα/νοῦς exists. Rather than positing the soul's disembodiment as the eschatological ideal, Paul instead posits the soul's reembodiment.[75] Seen in this way, Paul draws a caricature in 1 Cor 15:44 between two embodied extremes—on the one hand, the ensouled earthly body (σῶμα ψυχικόν); on the other, the enspirited risen body (σῶμα πνευματικόν). He contrasts two different embodied states—the body informed by ψυχή(/σάρξ) vis-à-vis the body informed by πνεῦμα(/νοῦς)[76]—neither of which

---

75. On this point, Paul stands in contrast to Philo and perhaps his Corinthian interlocutors.

76. The language of "informed by" is preferable to the standard scholarly parlance of "subjected to" for three main reasons. First, while "subjected to" implies a more ontological distinction between subject and object, the language of "informed by" makes no such distinction and thus retains the character of the one-world model advocated here. Accordingly, "informed by" implies something similar to the Aristotelian *hylomorphic* notion of body and soul as "two mutually complementary and inseparably connected aspects." For Aristotle, such conjunction "is necessary for life ... [and constitutes] a natural and good relationship" (Eijk 2000, 63). Second, the limits of this integrative "informed by" is found in the fact that, while Paul (like Aristotle) speaks of body-soul intermixing, he also follows something closer to a Platonic notion of body-soul tension or hostility, not between ψυχή (or πνεῦμα) and σῶμα per se, but rather between πνεῦμα and earthly σῶμα (and ψυχή and heavenly σῶμα). The language of "informed by," then, reflects Paul's conviction that bodies interact with ψυχή or πνεῦμα in ways—either harmonious or hostile—relative to their cosmo-somatic loca-

is characteristic of believers in the present.⁷⁷ With the exception of certain moments of rhetorical critique (e.g., 1 Cor 3:1–3), Paul otherwise characterizes life in Christ as an embodied existence that lies between these two poles—that is, an enspirited earthly body.⁷⁸ Seen in this light, in 15:44 Paul is saying: if there is an ensouled body that is designed for and thus tends toward body-soul coherence on earth (i.e., fleshly existence), then there also is an enspirited body that is designed for and thus enables body-spirit coherence in heaven (i.e., pneumatic existence). As with Philo, where cosmology and anthropology coalesce, ethical imperatives follow—for Paul, life as an enspirited earthly body in the present has a decidedly eschatological outlook in as much as one's ethical actions now anticipate one's future existence as an enspirited risen body (σῶμα πνευματικόν).

The key interpretive issue in all of this is the stress Paul places on body-soul interrelation, which can only be recognized when dualism in Paul is seen to stress integration rather than opposition. As noted earlier, the term *polarity* provides a way of conceptualizing this feature of Paul's thought—polarity implies an integrated and unified whole wherein opposing forces exist in interdependent tension. In chapter 4, I will more clearly identify this interrelation as intrasomatic polarity. At present, however, the key point to make is the recognition that such polarity is only resolved in the future resurrection when the πνεῦμα/νοῦς will be ideally matched within a heavenly glory-body. Consistent with the blending structure that I have mapped, Paul's focus is squarely upon the expectation of a transformed exterior, specifically one that does not exhibit intrasomatic tension with the πνεῦμα/νοῦς.

Returning to the second and third scholarly positions noted above (the first has already been addressed), Paul is stressing not so much an embodied existence that will be under the rule of the Spirit (position 3)

---

tions. Finally, the language of "subjected to" (or "under the rule of") implies a certain personification of πνεῦμα that seems alien to the first-century context and reflects, as Stowers (2008, 363) remarks, later developments in Trinitarian Christianity. The language of "informed by" is preferable because it retains the idea of distinct substances as intermixing and acting one upon the other rather than of individuated persons ruling one over the other.

77. Kooten (2008, 301) has similarly noted this caricature.

78. I refer here to the plethora of Pauline texts that speak of or presume the granting of divine πνεῦμα to Christ-devotees (Gal 5:16–26; 6:1; Rom 5:5; 8:9–11, 15–17; 1 Cor 2:16; 6:19 [perhaps 3:16]; 2 Cor 1:22; 3:3; 5:5).

as an embodied existence properly suited for life informed by πνεῦμα.⁷⁹ The stress very much is upon the somatic exterior: it will be a body that is qualitatively appropriate both for the heavens and the indwelling πνεῦμα (contra the present earthly body of flesh and blood). Throughout 1 Cor 15, however, Paul is largely ambiguous about issues of somatic composition (position 2). Though he certainly looks ahead to a body that is cosmologically appropriate for the heavens and thus ideally informed by πνεῦμα (just as an earthly body is suited toward ψυχή), Paul also characterizes this body as being one of glory (15:40–41). When seen within the context of Paul's other writings and the concentric circles noted above, Paul appears to conceptualize the σῶμα πνευματικόν as an angelomorphic glory-body (and thus framed by the RESURRECTION IS CELESTIAL LUMINOSITY metaphor).⁸⁰ While this body may or may not be compositionally pneumatic, it certainly is suited ideally for πνεῦμα.⁸¹ Accordingly, Paul is best seen as synthesizing various Greek and Jewish traditions while also working with a strong sense of interconnectivity between distinct cosmological and somatic elements.⁸²

To summarize the foregoing, the plant metaphor creates a conceptual space wherein Paul is able to focus on contrasting container states (sown *in* x, raised *in* y), demonstrating them to be of varying earthly and heavenly

---

79. It is possible that Paul has both human πνεῦμα and divine πνεῦμα (i.e., Christ, the πνεῦμα ζῳοποιοῦν, 1 Cor 15:45) in mind, whereby the efficacious power of the former is enabled through the granting of the latter. This point will be further elaborated in the next chapter (§4.2).

80. Elsewhere, Paul characterizes resurrection using the category of "glory" (e.g., Rom 8:17–18), and he often describes the risen Christ as having a "body of glory" (Phil 3:21; see also 2 Cor 3:18; 4:4–6).

81. That is, just as the risen Christ is both pneumatic (1 Cor 15:45) and characterized by a glory-body (Phil 3:21), so too will believers be. As we will see in ch. 4 (§4.3), there is good evidence in Rom 8 that Paul is happy to use the language of πνεῦμα when intimating the somatic container in which the resurrected dead will exist. This suggests that πνεῦμα and δόξα fall within the same conceptual domain for Paul (see also 2 Cor 3:7–4:6). In 1 Cor 15, however, while it is tempting to see glory-bodies as compositionally pneumatic, Paul never elaborates this point explicitly. Instead, he posits celestial glory-bodies as the ideal containers in which πνεῦμα exists.

82. A similar point is made by Engberg-Pedersen (2009, 124–29), who distinguishes between "apocalyptic or mytho-poetic" and "scientific" (in the Stoic sense) language in 1 Cor 15. While Engberg-Pedersen explores the "scientific" language in 15:35–49, in the present study I have demonstrated the need to revisit the "apocalyptic or mytho-poetic" language too.

qualities. What we find in the emergent structure of the plant metaphor is a consistent focus upon somatic opposition—the σῶμα of the grown wheat is visibly different and distinct from the seed that was sown. Despite such radical opposition, notions of trans-somatic continuity are nonetheless implicit. Indeed, Paul does not locate where such continuity is but rather draws a caricature between the ensouled earthly and enspirited heavenly bodies. In doing so, he stresses somatic transformation of the exterior (i.e., the body), thus looking ahead to a mode of embodiment perfectly suited for the πνεῦμα/νοῦς.

3.2.3. On Wearing a House: The Clothing/Housing Metaphor of 2 Corinthians 5:1–5

Given the CHANGE IS MOVEMENT metaphor is premised on a transposition of containers, it is not surprising that Paul elsewhere utilizes metaphors that stress this container aspect. This is particularly evident in the clothing and housing metaphors of 2 Cor 5:1–5 (and 1 Cor 15:49, 53–54), though it is already prevalent in the broader discourse of 2 Cor 3–5. Here Paul oscillates between outer and inner somatic referents (esp. 3:12–18), he refers to an inner shining light (4:6), he likens the body to a clay jar (4:7), and he draws a distinction between outer decay and inner renewal (4:16–18; for a full discussion see ch. 5 below). By the time his Corinthian readers arrive at chapter 5, Paul has already primed them for an understanding of resurrection as transposition from one container to another, and the images of clothing and housing take center stage.

Consistent with this study's broader theoretical framework, the body itself is the primary medium through which human beings experience containment; so Johnson (1987, 21), "we are intimately aware of our bodies as three-dimensional containers into which we put certain things (food, water, air) and out of which other things emerge (food and water wastes, air, blood, etc.)." The primary metaphor that arises from this aspect of human embodiment is the BODY IS CONTAINER metaphor, which enables descriptions of the human person configured around the IN-BOUNDARY-OUT axis of the CONTAINER gestalt. Put differently, the human body is understood as having both an interior and an exterior. Though the BODY IS CONTAINER metaphor emerges organically from embodied experience, it doubtless is constructed in diverse and various ways across cultures. I will examine both Jewish and Greek anthropological descriptions in §4.2, though at this point we should note that Paul fits within a broader cultural pattern that maps the human constitution along an IN-OUT axis. As we have seen all along, Paul's transformation ideals emphasize contrasting CONTAINER states. It is the BODY IS CONTAINER metaphor that enables such descriptions.[83] This is expressly clear in 2 Cor 5:1–5, where Paul elaborates two other CONTAINER-structured metaphors.

The first is cued in 5:1–2a, where Paul speaks of the body as a dwelling place. It goes without saying that buildings are conceptually perceived as containers that people constantly move in and out of (BUILDING IS CONTAINER). By virtue of this shared schematic structure, as well as other frame elements, the domains BODY (I_1) and DWELLING PLACE (I_2) are blended together so as to create the BODY IS HOUSE metaphor (fig. 3.6 on p. 124).[84] In 2 Cor 5:1–2a, Paul again contrasts two different somatic/dwelling states. On the one hand, the "earthly" (ἐπίγειος) is susceptible to "dismantling" (καταλυθῇ) and described as a "house, which is a tent" (οἰκία τοῦ σκήνους), a phrase that is at home in Greek philosophical traditions.[85] On the other hand, in a description that carries shades of Jewish apocalyptic,[86] Paul speaks of a "house" (οἰκίαν) or "building from God" (οἰκοδομὴν ἐκ θεοῦ) that is "not built by [human] hands" (ἀχειροποίητον) and thus "eternal in the heavens" (αἰώνιον ἐν τοῖς οὐρανοῖς). Again Paul is synthesizing Jewish and Greek traditions, and by virtue of the BODY IS HOUSE metaphor he posits both earthly and heavenly somatic dwelling places. (Note: The basic

---

83. It is partly for this reason that notions of containment were coherent within the plant metaphor. Despite the fact that seeds and plants are not usually thought of as containers, bodies are. Thus Paul is able to successfully contrast earthly and heavenly bodies. Paul further develops this line of thinking briefly in 1 Cor 15:49 and 53–54, where he characterizes eschatological transformation as a process of putting on clothing.

84. The content of this blend is composed of aspects associated with DWELLING PLACES, and includes structure such as Builders, Interior (IN), Exterior (OUT), a BOUNDARY, as well as qualitative associations such as Home (see tables 3.1 and 3.2). As Paul introduces the concept HOUSE, I_1 and I_2 are blended on account of their shared CONTAINER structure, thus creating the metaphor BODY IS HOUSE.

85. The appositional use of σκῆνος with οἰκία denotes the temporary nature of this dwelling (BDF §167; see also BDAG s.v. σκῆνος). The metaphor was common in Greek philosophical traditions (for more, see Aune 1995, 301–2).

86. The image of an eschatological building is common in Jewish (esp. apocalyptic) tradition (e.g., 1 En. 90:28–38). Though the focus of the present passage is not upon a renewed Jerusalem and/or temple, Paul's own description of the body as the temple of the spirit (e.g., 1 Cor 6:19; see also 1 Cor 3:16–17) suggests that we should not dismiss these associations out of hand.

blend has been sketched in fig. 3.6; the specific blending maps for both the EARTHLY and HEAVENLY BODIES are outlined in tables 3.1 and 3.2.)

The second CONTAINER-structured metaphor, introduced in 5:2b and 4, focuses on the concept of CLOTHING. We have already demonstrated that celestial transformation is commonly described by the dawning of a heavenly/angelic garment. While much Greek and Roman attire was designed to wrap around the body, it was common to conceptualize clothing via the CONTAINER schema. For instance, the verb ἐνδύω, which is commonly used to describe the act of putting clothing on, is also used to denote movement into an object or state (i.e., "go into" or "enter into" [LSJ]).[87] This sense of moving *into* and *out of* clothing is reflected in many garment designs as well. The χιτών/*tunica*, worn by both men and women, was (for lack of a better term) tubular in design and either slipped over the head and pulled down or stepped into and then pulled up so as to cover the length of the body.[88] It was not uncommon to wear two χιτῶνας (i.e., both an under- and overgarment), and these were usually covered over by another garment such as a ἱμάτιον (or Pallium/Palla).[89] Though this latter garment was not so much moved into as adorned (i.e., wrapped around the body), we can conclude that Greek and Roman dress consisted of several different layers, some of which were "put on" and all of which encompassed the torso.[90] This all points to an understanding of clothing

---

87. In this way, the embodied grounding of ἐνδύω is tied to the CONTAINER schema. The word itself is a compound formed from ἐν and δύω. The former is a familiar preposition that commonly denotes the state of being *in* a location (see §5.1.1). The latter is commonly glossed (LSJ) "to cause to sink or plunge into" (causative) or "to go into" (noncausative, particularly with respect to places and even clothing [e.g., Homer, *Il*. 5.845; 6.340; 18.416]).

88. For helpful visual depictions of the χιτών/*tunica* and other garments, as well as differences between male and female garb, see Goldman 2001. Much of my analysis deals interchangeably with Greek and Roman clothing; such descriptive flexibility is founded on Goldman's assertion that the basic design and structure of Greek and Roman dress was the same within the broader Greco-Roman period, despite differences in style and ornamentation (217).

89. Men would wear the ἱμάτιον draped over the left arm and wrapped around the torso, while women could wear the ἱμάτιον draped over the head (such that it covered the entire body) or simply over the arms. Roman citizens also wore the toga, which was similar in design though differed in cut. The garment functioned as Roman formal dress, and it was given as a rite of passage to signify a boy's transition to manhood (Dolansky 2008). At times women also wore the toga as a sign of adultery.

90. The garments listed here are by no means exhaustive, and one can also point

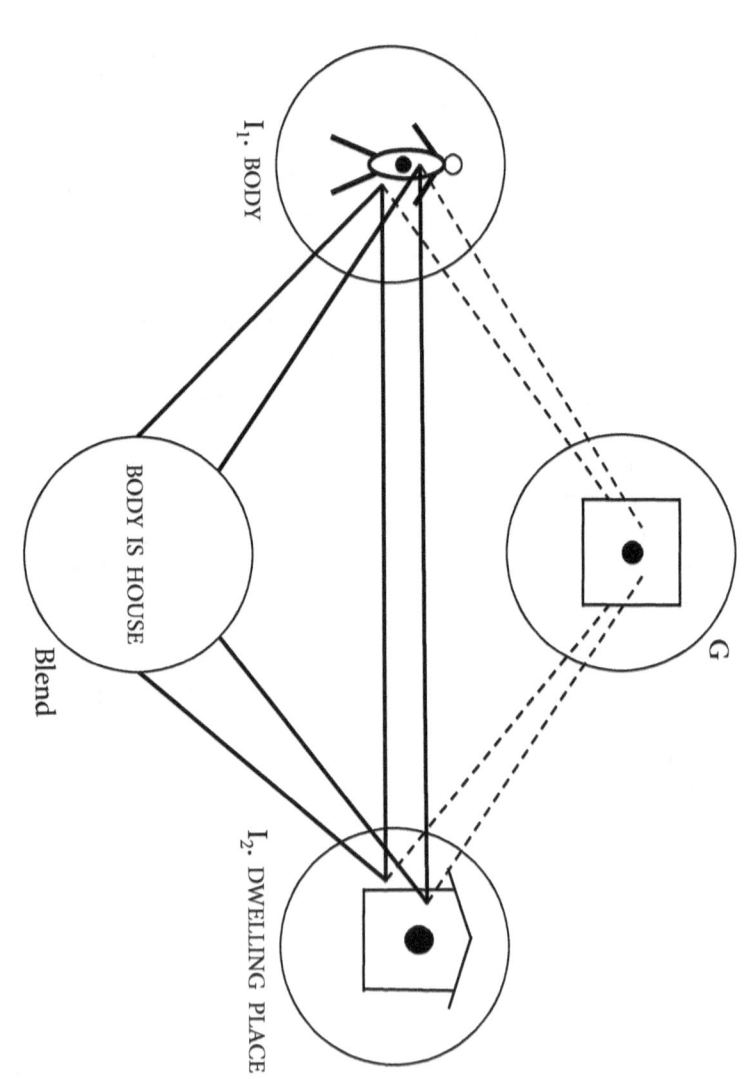

Figure 3.6. The BODY IS HOUSE Metaphor (2 Cor 5:1–2a)

Table 3.1. Blending Map for the EARTHLY BODY IS TENT Metaphor
(ἡ ἐπίγειος ἡμῶν οἰκία τοῦ σκήνους, 2 Cor 5:1–2a)

I_1. EARTHLY BODY	Generic Space	I_2. TENT
ἔσω ἄνθρωπος (2 Cor 4:16)	In	Interior
ἔξω ἄνθρωπος (2 Cor 4:16)	Boundary	Walls
Parents	Generator	χειροποίητος
Birth	Genesis	Assembly
Flesh/Blood (see 1 Cor 15:50)	Composition	Materials for a σκῆνος
Death	Termination	Dismantle (καταλύω)

Table 3.2. Blending Map for the HEAVENLY BODY IS HOUSE Metaphor
(οἰκοδομὴν ἐκ θεοῦ, 2 Cor 5:1–2a)

I_1. HEAVENLY BODY	Generic Space	I_2. HOUSE
ἔσω ἄνθρωπος (2 Cor 4:16)	In	Interior
ἔξω ἄνθρωπος (2 Cor 4:16)	Boundary	Walls
ἀχειροποίητος	Generator	χειροποίητος
parousia (but, baptism?)	Genesis	Construction
Materials that are αἰώνιος	Composition	Materials for an οἰκοδομήν/οἰκία
————	Termination	Destruction

as a type of container that humans move *in* and *out* of, thus reflecting the conceptual metaphor CLOTHING IS CONTAINER.[91]

Paul is concerned, however, not with the putting on of different clothes but rather with the putting on of a different body. When blended with the BODY IS CONTAINER metaphor, a relatively straightforward blend is created that establishes cross-space mappings between the BOUNDARY role-values, thus linking CLOTHING to BODY (fig. 3.7). Accordingly, Paul contrasts differing somatic states as instances of wearing different types of clothing, thus establishing the BODY IS CLOTHING metaphor. With respect to eschatological transformation, in 1 Cor 15:53–54 Paul insists that what is perishable and mortal must "be clothed with" (δεῖ … ἐνδύσασθαι) the imperishable and immortal. Similarly, in 15:49 he insists that though believers currently "wear" (ἐφορέσαμεν) the image of the earthly person, they will one day "wear" (φορέσομεν) the image of the heavenly person.[92] Returning to 2 Cor 5, Paul utilizes this metaphor as a way of describing the process of eschatological transformation. In 5:2b and 4 the apostle speaks of "clothing over" (ἐπενδύσασθαι). The image is that of one garment (i.e., the heavenly body) being put on over top of another (i.e., the earthly body).[93] As one reads on, Paul elaborates this image by blending the clothing and housing metaphors so as to describe postmortem transformation. The conceptual blend reflected in 5:2b and 4 is extremely robust, drawing on all the input spaces and conceptual metaphors that I have identified in the discourse thus far (see fig. 3.8 on p. 128).

The blend consists of three input spaces. The first (I_1) is composed only of the earthly human body and does not include notions of heavenly

---

91. My discussion has focused largely on the functional aspects of ancient Mediterranean clothing and the kinds of conceptual structures that arise from those practicalities. In addition to this, clothing also caries certain cultural and social values, all of which constitute and enrich the metaphorical frame-structures. For more on how clothing and dress convey status, membership, and power, see (generally) Batten 2010 and (on Paul specifically) Kim 2004.

92. The clothing metaphor may actually be introduced as early as 1 Cor 15:37, where Paul's description of the sown seed as "naked" (γυμνὸν κόκκον) coheres with the CLOTHING frame. See n. 65 above.

93. Via the BODY AS CLOTHING metaphor, the use of ἐπενδύομαι in both 5:2 and 5:4 (the only New Testament occurrences) points toward the idea that the earthly body/dwelling is a garment that will one day be clothed over by the heavenly body/dwelling. In this way, the image that Paul seeks to convey is not that of *container removal*, nor even container *replacement*, but rather *further containment*.

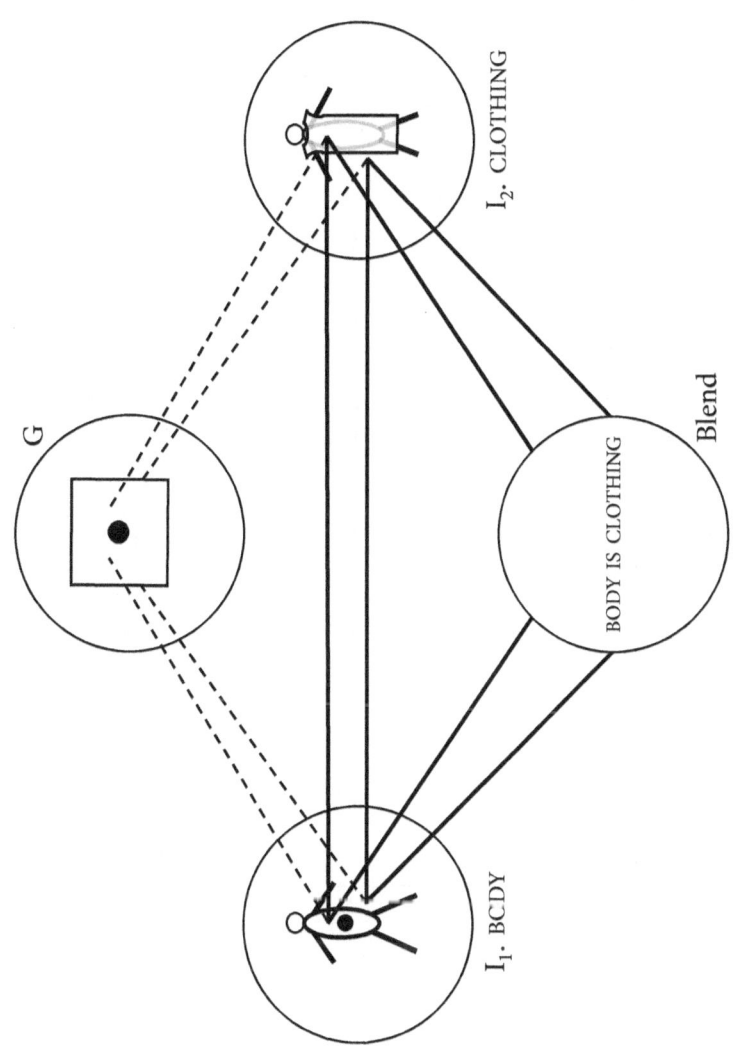

Figure 3.7. The BODY IS CLOTHING Metaphor (2 Cor 5:2b, 4)

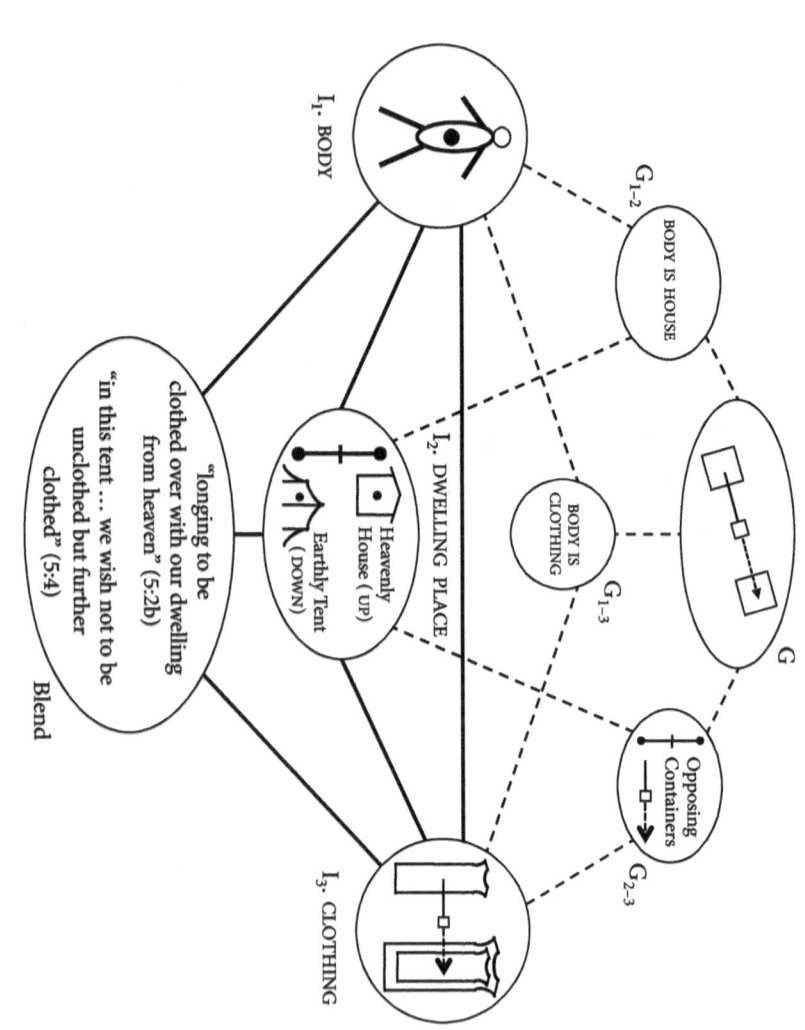

Figure 3.8. Putting on a House (2 Cor 5:2b, 4)

bodies, since this has not been the focus of Paul's address in the broader epistolary context.[94] The second input (I_2) consists of vertically configured earthly and heavenly dwelling places.[95] The final input (I_3) contains the process of putting one garment on over the top of another and thus includes the CHANGE gestalt. What links the three inputs together are a series of subgeneric spaces, which consist of the BODY IS HOUSE metaphor (G_{1-2})[96] and the BODY IS CLOTHING metaphor (G_{1-3}),[97] as well as the recognition of opposing containers, configured either vertically or along a PATH schema (G_{2-3}).[98] The generic space that ties these subgeneric mappings together is the CHANGE gestalt, which maps the opposing container elements as well as the process of transformation between the two.[99] The blended space itself consists of emergent meaning not found in any of the inputs. Most pointedly, Paul is able to characterize believers as "longing to be clothed over with our dwelling from heaven" (τὸ οἰκητήριον ἡμῶν τὸ ἐξ οὐρανοῦ ἐπενδύσασθαι ἐπιποθοῦντες, 5:2b) and further to speak of earthly/heavenly dwellings as garments that are worn (5:4). Not surprisingly, Paul caries this metaphor forward into 5:6–10, where he speaks of being at "home in the [earthly] body" (ἐνδημοῦντες ἐν τῷ σώματι) but desiring to be "away from the [earthly] body and home with the Lord" (ἐκδημῆσαι ἐκ τοῦ σώματος καὶ ἐνδημῆσαι πρὸς τὸν κύριον). Taken together, Paul's ability to speak of wearing a heavenly dwelling draws from all three inputs in that it presumes an earthly body (I_1) that puts on (I_3) a heavenly house (I_2).

---

94. Indeed, since 4:7 (and even as early as 3:2), Paul has been fixated on the earthly human body (see discussion in §5.2).

95. These dwelling places are vertically configured on account of the cosmological mapping (see 5.1), which presumes the VERTICALITY schema.

96. This was introduced already in 5:1–2a. Because I_1 lacks any kind of opposing structure, the vertical configuration of containers is not linked in the subgeneric space.

97. Because the PATH structure is not found in I_1, it therefore does not find articulation in this subgeneric space.

98. The two axes are not (yet) subsumed into one inclined PATH structure, but rather stand side by side so as to enable the blend of I_2 and I_3.

99. From G_{1-2}, the contrasting *earthly body/tent* and *heavenly dwelling* elements are mapped to the SOURCE and GOAL containers, respectively. Similarly, the (earthly) BODY AS CLOTHING element of G_{1-3} is mapped to the SOURCE element. Along with G_{1-2}, G_{2-3} similarly maps vertically opposing container structures onto the SOURCE and GOAL elements of the CHANGE gestalt, while also mapping the PATH structure itself. Taken together, both the VERTICALITY and PATH structures of G_{2-3} correspond to the inclined CHANGE gestalt in resurrection contexts.

The blend diagrammed in figure 3.8 is enabled in part because of a shared CONTAINER structure, but it is the CHANGE gestalt that organizes the various elements together. The blend is premised on an understanding of the human body as a container (i.e., BODY IS CONTAINER), and eschatological transformation is not a radical or ontological break but a transformation of somatic continuity within a unitary, one-world model. But what in all of this is continuous? Indeed, Paul is rather clear that the mortal is "swallowed" (καταποθῇ) by life (5:4b), an image of consumption that implies the terminal end of that which is ingested.[100] Perhaps an answer is to be found in 5:3, where the apostle rather curiously insists that, "when we have taken [the earthly body] off, we will not be found naked" (ἐκδυσάμενοι οὐ γυμνοὶ εὑρεθησόμεθα). Here Paul extends the frame-structure of the clothing metaphor to imply that believers already, in their earthly existence, possess some kind of heavenly-quality garment that is not disrobed at death.[101]

At this point, we can note the inherent logic of the CLOTHING frame: the act of putting on one garment entails taking off another whereby a period of nakedness ensues. Paul seems to have picked up on this logic in 5:3; and, presumably seeking to avoid notions of a disembodied soul, he posits some form of interim clothing. Having insisted that the earthly and heavenly bodies are differing *outer* garments, the logic of the CLOTHING frame provides Paul with an alternative to interim nakedness—an undergarment that persists once the outer clothing layers are removed.[102]

---

100. The swallowing metaphor denotes the destruction of the earthly tent through the process of eschatological consumption (to extend the SWALLOWING frame). It should not be overlooked that the swallowing metaphor also is premised on the CONTAINER schema. Here the movement of the mortal body *into* the risen body is characterized as the act of a perishable object (e.g., food) entering *into* a consumer's body. The same metaphor is found in 1 Cor 15:54, where it is similarly used in conjunction with the clothing metaphor.

101. Given that Paul may presume an intermediary state between death and parousia (see Dunn 1998b, 489–90), two points are worth noting. First, such an intermediary state is not without parallel in broader Jewish tradition (e.g., 1 En. 22; Josephus, B.J. 2.163). Second, Paul is not interested in describing such a state for its own sake, nor does he see it as the eschatological ideal (cf. the language of longing in 2 Cor 5:2 and 4). Paul remains clearly focused on risen embodiment, and if such an interim state exists, he insists that it too will be (in some fashion) embodied (= clothed).

102. As we have seen above, this is consistent with typical Mediterranean garb whereby both under- and overgarments are worn. To extend that discussion, Roman

What are these eternal-quality (under)garments that Paul perceives as having already been given and surviving death? The answer cannot be the earthly body, as Paul feels quite free to suggest that it can be destroyed (5:1) and will be taken off (5:3). Nor can this be the heavenly body, which is an overgarment (5:2, 4) and will be given in the future. The best answer is the indwelling πνεῦμα, which Paul here insists is the "deposit" or guarantee (τὸν ἀρραβῶνα τοῦ πνεύματος) of risen existence (5:5). While we must acknowledge that Paul does not speak of πνεῦμα as being put on, he does ubiquitously map πνεῦμα to the somatic interior, thus locating it *within* the earthly body (or underneath the earthly garment, to extend the metaphor). For Paul, Christ is πνεῦμα (2 Cor 3:17), and thus the apostle's various references to "putting on" (ἐνδύω) Christ can rightly be read in a pneumatic light (Gal 3:27; Rom 13:12–14; see also 1 Thess 5:8). Similarly, the baptismal rite is both an act of "putting on Christ" (Gal 3:27) and likely the means by which πνεῦμα is granted to believers (e.g., note the water imagery of 1 Cor 12:13; Rom 5:5). If we consider 2 Cor 5 within this broader Pauline context, the apostle envisions a strong degree of continuity between earthly and heavenly bodies, continuity that he maps to the somatic interior and links to the presence of πνεῦμα. Consistent with his emphasis on further containment, then, Paul extends the clothing metaphor to denote both inner and outer containers, one of which can be taken off at death, the other of which is permanent and survives death and thus ensures believers "will not be found naked" when their bodies are disrobed at death. Here, then, is the point of continuity across earthly and heavenly somatic existences, a point that I will flesh out in greater detail in chapter 4.[103]

In summary, we have seen that the clothing/housing metaphor of 2 Cor 5:1–5 is premised on the BODY IS CONTAINER metaphor. In light of the one-world model noted above, Paul conceptualizes transformation between these somatic states as a process of both difference and continu-

---

men and women had different kinds of undertunics. For example, the *indusium* (for a matron) and the *supparus* were specific kinds of female undertunics that were worn underneath the regular tunic; they were likely light and functioned as a kind of "slip" (Olson 2003, 201–3). Despite this, however, Olson suggests it is unlikely that either men or women regularly wore any kind of loincloth underneath the tunic (205–9).

103. This aligns with what we saw in 1 Cor 15:44, where the risen body is understood as a somatic existence that is perfectly suited for πνεῦμα.

ity; that is, while the external somatic states are cosmologically distinct, the internal πνεῦμα persists.

3.3. Conclusions

The overarching aim of this chapter has been to understand better the categories of reality that Paul works with, specifically with respect to cosmology and anthropology. Locating the apostle within a series of concentric cultural circles, we have seen that Paul holds to an integrational rather than oppositional dualistic framework; that is, Paul thinks in terms of unified wholes wherein opposing forces exist in interdependent tension with one another. With respect to Paul's transformation metaphors, the apostle envisions somatic states that are uniquely fashioned for their cosmological locations. In 1 Cor 15, Paul draws a caricature between the ensouled earthly body (σῶμα ψυχικόν) and the enspirited heavenly body (σῶμα πνευματικόν), both of which are qualitatively discontinuous with one another because of their cosmo-somatic locations. The difference between these two caricatures is drawn largely with respect to issues of intrasomatic polarity; that is, Paul contrasts two embodied extremes so as to stress the risen body as perfectly suited for the indwelling πνεῦμα. While notions of continuity are only implicit in 1 Cor 15, in 2 Cor 5 Paul points more specifically to the location of trans-somatic continuity (esp. 2 Cor 5:3 and 5). Here Paul envisions a process of radical discontinuity of the somatic exterior but sustained continuity of the somatic interior. For those in Christ, who have already received πνεῦμα and thus exist as enspirited earthly bodies, they are already clothed with Christ/πνεῦμα and thus have a deposit in anticipation of the enspirited heavenly body.

Returning to the secondary literature examined in chapter 1 (§1.3.2), we can now see that the standard scholarly constructions of dualism and monism are hermeneutically unhelpful and historically imprecise. On the one side, the strong dualism that is often attributed both to Jewish apocalypticism (generally) and Paul (specifically) is fallaciously overextended. As we have seen, Paul has a much more integrative cosmology. On the other side, strong assertions of anthropological monism are equally problematic. As the transformation metaphors of both 1 Cor 15 and 2 Cor 5 demonstrate, Paul is quite capable of understanding the human composition as partitively drawn. Indeed, we have seen strong evidence that suggests the BODY IS CONTAINER metaphor is extended not only to denote external transformation but also to map trans-somatic continuity of the interior (this point will be further elaborated in ch. 4). In this way, notions of anthropological dualism are germane to Paul's resurrection ideals. Taken together, Paul is best located between these two scholarly constructs—Paul upholds a one-world model that is partitively drawn and yet characterized by intracosmic and intrasomatic polarity.

4
Eschatological Somatology:
Identifying the Already and the
Not Yet in Paul

In chapters 2 and 3, I examined the use of metaphors for resurrection, both in Paul's epistles and in broader Second Temple Jewish literature. In so doing, two key aspects came to the fore. In chapter 2, I identified the constituent metaphors and image schemata that make up notions of resurrection and further demonstrated how this constellation of concepts—the RESURRECTION gestalt—structures much of Paul's thinking. In chapter 3, I built upon this foundation, specifically focusing on Paul's transformation metaphors in the Corinthian correspondence. In both analyses, I directed attention toward the temporal scaling of resurrection as an event in the future. This is how resurrection is traditionally configured within scholarly discussions, and it constitutes what usually is identified as "literal" or "actual" resurrection.

In this chapter and the next, I draw our attention toward instances where the RESURRECTION gestalt and its suite of metaphors are elaborated with respect to life in Christ prior to death. At issue is the extent to which Paul's resurrection ideals are oriented not merely toward the future but also toward the present. The issue is particularly evident in Rom 6, where Paul insists that believers have been "crucified with," "buried with," and thus have "died with Christ" (6:4–8). The absolute nature of such death is clear in Paul's address, as are the ethical implications: his readers in Rome are to consider themselves "dead to sin" (6:11). While participation in Christ's death is sure, the precise nature of resurrection within this passage is less clear. To be certain, Paul explicitly understands resurrection as something that has not yet happened (6:5, 8), and it cannot be denied that he uses the usual linguistic terminology (ἀνάστασις) when speaking of this future event. At the same time, however, the apostle insists that believers now "walk in newness of life" (6:4), that they present themselves as "those who are living from the dead" (6:13), and further that they consider themselves "alive to God" (6:11). The conceptual matrices of DEATH/RESURRECTION and DEATH/LIFE are lurking in the metaphorical intertextures of this passage. While such descriptions are not linguistically identified as ἀνάστασις, they nonetheless suggest (even presume) *some kind* of present resurrection experience. Rather than taking the linguistic sign as the sole indicator of Paul's soteriological ideals, we do far better to explore how the entire RESURRECTION gestalt is brought to bear on Paul's address in Rom 6.

Several problems emerge, however, when we speak of resurrection as already realized (in some sense). How does Paul configure this present life/resurrection? What exactly does it mean to be risen in the present? How does this present life/resurrection relate to the future life/resurrection that Paul explicitly stresses? Is it appropriate to speak of resurrection as something present, or should we speak rather of present life and future resurrection? In the present chapter, I will address issues such as these, all of which center on the larger concern of Paul's eschatological outlook, specifically his understanding of "already" and "not yet." Traditional scholarly treatments of Paul's theology have overwhelmingly insisted that the apostle modifies the Jewish eschatological expectation.[1] Given what I have already shown in chapter 2, it is important to recognize that the flexibility of the RESURRECTION gestalt necessarily problematizes such claims. Accordingly, part of this chapter's aim is to engage critically the nature of such supposed eschatological modifications.

The following discussion focuses specifically on Rom 6–8 so as to examine the extent to which Paul understands resurrection as not just a future but also a present experience. To anticipate my conclusions, I will demonstrate that Paul has a single resurrection event in mind, one that is

---

1. A few examples will suffice: C. H. Dodd (1963, 84 and 37) argues, "in the New Testament ... [we have] a profound difference" such that the church "proceeded to reconstruct on a modified plan the traditional scheme of Jewish eschatology." Vos (1961, 36–41) contrasts "the original scheme" of Jewish eschatology with "the modified scheme" that Paul employed. Cullmann (1962, 82) insists that "the new feature in the Christian conception of time, as compared with Jewish conception [*sic*], is to be sought in the division of time." Lincoln (1981, 170) contends, "Paul modified the sharp contrast between the two ages." Dunn (1998b, 463) asserts that Jesus "disrupted the previous schema and required it to be modified." Wright (2003, 372) suggests that the division of history into two resurrection moments is one of two "mutations within the Jewish worldview."

dynamically played out on the σῶμα such that the nexus of already/not yet is mapped onto the human body itself. To this end, Paul holds to an eschatological somatology that locates the human being in a trajectory of resurrection, thereby enabling partial resurrection in the present and full resurrection in the future.

4.1. Baptismal Death in Romans 6:1–11

In the ensuing discussion, I offer a blending analysis of Rom 6:1–11 (esp. v. 4) that highlights Paul's argumentative aims while also exploring— and this is more to my immediate point—the extent to which these aims are grounded in certain recurrent, particular, basic bodily practices. As I hope to demonstrate, the logic of Paul's address in 6:1–11 is premised on certain somatic movements that are enacted in baptism and that are meaningful precisely because they reflect conceptual structures that are shared between both performative and oral/written modes of communication. Put differently, for the apostle, baptism functions not as a literary metaphor or trope but rather as an embodied practice, one that enacts the conceptual structures of the VERTICALITY schema conveyed in Paul's proclamation of the risen Christ.

At the beginning of Rom 6, Paul turns his attention toward the relationship between grace and ethics. In response to his assertion in 5:20 that grace increases on account of sin, we find the rhetorical question of 6:1: "should we not continue in sin?" To his imagined interlocutor, Paul counters with the emphatic "by no means," and the rationale for what he takes as self-evident is the assertion that believers have already "died to sin" (6:2). The key text for our purposes is 6:4, which reads as follows:

> συνετάφημεν οὖν αὐτῷ διὰ τοῦ βαπτίσματος εἰς τὸν θάνατον, ἵνα ὥσπερ ἠγέρθη Χριστὸς ἐκ νεκρῶν διὰ τῆς δόξης τοῦ πατρός, οὕτως καὶ ἡμεῖς ἐν καινότητι ζωῆς περιπατήσωμεν.

> Therefore, we were buried with him through baptism into death, so that, just as Christ was raised from the dead through the glory of the Father, thus we too might walk in newness of life.

This passage betrays an elaborate blending structure that consists of three inputs as well as several generic spaces (fig. 4.1). Given the hermeneutical importance of this text, it is beneficial to examine the blend in detail.

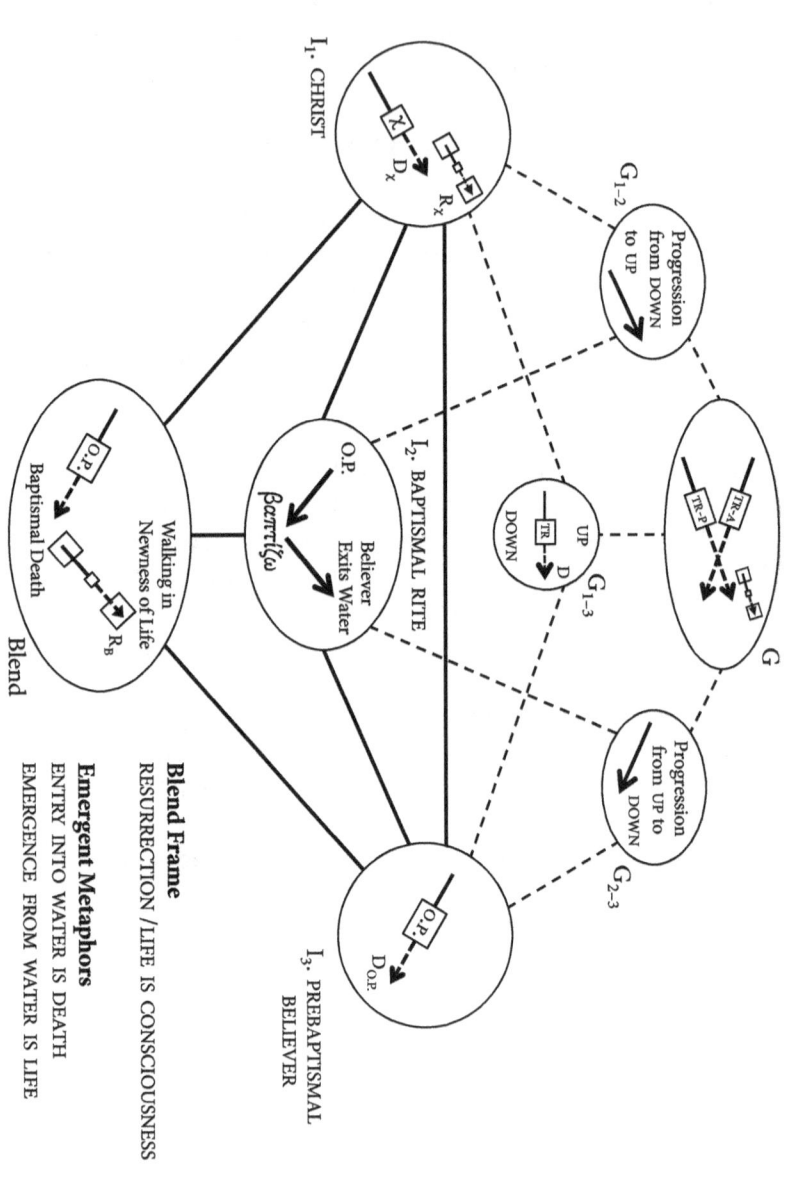

Figure 4.1. Baptismal Death and Resurrection (Rom 6:4)

The first and third input spaces (I_1 and I_3) are concerned with the figures of Christ and Christ-devotees, respectively. Given the focus in 6:4 on Christ's death and resurrection, the first input (I_1) is framed by the protagonist elements of the RESURRECTION gestalt. Accordingly, this space includes structural elements such as the protagonist's inclined PATH and subsequent transformation, as well as specific elements such as Christ himself (i.e., the TR-P, signified by χ), Christ's death (signified by D_χ, understood as an event along the macro-PATH), and Christ's risen existence (signified by R_χ). By contrast, the third input (I_3) is framed by the believer's *pre*baptismal state.[2] This space includes the structural element of the antagonist's declined PATH, as well as specific elements such as believers themselves (i.e., the TR-A, signified by O.P. ["old person," ὁ παλαιὸς ἡμῶν ἄνθρωπος, 6:6]) and the projected antagonist's death (signified by $D_{O.P.}$).[3]

The second input space (I_2) is more complicated, for it is this space that concerns the baptismal rite and thus requires a greater deal of description. We must acknowledge that describing this space is difficult, for the rite itself is ultimately lost to history. This does not mean, however, that we are completely unable to articulate aspects of how Paul and his readers in Rome might have practiced baptism. As much as possible, I want to focus on the practice itself. A fruitful way forward, which is grounded well in the theoretical commitments of the present study, is to look for correlations between literary descriptions of resurrection and performative enactments of baptism. As noted in chapter 1 (§1.4), because conceptual metaphors are conceptual in nature, they are thus multimodal and able to find expression in nonverbal contexts;[4] that is, in addition to language,

---

2. Since the entire pericope is premised on the contrast between pre- and post-baptismal states (e.g., 6:6, 11), I_3 consists of the former while the blended space consists of the latter.

3. The translation of ἄνθρωπος as "person" as opposed to the more traditional "man" or even "human" is preferable for the following reasons: (1) "person" denotes the gender generality of ἄνθρωπος, and (2) "person" points to the individuated nature of the baptizand, where such individuation must always be understood within a collectivist context. On this latter point, Paul's interests lie not in the salvation of individuals but rather in the resurrection of individuated-bodies-located-in-a-collectivist-context.

4. To say that conceptual metaphors are multimodal is to recognize that such metaphors undergird actions and performance as much as language itself. Accordingly, nonverbal performative dimensions of human culture can be as communica-

conceptual metaphors find expression in art, gestures, and even ritual.[5] By recognizing that the literary and the performative can convey the same conceptual structures, a promising way forward is to look for embodied, performative descriptions within the historical record.

Such conceptual coherence can be demonstrated through both linguistic and narrative analyses. To the former, in general usage the linguistic sign βαπτίζω[6] implies downward movement (dipping or submersing in liquid)[7] that often results in a tragic end (e.g., death);[8] thus Albrecht Oepke (1964, 530) notes that in the Hellenistic period "the idea of going under or perishing is nearer the general usage [of βαπτίζω]."[9] In linguistic expression, then, βαπτίζω is conceptually correlated with downward directionality (thus rendering the metaphor, ΒΑΠΤΙΖΩ IS DOWN). We see a similar trend within the limited narrative/written descriptions of early Christian baptismal practices, where we have good reason to suspect that the rite included some form of vertically configured somatic movement. Such is certainly the case with Jesus's baptism in Mark (and Matthew after

---

tive as verbal dimensions. On the multimodal nature of conceptual metaphor, see esp. Gibbs 2008, chs. 25–28; also Lakoff and Johnson 1999, 57.

5. The present cognitive linguistic analysis aligns in many ways with recent trends in the cognitive science of religion. Risto Uro (2010, 2011) offers a succinct primer of cognitive approaches to ritual studies as related to early Christianity, specifically identifying genealogical, functionalist, and symbolist approaches. The present analysis falls squarely within the symbolist camp, which focuses on the semiotics of ritual acts and explores the extent to which a given rite is a culturally interpreted communicative act that can be examined in relation to universally shared human cognitive structures (see Uro 2010, 224–26).

6. The verb βαπτίζω is used in 6:3, the noun βάπτισμα in 6:4. The latter points to the established practice, which is here understood instrumentally as the means by which "burial with" (συνθάπτω) Christ is achieved.

7. So LSJ, which glosses the term generally as "to dip" or "plunge." LSJ offers several other glosses too, many of which are premised upon downward movement (e.g., "to be drowned" [where one moves down into the water], or "to dye" cloth [a practice that likely used the act of plunging]).

8. The sign often is used in contexts that denote some kind of tragic end; for instance, it is used of sinking ships and drowning humans (e.g., Josephus, *B.J.* 3.525–527), of passions likened to water that threaten to destroy the soul (Philo, *Leg.* 3.18), and also (without reference to water) of Jerusalem's destruction (Josephus, *B.J.* 4.137).

9. Oepke particularly stresses this point in contrast to other meanings such as *to wash*.

him), and Acts 8:39 contains a related description.[10] Though the Didache may evince an alternative practice,[11] both Barn. 11:11 and Shepherd of Hermas, Mand. 4.3 (see also Sim. 9.16) explicitly describe this down-up procedure. The much later Hippolytus (third century CE) speaks similarly of a threefold immersion (*Trad. ap.* 21.14–19).[12] Though the practices of Paul, his communities, and Christ-devotees in Rome are ultimately lost to history, it seems reasonable that the baptismal rite involved some form of down-up somatic movement, thus enacting the VERTICALITY schema (i.e., ENTRY INTO WATER IS DOWN/EMERGENCE FROM WATER IS UP).[13]

Given this schematic correspondence, the insistence of many exegetes that there is no "clear analogy" between baptism and Christ's death/resurrection is overstated.[14] Grounded in the VERTICALITY schema, the baptismal rite was susceptible to cultic enactment of the DEATH IS DOWN/LIFE IS

---

10. Mark 1:10, "coming up out of the waters" (ἀναβαίνων ἐκ τοῦ ὕδατος); Matt 3:16, "he came up from the waters" (ἀνέβη ἀπὸ τοῦ ὕδατος); and Acts 8:39, "they came up out of the water" (ἀνέβησαν ἐκ τοῦ ὕδατος). It is not clear whether this "coming up out of the waters" implies the act of getting out of the water or simply emerging from underneath the water. The key point for our purposes is the recognition of upward movement (thus implying a prior downward movement).

11. Didache 7:1–4 prefers baptism "in living water" (ἐν ὕδατι ζῶντι), which likely is a reference to a running stream (Niederwimmer 1998, 127). The passage makes no mention of vertical movement into or out of the water, though neither does it describe the practice at all. In vv. 2–3, concessions are made for the absence of ὕδωρ ζῶν; while v. 3 speaks of thrice pouring water over the head of the baptizand, it is unknown if such an act would be practiced in the preferred context of ὕδωρ ζῶν.

12. The thrice immersion is recounted in all the surviving traditions (see Bradshaw, Johnson, and Phillips 2002).

13. Wayne Meeks (2003, 155), moreover, has conjectured that baptism was accompanied by several other vertically structured practices (e.g., recitation of Phil 2:6–11, a text that is rich in vertically concepts).

14. I here cite Robert Tannehill (1967, 34), who is worth quoting in full: "there is no clear analogy between the act of entering the water and Christ's death, for Christ was not drowned. Nor is there a clear analogy between entering the water and burial, for burial at sea is not the normal means of burial." Tannehill's judgment seems to be made on the basis of genealogical or thematic parallels, and at this level he indeed is correct that analogy cannot be found. One of the main problems in this approach is that baptism in Rom 6 is treated not as a ritual practice but only as a literary construct. Paul's rhetoric about the rite is viewed as a linguistic arena in which the myth can be explored. What the Romans or any other first-century Christ-devotees actually are doing with their bodies is set to the side, presumably becoming an issue of secondary concern. Such tropification of the rite has confounded many scholars as to why Paul

UP conceptual metaphors. Indeed, it is perhaps significant that in Rom 6 baptism is *not* signified to resurrection through the metaphor of washing. Though the idea of washing would naturally fit both the ritual act and the linguistic sign (perhaps see 1 Cor 6:11), the washing image does not lend itself as easily to notions of death/resurrection. In this way, Paul exploits in Rom 6 those aspects of the ritual that enable blending with Christ's death and resurrection. Retuning to 6:4, one can reasonably construct I_2 to include sequential vertical movement composed of the old person's (O.P.) initial descent into water (βαπτίζω) followed by an ascent out of water. Though the space is conceptual in nature, it is both grounded in and thus constructed through the performance of the rite.

Taking the entire blending structure of figure 4.1 together, the subgeneric spaces are all cross-mapped with one another by virtue of the RESURRECTION schematic structure (G),[15] which here functions as a gestalt in that all the elements work interdependently.[16] Simply put, it is the logic of death and resurrection that makes Paul's address coherent and meaningful. Significantly, in the blended space, we find emergent meaning not found in any of the inputs alone. The most important aspect of this emergent meaning is the joining of the antagonist's declined PATH to the protagonist's transformation/change PATH, both of which are projected from I_3 and I_1, respectively, though structured by the down-up movements enacted in the baptismal rite (I_2). In the blended space, the two death events of I_1 and I_3 are cross-mapped with one another ($D_\chi \rightarrow D_{O.P.}$). Accordingly, Christ's death/resurrection is correlated with the baptismal act in the blended space, thus creating the element of baptismal death (which is seen as the terminal end of the "old person" and the point of

---

links baptism to death/resurrection in Rom 6. Tannehill's puzzlement is echoed by Dunn (1988, 1:312) and more recently by Robert Jewett (2007, 398).

15. Of the subgeneric spaces, G_{1-3} includes several elements (e.g., PATH structure, a death event [D] correlated with the path's GOAL, and the opposition of UP and DOWN) that specifically cross-map the TRAJECTORS ($\chi \rightarrow$ O.P.) and their respective deaths ($D_\chi \rightarrow D_{O.P.}$). On the other hand, I_2 is cross-mapped with I_1 and I_3 via opposing vertical structures such that G_{1-2} denotes progression from DOWN to UP (i.e., vertical incline) and G_{2-3} denotes progression from UP to DOWN (i.e., vertical decline). In both cases, the progression corresponds to the event sequences in the various input spaces, while the vertical structure corresponds either to baptismal motion (I_2) or trajector movement (I_1 and I_3).

16. In this way, the RESURRECTION gestalt brings together the various elements of each subgeneric space.

transference between the two paths). Because the death event is the key focal point of the entire system, only the protagonist's transformation/change PATH is projected from I_1 to the blended space.[17] This is evident in that Paul characterizes baptismal effectiveness as a transformation between contrasting container structures; that is, from living "in sin" (ἐν αὐτῇ [namely, ἁμαρτία], 6:1-2) to walking now "in newness of life" (ἐν καινότητι ζωῆς, 6:4). What emerges in the blended space, then, is the conceptualization of believers as having once traversed the antagonist's declined PATH but currently transformed through baptismal death into a new, transformed state.[18] Conceptually speaking, because baptismal death has happened, so has baptismal resurrection.

Though Paul's address in 6:1–11 is focused unmistakably on baptismal death with Christ, notions of a conjoined resurrection are naturally entailed. That is, the correlation of death with the verb βαπτίζω results in the conceptual metaphor ENTRY INTO WATER IS DEATH and thus entails—within the logic of the RESURRECTION gestalt—the obverse metaphor, EMERGENCE FROM WATER IS LIFE. Within the performative context of the rite, the two metaphors are inextricable. Though coburial/death may be the dominant point that Paul stresses at human scale, coresurrection is no less implicit.[19] Such a conclusion presumes, however, a correlation of baptism with life/death that is premised on embodied rather than thematic parallels. Baptism is linked to Christ's death and resurrection for the simple fact that the rite itself becomes a communicative site for the same conceptual

---

17. This is confirmed in two ways. First, in 6:4 Paul is focused on Christ's risen state, and thus the believer's postbaptismal state is likened not to Christ's preresurrection state (i.e., protagonist's inclined PATH) but rather to his existence as a risen, transformed being (i.e., transformation/change PATH). Second, Paul's focus in 6:1–4 is upon baptism as a watershed moment in which transformation is enacted.

18. Such transference was not possible in the RESURRECTION gestalt by itself. This further underscores the porous (rather than oppositional) nature of soteriology in Paul's thought. There is a dualism present here, though it is a dualism premised on permeability.

19. With regard to other baptismal texts, in Gal 3:27 Paul explicitly links the rite to the activity of being "clothed" with Christ. We have already seen that the clothing metaphor has resurrection overtones, which suggests the imparting of risen existence at baptism. More enigmatic is the Corinthians' practice of baptism on behalf of the dead, to which Paul makes a passing reference as a rationale for why the dead are in fact raised (1 Cor 15:29). Here the apostle may well presume the efficacy of the EMERGENCE FROM WATER IS LIFE metaphor (albeit extended beyond the baptizands themselves).

structures that constitute the myth. Ritual exists as a kind of metaphorical gesture (or, gesture of metaphor) in which abstract ideals are transmitted and obtained in the concrete reality of the adept. The rite serves as a communicative act enabled by and fashioned upon the mutuality of shared human experiences. It is not so much that ritual embodies myth or that myth embodies ritual but rather that both myth and ritual become communicative mediums through which concepts and ideas are expressed.[20] This is similar to Gregory Nagy's (2002, 243) notion of myth-performance: "myth itself is a form of ritual: rather than thinking of myth and ritual separately and only contrastively, we can see them as a continuum in which myth is a verbal aspect of ritual while ritual is a nonverbal aspect of myth."

For Paul, soteriology is ritually embodied. Baptismal death is not so much a conceptual as a performative issue. The somatic actions of the baptizand do not merely represent the transference from death to life; they actually constitute it.[21] This becomes clear when we recognize that, were we to remove the somatic actions of I_2 from the network, the entire blend would fall apart and the emergent structure of the blended space would vanish. For this reason, propositional descriptions that speak of baptism simply as a literary metaphor fail to capture the performative underpinnings of Paul's address.[22] Further in this vein, while transference is somatically enacted in the ritual, transformation is somatically

---

20. This is not to suggest that myth and ritual need always coalesce, nor that they always are mutually dependent and/or supportive. A century of ritual studies has rightly discredited the notion that myth is merely the text of ritual and ritual the enactment of myth. Nonetheless, R. Segal (2006–2007, 1:120) is right to note that, in many cases, myth and ritual do work tightly together in such a way that "myth ... becomes part of the ritual itself."

21. Though my argument here may seem banal to some, the implications of this analysis are far reaching. In important respects, standard scholarly treatments of Rom 6:1–11 reflect the deep rupture between language and experience that was outlined in ch. 1 (§§1.2 and 1.3.3). By providing a more robust understanding of how language and performance mutually interlace one another, Paul's address in Rom 6 becomes more intelligible when the performative aspects of the baptismal rite are incorporated into the linguistic and conceptual meaning-making procedures of the readers/hearers. Accordingly, the logic of Paul's address both presumes and necessitates this kind of embodied congruence between language and experience.

22. See, e.g., Tannehill (1967, 42–43), "baptism refer[s] to the *significance* of Christ's death"; and Wedderburn (1987, 358), baptism "remind[s]" believers of Christ's death/resurrection. To these we can also compare Dunn (1999, 310), who, in viewing the baptismal metaphor as a literary device, opposes metaphor and sacrament (or

enacted in believers' postbaptismal lives. Thus Paul's insistence that, just as Christ was raised, so believers "walk in newness of life" (ἐν καινότητι ζωῆς περιπατήσωμεν, 6:4). The image is that of an upright, erect human being "walking" about. Paul here extends the logic of the RESURRECTION/ LIFE IS CONSCIOUSNESS metaphor to frame postbaptismal (= postmortem) existence. Herein lies the ethical rationale that was presumed in 6:2: death with Christ entails conscious, risen life with Christ, thus enabling one to walk in new life and to live in self-mastery (this point will be elaborated in greater detail below).[23] It is for this reason that Wedderburn's (1987, 232) characterization of Rom 6:4 as "asymmetrical" is erroneous.[24] Paul may be foregrounding the experience of death with Christ, but the entire resurrection equation is in mind.

It cannot be overlooked, however, that although Paul's description of baptism in 6:4 entails a present conjoined resurrection with Christ, the apostle nevertheless retains a strong degree of eschatological reserve. This is expressly clear in 6:5 and 8, where the apostle uses the future tense to denote resurrection as a still unfulfilled expectation.[25] We here push up

---

language and experience): "metaphor belongs more with a theology of the sacramental universe than with the theology of particular sacraments."

23. Thus Paul insists that believers are no longer enslaved to sin (6:6) and should present themselves to God as those who are "living from the dead" (ἐκ νεκρῶν ζῶντας, 6:13).

24. At issue here is the logic by which Wedderburn arrives at his conclusion. Wedderburn insists, for example, that though Christ's death could be shared now, it was the literal and physical nature of resurrection that precluded a similar participation in the present (1987, 395; cf. 160–232). Given this insistence on literal resurrection, it is not readily apparent why a literal understanding of death and burial should not also be understood. Indeed, was not Christ's death a literal, physical event too (to extend Wedderburn's reasoning)? On this logic, then, why should participation be extended to the one but not the other? Surely the apostle is interested in both, for even though Paul is cautious to place believers' resurrection in the future (Rom 6:5), the baptismal analogy is drawn according to both Christ's death and resurrection (6:4), and Paul later instructs believers to present themselves as "those who are living from the dead" (ἐκ νεκρῶν ζῶντας, 6:13). While Wedderburn suggests that believers presently participate in a kind of "true 'life'" (294) that is different from resurrection, such an assertion seems artificial in that it obscures the logic of the baptismal metaphor.

25. We should not miss Paul's terminological shift in 6:4–5, where he moves from speaking of the present (ἐν καινότητι ζωῆς περιπατήσωμεν) to the future (σύμφυτοι … τῆς ἀναστάσεως ἐσόμεθα), thereby relegating the terminology of ἀνάστασις to the future. In this chapter and the next, I hope to substantiate the claim that any differen-

against the already/not-yet nature of Paul's thought, and how we account for this nuance is crucial. Rather than retreating to the dubious distinction between a future literal and present metaphorical resurrection or to the tendency among modern scholars to stress baptismal death at the expense of baptismal life,[26] we must chart a course that takes seriously the soteriological embodiment just outlined. Put differently, Paul's language is pregnant with some kind of present resurrection. The task at hand is to delineate more clearly not only what this present dimension is, but also to show how it relates to the ἀνάστασις that Paul reserves for the future. It is to the former issue that I now turn with respect to Rom 7. I will examine the latter with respect to Rom 8:9–11 in §4.3.

4.2. Anthropology and Ethics in Romans 7

It is perhaps significant that Paul's description of the "old person" who died in baptism (6:6) is *not* correlated with a parallel reference to a "new person" who now lives. Paul does, however, speak of the "inner person" (τὸν ἔσω ἄνθρωπον) who delights in the law of God (7:22); and while Paul is speaking here not as a Christ-devotee but rather as a rhetorical "I"-under-the-law, he elsewhere uses the same expression with respect to those in Christ (see 2 Cor 4:16).[27] Indeed, throughout Rom 6–8 Paul locates the locus of the believer's present transformation as being in the somatic interior. Believers have become obedient "from the heart" (ἐκ καρδίας, 6:17) and are to prevent sin from reigning "*in* [their] mortal bodies" (ἐν τῷ θνητῷ

---

tiation between present ζωή and future ἀνάστασις ultimately reflects Paul's larger vision of resurrection as an ongoing process that is happening to the human σῶμα. This is underscored in Rom 6 by the fact that, though Paul uses the language of "life" in the temporal present (e.g., ζωή, συζάω, ζάω in 6:4, 8, 11, 13), such language shares many conceptual and schematic correlations with ἀνάστασις (as demonstrated in §2.1.1). Both ζωή and ἀνάστασις belong within the same semantic field, as there is nothing in Paul's use of "life" terms vis-à-vis ἀνάστασις that implies categorical difference (indeed, in 6:10 Paul uses the language of *living* to describe the risen Christ). Accordingly, Paul's placement of ἀνάστασις in the future should not be seen as an absolute relegation of resurrection to the eschaton but rather as a teleological reservation regarding the transformative development of those who are in Christ.

26. So Wedderburn (1987) and other commentators, noted in ch. 1 (§1.3.3).

27. For the history of the phrase ὁ ἔσω ἄνθρωπος, which is Greek in origin and has specific Platonic nuances, see Burkert 1998 and Betz 2000.

ὑμῶν σώματι, 6:12).²⁸ While the exterior μέλη can be directed to opposing ethical practices, it is the renovation—better, *resurrection*—of the somatic interior that enables the μέλη to serve God rather than sin (6:18-19). In this regard, though Paul contrasts ethical states via opposing container descriptions (i.e., either being "in sin" or "in new life" [6:1-4]), his rationale for doing so is directed toward the somatic interior.

I have already introduced the BODY IS CONTAINER metaphor (see §3.2.3), which emerges organically from embodied human experiences. Though strong emphasis has been placed on the universality and shared experiential grounding of this conceptual metaphor, cultures differ from one another in their appropriation and elaboration of the metaphor's schematic elements.²⁹ With respect to the ancient Mediterranean and Near East, Walter Burkert (1998, 63-69) has demonstrated that both Greek and Semitic traditions preserved in the Homeric hymns and the Akkadian language (respectively) understand phenomena such as thought and emotions as being correlated with organs such as the heart, liver, bowels, and even the diaphragm. At these more ancient stages, such descriptions do not represent a strong bifurcation of the human being, though they do attribute to the organs those activities that are later given to the soul.³⁰ In Greek tradition, it is only in the Hellenistic period that this inner referent becomes abstracted and the soul becomes an independent entity.³¹ Personhood (or consciousness) is no longer correlated to the organs but instead stands on its own, still located within the body though variously thought to be composed of πνεῦμα, fire, αἰθήρ, or some other substance

---

28. The use of μέλος in 6:12-13, 19 suggests τῷ θνητῷ ... σώματι is understood best as the visible, outer body.

29. See, e.g., Charles Taylor (1989, esp. 111-207), who traces various notions of inwardness and the development of the self in the Western tradition. Of particular note is Taylor's recognition, albeit in passing, that in-out somatic mappings have a certain universal recognition across human cultures (112). By drawing on cognitive linguistics and rooting transcultural meaning foundations in the body, I have in the present study sought to do justice to what Taylor identifies as the "really difficult [task of] distinguishing human universals from ... historical constellations."

30. Thus Burkert (1998, 69) notes, speaking of the Homeric and lyric poets, "there is no separation of corporeal organs and activities of the soul."

31. As a complement to Burkert (1998), Taylor (1989, 118-20) maps this development as a transition from the fragments of the self in Homer to Plato's more unified and articulated soul.

(or a mixture thereof).³² A little later, though the Hellenistic philosophical traditions differ on the precise description of the soul, all locate it within the body and further understand it as the center of human intelligence.³³ In contrast, classical Hebraic culture continues to locate the epicenter of personhood/consciousness with the "heart" (לב or לבב) or the נפש,³⁴ thus retaining stronger correlations between the physical organ and the self.³⁵ In both traditions, however, the locus of personhood/consciousness is correlated with the somatic interior (the soul or some physical organ) vis-à-vis the visible exterior (the body or some body part).³⁶ These trends indicate that both Greek and Semitic traditions have a proclivity toward weak folk dualism (see §1.3.2 above), which is premised on the very basic BODY IS CONTAINER metaphor.³⁷ Even though some Greek traditions eventually lean in stronger dualistic directions, certain capacities (in this case, personhood or consciousness) tend to cluster together and gravitate toward certain poles (in this case, somatic interior vis-à-vis the visible exterior).

---

32. Burkert 1998, 70–71; see also Martin 1995, 115–20.

33. See Aune (1995, 294–95), who differentiates various philosophical traditions from one another and then offers a synthesis of seven commonly held views regarding the soul.

34. The noun נפש (the verb means "to inhale, breathe" [*HALOT* 2:711]) refers variously to many things that are somatically inward (e.g., "throat, breath" [*HALOT* 2:711–13]; in Lev 17:11 נפש is specifically located in the blood). Moreover, נפש is understood as something that leaves the body at death and comes back at life (e.g., Gen 35:18), and it seems at times to convey the idea of the human being him- or herself (hence the translation "person, personality, life" [*HALOT* 2:712–13; BDB 659–60]).

35. Though he only indirectly explores the scriptural backgrounds (Jewett 1971, 305–33 and 447–48).

36. This is not to say that ancient thinkers understood human consciousness as a unified singularity that was neatly mapped to the somatic interior. We have already seen (§3.1.3) that Philo (and Plato before him) distinguished not simply between body (OUT) and soul (IN), but rather between the irrational and rational parts of the soul, which both are internal (IN) and align with either the body (OUT) or the divine/reason (UP), respectively. Accordingly, human consciousness or personhood is partitively constructed and includes differentiated components that connect to differing external referents.

37. To further my discussions in chs. 1 and 3 (§§1.3.2 and 3.2.3), the BODY IS CONTAINER metaphor contributes conceptual structure necessary for intuiting notions of mind-body distinction. These notions are certainly not uniform, and they need not be consistent across cultures, though the basic IN-OUT structure of the BODY IS CONTAINER metaphor functions as one of the central axes along which dualistic notions develop.

4. ESCHATOLOGICAL SOMATOLOGY

One of the most explicit Pauline descriptions of this in-out somatic interplay is found in Rom 7:14–25. Here Paul repeatedly refers to sin as dwelling "in him" (ἐν ἐμοί, 7:17, 18, 20, 23; see also 7:8), as well as to the tensive relationship between exterior and interior.³⁸ The distinction is made explicit in 7:22–24, where Paul characterizes a futile intrasomatic battle (ἀντιστρατευόμενον) between the "inner person/mind" (τὸν ἔσω ἄνθρωπον/τοῦ νοός μου [IN]) and the "body parts/body of death" (τοῖς μέλεσίν μου/τοῦ σώματος τοῦ θανάτου [OUT]). The logic of the passage is premised on an interconnection of the somatic interior and exterior, where IN affects OUT and vice versa—if sin is inner, Paul is helpless to do the good that he wants because the sin-ruled somatic exterior precludes him from such action (7:20).³⁹

The rhetorical sketch that Paul draws in Rom 7:14–25 (really vv. 7–25) is particularly important in that it points to a teleological trajectory of somatic transformation, one that extends from the prebaptizand through the baptismal rite and looks ahead to the ideal risen form. I take it as axiomatic that Paul is speaking in 7:7–25 not of his own experiences of uninhibited moral abasement—either past or present—but rather draws a rhetorical caricature of torah observance portrayed from the perspective of his (Paul's) present life in Christ.⁴⁰ This is not to say that the experience described is completely unrelated or detached from Paul's (or believers') present ethical situation(s). Indeed, the apostle speaks as a rhetorical "I"

---

38. From the perspective of the rhetorical "I," the exterior is only described negatively (σάρξ, 7:18 [see also 7:14]; various kinds of "actions," 7:15–17, 19–20), while the interior is described both positively (ἔσω ἄνθρωπον, 7:22; the speaker's θέλω, 7:18; νοῦς, 7:23) and negatively (ἁμαρτία, 7:17, 18, 20, 23). In terms of Paul's anthropology, this passage is not easily systematized and instead betrays the apostle's transformational ideals. When taken as a whole, in Rom 6–8 Paul locates the body within a trajectory of transformation (as outlined in this chapter, §§4.3–4), the individual stages of which contain somatic compositions that conflict or contradict one another.

39. See further 7:25, where νοῦς (IN) and σάρξ (OUT) are explicitly contrasted and correlated with the "law of God" and the "law of sin," respectively.

40. On this, Engberg-Pedersen (2000, 243) seems correct when he says: "*viewed in light of that (new) possibility* [namely, life *in Christ*], life under the law *should* be experienced as being inescapably entangled in sinfulness in the way he explains in 7:7–25" (emphasis original). The closest historical parallel to such an address is the Greek literary technique προσωποποιία (or "speech-in-character"; see Stowers 1995). The precise identity of this rhetorical "I" is a matter of much dispute (see Jewett 2007, 441–45).

under the law so as to demonstrate the efficacious moral potential of present life in Christ (hence 8:1–30). In this way, 7:7–25 presumes traditions of ancient moral psychology and self-mastery,[41] and Paul's understanding of resurrection is thus elaborated within such frame-structures.[42]

Working in this vein, Wasserman (2007, 2008) has compellingly argued that 7:7–25 reflects an anthropological mapping that exploits the so-called worst-case scenario of extreme immorality as envisioned in Platonic moral psychology. In this tradition, the soul's irrational faculty rebels against and rules over its rational faculty, thus resulting in the passion-ruled self.[43] In 7:7–25, Paul draws on these traditions, envisioning the soul as split between its rational bit (νοῦς or ὁ ἔσω ἄνθρωπος, 7:22–25) and irrational bit (ἁμαρτία, 7:20).[44] By describing what happens when the lower soul subjects the higher, Paul thus contrasts a past state of unmitigated immorality with the efficacious moral aptitude enabled in Christ. Present life in Christ is characterized by the need to mediate continually this intra-soul tension (see 6:12–14) and thus 7:7–25 has both a rhetorical function in describing an imagined past ineptitude and an exhortative function in describing an attainable present potential.

---

41. In addition to Engberg-Pedersen (2000) and Stowers (1995, 2003), see more recently Wasserman (2007).

42. It cannot be overlooked that the immediate epistolary context of Rom 7 is concerned with torah observance vis-à-vis unmitigated sin. In this regard, after demonstrating that patterns of self-mastery were promoted variously across Hellenistic philosophical schools, Stowers (2003, 531–34) points specifically to Jewish traditions wherein the Mosaic law was understood as a tool by which self-mastery was achieved. In this light, self-mastery seems the best historical and contextual analogue for Paul's address in 7:7–25.

43. Wasserman (2007, 2008) finds comparative analogues in Plato (esp. *Resp.* 9.571–577), Philo (*Leg.* 1.105–108; *Deus.* 111–113), Plutarch (*Virt. vit.* 101A), and Galen (*On the Diagnosis and Cure of the Soul's Passions*). While the earlier Platonic material demarcates a trichotomous soul (i.e., the reasoning, spirited, and appetitive parts), many Middle Platonic authors conflate the irrational faculties into a single lower soul that is distinct from the higher reasoning faculty (Wasserman 2007, 809). Paul seems to stand most comfortably within this latter tradition.

44. As the personification of the irrational soul, ἁμαρτία is described as living in the speaker (7:20) in as much as ἁμαρτία is part of the anthropological composition. On this point, Wasserman has compellingly argued that sin is neither a helpless state to which unregenerate humanity is predisposed (so Bultmann) nor an external cosmic power (i.e., Sin) that governs the individual prior to their coming under the lordship of Christ (so Käsemann).

4. ESCHATOLOGICAL SOMATOLOGY   151

That Paul does not use the term ψυχή in Rom 7 should not deter us from this reading. The anthropological division of body and soul was quite widespread by the early imperial period (see Martin 1995, 112–17). Kooten (2008, 298) finds in Paul a notion of the soul that is, "despite some distinctively Jewish features,... basically Greek."[45] The strength of Wasserman's reading is her recognition that, though Plato and others do at times pit body against soul, such an antithesis cannot and should not be understood as a summary of Plato's thinking. Wasserman (2008, 58) rightly notes that the opposition of body and soul at death neither implies nor requires a similar opposition during life. Indeed, during life "the goal is not to destroy or be rid of the body but to use reason to subdue and dominate the lower parts of the soul and its menacing allies" (Wasserman 2013, 264). When approaching Paul's anthropology from the perspective of self-mastery, it is far better to stress notions of the present embodied soul rather than future body-soul opposition. This coheres with my findings in chapter 3, where Paul was seen to work within a one-world model characterized by dualistic interrelation. Anthropologically speaking, this can be expressed as an intrasomatic polarity of parts within a system.

The apostle's most pointed description of the passion-ruled state in Rom 7 is via the death metaphor (7:9–13). Though death metaphors are not often used of the soul in Platonic discourses,[46] Wasserman points to an important parallel in Philo where the souls of Adam and Eve are described as dying in the lapsarian event.[47] Following this Philonic context, Wasserman (2007, 811) understands life and death as "moral-psychological metaphors for dominance," and thus Paul uses the death metaphor to characterize the soul's ineptitude. From the present study's perspective, however, the use of the DEATH frame necessarily imports a conceptual structure that differs from that imparted by the metaphors of dominion, slavery, and war that otherwise characterize Rom 6–7 (esp. 6:14–23; 7:23). Though correlations exist, the metaphors are certainly not the same.

---

45. For a general discussion, see Kooten (2008, 298–302), who demonstrates that even those Pauline uses of ψυχή that are usually labeled as Septuagintal find parallel in broader Greek usage.

46. Likely due to the soul's immortality (Wasserman 2007, 808).

47. Philo also uses the death metaphor for moral inability: "the death of the soul is the decay of virtue and the acquirement of wickedness." It is a "peculiar and special death, which is the entombing of the soul in passions and every kind of wickedness" (*Leg.* 1.105–107).

Indeed, for Paul death is not a terminal but rather a transformative event, which is to say that the death metaphor of 7:9–13 is understood best in the context of the apostle's broader description of baptismal death/resurrection in 6:1–11. Paul is describing not only intrasoul subjection (Rom 7) but also articulating a more fundamental transformation (as seen in the argumentative thrust of Rom 6–8). His concern in Rom 7 is not the articulation of life-under-the-law for its own sake, but rather the articulation of how baptismal death brings the morally inept back to life. The rhetorical soul of Rom 7 is set right not just in terms of hierarchical domination; it actually transitions from death to life through the process of baptismal death/resurrection (Rom 6) and the reception of divine πνεῦμα so as to enable self-mastery (Rom 8).[48] In this way, Paul's use of self-mastery traditions are incorporated into his resurrection ideals, thus locating present baptismal resurrection in the somatic interior. For Paul, Christ-devotees are dead to sin (i.e., no longer dominated by the soul's irrational bits [6:2, 7, 11]) and able to live morally by virtue of the pneumatically informed risen interior.

This is not to say that self-mastery and resurrection are the same. They are not. It is to say, however, that Paul integrates moral psychology traditions into his broader resurrection ideals as a way of characterizing the resurrection effected in baptism. Looked at from another angle, baptismal resurrection is the efficacious process by which self-mastery becomes possible. So Gerd Theissen (2007, 89):

> Paul leaves no doubt: the redeemed has overcome the fleshly (sarkic) essence [*Wesen*].... The overcoming has taken place through the "killing" of the sarkic affects, through the crucifixion of the flesh together with its passions and desires (Gal 5:24). The idea of an eradication of passions is familiar in antiquity.[49]

---

48. Romans 6:1–11 describes a process of death, while 7:9–13 presumes the state of being dead. Though this difference is important, it is not detrimental to my reading. Indeed, as noted in §2.2.3 above, Paul conceives of Christ as imparting Definitive Life vis-à-vis Adam's Definitive Death, and the process of such transformation is resurrection.

49. My translation. German original: "Paulus lässt nämlich keinen Zweifel daran: Der Erlöste hat das fleischliche (*sarkische*) Wesen überwunden.... Die Überwindung geschah durch 'Tötung' der sarkischen Affekte, durch Kreuzigung des Fleisches samt seinen Leidenschaften und Begierden (Gal 5,24). Die Vorstellung von einer Ausrottung der Leidenschaften ist der Antike vertraut."

Importantly, Paul works this out with respect to πνεῦμα. For Paul, just as the future resurrection is characterized by an organic interlacing of believers into Christ's body (Rom 8:29; Phil 3:21), so too human and divine πνεῦμα interlace each other in the present. While Paul does speak of human πνεῦμα (1 Thess 5:23) and even contrasts it with divine πνεῦμα (e.g., Rom 8:16; 1 Cor 2:11), in many instances it is not easy to distinguish the two from one another (e.g., Rom 8:4–6, 10).[50] Though perhaps we do not need to. Paul likely has in mind the idea of Christ-devotees being informed both by human πνεῦμα and divine πνεῦμα, which is to recognize that the former's ethical aptitude is enabled through the granting of the latter. To this end, the imparting of divine πνεῦμα results in the coming-back-to-life— the resurrection—of human πνεῦμα.[51] The two are interwoven together, and this highlights the participationist nature of Paul's resurrection ideals (both future and present).

As a cosmo-somatic category, πνεῦμα is correlated with both the heavens (UP) and the soul (IN).[52] Similarly, as a divine substance, πνεῦμα is correlated with both the risen/exalted Christ (UP) and the indwelling Christ (IN).[53] These tight pneumatic correlations between UP and IN thus enable Paul to project his resurrection ideals onto the present. That is, space and time are coordinated such that πνεῦμα links both future (UP) and present

---

50. So noted by Dunn 1998b, 75–76.

51. Though expressed differently, this is in line with Kooten's (2008, 382–83) insistence that "through Jesus Christ ... man's mind once again becomes fully operative." Kooten argues for a trichotomous anthropology throughout Paul's letters, and in Romans he sees Paul developing a universalist anthropology whereby Christ enables the renewal of the debased mind (340–92). Kooten understands this renewal as a restoration back to the original Adamic state. While this may indeed be the case in Romans (see esp. Rom 1:18–32), we have seen above that such a thesis cannot be extended to the Corinthian correspondence (§§2.2.4 and 3.2.2).

52. Recall Philo, where the soul's higher rational faculty is correlated with the divine breath (*Her.* 55; see also *Opif.* 135). Martin (1995, 120) has also noted the generally accepted idea that "whatever substance comprises the stars ... also comprises the soul." In this way, we see a correlation of somatic interior (IN) with the cosmological apex (UP).

53. For Paul, the risen/exalted Christ (UP; see Rom 8:34) is also the indwelling pneumatic presence (IN; see Rom 8:9–11). Paul describes the risen Christ as πνεῦμα (e.g., 1 Cor 15:45; 2 Cor 3:17–18; Rom 1:4) and also uses πνεῦμα synonymously with "Christ" (e.g., Rom 8:1, 9–11). Paul also ascribes similar roles to the two (compare Rom 8:26–27 with 8:34) and elsewhere refers to both Christ and the divine πνεῦμα as the "firstfruits" of the resurrection (compare 1 Cor 15:20, 23 and Rom 8:23).

(IN) resurrections. It is in this sense that the indwelling πνεῦμα functions as the deposit (2 Cor 1:22; 5:5) of that which is to come, a guarantee that is located within the believer's body (2 Cor 1:22; 3:17–4:6; see also Gal 4:6). Given that this interior transformation results in exterior moral actions, it is not surprising that Paul describes such activities pneumatically, for example, living according to πνεῦμα (Rom 8:4–17; Gal 5:16–26) and the bearing of pneumatic fruits (Gal 5:22–23). Moreover, Paul locates divine/human fellowship (NEAR) as a present pneumatic experience within the believer (Rom 8:16). With respect to Paul's broader resurrection ideals, time is curtailed that what is traditionally understood as FUTURE/UP/NEAR is now understood as PRESENT/IN/NEAR.

As we can see, then, Paul's resurrection ideals are tightly interwoven with his anthropological understanding. In the wake of baptism, the granting of divine πνεῦμα into believers' bodies (Rom 5:5; 8:15) thus properly orders the somatic interior and enables moral behavior; or, as Paul puts it in Rom 8:5–6, it enables the possession of a "spiritual mind" (φρόνημα τοῦ πνεύματος) and thus to live "according to spirit" (κατὰ πνεῦμα). Just as eschatological resurrection produces a somatic transformation, so too does baptismal resurrection. The former is external, the latter internal.[54] This, in turn, gives rise to a novel resurrection metaphor: RESURRECTION IS IN. In Rom 6–8, Paul frames this metaphor via the cultural notion of SELF-MASTERY, which is itself premised on the BODY IS CONTAINER metaphor. Here the lower faculties (DOWN) implicate the body/flesh (OUT) vis-à-vis the higher faculty of reason (UP/IN). What we see, then, is a schematic correlation of DOWN/OUT and UP/IN, which enables Paul both to combine and fluidly move between the metaphors RESURRECTION IS IN and RESURRECTION IS UP. Moreover, the SELF-MASTERY frame enables this inner resurrection to find external expression in ethical praxis and thus further clarifies Paul's use of the RESURRECTION IS CONSCIOUSNESS metaphor in Rom 6:4. Taken together, Paul's resurrection ideals are projected onto the human constitution itself, and baptismal death is understood to enact a transformation of the somatic interior.

---

54. So Kooten (2008, 381): the baptismal "break with the past … has radically changed [the believer's] anthropological constitution." Taken in another direction, Engberg-Pedersen's emphasis on the material nature of πνεῦμα further underscores this somatic alteration. Thus Engberg-Pedersen (2010, 71) insists that the reception of πνεῦμα was a "physical, literal take over (if only an incipient one) brought about by a literal infusion of physical *pneuma* coming from above."

In summary, Paul sets out a vision of the baptized Christ-devotee as one who already is resurrected internally, but who still awaits resurrection of the somatic exterior. In this way, Rom 6–7 points to what was also identified in 1 Cor 15, namely, Paul's understanding of believers presently existing as enspirited earthly bodies (vis-à-vis the rhetorical "I's" ensouled earthly body [7:7–25]). For Paul, the human form is partitively drawn, not via an opposition of body and soul but rather an intrasomatic polarity of in and out. Within the context of self-mastery traditions, to say that resurrection has happened to the somatic interior is to insist that the properly aligned interior enables exterior ethical actions (understood by Paul via the RESURRECTION IS CONSCIOUSNESS metaphor). Turning our attention now to Rom 8, we will see that this intrasomatic polarity characterizes present life in Christ and also anticipates the idyllic eschatological form (i.e., the enspirited risen body).

4.3. Trajectories of Transformative Embodiment in Romans 8:9–11

To say that believers exist as enspirited earthly bodies is to locate human existence within a trajectory of transformative embodiment. For Paul, the baptizand's body is somatically altered through the granting of divine πνεῦμα, thus enabling ethical action in the present and anticipating the transformation of the somatic exterior in the future. Such is the direction in which Paul moves in Rom 8, where the apostle now outlines the pneumatic nature of present life in Christ. As I will show in the following discussion, the present baptismal resurrection is not a separate resurrection event (as though Paul were speaking of two resurrections—one present, the other future), nor is it a temporally curtailed resurrection (as though the future event is brought back into the present), but rather an initial first part of the anticipated eschatological resurrection. That is, the baptismal resurrection of the human πνεῦμα connects to the future resurrection of the human σῶμα such that both are interconnected aspects of a single resurrection event.[55]

To better understand this temporal trajectory between somatic states, it is important first to recognize that Paul perceives intrasomatic polarity as the hallmark of embodied earthly existence. This is true for both the

---

55. A similar argument has recently been articulated by Engberg-Pedersen (2009), who offers a more philosophically descriptive account that largely coheres with the cognitive linguistic reading advanced in this study.

rhetorical "I" (the ensouled earthly body) and Christ-devotees generally (enspirited earthly bodies). I have already demonstrated the former, where the "inner person/mind" (IN) and the "body parts/body of death" (OUT) exist within a futile combative tension.[56] The latter is evinced throughout Rom 6–8 more broadly, where Paul instructs the Romans to continually subject their lower soul/body (DOWN/OUT) to the higher soul (UP/IN).[57] In Rom 8:5-17, believers either set their minds on πνεῦμα (correlated with life [UP/IN]) or on σάρξ (correlated with death [DOWN/OUT]).[58] Though the baptismal resurrection of the human πνεῦμα enables self-mastery through the transformation of the somatic interior, the same intrasomatic dynamic remains because believers exist as earthly bodies. As such, intrasomatic polarity underscores earthly embodiment. This demonstrates the extent to which Paul's anthropology in Rom 6–8 is characterized not by neat partitions of in and out, nor by intrasoul division, but rather by conjoined parts within a whole. The human subject is a unified polarity of parts.[59]

---

56. Though Wasserman (2007; 2008) correctly locates the struggle of Rom 7:7-25 as an intrasoul struggle (i.e., between the higher and lower faculties), it is perhaps more accurate to say that Paul generally envisions an *intrasomatic* struggle. The apostle views the soul's lower faculties as so intertwined with the body that it becomes impossible to distinguish the two. This is seen in the rhetorical "I's" insistence that immorality exists "in my flesh" (ἐν τῇ σαρκί μου, 7:18) and his later yearning to be free from the "body of death" (τοῦ σώματος τοῦ θανάτου, 7:24). In both instances, the soul's lower faculty (ἁμαρτία [DOWN]) is conflated with the somatic exterior (σάρξ/σῶμα [OUT]).

57. See, e.g., Rom 6:12-14, 19; 7:5-6; and 8:5-13.

58. Accordingly, believers must continually orient the somatic interior (i.e., the "mind" [φρόνημα, 8:6-7] or the πνεῦμα [8:13, 16]) not toward the earthly exterior (i.e., the σάρξ or "deeds of the body" [τὰς πράξεις τοῦ σώματος, 8:13]) but rather toward the divine πνεῦμα (8:9-11).

59. Given the centrality of the somatic interior for the argument advanced in this study, it is imperative to demarcate clearly how the boundaries of IN-OUT are to be viewed as useful conceptual schemata for reading Paul. I have already noted the importance of recognizing the multifarious nature of that which is IN (see §3.1.3, and n. 36 above); accordingly, rather than looking for 1:1 binaries, one must recognize the flexibility of the schematic typology. To this one can also add that in-out are not systematized for Paul, and thus the apostle is able to alternate his terminology both for the somatic interior (πνεῦμα, νοῦς, καρδία, etc.) and exterior (σῶμα, σάρξ, μέλος, etc.) with much variety. Indeed, Paul's anthropological terminology is quite various and contextually determined (Jewett 1971). In an equally important respect, however, it is helpful to locate Paul in relation to other ancient thinkers regarding the partitioning of the body. I follow Charles Taylor's (1989, 127-42) caution against placing too much

Though polarity characterizes earthly embodiment, Paul's resurrection ideals anticipate a future suspension of such polarity, namely, the anticipated enspirited risen body. We have already seen this in 1 Cor 15, where the σῶμα πνευματικόν is best understood as a body perfectly suited for the indwelling πνεῦμα, thus marking the cessation of such intrasomatic tension. In a similar manner, Paul insists that believers currently "groan" (στενάζω) inwardly in the earthly body, looking ahead with anticipation for the swallowing of the mortal by the immortal (2 Cor 5:2, 4; see also Rom 8:22–23). The already risen interior thus awaits the achievement of the not yet risen exterior, and in this way the enspirited earthly body has a decidedly future orientation. This can be demonstrated nicely by examining Rom 8:9–11, where Paul locates present human embodiment within his larger resurrection outlook. The passage reads as follows:

> But you are not in flesh [ἐν σαρκί] but in spirit [ἐν πνεύματι], just as the Spirit of God dwells in you [οἰκεῖ ἐν ὑμῖν]. But if anyone does not have the Spirit of Christ, they are not his. But if Christ is in you [Χριστὸς ἐν ὑμῖν], though the body is dead because of sin, the spirit is life because of

---

emphasis on the somatic interior, as this is unhelpful and anachronistic when reading writers prior to Augustine. Indeed, it was Augustine who made the somatic interior the independent or self-contained seat of selfhood. By contrast, Taylor notes that when reading Plato's notion of self-mastery, in-out formulations can be misleading. For Plato, the moral sources to which one accedes are not within but rather outside of the subject. Plato puts forth a vision of the larger order of Reason into which subjects connect up (123). Paul too has an element of connecting up into a larger order of being (namely, πνεῦμα/Christ), just as he also has an element of stressing the somatic interior vis-à-vis the exterior. That being said, the apostle's focus in both instances evinces a greater degree of somatic embeddedness than either Plato or Augustine. This is particularly evident in the emphasis Paul places on somatic transformation: so Theissen (2007, 83), "The point of emphasis for Paul is not the opposition between inside and outside, but the transition from the old human being to the new human being" (my translation; German original: "Die Pointe bei Paulus ist aber nicht der Gegensatz zwischen Innen und Außen, sondern der Übergang vom alten zum neuen Menschen"). Accordingly, Paul lies somewhere between Plato and Augustine (not just temporally, but conceptually too). He locates the center of right living neither in something external to the human being (so Plato) nor in something internal to the human being (so Augustine) but rather advances a vision of the internal and external as mutually interlacing. All of this points in the same direction as the conclusion of the previous chapter: intrasomatic polarity. Again, polarity functions as the key concept in Paul's vision of resurrection, and the body becomes the primary location in which this polarity is worked out.

righteousness. But if the Spirit of the one who raised Jesus from the dead dwells in you [οἰκεῖ ἐν ὑμῖν], the one who raised Christ from the dead will make alive your mortal bodies through his Spirit that dwells in you [ἐν ὑμῖν].

As with a number of the passages examined above, Paul again contrasts two opposing container states. On account of the indwelling πνεῦμα, believers are no longer ἐν σαρκὶ but rather ἐν πνεύματι (8:9; = ἐν Χριστῷ, 8:1). Standard scholarly treatments of these opposing containers have largely followed Ernst Käsemann's (1971c; 1980) notion of apocalyptic anthropology, where human beings exist as passive participants within one of two opposing aeons or "sphere[s] of subjection" (1980, 223).[60] The problem with this interpretation is that it is founded on an overdrawn dualism and, further, that it objectifies the so-called "spheres of influence" in a way that detaches them from the realm of human experience. As noted in chapter 1 (§1.3.3), this results in an exceedingly cognicentric view of life in Christ, one where believers participate in the conditions that Christ enables rather than in/with Christ himself.

A better and more promising step forward is to view Paul's descriptions in 8:9-11 as premised on his resurrection ideals, specifically with respect to alternative somatic states. This is preferable for three reasons. First, 8:11 points toward the future event of resurrection, thus contextualizing this passage within the RESURRECTION frame-structure.[61] Second, the use of σάρξ as a CONTAINER is congruent with Paul's broader somatic mappings,[62] and the corresponding use of πνεῦμα as a CONTAINER finds

---

60. More recent examples include Dunn (1988, 1:444): Paul insists a "decisive transfer of allegiance and lordship has already taken place"; Jewett (2007, 489): believers are "members of the realm of Christ"; and Matera (2010, 195): believers are "not in the realm of flesh but in the realm of the Spirit."

61. This is evident in Paul's choice of verbal tenses, which are aorist, imperfect, and present in 8:1-10 but shift in 8:11 to include the future. Of note, the language of 8:9-11 is not unlike that of 6:1-14 in that past, present, and future all interlace one another in ways that draw participatory analogues between Christ's and believers' resurrections. This suggests that the two passages speak similarly to Paul's vision of resurrection as a singular, transtemporal event that includes the present inner pneumatic resurrection that we have been exploring throughout this chapter.

62. In light of the BODY IS CONTAINER metaphor, σάρξ is the material structure of the container.

parallel resonance with Paul's understanding of the risen body.[63] Third, the description of the body in 8:10 and the language of the indwelling πνεῦμα/Christ suggests strongly a somatic interpretation. Taking these together, 8:9-11 contrasts not opposing aeons or apocalyptic spheres, but rather differing somatic states. Accordingly, the pericope has an inherent temporal dimension, bringing the ensouled earthly and enspirited risen bodies to bear on the enspirited earthly body.

The blending structure reflected here consists of two input spaces (see fig. 4.2). The first (I_1) is cued by Paul's container descriptions in 8:9a, though fully framed by the reference to resurrection in 8:11. This space is specifically marked by the transformation of the ensouled earthly body into the enspirited risen body. In an important respect, the two bodies are imaginative caricatures. The former is understood in light of Rom 7 as a σάρξ-ἁμαρτία unity (signified by σ and α, respectively),[64] while the latter is understood as a pneumatic unity (signified by π).[65] Both bodies function as values that are mapped onto the CONTAINER roles of the CHANGE gestalt. The second input (I_2) consists of the present, postbaptismal body

---

63. As noted in §3.2.2 above, Paul understands the σῶμα πνευματικόν of 1 Cor 15 to be an apocalyptic glory-body, something not unlike what the angels possess, or what an ascender to heaven is transformed into. Here in Rom 8:9 Paul is quite willing to use the language of πνεῦμα so as to articulate the container state into which one is transformed. This suggests that, while the σῶμα πνευματικόν need not be compositionally pneumatic (see §3.2.2, and esp. nn. 74 and 81 in ch. 3), it nevertheless is pneumatically oriented and configured. Of significant importance in the present passage is the description of being ἐν Χριστῷ (see 8:1 and 10), which may imply the Christic somatic state (as in 1 Cor 15:22, 45-49; see §§2.2.4 and 3.2.2) and thus suggests a degree of pneumatic existence (see 2 Cor 3:17). That is, like Christ, resurrected believers also will be pneumatic and characterized by a glory-body.

64. In this blending diagram, I follow Paul's anthropological mapping of the body as characterized by σάρξ-ἁμαρτία. Consistent with this chapter's discussion (§4.2), this body should be understood as a trichotomous σῶμα-ψυχή-νοῦς/πνεῦμα (where the πνεῦμα in question is human πνεῦμα).

65. The presence of the phrase ἐν πνεύματι in 8:9 indicates πνεῦμα is configured as the container itself. On account of the many references in Paul's writings to the indwelling πνεῦμα (Gal 5:16-26; 6:1; Rom 5:5; 8:15-17; 1 Cor 2:16; 6:19; 2 Cor 1:22; 3:3; 5:5), as well as the indication in the Corinthian correspondence that pneumosomatic resolution stands as the eschatological ideal (1 Cor 15:44; 2 Cor 5:5), I have also included πνεῦμα as that which is contained in the container. In this ways, though Paul in Rom 8 does not explicitly describe the risen body, the blended space is reasonably configured in terms of this IN-OUT pneumatic construction.

of the Christ-devotee. The space is cued in 8:9b–10, where Paul's description shifts from contrasting external referents to focus instead on the interior referent. Framed by the BODY IS CONTAINER metaphor, this space is characterized by the intrasomatic polarity of inner πνεῦμα (signified by π) and outer σάρξ (signified by σ).[66]

The two inputs are blended on account of the generic space (G), which includes the general metaphor BODY IS CONTAINER (including somatic interior and exterior), as well as the recognition of a transitional somatic state.[67] This transitional state is the focus of the blended space, where the TRAJECTOR of I_1 is cross-mapped with the baptized Christ-devotee of I_2. From I_1 the entire CHANGE gestalt is projected, while from I_2 the CONTAINER structure of the baptizand's body is projected onto the TRAJECTOR role-value.[68] In this way, the TRAJECTOR of I_1 is now identified as a transitional somatic existence that is partly drawn from the SOURCE-CONTAINER (σάρξ [OUT]) and partly from the GOAL-CONTAINER (πνεῦμα [IN]).[69] In the blended space, then, believers are placed within an overarching trajectory of transformation wherein part of the body has been already transformed (the interior), while other parts (the exterior) still await transformation.

Three aspects of this blended space are particularly noteworthy. First, we see that Paul understands the process of resurrection transformation not as a future reality but rather as one that is somatically enacted in the present. That is, Paul does not envision two resurrection events (one in baptism and one at the eschaton), nor does he stress either a present or a

---

66. As with I_1, this anthropological mapping should be understood as a trichotomous σῶμα-ψυχή-νοῦς/πνεῦμα, though in this instance the πνεῦμα in question is divine πνεῦμα (see n. 64 above).

67. By transitional state, I do not mean a postmortem intermediary state but rather a midway somatic existence that stands between the somatic states of the SOURCE and GOAL elements.

68. In fig. 4.2, I have signified the projection of structure by the two contoured arrows that extend from I_1 and I_2 to the blend space. The gray arrow from I_1 denotes the projection of the CHANGE gestalt, while the black arrow from I_2 denotes the projection of both the CONTAINER gestalt and the IN (πνεῦμα) and OUT (σάρξ) values associated with that gestalt. Because structure is projected from both inputs, the overall network is what Fauconnier and Turner (2002, 131–35 and 340–45) refer to as a double-scope blend.

69. Note the cross-space mapping, where the interior πνεῦμα of I_2 is linked to the interior πνεῦμα of the GOAL-CONTAINER in I_1, and the exterior σάρξ of I_2 is linked to the exterior σάρξ of the SOURCE-CONTAINER in I_1.

4. ESCHATOLOGICAL SOMATOLOGY

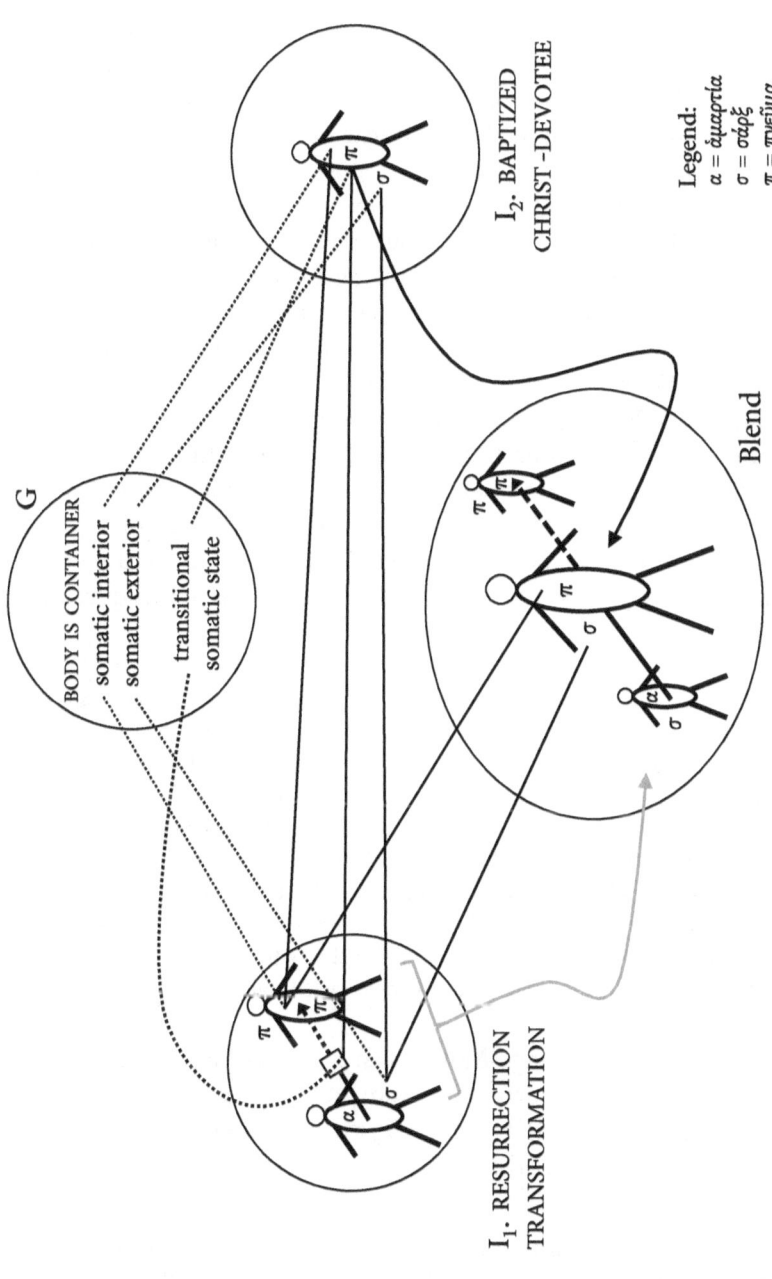

Figure 4.2. The Enspirited Earthly Body (Rom 8:9–11)

future resurrection in favor of the other. Instead, he envisions one ongoing process of transformation that spans past, present, and future. Rather than relegating the CHANGE gestalt to a future period, Paul instead locates it in the present and temporally scales it such that believers are currently in the midst of being transformed. This is the trajectory of transformative embodiment to which I alluded at the outset of this section.

Second, we can see with somewhat better clarity what continuity and discontinuity look like in Paul's resurrection ideals. Very little is continuous between the ensouled earthly body and enspirited risen body. In the caricature that Paul constructs of the σάρξ-ἁμαρτία subject, both the somatic exterior and interior are destroyed and replaced with their risen counterparts. When this caricature is viewed within the context of the trichotomous σῶμα-ψυχή-νοῦς/πνεῦμα subject (where νοῦς/πνεῦμα = ἔσω ἄνθρωπος), the νοῦς/πνεῦμα functions as the point of continuity, though only because the νοῦς/πνεῦμα has been brought to life through the granting of divine πνεῦμα in baptismal resurrection. In essence, then, it is very difficult to point to that which is continuous between the ensouled earthly body and enspirited risen body, for the whole of the subject has undergone transformation. Vigdis Songe-Møller (2009, 118–19) is worth quoting at length here:

> The individual is, in some way or other, *the same* before and after resurrection; and this sameness has something to do with the body.... [But] we cannot point to any special part of the individual that remains the same. The continuity of the person before and after resurrection can, it seems, only be put in negative terms: it does not seem to depend on an unchanging element, an element which remains the same before and after death and which, like the Platonic soul, does not ever, and cannot, undergo any kind of change. Or, to put it differently: continuity is not based on the essence of the individual, on that which determines what kind of being this individual is.... The change is total.[70]

On my reading, though Songe-Møller is largely on target, she perhaps has overstated the case in as much as there are hints in Paul's writings that the somatic interior (generally) and the νοῦς/πνεῦμα (or ἔσω ἄνθρωπος) (specifically) are to be viewed as the point of continuity between terrestrial and

---

70. Earlier in the same article, in a manner that coheres with the findings of this study, Songe-Møller (2009, 112) notes that Paul parallels the "[future] transformation of the body (in death) and the [present] transformation of the mind (in life)."

4. ESCHATOLOGICAL SOMATOLOGY 163

heavenly existences. This is only the case, however, because a complete transformation has taken place. Prior to baptism, the νοῦς/πνεῦμα (or ἔσω ἄνθρωπος) of the ensouled earthly body is unable to live in self-mastery—that is, unable to "walk in newness of life." Once brought to life by divine πνεῦμα, however, this interior referent is transformed and able to sustain death.[71] Thus continuity is to be found at the level of the risen somatic interior, which already is realized in the present and sustains through the eschaton.

Finally, it now becomes clear that, for Paul, the baptized σῶμα functions as the location of eschatology. Resurrection is projected onto the body itself, specifically according to the IN-OUT axis of the BODY IS CONTAINER metaphor. In this respect, Paul's eschatology and anthropology are intertwined, which is to say that temporal polarity and anthropological polarity interlace. Paul thinks neither in terms of body-soul nor present-future opposition, but rather conceptualizes both in terms of tensive interrelation that exists at the nexus of the human σῶμα. In this way, eschatology is somatically drawn such that resurrection is embodied in the present.[72]

In summary, then, Paul locates present human embodiment within a larger trajectory that anticipates the future pneumatic alignment of both the somatic interior and exterior. For Paul, eschatology and anthropology are inextricable, and both are projected onto the baptized σῶμα such that believers simultaneously look ahead to and participate in resurrection. Paul has a singular resurrection event in mind, one that has already begun. In this way, one can identify both the already/not-yet nature of Paul's resurrection ideals and the nature of (dis)continuity across earthly and risen existences.

---

71. This is, in effect, the eternal-quality (under)garments noted in 2 Cor 5:3, though in Rom 8:9–11 Paul has dropped the clothing metaphor.

72. Given this third point, it indeed is appropriate to speak of opposing spheres of influence in 8:9–11, not because of a supposed apocalyptic opposition of cosmic aeons or lordship, but rather because of the intrasomatic polarity that characterizes human embodiment. The language of spheres is appropriate given Paul's ubiquitous use of the BODY IS CONTAINER metaphor. To be ἐν σαρκί is to have one's moral actions governed by the lower soul (personified by sin). Conversely, one is ἐν πνεύματι if they, on account of the indwelling divine πνεῦμα, practice self-mastery. Being ἐν σαρκί or ἐν πνεύματι, then, refers to opposing modes of human embodiment, and the language of spheres is appropriate in that it captures the container nature of Paul's thinking. Embodiment and the intrasomatic polarity that characterizes human existence are the way in which such spherical influence is best understood.

4.4. Paul's Eschatological Somatology

The foregoing discussion demonstrates how Paul utilizes and metaphorically extends the RESURRECTION gestalt so as to frame a vision of life in Christ for his readers in Rome. In what remains of this chapter, I explore some of the implications of this reading of Rom 6–8, specifically for Paul's eschatology more broadly. As outlined already (see n. 1 above), modern scholars have often claimed that Paul modifies the eschatological expectations that he inherits from his fellow Judeans. We have already seen that Paul's resurrection ideals fit squarely within a Jewish framework (§2.2), but to what extent do his eschatological ideals fit here too? In the following discussion, I will demonstrate that, though Paul's eschatological outlook does display novelty, claims of mutation or even modification are overdrawn. I will argue this point in light of the theoretical commitments outlined in chapter 1. These commitments enable a more precise understanding of the eschatological structure with which Paul works.

It is important to recognize that the already/not-yet paradox in Paul's thought is not limited to his resurrection ideals. The watershed moment within this paradox is the Christ event. With the coming of Christ the "fullness of time came" (ἦλθεν τὸ πλήρωμα τοῦ χρόνου, Gal 4:4); the location of Christ's resurrection as a past event means that the eschaton has (in some sense) already dawned. In other passages, Paul speaks of an eschatological crisis that is either "present" or "impending" (τὴν ἐνεστῶσαν ἀνάγκην, 1 Cor 7:26–31),[73] and he insists (in passing) that the conclusion of the old aeon has arrived (1 Cor 10:11).[74] With equal consistency, however, and across the undisputed corpus, one can also point to several

---

73. Elsewhere in Paul, ἐνίστημι always is used of the present in contrast to that which is future (Rom 8:38; 1 Cor 3:22; Gal 1:4). For this reason, it seems best to see the crisis (ἀνάγκη) of 7:26 as a present reality. In the broader period literature, ἀνάγκη is used to denote the distress of the eschaton (e.g., 1 En. 1:1; 100:7; 103:8; Luke 21:23). Paul's own view on the nature of this crisis is not clear.

74. The precise meaning of the phrase τὰ τέλη τῶν αἰώνων κατήντηκεν is contested, though it is translated variously as either "the ends of the ages have come" or "the ends of the ages have met." In the former, stress is placed on the conclusion of the previous/present aeon, while the latter stresses the intersection of two opposing aeons. For my purposes, the issue perhaps is moot, as the point to be made is that the aeonic conclusion/intersection has now arrived—hence καταντάω, which is commonly glossed "to come, arrive," in the sense of reaching a destination (LSJ, BDAG, LEH). The verb fits marvellously within the PATH structure of the RESURRECTION gestalt, whereby the

instances where eschatological judgment and resurrection are understood as looming in the (admittedly near) future. For example, Paul speaks of Christ returning during the apostle's own lifetime (1 Thess 4:15, 17; 1 Cor 15:51–52; see also 1 Cor 1:7), and elsewhere he expresses that salvation is nearer now than it was before (Rom 13:11–14), that Christ's parousia could happen at any time (1 Thess 5:1–3), and that the end is very close (Rom 8:18; 16:20; 1 Cor 7:29–31). Taking these texts together, there exists a temporal oscillation of already and not yet in Paul's thought.

In line with the general scholarly trend toward cognicentrism identified in chapter 1, descriptions of eschatological modification are largely understood as a doctrinal or propositional problem. Paul is understood as encountering a problem of logic, one that required resolution precisely because the rational structure of the existing model—Jewish eschatology—failed to accommodate the Christ event. Such was the approach taken by Albert Schweitzer (1968, 97), who posited a number of presumed eschatological puzzles that led "Paul as a thinker to his Mysticism." More recently, Andrew Lincoln (1981, 172) has configured issues of transcendence and imminence both spatially (up and down) and temporally (now and then) while at the same time locating the already/not-yet paradox in heaven: "In thinking about the believer's present experience of the age to come Paul's focus can be in heaven, because for him, with Christ's resurrection and exaltation, the eschatological center of gravity had moved to the heavenly realm." Lincoln is heavily indebted to his analysis of Colossians and Ephesians, and by stressing heaven as the eschatological center, he has overlooked the fact that notions of verticality and horizontality alone do not bring eschatology into the present. Indeed, both refer to locations out there (either up or then) that the believer must embrace propositionally.[75] I will return to this point below.

A final cognicentric tendency is advocated by those who assert that the Christ event was of such uniqueness that it spurred the aforementioned mutation. Thus Wright (2003, 373): "what caused these developments-from-within?… Paul himself would have answered: it was Jesus' own resurrection."[76] Despite it being far from clear that Paul would have rec-

---

GOAL (i.e., destination) has already been reached (note the perfect tense, κατήντηκεν). For scholarly discussion, see Fitzmyer 2008, 387–88; Thiselton 2000, 743–46.

75. In this way, "the believer's present experience of the age to come" is a theological assertion that one intellectually embraces (Lincoln 1981, 172).

76. A similar assertion underscores W. Davies's (1962, 290) much earlier state-

ognized any kind of mutation within his own thought,[77] assertions of this kind remove notions of resurrection from their cultural frame-structure, thus presuming that Christ's resurrection was self-evident and further that the categories of Jewish eschatology were not ultimately needed to identify Jesus as resurrected.[78]

Taken together, these perspectives all configure eschatological modification as a matter of fixed propositions. Paul is backed into a cognicentric corner by insisting that his variance from the tradition necessarily reflects a sui generis categorical difference.

It cannot be denied that specific motifs and/or elements of Paul's eschatology differ from those of his contemporaries. I have already demonstrated this in chapter 2 (§2.1), where the variety of resurrection belief in Second Temple Judaism is notable. This cultural diversity betrays the richness of eschatological expectations across the period literature, and one should not overlook the breadth of such narratological variety.[79] But

---

ment, "the character of [Paul's] eschatology was determined not by any traditional schema but by the *significance* which Paul had been led to give to Jesus.... His eschatology was subservient to his faith and not constitutive of it."

77. Indeed, Paul's own self-perception is of "calling" rather than conversion (see Gal 1:15–16). While the apostle at times presents his calling in radical terms (e.g., Phil 3:1b–11), he continues to employ categories such as law, covenant, and judgment so as to articulate his identity in Christ.

78. For Wright, the only tenable conclusion can be that Jesus indeed did rise from the dead (2003, 706–10), which he further insists cannot "mean that [Paul] was simply having a 'religious experience' without any objective correlate" (378). Accordingly, the resurrection of Christ can only be a self-evident historical event. Indebted to a form of critical realism, Wright defends this claim by insisting, "All experience is interpreted experience, *but not all experience can be reduced to terms of the interpretation*" (378, emphasis added). In light of my findings in the present study, notions of resurrection do not constitute the kinds of experiences that one can critically posit as foundations of meaning, or that can function substantively—even self-evidently—in the way Wright presumes. As we have seen, resurrection is a complex and varied concept that always is metaphorical, necessarily embedded within broader networks of cultural frames, and built up by image schemata. Accordingly, resurrection cannot function as a self-evident "experience ... [ir]reduc[ible] to [the] terms of the interpretation," for resurrection can only be recognized within particular cultural, historical, and embodied contexts.

79. One need look no further than Schweitzer's (1968, 75–100) maximalist account to see that any attempt to fit Paul into a static narrative is doomed to failure. Schweitzer errs in that he works at the level of human scale, thus seeking to identify a coherent and singular narrative that accounts for all the details of Paul's

this is not the point. What is at issue is the more substantial claim that the underlying structure of Paul's eschatology has undergone mutation, that Paul stands in some degree of unique contradistinction from his fellow Judeans of the period. This is particularly evident in the "schematic" diagrams that scholars like Geerhardus Vos (1961, 36–41) and Dunn (1998b, 461–66) construct (reproduced in fig. 4.3).[80] Here the "traditional" Jewish view, which is often one-dimensional and strictly teleological, is contrasted with Paul's "newly modified" view, which is two-dimensional and consists of temporal (Dunn) and/or cosmological (Vos) overlap.

It should not be overlooked that neither Dunn nor Vos uses the term *schema* with the same degree of technicality that I have. Both (seem to) use schema to denote an ordered and recurrent system, and despite their claim to have represented the underlying structure of Paul's eschatology, their analyses are conducted exclusively at the level of human scale (thus attending to things like recurrent motifs and specific events). For this reason, their analyses cannot help but uncover a modified schema, for neither Dunn nor Vos has penetrated beyond the narratological level. Extending from my findings in chapter 2 (§2.1), this study's more technical understanding of schema enables a precise analysis of Paul's eschatology and any schematic alterations he may have made.

In light of the foregoing discussion of Rom 6–8, Paul's eschatology is seen not to reflect mutation but rather strong coherence with the RESURRECTION gestalt that he shares with his Judean contemporaries (see fig. 4.4, where I diagram the schema so as to denote Paul's appropriation of the RESURRECTION gestalt in light of the CHRIST frame). Proceeding from the perception that Jesus has been raised from the dead,[81]

---

various eschatological descriptions (including a doctrine of the two resurrections, an understanding of two different streams of Jewish eschatology, an insistence upon two kingdoms, etc.).

80. The extent to which diagrams of this kind pervade Pauline scholarship is evinced by their inclusion in standard introductory works (e.g., Horrell 2006, 70–71).

81. I use the term *perception* in this sentence to denote the whole of Paul's subjective experience. Consistent with the broader tenets of this study, such perception is grounded in particular kinds of experiences of the risen Christ (e.g., ecstatic, ritualistic, communal) and conceptualized in such a way that the risen Christ is materially present (through πνεῦμα) in Paul and his communities. In these ways, Paul's perception of Christ's resurrection is thoroughly embodied. That I speak of *Paul's* perception should not be taken in a strong individualistic sense. Paul very much

168 RESURRECTION IN PAUL

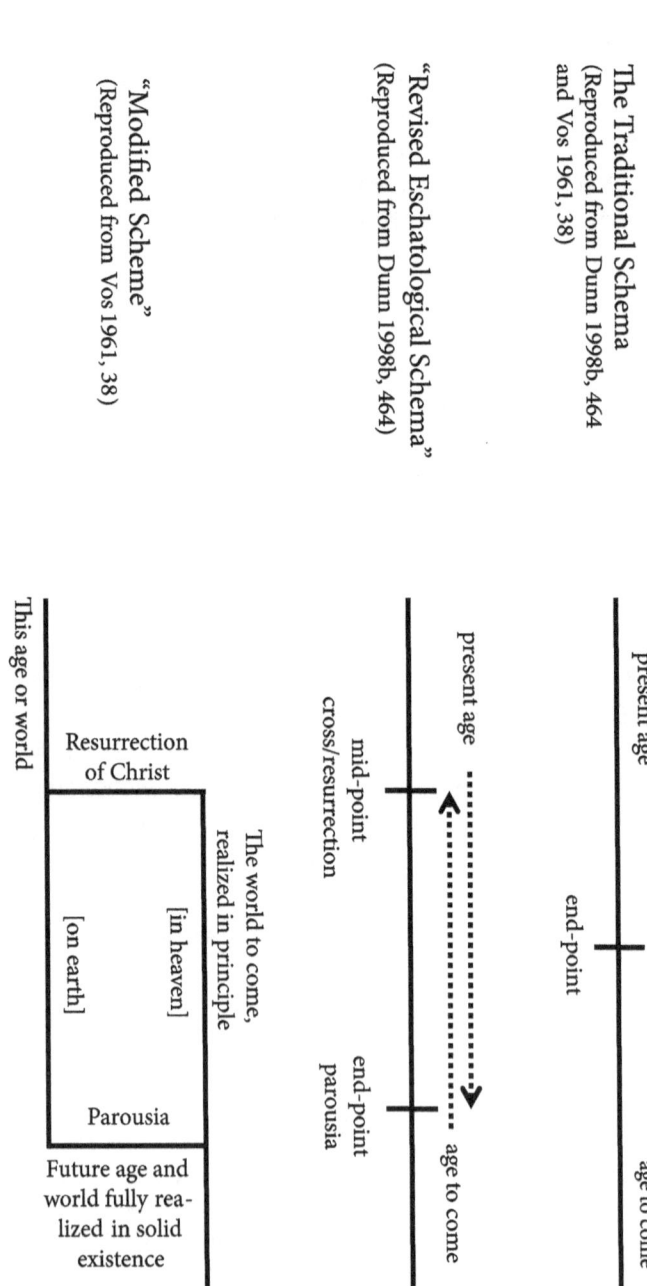

Figure 4.3. Scholarly Depictions of Paul's Modified Eschatological Schema

4. ESCHATOLOGICAL SOMATOLOGY

Paul perceives the eschaton to have dawned and thus locates himself and Christ-devotees in the macro-GOAL of the RESURRECTION gestalt. Christ's parousia (signified by θ/p) stands at the macro-GOAL's still-expected completion. While it is Christ's death/resurrection (signified by †) that cues this emphasis on the macro-GOAL, it is baptism into Christ's death (signified by β) that sets the believer on this particular trajectory. Accordingly, the two events of baptism/death and parousia are mapped onto the RESURRECTION gestalt. While they mark frame-specific content in Paul's appropriation of the gestalt, they themselves are not inherent to the overall structure (which retains its general elements and systematicity [compare with fig. 2.9]). That being said, Paul's appropriation of the RESURRECTION gestalt is not without novelty. As we saw in Rom 6–8, such novelty is found in the transformative PATH structure, which is scaled temporally so as (1) to include the terrestrial transformation of the baptizand's σῶμα and (2) to denote an ongoing process of IN-OUT transformation toward Christ's parousia. By virtue of baptismal death, Christ-devotees are inwardly raised and in the midst of transformation from one somatic state into another. Paul has a single, drawn-out process of resurrection in mind.

I must stress, however, that none of this is a mutation or even modification, for the RESURRECTION gestalt does not change. Paul neither adds to nor subtracts from the schematic elements but rather frames the entire gestalt in light of the Christ-event-experienced-in-baptism. As demonstrated above, baptism sets Christ-devotees on a transformative PATH (fig. 4.1), which they now progress as part of their achievement of the macro-GOAL (figs. 4.2 and 4.4). This produces distinct resurrection ideals at human scale that are not found in the comparative traditions analyzed in chapter 2 (§2.1).

What we see in Paul, then, is not an aeonic overlap or a bringing of the future back into the present, but rather a somatically drawn polarity of IN and OUT such that the human interior becomes the location of revelation and the exterior the location of earthly persistence. In this way, Paul does not work with temporal linearity so much as an intrasomatic polarity between σάρξ and πνεῦμα (IN-OUT), now and then (SOURCE-GOAL), and

---

exists within communities of Christ-devotees and is a participant with his fellow coworker in establishing and maintaining such communities. Indeed, 1 Cor 15:1–11 indicates that the perception of Christ's resurrection is a matter of emerging Christian tradition.

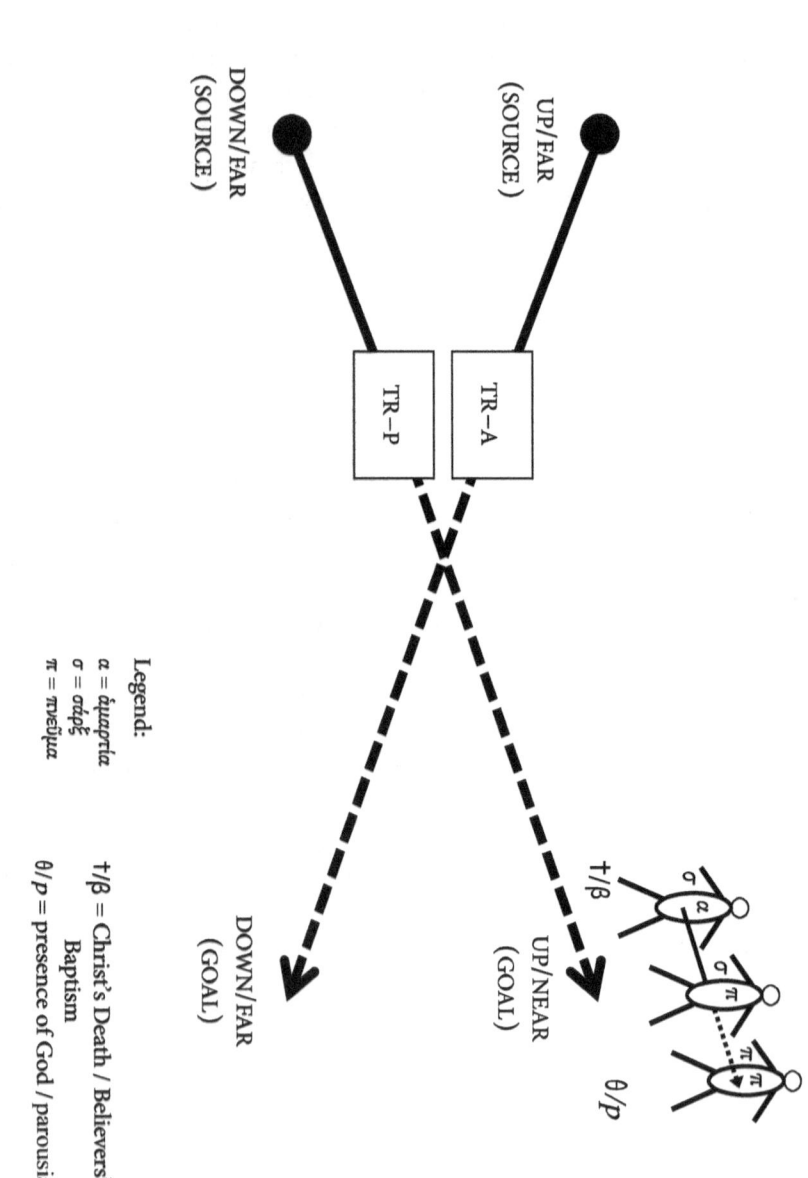

Figure 4.4. Paul's Appropriation of the RESURRECTION Gestalt

Legend:
α = ἁμαρτία
σ = σάρξ
π = πνεῦμα

†/β = Christ's Death / Believers' Baptism
θ/p = presence of God / parousia

earthly and heavenly (UP-DOWN). At the center of all this is the human σῶμα. For Paul, eschatology is somatically mapped. It is eschatological somatology. To highlight this, we can return briefly to the work of Lincoln noted above. Though rightly stressing the relationship between Christ and believers as the location of imminence,[82] Lincoln's (1981, 172) relegation of the "eschatological center of gravity … [to] the heavenly realm" thus produces a strenuous emphasis upon the heavenly, exalted Christ that is not sufficiently counterbalanced with Paul's focus on the indwelling, pneumatic Christ.[83] Though Lincoln rightly focuses on cosmology (earth and heaven) and temporality (now and then), my present analysis suggests that Paul's eschatology must also be extended to include anthropology (somatic interior and exterior).[84] In this way, that which is traditionally ascribed to the cosmos (up) and temporal future (then) must also be correlated with the somatic interior (in). It is this third dimension of anthropology (specifically somatology) that enables imminence in Paul's eschatological outlook and further constitutes the demarcation of already and not yet in Paul's thought.

4.5. Conclusions

It may seem odd to the reader that I have employed throughout this chapter the language of *resurrection* with respect to the past/present when Paul clearly relegates terms such as ἀνάστασις to the future. With respect to this

---

82. For Lincoln (1981, 170), this is expressed through the recognition that Paul's understanding of heaven has a much more immanent nature than usually is ascribed to dualistically configured Jewish apocalyptic thought. For Lincoln, Paul represents a "decisive break" with such a dualistic worldview, further underscoring the claim to modification.

83. Even where Lincoln (e.g., 1981, 187) does stress the pneumatic presence of Christ in believers, the focus of discussion moves toward Christ's heavenly position rather than his pneumatic indwelling. Adolf Deissmann's (1957, 140) much earlier critique finds renewed resonance here: "This certainty of the nearness of Christ occurs far more frequently in Paul's writings than the thought of the distant Christ 'highly exalted' in Heaven."

84. Lincoln does address issues of anthropology in his discussion of 2 Cor 5, though his treatment moves toward spatial and temporal issues rather than any kind of somatic mapping. Thus Paul does *not* hold an "anthropological dualism but rather a temporal duality" (1981, 70). In Lincoln's view, this future age to come already exists in heaven and thus is abstracted from the believer him- or herself.

past/present dimension, some may prefer to use the language of *transformation*, which perhaps conveys the same meaning though in a less charged way (especially when the deutero-Paulines are so naturally on the periphery of our modern view). But such a capitulation misses the more important claim of this chapter, which can be expressed in two parts as both reminder and thesis: (1) notions of resurrection are not reducible to lexical signs, and thus the whole of the RESURRECTION gestalt cannot be limited to lexemes but rather reflects a constellation of interlocking concepts; and (2) Paul utilizes the logic of the RESURRECTION gestalt as a frame-structure in which to articulate a vision of Christ-devotee identity, one that is for both Judeans and gentiles and that enables self-mastery as the mode of the "new life" effected in baptism (cf. 6:4). At one level, for Paul RESURRECTION proves to be a good concept with which to frame life in Christ.

But RESURRECTION is not just a good concept with which to think, but rather something the apostle takes as really real. For Paul, Christ-devotees find themselves in the midst of the resurrection process. Their bodies exist in a state of intrasomatic polarity whereby they are currently dying and coming back to life. This present experience of resurrection is mapped chiefly to the somatic interior (RESURRECTION IS IN). Cosmology and chronology interlace at the nexus of the σῶμα. Christ-devotees exist as enspirited earthly bodies that are in the process of transformation from ensouled earthly bodies to enspirited risen bodies (fig. 4.2). In positing this transformative trajectory, however, Paul does not modify or mutate his eschatological expectations but rather intuits this view within the frame-structure that governs his thought—Paul's perception of the crucified and risen Christ.

Without recourse to eschatological modification, we have seen more clearly the nature of Paul's already/not-yet ideals: eschatology is somatically grounded such that believers are already raised inwardly but not yet raised outwardly. Christ-devotees are in the process of being resurrected, a conviction that is expressed in Rom 6–8 through the RESURRECTION IS CONSCIOUSNESS metaphor, here framed through the conceptual category of SELF-MASTERY. To this end, believers are able to exercise self-mastery because they are informed by the divine πνεῦμα (i.e., the πνεῦμα ζωοποιοῦν, 1 Cor 15:45), the indwelling presence of which enlivens the ἔσω ἄνθρωπος (or νοῦς, or human πνεῦμα) and thus constitutes the resurrection of the somatic interior.

Returning to the scholarly literature examined in chapter 1 (§1.3), I can summarize the present chapter's major contributions as follows. First, while many exegetes locate participation in Christ's death and resurrection as past and future events (see §1.3.3), we have seen that Paul holds to a single resurrection event that is temporally drawn out and somatically mapped. For Paul, resurrection is an ongoing experience that has both present and future manifestations. Both are important, and it is erroneous to draw a sharp distinction between future literal and present metaphorical resurrections (see §1.3.1). Accordingly, we have also seen the fundamental importance of recognizing Paul's present resurrection assumptions, which are expressed in Rom 6–8 as ethics (RESURRECTION IS CONSCIOUSNESS) rather than transformation of the somatic exterior (RESURRECTION IS CELESTIAL LUMINOSITY, as in 1 Cor 15 and 2 Cor 5).[85] Second, by identifying the location of present resurrection, we have uncovered the location of continuity across earthly and risen forms: namely, continuity is mapped to the somatic interior and correlated with πνεῦμα (both divine and human). In contrast to Käsemann's (1971c) dualistically drawn discontinuity and Bultmann's (1951–1955) Cartesianesque continuity of self (see §1.3.2), my analysis has grounded trans-somatic continuity in the transformed somatic interior. Finally, in contrast to the notion of dying and rising with Christ as a passive participation in dualistically drawn aeonic spheres (see §1.3.3), we have seen that Paul's focus is squarely and concretely on the body. The somatic interior becomes the location of transformation, and proper ethical praxis with one's body serves as the hallmark of the resurrected interior. To this end, participation in Christ's resurrection is a matter of oneness with the indwelling divine πνεῦμα.

---

85. The principal exception to this is Rom 8:18–25, where Paul looks ahead to the future transformation of the somatic exterior.

5

PARTICIPATING IN RESURRECTION:
UNION, MUTUAL AFFECTIVITY, AND ETHNICITY

In the previous chapter, we saw that Paul's language of being ἐν σαρκί and ἐν πνεύματι reflects differing embodied states that place Christ-devotees within a transformative trajectory. Paul is blending his anthropology with his eschatology, thus understanding resurrection as a process in which the human body engages. To follow this conclusion through, however, requires that we examine the full range of Paul's container descriptions, which include not only references to being ἐν πνεύματι but also (and more pervasively) ἐν Χριστῷ.

Like so much of his soteriology, Paul's resurrection ideals are always tending toward participationist expressions. Paul speaks not only of believers participating in Christ's death and resurrection but also of their being enmeshed with Christ in the process of so doing. Thus in Rom 6:5 believers are "grown together with" (σύμφυτοι) the likeness of Christ's death; and in Phil 3:21 believers will be "morphed together with" (σύμμορφον) Christ's risen existence (see also Rom 8:29). The former image—σύμφυτος—has resonance in horticultural and biomedical frame-structures, both of which denote two separate entities that are united into a living singularity.[1] This image, which conveys "indivisible, organic unity with Christ"

---

1. The adjective σύμφυτος occurs only here in the New Testament, and its precise meaning is contested. For some, it implies a horticultural frame whereby believers and Christ are grafted or implanted together, thus denoting the image of a plant and a branch organically growing together (so Fitzmyer 1993, 435). This interpretation fits with Paul's description of the gentiles being grafted into the olive tree (Rom 11:17–24), which admittedly has a different flavor than Rom 6:5 (though perhaps not unrelated). Others suggest a biomedical frame whereby the two edges of an open wound are sewn together (Dunn 1988, 1:316). It also is worth noting our adjective's cognate verb, συμφύω, is used in both senses noted here (thus LSJ: "[to] make grow together,

(Jewett 2007, 400), concurs with the genealogical dimensions of Paul's participationist and resurrection ideals that we will explore below.[2] The latter image—σύμμορφος—is similar to our metamorphosis "but with a more intimate and transformative meaning.... It [suggests] that the reformation will explicitly take place 'together with' (*syn-*) [Christ's] glorious body" (A. Segal 2004, 419).[3] Passages such as Rom 6:5, 8:29, and Phil 3:21 point not to a propositional assertion of participation in/with Christ but to an experience of divine/human oneness. As Engberg-Pedersen (2010, 151) notes with regard to Phil 3:10–11, Paul's language "comes out as being extremely experiential.... Paul is merging into Christ." The apostle understands resurrection as a joining together, a kind of intertwining of Christ and believers. His descriptions tend not just toward being in the Christic form but also toward a more complete and unitary engulfment into Christ himself. This understanding of resurrection is related to but differs markedly from the traditional metaphors examined in chapter 2 (§2.1). The emphasis is less on renewed corporeality (RESURRECTION IS UP) and more on divine/human proximity (RESURRECTION IS NEAR). Indeed, not just proximity

---

unite [a wound]"). In both horticultural and biomedical frame-structures, however, σύμφυτος certainly denotes an organic image of joining together.

2. Johnson Hodge nicely demonstrates this with respect to Rom 8:29, where she argues that Paul's *image* (εἰκών) language is best read in the context of patrilineal descent; that is, "according to Paul, baptized gentiles have been *reconceived*, *shaped into* Christ's form, and given a *new birth*.... [They] have been *conceived* and *formed* by a procreative God" (2007, 115–16, emphasis added). Extending Johnson Hodge's analysis may have implications for Paul's resurrection ideals, specifically the description of baptism as an intertwining of believers into the likeness (ὁμοίωμα) of Christ's death and resurrection (Rom 6:5). Though Johnson Hodge does not address Rom 6:5 specifically, the semantic overlap of εἰκών with ὁμοίωμα (e.g., LXX Gen 1:26; see Johnson Hodge 2007, 111–12) suggests Rom 6:5 might be read in a way similar to Rom 8:29: that is, "God [is understood] as the 'molder' shaping his newly adopted sons after the image of his firstborn, Christ. Like fetuses, the gentiles-in-Christ need to be altered, formed, and molded into new beings belonging to a new family" (113). Adding support to this line of inquiry is Johnson Hodge's own insistence that baptism functions as a ritual of adoption (67–77), one in which the patrilineal line of descent is connected materially through shared πνεῦμα rather than shared blood.

3. While I understand Segal as working in the right direction, it should be noted that σύμμορφος can simply denote the morphing together of two distinct entities into a "similar shape or form" (LSJ, BDAG) and thus does not necessarily denote the organic unity that σύμφυτος does.

5. PARTICIPATING IN RESURRECTION 177

but a kind of hyperproximity—Paul is looking ahead to being completely and fully subsumed into Christ (RESURRECTION IS IN).

In the present chapter, I explore these issues and their attendant dimensions in detail, particularly examining the interrelation of Paul's participationist language with his understanding of resurrection as an unfolding and ongoing process. The scope of analysis is admittedly far reaching. Consistent with this study's emphasis on the vertical integration of cognition and culture, the following discussion will range from the embodied foundations of grammatical meaning (§5.1) to the sociorhetorical aims of Paul's epistolary addresses (§5.2), from the neurobiological happenings of ecstatic experience to the literary and cultural frames in which Paul's participationist language is elaborated (§5.3). While Pauline specialists often treat many of these issues in isolation from one another, I hope to demonstrate that the notion of resurrection as joining together comes into clearer focus when one coordinates disparate categories. As I will show, Paul's present experience of resurrection is a participatory experience that garners certain patterns of embodiment that structure the identities and existences of Christ-devotees. While these patterns are most clearly seen in 2 Cor 3–4 and Gal 3–4, evidence will be adduced from all of Paul's epistles so as to demonstrate their presence across the whole of the undisputed corpus.

5.1. Resurrection and UNION

Paul's participatory language is one of the most important yet diversely contested themes in the undisputed letters. The most common phrases Paul uses to articulate these ideals are the ubiquitous ἐν Χριστῷ and the less common (though still pervasive) σὺν Χριστῷ, both of which convey related though distinct ideas of union between Christ and Christ-devotees. Before turning to the interrelation of Paul's participationist and resurrection ideals, it will be helpful first to examine the conceptual structures that undergird Paul's linguistic descriptors. In what follows, I offer a cognitive linguistic analysis of Paul's *in/with Christ* ideals, with specific attention given to the concepts conveyed by the linguistic signs themselves.

5.1.1. Ἐν Χριστῷ in Cognitive Linguistic Perspective

From a cognitive linguistic perspective, traditional grammatical assessments of how prepositions such as ἐν or σύν contribute meaning to Paul's broader participationist ideals are in need of revision. Of particular note is the fracturing of the linguistic sign into multiple, homophonous meanings. Consider the preposition ἐν, for instance, which often is described as the "maid-of-all-work" among Greek prepositions.[4] While some grammarians limit the functions of ἐν to a handful of broad categories,[5] others have fragmented the preposition into as many as twelve (or more) distinct functions.[6] In large part these categories are defined on contextual grounds: for example, a locative ἐν is identified when someone is "in the market" (ἐν τῇ ἀγορᾷ, Matt 20:3).[7] This creates problems, however, when the context in question is not entirely self-evident, as is the case for Paul's *in Christ* descriptions. Indeed, Paul's language of being ἐν Χριστῷ has been identified as "utterly def[ying] definite interpretation" (BDF §219.4), and the use of ἐν in such contexts is sometimes listed as a separate and unique prepositional category (S. Porter 1999, 159).

Contextual concerns are not to be neglected, for the function of a preposition like ἐν is realized only in the midst of linguistic usage. This does not mean, however, that the preposition itself does not impart meaning or conceptual structure to the discursive unit. Indeed, from a cognitive linguistic perspective, it is only because a lexeme such as ἐν triggers certain conceptual mappings that it is meaningful within discursive contexts. In her recent analysis of ἐν Χριστῷ in 1 Peter, Bonnie Howe (2006, 233–48, esp. 235–37) has outlined the cognitive linguistic perspective succinctly. Unlike standard grammars, Howe insists (237):

> We do not have five (or more) different, homophonous words, ἐν. Instead, we have one *emergent concept* 'EN, one word for that emergent

---

4. So Moulton, Howard, and Turner 1906, 1:103; cf. BDAG 326, s.v. ἐν: "the uses of this prep. are so many and various, and oft. so easily confused, that a strictly systematic treatment is impossible. It must suffice to list the main categories, which will help establish the usage in individual cases."

5. Dana and Mantey (1939, 105–6), for example, list what they deem the root meaning ("within") and two resultant meanings ("locative" and "instrumental"). They also note three remote meanings.

6. For example, BDAG (326–30, s.v. ἐν) lists twelve different categories, many of which have subdivisions therein. Similarly, Daniel Wallace (1996, 372) lists ten basic usages, which he insists are "painted with broad strokes" (thus implying that more should ideally be added). A. Robertson (1919, 584–91) lists eight categories.

7. Thus Dana and Mantey (1939, 98–99): "the best way to determine the meanings of a preposition is to study it in its various contexts and note its various uses."

concept, and multiple metaphorical concepts in which 'EN serves to partially define emotional states, theological relationships between beings, the nature of instrumentality, and so on.

Howe perhaps overstates the case a bit here, as she also (more accurately) notes that the same lexical sign can, depending on the context, trigger other conceptual structures.[8] Central here is the recognition that the embodied grounding of the linguistic sign—that is, the underlying emergent concept ('EN)—is generative in the meaning-making and meaning-conveying processes. The crucial point is that the lexeme itself triggers conceptual structures that are essential to understanding the discursive context. Such conceptual structures are image-schematic in nature, drawing on embodied experiences of CONTAINMENT (as in most uses of ἐν) or PROXIMITY (as in most uses of σύν). Accordingly, a preposition like ἐν is not defined *only* by usage within specific contexts. Rather, ἐν imports meaning to the discourse itself, drawing on embodied human experiences so as to create and to convey meaning.

Rather than positing multiple, homophonous meanings for prepositions such as ἐν, cognitive linguists instead assert the polysemy of such signs. Pietro Bortone (2010, 71–75) has explored the implications of this approach, specifically applying George Lakoff's (1987) theory of categorization to illuminate diachronic and synchronic usages of Greek prepositions. As Bortone (2010, 72) notes, "the key to comprehending polysemy is our tendency to re-apply images to new concepts, to graft the structure of one semantic field onto other (especially abstract) domains." Bortone continues,

> In the cognitive view,... meaning is a radially-structured network: there is a core item from which other ones are spawned.... The relation of the derived members to the prototypical element becomes less obvious as the chain expands: outer items (Lakoff 1987: 84) cannot be predicted, and have to be learnt.... Traditionally, the lack of traits between two uses of the same word has been taken as proof of homonymity, rather than polysemy. With the interpretation of polysemy as a network of family-

---

8. Thus Howe (2006, 235), "a single word like ἐν can evoke multiple image schemas," and again later, "the word [ἐν] is the same in each case, but the conceptual structuring is different" (236). In such cases, the linguistic sign itself evinces association with several different emergent concepts, some of which may well be independent from one another. Such is the case with the *causal* use of ἐν, whereby the assertion that X happens because of or on account of Y has no necessary dependency on the CONTAINER schema (e.g., Acts 7:29).

like relation, the alleged meaninglessness of prepositions and case forms ... becomes all the more untenable: "that prepositions are meaningful even as 'pure grammatical' elements follows directly from the basic tenets of ... cognitive grammar."⁹ (73)

In the case of ἐν, the core meaning in question concerns the CONTAINER schema while radial meanings are metaphorically elaborated (in ways that are not necessarily predicable) so as to extend the sign ἐν to cue other image-schematic structures.¹⁰

Several implications proceed from the assertion that prepositional meanings are rooted in embodied experiences. Though many grammarians (rightly) suggest that prepositions evince a basic spatial sense that is then metaphorically elaborated in various ways,¹¹ many of these same grammarians do not commonly recognize that a single schematic structure can constitute various senses of prepositional usage. For example, while some distinguish between a locative and spherical use of ἐν (e.g., S. Porter 1999, 156–57), cognitive linguists question the degree to which these senses differ. Both the locative and spherical utilize the CONTAINER schema in constructing meaning, the former with respect to geographical placement and the latter with respect to influence and hegemony. For this reason, the relegation of Paul's ἐν Χριστῷ descriptions to their own category of prepositional usage is problematic. Such is the approach taken by Stanley Porter (1999, 159), who posits a unique spherical usage of ἐν that is indebted to a certain form of apocalyptic dualism and cosmic subjection (namely, to be in Christ is to be controlled by Christ; to be in Adam is to be controlled by Adam). A similar move is made in A. T. Robertson's (1919, 587–88) relegation of Paul's *in Christ/Adam* language to a separate category of prototypical association; this is something closer to the theory of representational figures. Both Porter and Robertson theologize the preposition, thus isolating Paul's ἐν Χριστῷ descriptions and detaching them from broader patterns of linguistic usage. Little concern is given to the preposition itself, which is imbued instead with ideological content quite apart from any kind of embodied grounding.

---

9. Here, Bortone cites Langacker 1992, 287.
10. For examples, see n. 8 above.
11. See, e.g., S. Porter 1999, 142; and Dana and Mantey 1939, 99. More preferable is the work of Bortone (2010, 47–57), who contrasts both cognitive and generative linguistic approaches to the spatial dimensions of prepositions in historical Greek usage.

At the same time, we do well not to ignore the more basic locative senses with which prepositions function and specifically to begin exegesis with the more concrete spatial meanings before asserting secondary, more abstract meanings. This stands in contrast to Maximilian Zerwick (1985, §§116–18), who understands Paul's ἐν Χριστῷ language as reflecting a "sociative" use of ἐν, which is "practically reduced to the expression of a general notion of association or accompaniment, which would be rendered in English by 'with'" (§117). Here Zerwick understands ἐν in light of a radial image schema—that of PROXIMITY rather than the more central CONTAINMENT schema. As I will show, there is perhaps good reason to stress this "sociative" dimension, for Paul is concerned not only with Christ-believer oneness (CONTAINMENT) but also togetherness (PROXIMITY). Nonetheless, there is ample evidence in Paul's letters that the CONTAINER rather than PROXIMITY schema is conceptually more germane in the apostle's usage of ἐν Χριστῷ. Accordingly, we do better to start from the point of common usage—ἐν as denoting CONTAINMENT—before pivoting to alternative emergent concepts.

In light of the foregoing, it is problematic to overly fragment or even isolate Paul's ἐν Χριστῷ language. Rather than positing unique theological usages, we do better to examine the conceptual structures that 'EN imparts to Paul's participationist ideals. As we will see below, ἐν is best understood as triggering the CONTAINER schema, thus conceptualizing Christ as a container in which believers exist, and thus giving rise to the CHRIST IS CONTAINER metaphor. To say that ἐν triggers the CONTAINER schema means that Paul utilizes the lexeme to understand abstract experiences or ideas by means of the common physical experience of being spatially contained. It is not that Paul necessarily understands Christ (or πνεῦμα, or Adam, or Abraham) as actually being a container (though in many instances he does: see §§2.2.4, 3.2.2, 4.3, and 5.3), but rather that the CHRIST IS CONTAINER metaphor enables a conceptual system wherein Paul is able to describe the relationship between Christ and believers via the categories and structural relations inherent in the CONTAINER schema (e.g., being located *in* or *out*, passing *through*). In this way, prepositions such as ἐν impart conceptual structure that is fundamental to understanding Paul's participationist ideals.

5.1.2. Conceptual Patterns in Paul's Participationist Language

When we speak of Paul's participationist language, we are really speaking of two interrelated though distinct sets of descriptions. The first is Paul's language of *oneness*, which is premised on the CONTAINER schema and reflected in phrases such as ἐν Χριστῷ, εἰς Χριστόν, and even διὰ Χριστοῦ. The second is the language of *togetherness*, which is premised on the PROXIMITY schema and reflected in σύν phrases and σύν- prefixed words. To a large extent, the former (oneness) functions as the dominant idea, though this is only because the two expressions are inextricable and reflect the more general gestalt structure UNION. Before I articulate this UNION gestalt specifically, it will be helpful to examine the oneness and togetherness dimensions separately.

Paul articulates oneness between Christ and believers in a number of different ways, all of which are premised on the CONTAINER schema. The best known and most obvious is the phrase ἐν Χριστῷ (Ἰησοῦ) and its correlates,[12] which conveys a mental space wherein Christ is conceptualized as a container that believers exist in. The ubiquity of the CHRIST IS CONTAINER metaphor is evinced in other prepositional phrases as well. One example is the διὰ Χριστοῦ construction,[13] which Paul almost always expresses as διά + genitive (*through*) rather than διά + accusative (*on account of*).[14] The sense for Paul is not only the instrumental means by which God and believers act, but more fundamentally the spatial proximity between God and believers. Interactions between the divine and humanity happen through Christ. Paul further describes believers as having entered εἰς Χριστόν,[15] a movement that takes place in baptism (Gal 3:27) such that

---

12. On ἐν Χριστῷ (Ἰησοῦ), see, e.g., Gal 1:22; 3:26; 5:6; Rom 6:11; 8:1; 15:17; 16:3; 1 Cor 1:2; 4:17; 2 Cor 3:14; 5:17; 12:2; Phil 1:1; 3:9, 14; 4:7; 1 Thess 2:14; 4:14; Phlm 8, 20. Related phrases include ἐν κυρίῳ (e.g., 1 Thess 1:1; Rom 14:14; 16:2, 8, 11–13, 22; 1 Cor 4:17; 9:1; 11:11; Phlm 20), ἐν πνεύματι (e.g., Rom 8:9; 14:17; 1 Cor 6:11; 12:3, 9, 13; 1 Thess 1:5), ἐν αὐτῷ (e.g., 1 Cor 1:5; 2 Cor 1:19–20; 5:21; Phil 3:9), and perhaps ἐν θεῷ (1 Thess 1:1; see also Rom 5:11 and 6:11).

13. In addition to διὰ Χριστοῦ (e.g., 2 Cor 1:5; 3:4; 5:18), see also διὰ Χριστοῦ Ἰησοῦ/Ἰησοῦ Χριστοῦ (e.g., Rom 1:8; 2:16; 5:21; Gal 1:1; Phil 1:11), δι' αὐτοῦ (1 Cor 8:6; 2 Cor 1:20), διὰ τοῦ κυρίου Ἰησοῦ Χριστοῦ (Rom 5:11; 15:30), and διὰ πνεύματος (Rom 5:5; 1 Cor 2:12; 12:8). To these one might also add the subjective genitive reading of διὰ πίστεως (Ἰησοῦ) Χριστοῦ (Rom 3:22; Gal 2:16; Phil 3:9).

14. So noted by Dunn 1998b, 406. Exceptions to this rule include 1 Cor 4:10 and Phil 3:7. Importantly, it is worth noting that διά + accusative can also denote spatial orientation (cf. BDF §222; Wallace 1996, 369), a sense that may well be operative in Paul's two διὰ (τὸν) Χριστόν usages (1 Cor 4:10 and Phil 3:7).

15. In addition to εἰς Χριστόν (e.g., Gal 3:27; 2 Cor 1:21; see also Rom 16:5; 1 Cor 12:13; Phlm 6), see also εἰς Χριστὸν Ἰησοῦν (e.g., Rom 6:3 and perhaps Gal 2:16), and contrast with εἰς τὸν Μωϋσῆν (1 Cor 10:2).

the baptizand "puts on" (ἐνεδύσασθε) Christ. The clothing image clearly coheres with the CHRIST IS CONTAINER metaphor, and both it and the baptismal image find resonance within Paul's resurrection ideals.

Perhaps Paul's most vivid expression of Christ-believer oneness is the image of the church as the body of Christ.[16] It is not surprising that some exegetes read Paul's ἐν Χριστῷ phrases as denoting one's presence within the ecclesial community,[17] though we overstep if we equate ἐν Χριστῷ to a mere synonym of ἐν τῇ ἐκκλησίᾳ.[18] We are on firmer ground when we recognize that coherence between the ecclesial metaphor and Paul's ἐν Χριστῷ descriptions results from a shared container structure mapped onto the figure of Christ vis-à-vis Christ-devotees. The ecclesial metaphor is but one expression of Paul's broader description of Christ-believer oneness. As a metaphor for oneness, this corporate image is an exceptionally lucid expression of the CONTAINER schema. Via the BODY IS CONTAINER metaphor, being ἐν Χριστῷ denotes being part of his very body.

---

16. See 1 Cor 12 and Rom 12:4–8. To a large extent, the body imagery in 1 Corinthians serves Paul's rhetorical aims. Margaret Mitchell (1991) has demonstrated that 1 Corinthians is a unified, deliberative epistle that draws on common political terms and topoi in the service of combating factionalism and urging proper concord within the Corinthian ἐκκλησία. A key concept in this rhetorical strategy is the CHURCH IS BODY (OF CHRIST) metaphor, which is a particular expression of the more general and widely used SOCIETY IS BODY metaphor (for a discussion of the ideological nuances and widespread use of this trope, see Mitchell 1991, 157–64; Martin 1995, 92–96). Though the fashioning of a group as a body is commonly used in the promotion of social unity and the maintenance of social hierarchy, in 1 Corinthians Paul inverts this logic and thus constructs a countervision of oneness/togetherness wherein "the lower is made higher, and the higher lower.... The dominant Greco-Roman common sense—that honor must accord with status and that status positions are relatively fixed by nature—is completely, albeit confusingly, thrown into question" (Martin 1995, 96).

17. So Ernst Käsemann (1971d, 106), who argued that the concepts of being in Christ and of the ecclesial body of Christ "belong together in that they mutually interpret one another." For Käsemann (2010, 46), the "Body of Christ of the Church … is the earthly sphere of the lordship of Christ." Richard Hays (2008, 344) leans in a similar direction when he asserts, with reference to Sanders (1977, 522), "[ecclesial participation] is as close as we are likely to get to the category that lies between magical transference and revised self-understanding."

18. The only occurrences of ἐν τῇ ἐκκλησίᾳ are in 1 Cor 6:4 and 12:28, where Paul is speaking of the Corinthian congregation itself. Moreover, though the dative ἐκκλησίᾳ occurs far more frequently in Paul's letters, it always denotes the community itself, not union between Christ and believers.

In an interesting way, the CHURCH IS BODY (OF CHRIST) metaphor provides Paul a structure within which to organize part and whole in relation to one another. This is true not just for the relationship between believers and Christ, but also for locating the individual vis-à-vis the community.[19] Within the frame-structure of the BODY IS CONTAINER metaphor, the distinction between integrative parts within a whole is upheld—this is true not only of the constituent elements of the CONTAINER schema (namely, that which is IN vis-à-vis that which is OUT) but also of the potential for several individuated contents within the container. Paul accordingly can stress either side of the container equation: that the members of Christ's body are not their own but belong to one another and to Christ (Rom 12:5; 1 Cor 6:19) or that the individual is interdependent within the collective (e.g., 1 Cor 12:7 and 26). This sense of oneness is premised on the idea of many parts being contained within a single whole.[20] Conversely, in 1 Cor 6:15–20 Paul can address the community (ὑμῶν) while speaking of the πνεῦμα dwelling in the singular σῶμα, thus exhorting the Corinthians to glorify God in their (plural) body (singular): ἐν τῷ σώματι ὑμῶν (6:20). The lines between the individual and the community are blurred here—οὐκ ἐστὲ ἑαυτῶν (6:19)—despite the fact that Paul's primary interest is an instructional address concerning individual bodies (6:15; cf. also the singular ὁ in 6:17). Comparing 6:19 with 3:16 further underscores the mutuality of individual and community. In 3:16, Paul insists that the community is the temple of divine πνεῦμα, while 6:19 denotes the individual's body as the temple of ἁγίου πνεύματός. Both descriptions presume the BODY IS CONTAINER metaphor and map the pneumatic presence of Christ to the interior. In this way, Paul simultaneously thinks of the individual and the community as somatically interdependent. The apostle makes no sharp divide between the individual and community (i.e., between part and whole), nor does he monistically subsume one into the other; rather,

---

19. The most explicit text is 1 Cor 12:12–13, where Paul makes a distinction between the whole "body" (σῶμα) and specific parts such as "limbs/members" (μέλος) and cross-maps this somatic construction onto the general community and specific individual Christ-devotees. What results is a view of the community that acknowledges the individual within the context of the communal, with the focus resting on the intrasomatic polarity of part and whole.

20. This sense of mutual interrelation permeates Paul's letters, especially with respect to notions of togetherness (as I will discuss below; e.g., 1 Cor 4:8; 12:26; 2 Cor 7:3; Phil 1:7, 27; 2:2, 17–18; 4:14; Gal 5:13–15, 22–26; 6:1–5; see also Phil 2:1–5).

intrasomatic polarity extends to the community via the CHURCH IS BODY (OF CHRIST) metaphor.

In addition to Paul's language of Christ-believer oneness is the related language of *togetherness*. Whereas Paul's oneness descriptions are premised on the CONTAINER schema, his togetherness descriptions are structured by the PROXIMITY schema and thus characterize believers as participating with Christ (i.e., NEAR rather than IN). The most pervasive way togetherness is articulated is through the expression σὺν Χριστῷ and (especially) Paul's various σύν- compounds, thus describing believers as existing and acting with Christ.[21]

Paul evinces weak and strong expressions of togetherness, both of which demonstrate the extent to which oneness and togetherness interlace each other. In its weaker form, divine-human propinquity is expressed via notions of belonging such that believers are understood as God's possession. This is particularly evident in Rom 8, where the language of *belonging to Christ* (v. 9) is used in conjunction with the reciprocal *Christ in you/you in Christ* description.[22] Thus Sanders (1977, 462): "to belong to Christ is not different from being 'in' him.... we see [in Rom 8] the close connection between belonging, indwelling and being indwelt." A similar sense of belonging is also found in Gal 3:28–29, where "[being] of Christ" (ὑμεῖς Χριστοῦ) denotes being both ἐν Χριστῷ Ἰησοῦ and "of Abraham's seed" (τοῦ Ἀβραὰμ σπέρμα). In passages such as these, the image of being Christ's possession denotes divine-human proximity (NEAR) such that oneness and togetherness closely correspond with each other.

In its stronger form, Christ-believer togetherness denotes not only proximity but shared ontology. This is most explicit in Paul's descriptions of believers becoming organically enmeshed with Christ (e.g., σύμφυτος, Rom 6:5; σύμμορφος, Rom 8:29; Phil 3:21). Each of these instances con-

---

21. The phrase σὺν Χριστῷ occurs only in Rom 6:8 and Phil 1:23 (used in the former to denote past baptismal death with Christ and in the latter to denote postmortem life with Christ), though compare further the phrases σὺν Ἰησοῦ (2 Cor 4:14), σὺν αὐτῷ (e.g., Rom 8:32; 2 Cor 13:4; 1 Thess 4:14; 5:10), σὺν κυρίῳ (1 Thess 4:17), as well as the obverse σὺν τῷ κόσμῳ (1 Cor 11:32). Dunn (1998b, 402–3 nn. 62–63) has conveniently listed forty-three different σύν- prefixed nouns and verbs, spanning both the undisputed and disputed Paulines.

22. On believers belonging to Christ, see 1 Cor 3:23; 6:19–20; 15:23; Gal 5:24; and Rom 14:8. Further examples include Paul's use of the slave metaphor, in which believers now have a new owner (e.g., Rom 6:16–23). Paul also frequently describes the churches of God (e.g., ἐκκλησίᾳ τοῦ θεοῦ, 2 Cor 1:1).

veys the idea of two separate entities that are united into an organic and living singularity.²³ The teleological focus of these passages indicates that Paul is looking ahead to the cessation of intrasomatic polarity that will accompany the final transformation into the enspirited risen body. Believers will thus exist in a somatic unity with Christ, the πνεῦμα ζῳοποιοῦν (1 Cor 15:45). In such σύν- compounds, then, the stronger shades of Paul's togetherness descriptions intimate a kind of hyperproximity that is marked by conjoined participation in the salvific drama. Togetherness and oneness are not only closely related; they actually bleed together in Paul's descriptions.

The foregoing discussion of both oneness and togetherness indicates that Paul's participationist ideals move in a particular image-schematic direction—from proximity (NEAR) to hyperproximity (IN/NEAR) to containment (IN). This spectrum of expression, which is structured by CONTAINER and PROXIMITY schemata, characterizes the breadth of Paul's participationist ideals: believers participate with Christ because they are both *in* and *near* Christ, and Christ is both *in* and *near* them.

In an important respect, however, this interplay of *in* and *near* reflects a more general schematic structure—the UNION gestalt—that correlates the CONTAINER and PROXIMITY schemata with one another.²⁴ The gestalt structure is diagrammed in figure 5.1, where it is portrayed as a container with a bidirectional PATH that enables a TRAJECTOR to move between IN-NEAR and OUT-FAR positions. As we can see, both the CONTAINER (IN-OUT) and PROXIMITY (NEAR-FAR) schemata naturally integrate with one another, and this is readily apparent in a number of embodied experiences of union. One of the richest and most primal of such experiences is the gestation process, where both mother and child experience union as CONTAINMENT during the gestation period and PROXIMITY as two separate human beings once birth has taken place.²⁵ Similarly, in sexual intercourse, partners who were once disconnected (FAR) come together (NEAR)

---

23. See discussion in nn. 1–3 above.

24. Though the meaning of the concept of UNION is undoubtedly constructed variously in different cultures, what is of immediate interest here is the image-schematic gestalt that emerges from recurrent patterns of human embodiment.

25. More precisely, in the gestation process both mother and child are connected as one, and the child actually grows *within* the mother until it is delivered *out* of the mother's body and thus becomes a separate human being.

such that the one is able to penetrate (IN) the other.²⁶ In these ways, the UNION gestalt integrates both the CONTAINER and PROXIMITY schemata in ways that are grounded in recurrent patterns of human embodiment. Indeed, the integration is so tight that the one schema (CONTAINER) actually entails the other (PROXIMITY). That is, being inside (IN) the container is a kind of hyperproximity (NEAR/IN), whereas movement away from the container places the trajector both OUT and FAR. Accordingly, there are conceptual correlations that link IN/NEAR vis-à-vis OUT/FAR. Being *in* something entails nearness, while being *out*side entails varying degrees of distance.

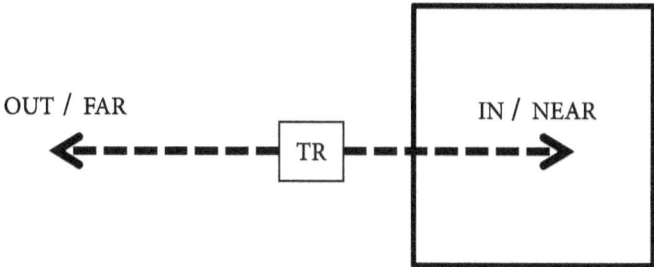

Figure 5.1. The UNION (CONTAINER-PROXIMITY) Gestalt

From an image-schematic point of view, the interconnection of Paul's oneness and togetherness descriptions is intuitive in that these two aspects reflect dimensions of the one UNION gestalt. For this reason, it is perhaps not surprising that the sex metaphor is not absent from the apostle's participationist descriptions. In 1 Cor 6:12–20, Paul describes believers as being united to God as one πνεῦμα via the metaphor of a man and a prostitute being united as one σάρξ in sexual intercourse (6:16–17). The context here is an appeal made on resurrection grounds (6:14), thus insisting that the future pneumatic state has present pneumatic implications. Within the metaphor, Paul insists that both fleshly and pneumatic unions are bodily

---

26. What is in view here is the physical act of intercourse and not the social values and constructions of that experience. In Greco-Roman antiquity, sexual relations were widely understood as asymmetrical, consisting of one active, superordinate participant and another passive, subordinate partner. For more, see Brooten 1996; and Osiek and Pouya 2010.

in nature. The preferred union is that between believers and God, which constitutes oneness of πνεῦμα rather than flesh. Sanders (1977) has rightly noted that the issue for Paul is not the immorality of fornication with a prostitute but rather the assertion that such fornication produces a union that is mutually exclusive to that shared between Christ and believers.[27] Believers constitute one body with Christ, not a fleshly body (as in sexual union) but rather a pneumatic body (as in resurrection union); that is, the character of this union is not only somatic but specifically pneumosomatic.[28]

In summary, Paul's participationist ideals are conceptually premised on the UNION gestalt, thus enabling notions of oneness (CONTAINER) and togetherness (PROXIMITY) to interlace in the apostle's thought. Paul's participationist language tends toward notions of IN/NEAR, thus characterizing the relationship of Christ and believers via descriptions of hyper-proximity (both indwelling and propinquity).[29] This is primarily achieved through the CHRIST IS CONTAINER metaphor, which enables Paul to conceptualize believers as existing *in* Christ, acting *through* Christ, standing *near* to Christ, and participating *with* Christ. Such descriptions are particularly prevalent in Paul's resurrection ideals, where the process of dying and rising with Christ is characterized not simply by participation but by a more fundamental entwining of Christ with believers. That is, Paul has a view toward pneumosomatic union, both in the present and the future.

5.1.3. Resurrection, UNION, and Patterns of Embodiment

It is perhaps not surprising, then, that Paul's participationist and eschatological ideals interlace one another in the ways they do. In the previous chapter (esp. §4.4) we saw that Paul's CHRIST-framed eschatology locates Christ-devotees in the eschaton (i.e., the macro-GOAL), thus traversing

---

27. Thus Sanders (1977, 455): "it is easy to miss how strange the logic behind it is for us and how natural to Paul.... To say that one should not fornicate because fornication produces a union which excludes one from a union which is salvific is to employ a rationale which today is not readily understood."

28. Closely related is the idea of believers existing in one πνεῦμα. The phrase is explicitly used in 1 Cor 6:17 (ἓν πνεῦμά ἐστιν), and Paul elsewhere speaks of the baptism of believers into one body as happening ἐν ἑνὶ πνεύματι (1 Cor 12:13).

29. Indeed, given that the CONTAINER schema is the dominant aspect of the UNION gestalt, it is not surprising that notions of oneness (e.g., ἐν Χριστῷ/πνεύματι) dominate Paul's participationist ideals.

the protagonist's transformation/change PATH as part of their achievement of the macro-GOAL (fig. 5.2 [= fig. 4.4]). The correlation of these two schematic elements with one another fosters two important foci: first, an emphasis on divine-human proximity (since the macro-GOAL is characterized by NEARness);[30] and second, an emphasis on somatic containment (since eschatology unfolds at the IN-OUT intersection of the TRAJECTOR's body).[31] It is too much to suggest, as Schweitzer (1968, 99) does, that Paul's eschatology created "the conditions for a peculiar Mysticism." An argument of this kind is hard to substantiate, and there are better generative grounds in which to root Pauline participation in/with Christ (see below, §5.3). Rather, we do better simply to recognize that certain conceptual affinities exist between Paul's participationist and eschatological ideals and further that these affinities enable the proliferation of participation and eschatology with one another.

We must recognize, of course, that Paul's language of Christ-believer participation has an important temporal dimension. Joseph Fitzmyer (1989, 89) has articulated this dimension well: "*syn* pregnantly expresses two poles of the Christian experience, identification with Christ at its beginning, and association with him at its term. In the meantime the Christian is *en Christō*."[32] Here Fitzmyer intuitively intimates the transformation/change PATH element of Paul's eschatological outlook. While these trends are certainly identifiable in Paul's letters, they are best seen as interrelated rather than distinct. As we have seen, Paul locates Christ-devotees in a participationist trajectory of transformation that progresses from death with Christ to a future rising with Christ. The entire process consists of dynamics that are worked out at the IN-OUT nexus of the human σῶμα,

---

30. As outlined in §2.1.3, the GOAL element of the RESURRECTION gestalt is structured partially by the NEAR element of the PROXIMITY schema. Seen within the context of Paul's CHRIST-framed eschatology, notions of Christ-believer propinquity are so pervasive precisely because Paul perceives himself and believers as existing in the eschaton (the GOAL, where divine-human nearness is strongest).

31. As I demonstrated in §4.4, Paul's CHRIST-framed eschatology temporally scales the transformation/change PATH such that the TRAJECTOR him- or herself comes into focus. In so doing, this TRAJECTOR is viewed as a CONTAINER-structured σῶμα (note the BODY IS CONTAINER metaphor), thus enabling Paul to develop an IN-OUT dynamic that is projected onto the human body.

32. See also Sanders (1977, 463): "just as Paul describes the state of the Christian as being in Christ, in the body of Christ, in the Spirit and the like, so he describes the means of entering that situation as dying with Christ."

with Christ-devotees moving closer and closer toward divine-human union. The hyperproximity (IN/NEAR) of oneness with the divine thus functions as the chief aim of Paul's resurrection ideals.

Because this participationist trajectory of transformation is currently unfolding on/in the Christ-devotee's σῶμα, Paul thus promotes recurrent patterns of embodiment wherein the RESURRECTION gestalt and its constituent metaphors are used to frame present life in Christ. Resurrection becomes not just a good concept with which to think. It also functions as a metaphor that Paul and his communities live by. We have already seen this in Rom 6–8, where death and resurrection frame the whole of the believer's existence. In contrast to Schweitzer's (1968) doctrine of mysticism, we do better to identify patterns or modes of embodiment wherein notions of RESURRECTION and UNION are seen to converge in the human σῶμα. In the remainder of this chapter, I will explore two aspects of such embodied patterns, specifically illuminating in greater detail Paul's understanding of participation *in* and *with Christ*.

5.2. Patterns of Embodiment 1: Life in Death

At several points in Paul's letters, life in Christ is characterized not by strength or power, but by weakness and humility. Both suffering and death are to be embraced with the expectation that life is inevitable.[33] At the heart of this motif is the concept of REVERSAL, which, as I have shown, is an entailment of the RESURRECTION gestalt and reflects the RESURRECTION IS REVERSAL metaphor (§2.1.2.1). Within the CHRIST frame, though

---

33. The theme finds articulation throughout Paul's letters (e.g., Rom 8:12–17; Gal 2:19–20; 1 Thess 2:13–16), though it is especially prevalent in the Corinthian correspondence and Philippians. For example, in an effort to redefine status hierarchies within the Corinthian *ekklēsia*, Paul generally prioritizes that which is foolish, weak, and low by insisting that God has shamed the wise, strong, and high (see 1 Cor 1:17–2:5). A similar logic is carried over into 2 Corinthians, too. In his so-called "fool's speech," Paul boasts in his weaknesses so that Christ's power might be made perfect in him (2 Cor 12:9–10; see also Phil 4:11–13). In Philippians, this paradox is expressed as a radical reorientation of values (Phil 3:4–11), and it also undergirds communal ethics that are modeled on Christ (Phil 2:1–11). The former is a reversal of social values, the latter a reversal of social structures. Beyond the undisputed letters, the image of the suffering apostle becomes a focal point of Paul's veneration in later Christian writings (e.g., the deutero-Paulines, the Pastoral Epistles, and even the apocryphal acts; see Pervo 2010, 16–18).

5. PARTICIPATING IN RESURRECTION 191

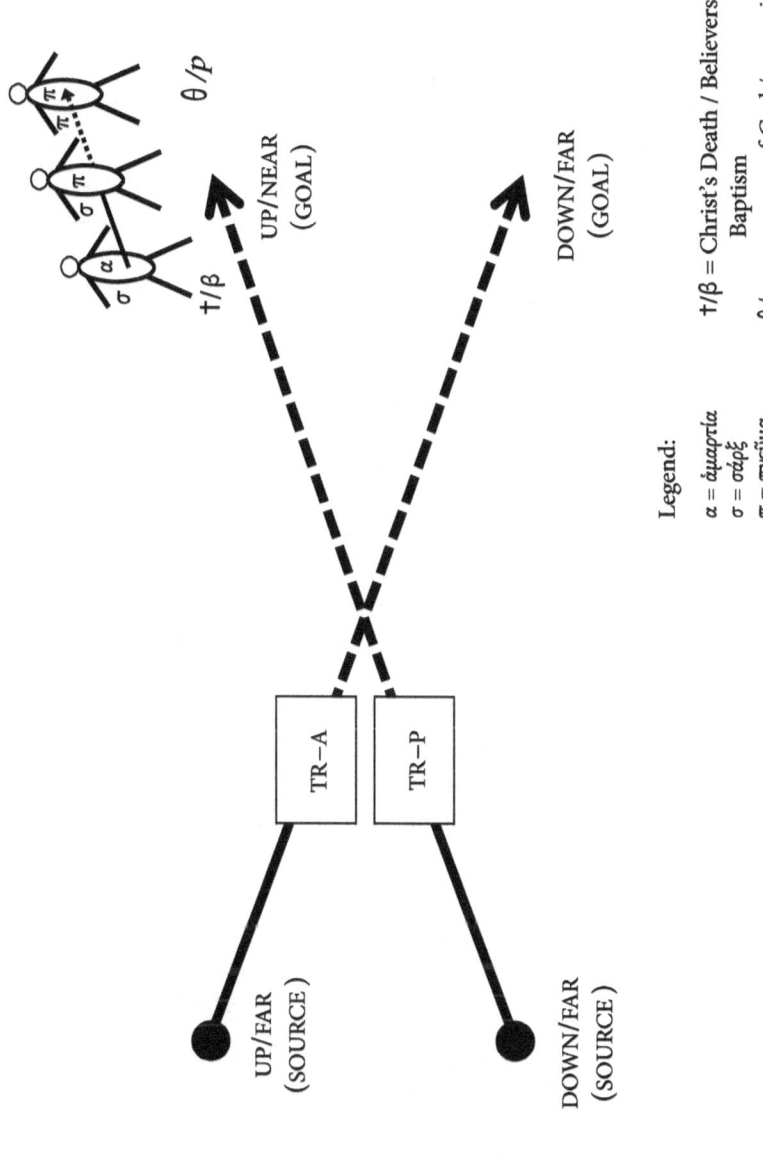

Figure 5.2. Paul's Appropriation of the RESURRECTION Gestalt

Christ's death and resurrection stand as the programmatic example of this reversal pattern (2 Cor 13:4), the RESURRECTION IS REVERSAL metaphor is most strongly expressed in Paul's insistence that participation in Christ's sufferings paradoxically brings Christ-devotees into closer fellowship with the pneumatic Christ and the ecclesial body (Phil 1:29; 3:10–11; 2 Cor 1:3–9).

Pauline scholars often characterize this paradox as the motif of dying and rising with Christ. Tannehill (1967, 75) correctly sees this as the "structure of the new life,"[34] and Engberg-Pedersen (2010, 45) describes Paul's thought as consisting of a "through death to resurrected life" pattern. Wedderburn (1987, 360–90, esp. 382), on the other hand, acknowledges the life through death motif but prefers to speak of life *in* death, which he sees as the more prominent Pauline theme. A key distinction for Wedderburn is the assertion that life *through* death speaks primarily of past and future events (so Rom 6:5), while the motif of life *in* death is oriented to the temporal present (so 2 Cor 4:10–11). In the ensuing discussion, I want to demonstrate the artificial nature of this distinction. As I have already shown, Paul evinces a strong degree of coherence between UP/IN and DOWN/OUT schematic role-values (§4.2), thus enabling the apostle to conceptualize life and death via VERTICALITY and CONTAINMENT schemata so as to yield complementary metaphors: LIFE IS UP/IN and DEATH IS DOWN/OUT. Given this correlation, Paul can speak interchangeably of DOWN to UP via PATH (i.e., life through death) and OUT to IN via PATH (i.e., life in death).[35]

It is this latter conceptual structure—OUT to IN via PATH—that I want to illuminate here (the DOWN to UP via PATH structure has already been discussed in §§4.3–4). As I will show, Paul maps the RESURRECTION gestalt's DOWN to UP via PATH structure onto the IN-OUT dimension of the human body, thus enabling the apostle to speak both of life *through* death and life *in* death. Metaphors of VERTICALITY are blended with those

---

34. So quoted from the title of Tannehill's (1967, 75–129) extended chapter on the topic. Tannehill stresses Paul's pastoral concerns as the impetus for this structuring: "this continuing participation in death ... prevent[s] the believer from trusting in himself and so falling back into the old life" (77; see also 127).

35. As I have stressed throughout this study, conceptual coherence does not imply systematicity at human scale. Wedderburn (1987) is certainly correct that life *through* death has a more sequential nature that lends itself to temporal expressions, while the life *in* death pattern has a more immediate orientation. The key point I stress, however, is that these expressions are not disconnected but rather reflective of interrelated aspects of Paul's resurrection ideals.

of CONTAINMENT in such a way that the inclined transformation/change PATH is projected onto the somatic strictures of the human subject him- or herself. This results not only in the framing of life in Christ via notions of resurrection but also in the more fundamental assertion that resurrection is currently happening to the body itself through a process of ongoing outer death and inner life. Accordingly, the embodied nature of participation in Christ's death/resurrection comes to the fore.

5.2.1. IN-OUT Affectivity in 2 Corinthians 3:12–4:6

We encountered in chapter 4 (§4.2) the notion of intrasomatic polarity as a mutually affective interplay of IN and OUT, which is to say that what happens inwardly affects what happens outwardly, and vice versa (IN ⇌ OUT).[36] In Rom 6–8, this interplay is framed by self-mastery ideals such that the properly aligned interior produces external, ethical actions. In 2 Cor 3–4, Paul again stresses IN-OUT affectivity. The key passage in this context is 4:7–18 (esp. 4:10–11 and 16–18), where the IN-OUT dynamic is understood as a process of carrying Jesus's death in one's body such that Jesus's life may be made visible in that same body (4:10–11). Paul's participationist ideals are particularly evident here, as the process of dying and rising with Christ is seen as a present (rather than past and/or future) dynamic at work in the body.

Before turning to 4:7–18, however, it will be helpful first to trace Paul's argument in 3:12–4:6. This is particularly important because the entire discourse of 2 Cor 3–4 presumes a somatically drawn IN-OUT affective dynamic.[37] In 3:12–4:6, this dynamic is framed not by notions of self-

---

36. I use the term *affective* and cognates (*affectiveness*, *affectivity*, etc.) to denote not emotional states (e.g., moods, feelings) but rather influence. That is to say, IN-OUT affectivity indicates the extent to which OUT affects IN, which in turn affects OUT. The term denotes a dynamic process of reciprocal influence.

37. Indeed, this interplay permeates the entire fragment that constitutes this section of 2 Corinthians (2:14–6:13; 7:2–4). Already at the outset (2:14–15), the tone of this address is geared toward public (= outward) displays of credentials, and the fragment concludes with a restatement of Paul's invitation into one another's hearts with the hope that such inward conjoining will produce external boasting (6:11–13; 7:2–4). In 3:2–3, Paul characterizes the Corinthians as a letter written on the human heart with pneuma (ἐγγεγραμμένη ἐν ταῖς καρδίαις ἡμῶν ... ἐγγεγραμμένη οὐ μέλανι ἀλλὰ πνεύματι θεοῦ ζῶντος). The frame of reference is clearly the somatic interior, though Paul also insists that this inner letter is public and able to be "known and read by all" (3:2). Paul

mastery but rather by Jewish ascent and divine glory traditions.[38] A major point of comparison for Paul is the contrasting of old and new covenants, both of which are characterized by "glory" (δόξα). According to the apostle, the glory of the new surpasses that of the old (3:9–10). Indeed, Paul insists the glory of the old has been "nullified" (καταργέω, 3:7, 11; see also 3:10), and he goes on to characterize the new (i.e., the ministry of πνεῦμα) as something that will come in glory (3:8, 12) and yet already abounds in glory (3:9, 11, 16–18). Again, we encounter an already/not-yet dynamic, and here—as in Romans—this interplay is mapped to the IN-OUT axis of the human σῶμα. This is expressly clear in 3:12–4:6, where the logic of

---

is here linking that which is somatically inward with that which is outward such that what happens inwardly is connected directly to what happens outwardly. Though the Corinthians are written on the hearts of Paul and his companions, those same Corinthians are on public display and thus stand as the only "letter of recommendation" that Paul needs. The theme carries on into ch. 5 (esp. vv. 11–17), where Paul hopes that he and his companions are known in the "conscience" (ἐν ταῖς συνειδήσεσιν ὑμῶν) of the Corinthians. Paul hopes that such inward knowledge will, by implication, result in the Corinthians outward boasting about the apostles, not like the super-apostles, who "boast in appearances but not in the heart" (τοὺς ἐν προσώπῳ καυχωμένους καὶ μὴ ἐν καρδίᾳ, 5:12). This ultimately leads Paul back into his σάρξ/πνεῦμα distinction, now articulated with respect to the absence of Christ's fleshly existence (5:16) and the (presumed) presences of Christ's pneumatic existence (3:17). Ultimately, Paul's knowledge of the pneumatic rather than fleshly Christ is tied to the apostle's experiences of heavenly ascent, which themselves are correlated in important ways with IN-OUT somatic affectivity at the eschaton (5:1–5) and in the present (3:12–4:7; 5:6–10, 13). These latter themes are discussed below (§5.3).

38. The principal intertexts concern the scriptural accounts of the giving of the law and Moses's repeated encounters with Yahweh's glory (esp. Moses's veiling practice; see esp. Exod 19:9b–25; 24:9–18; 33:7–23; 34:1–35; 40:34–38). Specific allusions are found in 2 Cor 3:7, 13, and 16, the latter of which is an allusion to Exod 34:34. Other scriptural passages lurking in the intertextual shadows of 2 Cor 3:1–4:6 include Jer 31:31–33 (which speaks of a "new covenant" that is mapped to the somatic interior), Ezek 36:26–27 (which speaks of a "new heart"), and Gen 1:3, Ps 112:4, and Isa 9:1 (which find expression in 2 Cor 4:6). Beyond these biblical texts, also relevant are the many extrabiblical traditions wherein Moses is interpreted as an ascender to heaven, not only extending his Sinaitic journey (e.g., LAB 12:1; 2 Bar. 4:2–7; 59:3–11; Ezek. Trag. lines 68–72) but also asserting a related ascent at the end of his life (e.g., Philo *Mos.* 2.288–292; *Virt.* 72–79; see also QG 1.86). For further examples, see Meeks 1967, 122–25, 156–59, 205–11, and 241–46. Given the interplay between Jesus and Moses in 2 Cor 3:12–4:6, it is perhaps not insignificant that these Mosaic ascents often result in the apotheosis or divination of the prophet (e.g., Philo QE 2.40; *Mos.* 1.155–158; perhaps 4Q374 2 II [as suggested by Fletcher-Louis 1996]).

5. PARTICIPATING IN RESURRECTION 195

Paul's argument flows from the somatic exterior to interior (OUT to IN) and then again from interior to exterior (IN to OUT). I examine each movement in turn.

In 3:13, Paul recounts an initial outward action—that of Moses veiling himself (Exod 34:29–35). Moses does this, in Paul's view, to hide or conceal the diminishing glory of the old covenant.[39] The veil functions as a kind of container (CLOTHING IS CONTAINER metaphor) that shields the visible glory upon Moses's face from the eyes of the Israelites.[40] The frame of reference is clearly the external σῶμα, as Paul is speaking of a garment that Moses puts over his face. From this external referent, Paul next turns his attention somatically inward, insisting that the "minds" (τὰ νοήματα αὐτῶν, 2 Cor 3:14) of those Israelites who looked upon Moses were hard.

---

39. That is, "to prevent the sons of Israel from looking at the end of the [glory being] nullified" (2 Cor 3:13). The construction πρὸς τὸ μὴ ἀτενίσαι denotes purpose (πρός + an articular infinitive), which suggests that Paul sees Moses's veiling as an intentional act (see Harris 2005, 297). Though this suggests an act of deception on Moses's part, it is worth noting that earlier (3:7) Paul has described the veil as shielding Moses from the Israelites "*because of* the glory of his face." This earlier reference suggests the glory was in need of mitigation rather deceptive hiding. Of note, the scriptural intertext (both MT and LXX) recounts Moses's veiling as a means of keeping the Israelites from being afraid of him (Exod 34:30).

40. While it may seem odd for a veil to be considered a container, such a conceptualization is supported on account of (1) its function as an article of clothing (recall the CLOTHING IS CONTAINER metaphor) and (2) the recognition that, when dealing with a physical instantiation of the CONTAINER schema, the boundary of the container restricts one's view (in this case, the veil hides that which it covers; see Lakoff and Johnson 1999, 32). The word κάλυμμα ("veil") occurs only four times in the New Testament (all in our passage), and it is the same word used in the LXX version of the intertext (Exod 34:33–35). In addition to Exod 34, the LXX uses κάλυμμα variously to refer to a curtain (Exod 27:16), a covering for various furnishing from the tent of meeting (Num 4:8–14), and even as a synonym for bodily clothing/armor (1 Macc 4:6), all of which suggest the CONTAINER schema and the kinds of entailments identified in point 2 above. The exact nature of what kind of "veil" Paul has in mind is not entirely clear. From the Homeric period to the Roman era, a κάλυμμα was a woman's veil (often worn by a bride), and it was also superficially connected with mourning and other social experiences (Cleland, Davies, and Llewellyn-Jones 2007, 101–2). It should be noted that, according to LSJ, a κάλυμμα can refer to a "hood," and while this would cover/contain the entire head, we cannot be certain that this is what Paul has in mind. In any event, there is enough evidence to suggest that a κάλυμμα would be conceptualized as a container, and Paul's logic in 2 Cor 3 seems to lend itself to this conclusion.

The direction of affect is explicit here in that Moses's external veil has an internal effect: as Paul insists, whenever Moses is read (note the MOSES FOR SCRIPTURE metonymy), the Mosaic veil exists upon the "hearts" of those who hear (τὴν καρδίαν αὐτῶν, 3:15). Paul's CONTAINER-structured anthropology is presumed here, and the mutually affected internal-external dynamic is explicit. What happens externally affects the internal, and this even crosses interpersonal and temporal planes.[41] Just as Moses wore a veil when he was away from the Lord's presence (FAR), so those who read the Scriptures are internally veiled and similarly separated from the Lord's presence (FAR).

Such is Paul's move from the somatic exterior to interior (OUT to IN). In 3:16–4:6, this movement is reversed. The scriptural intertext—which contains the whole of Moses's movements to and from Yahweh's glory in Exodus[42]—is important in that Paul keys his Corinthian address into certain constellations of ideas that are both schematically and thematically present therein. The episode at Sinai is premised on a CONTAINER structure that has a vertical point at its center and that has a natural entailment of proximity whereby nearness means both going to the center of the container and to the highest point of the vertical structure.[43] Accordingly, the

---

41. The use of "until today" (ἕως σήμερον) and "whenever" (ἡνίκα ἄν) in 3:15 indicates both generality and temporal length (i.e., the veil has always been there and is present in all readings of the Torah).

42. The principal intertexts have been discussed above, n. 38.

43. Two schematic aspects of the intertext are worth noting in detail. First, the site of Moses's encounter with the "glory of Yahweh" (כבוד יהוה/ἡ δόξα τοῦ θεοῦ, Exod 24:16; see also 24:17; 33:18, 22) is at the top of Mount Sinai, thus requiring both ascent (19:20; 24:1, 9, 12, 15; 32:30; 34:4) and corresponding descent. Accordingly, both VERTICALITY and PROXIMITY are correlated in this text such that divine "glory" is characterized by UP and NEAR role-values. Second, this correlation is complemented by a CONTAINER structure that is imposed upon Sinai itself. This CONTAINER structure is concentrated on proximity to Yahweh's presence at Sinai's peak (19:12–13, 17, 21–25; 20:21; 34:3) vis-à-vis exclusion from such presence at the base of the mountain. According to Exod 19, Moses is to "set up a boundary" (גבל/ἀφορίζω) between the mountain and the people that the Israelites are not to penetrate (19:12–13, 21–25 [esp. vv. 12 and 23]). Only Moses and a select few are permitted past the boundary and thus ascend the mountain to the presence of the Lord (19:20; 20:21; 24:9–18; 34:3), and it is only Moses who can stand before the Lord (24:1–2). In this way, the scriptural intertext already contains the schematic mappings that Paul is stressing, thus blending notions of VERTICALITY (ascending Sinai), CONTAINMENT (boundary definition), and PROXIMITY (movement to and from the "glory of Yahweh") with one another.

Exodus narrative draws schematic correlations of UP/NEAR/IN with "glory" and, conversely, DOWN/FAR/OUT with "nonglory" (or "veiled glory").[44] In 2 Cor 3:16, Paul plays on these correlations. The removal of the veil is marked by approaching the Lord's presence (NEAR), though for Paul the frame of reference is no longer the prescribed Sinaitic boundary but rather the interior of the human body: when the veil is removed, it is taken off of the human καρδία (generally) and not Moses's face (specifically, as implied by 3:15). Within this context, the intertextual echo in 3:16 (i.e., Exod 34:34) resounds with the insistence that, when one turns to the Lord (NEAR), the veil is no longer present on the somatic interior.[45] However, the subject who "turns to the Lord" in 2 Cor 3:16–18 is not Moses but rather those who believe in Christ. By cross-mapping mountainous (even heavenly) ascent to the somatic strictures of the body, the apostle is able to recast Christ-devotees as unveiled in the somatic interior. Significantly, Paul casts this inner unveiling as part of an ongoing process of "transformation" in which believers transition "from glory to glory" (μεταμορφούμεθα ἀπὸ δόξης εἰς δόξαν, 3:18). Here again Paul casts the somatic interior as the location in which transformation has already taken place; that which is inward (the καρδία) is already unveiled and near to the Lord (indeed, allowed to see the face of Jesus, God's Great Glory [4:6]).

In light of this inner unveiling, in 3:18 Paul reverses the spatio-somatic movement of 3:13–15 so as to draw attention to believers' already "unveiled faces" (ἀνακεκαλυμμένῳ προσώπῳ; note the use of the perfect tense).[46] Here the mutually affective relationship of IN and OUT (IN ⇌ OUT) is brought to

---

44. As discussed in §4.2, πνεῦμα functions as a category that conceptually is UP and IN, thus enabling the somatic interior (rather than Sinai's peak) to function as the location of divine-human propinquity. For Paul, the glory of the Lord is pneumatic in nature (2 Cor 3:17–18; 4:6), which is to say that the pneumatic glory encountered inside the human σῶμα (4:6) is the same glory that Moses encountered at Sinai's peak. Though there has been much exegetical debate as to the identity of κύριος in 3:16, 17a, 17b, and 18 (e.g., Thrall 1994, 1:278–82), I presume that Paul makes no firm distinction between the κύριος of the intertext and the κύριος whom he has encountered pneumatically. That is, the two figures are conflated for Paul.

45. To recall 3:12, it is this activity of being IN and NEAR that constitutes the great boldness with which believers act, boldness that those associated with Moses did/do not have in that they were/are veiled (both externally and inwardly). The NEAR/IN correlation happens within the believer him- or herself (an unveiling of the καρδία), thus reversing what is described in 3:15.

46. It is for this reason that Paul can later insist those in Christ are "new creations"

the fore, as the already unveiled inner heart results in the already unveiled external face. That Paul has the somatic exterior in mind is suggested by his use of κατοπτρίζω, which occurs here in the middle sense of "beholding oneself in a mirror" (κατοπτριζόμενοι, cf. LSJ; BDAG; L&N §24.44; see also Thrall 1994, 1:290–95). The mirror metaphor is apt precisely because it enables Paul to express the functional relationship of how the internal can view the external.[47] It is a determinative limitation of the human body that one is unable physically to see one's own face without an external reflective aid. A mirror facilitates such sight, and Paul here uses this metaphor as way of characterizing the unveiled, transformed, already radiant heart as looking out at the external, physical face that awaits future pneumatic glory.[48] What is in view is the external human σῶμα, which is characterized as already unveiled precisely because it is currently engaged in a trajectory of transformative embodiment.[49] We should of course not preclude the possibility that this mirrored reflection is imprecise or dim (compare with 1 Cor 13:12),[50] and thus the transformed inner heart sees the earthly, exterior face only partially reflecting the glory of the Lord (i.e., the face

---

(καινὴ κτίσις) and are to be regarded not according to the somatic exterior (κατὰ σάρκα) but rather according to the pneumatic nature they share with Christ (5:16–17).

47. It is perhaps not insignificant that Paul contrasts the veil with mirrored sight in 3:18. Both a veil and a mirror affect one's sight, though they differ in that the former inhibits while the latter facilitates sight.

48. This stands in contrast to those who suggest that Christ is the mirror in which believers view the glory of the Lord (see, e.g., Furnish 1984, 239; Thrall 1994, 1:284). Such a view is made on comparison with the personification of Wisdom in Wis 7:25–26, though this is problematic because (1) it fails to recognize Paul's spatio-somatic movement from OUT to IN and IN to OUT, and (2) Paul does not equate either Christ or the Lord's glory with the mirror itself but rather speaks of seeing the Lord's glory in the mirror.

49. This IN-OUT mapping is thus temporally correlated (IN with already; OUT with not yet), and Paul has the transformation of the entire person in mind. It is in this sense, then, that believers are transformed "from glory to glory" (ἀπὸ δόξης εἰς δόξαν, 3:18), that is, from an inner glory to an outer glory.

50. Contra Furnish (1984, 239), who insists that one not read 1 Cor 13:12 into the present context. Of note, in 13:12 Paul uses the mirror metaphor teleologically (i.e., he can only partially see now, but will fully see then), whereas here in 2 Cor 3:18 his usage is anthropological (i.e., the transformed somatic interior looks at the being-transformed somatic exterior). Because dimensions of teleology (now/then) and anthropology (in/out) are interrelated in Paul's writings (see above, §4.4), it seems warranted to compare 1 Cor 13:12 with 2 Cor 3:18.

is unveiled but not fully transformed). In the present passage, however, Paul makes no reference to the quality of the mirrored image.[51] He simply stresses believers' physical, external faces as being unveiled on account of the inner heart's unveiling while at the same time locating these already "unveiled faces" within a process of transformation "from glory to glory." For Paul, what happens to the somatic interior affects the somatic exterior, even if those effects are not yet fully realized.

To summarize, in 3:12–4:6 Paul's argument progresses from the somatic exterior to interior and back again, specifically stressing the mutually affective interplay of IN and OUT (IN ⇌ OUT). For Paul, ascent is simultaneously a movement into the body. The apostle draws a contrast between Moses, who ascended to the presence of God, and those who are in Christ, who similarly ascend to the presence of God, though they are privy to see the face of Jesus, God's Great Glory (4:6). Accordingly, those who see the face of God's Glory do so not at a mountainous/heavenly pinnacle but rather in their own body's interior—indeed, in their καρδία (3:15–16; 4:6). In constructing this cosmo-somatic mapping, Paul advocates an integrative vision whereby the somatic exterior determines the interior, and vice versa. Because inner and outer mutually affect one another, believers' bodies (specifically their faces) are unveiled and thus in the process of transformation precisely because their somatic interiors (specifically their hearts) are already unveiled and transformed.

5.2.2. IN-OUT Affectivity in 2 Corinthians 4:7–18

Though Paul does not use common resurrection vocabulary in 3:12–4:6, in 4:7–18 he now elaborates this IN-OUT affective dynamic as it relates to the life through death pattern of the RESURRECTION gestalt. In 4:7, Paul makes the BODY IS CONTAINER metaphor explicit when he refers to the earthly body as a "clay jar" in which the "treasure" of renewed life is stored.[52] Paul

---

51. Thrall (1994, 1:293–94) notes that ancient mirrors varied in quality, and thus there would be no automatic association of diminished sight with mirror viewing. Nonetheless, she rightly notes that though "the idea of defective vision is alien to the context, it remains true that mirror-vision is in some sense indirect vision."

52. The precise identification of this treasure is contested (see Thrall 1994, 1:321–22). It has been variously identified as the gospel (following 4:4), as the ministry of the gospel (following 4:1), and as the inner revelation of divine glory (following 4:6). Given the pervasive emphasis on IN-OUT affectivity that we have noted, the third

here is describing the enspirited earthly body, and he goes on to characterize death/resurrection as a process of intrasomatic IN-OUT affectivity. This is particularly evident in Paul's description of an "extraordinary power" (4:7) that has been given him by God. In 4:8-12 he describes this power through a rhetorical contrast of bad-and-worse experiences, all of which culminate in the organizing concepts of DEATH and LIFE (4:10-11). In Paul's view, ongoing suffering is an experience of carrying Christ's death in one's body such that Christ's life is revealed in that same body. The "extraordinary power" described in 4:7 refers to this ongoing process of Christ's death and resurrection enacting itself *in* the apostolic body; that is, Paul perceives the power of Christ's resurrection to be fully integrated into his (Paul's) somatic composition, and it functions as a sign of Paul's apostleship to the Corinthians.[53]

The precise location of this resurrection power is worth noting, as Paul envisions no less than three somatic locales. First, in 4:10-11 Paul maps both death and life to the somatic exterior (ἐν τῷ σώματι, 4:10; ἐν τῇ θνητῇ σαρκί, 4:11), thus muting the internal referent and instead stressing only the death and life dynamism of the external body. Second, the full process of IN-OUT affectivity is expressed in 4:16-18, where Paul distinguishes between the inner and outer person (ὁ ἔσω ἡμῶν [ἄνθρωπος] and ὁ ἔξω ἡμῶν ἄνθρωπος) so as to denote the ongoing renewal of the former and the ongoing destruction of the latter. Engberg-Pedersen (2010, 47-48) sees in these verses an image of an exterior body that is dead and decomposing while the interior is continually being given life. This is, however, only partly correct, for Paul understands IN and OUT as mutually affecting life upon one another (hence 4:10-11, where life is mapped to the somatic exterior). Third, this mutually affective movement is not just spatio-somatic but also communio-somatic. We have already seen this with Moses: what he does

---

option seems best. Accordingly, Paul is now making the IN-OUT somatic mapping explicit, and the inner revelation of divine glory is part of the risen, interior life.

53. In addition to the present text, in Phil 3:10 Paul speaks of the "power of [Christ's] resurrection" (τὴν δύναμιν τῆς ἀναστάσεως αὐτοῦ) as something he wishes to know, and he further correlates this with an ongoing experience of Christ's sufferings. Paul elsewhere insists that both resurrection and somatic transformation specifically happen by the "power" of God (δύναμις, 1 Cor 6:14; 2 Cor 13:4; ἐνέργεια, Phil 3:21). Other connections between resurrection and power can be found in Rom 1:4, 1 Cor 15:43, and perhaps 2 Cor 12:9. To this one should add also those passages that speak of πνεῦμα as the instrument of resurrection (e.g., Rom 8:11). Elsewhere Paul similarly correlates πνεῦμα with God's power (e.g., 1 Cor 2:4-5; Rom 15:13, 19; 1 Thess 1:5).

with his face affects all those who read him (2 Cor 3:13–15). Paul extends this communio-somatic logic to his own relationship to the Corinthians. In this third somatic locale, the sufferings and hardships that Paul and his companions endure in their apostolic bodies are viewed as effecting life in the ecclesial body. No doubt this plays into Paul's polemic with the so-called super-apostles, but the logic by which it does so is as follows: what happens to the individual (in this case, the apostle and his companions) affects the community (the Corinthians). So Paul, "death is at work in us [ἐν ἡμῖν], but life in you [ἐν ὑμῖν]" (4:12; see also 4:15). Paul's suffering/dying produces life for the Corinthians.

Taking these three somatic referents together—the external body, the internal body, and the communal body—Paul outlines an intrasomatic polarity whereby IN and OUT mutually affect one another. Death on the somatic exterior enacts life on the somatic interior (4:16–18), which in turn enacts life on the somatic exterior, both for the individual apostle (4:10–11) and the Corinthian ἐκκλησία (4:12). Given the richness and complexity of this somatically mapped life through/in death pattern, it is worth exploring the underlying blending network in detail (see fig. 5.3). Three inputs are in play here. The first (I_1) is cued in 4:7 and consists of the believer's body, which is conceptualized as a container on which death and life are mapped to the exterior and interior, respectively. The second (I_2) is composed of Paul's Christ-framed eschatology (specifically his transformational ideals) and is cued by both the apostle's temporal outlook (4:17–18) and his insistence that death leads to life (4:10–12). The final input (I_3) is composed of the IN-OUT affective relationship (IN ⇌ OUT) that Paul has been describing since 2 Cor 3:12. The three inputs are blended on account of a series of subgeneric spaces, all of which are linked via the RESURRECTION gestalt and its various conceptual metaphors (G).[54]

The blend created in 4:7–18 is perhaps the most robust of those examined in this study. Its novelty is found in the way I_2 and I_3 are projected onto the somatic container of I_1.[55] The key element in the blend is the projection of IN-OUT affectivity (from I_3), which now is blended with the

---

54. The subgeneric spaces all include familiar content: G_{1-2} includes the identification of believers as TRAJECTORS in the RESURRECTION gestalt; G_{1-3} includes the metaphors LIFE IS IN/DEATH IS OUT as well as the CONTAINER schema; and G_{2-3} includes the CONTAINER schema as well as Paul's assertion that the human interior and exterior are interdependent.

55. Note: the CONTAINER in the blended space of fig. 5.3 should be understood as

202 RESURRECTION IN PAUL

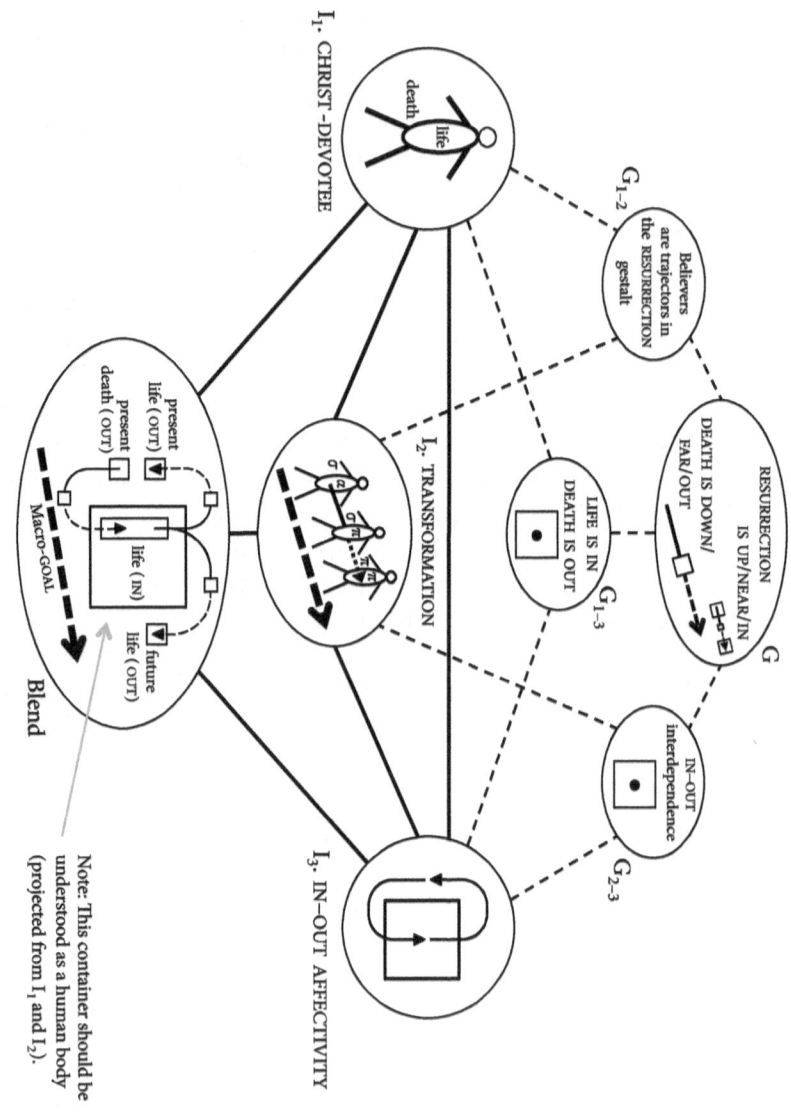

Figure 5.3. Resurrection and IN-OUT Affectivity (2 Cor 4:7–18)

Note: This container should be understood as a human body (projected from I₁ and I₂).

CHANGE gestalt of I_2 to denote an IN-OUT affective transformation (i.e., OUT to IN via TRANSFORMATIVE PATH). It is not just that exterior and interior affect one another; rather the nature of their affective relationship is now characterized as transformation (hence the three curved CHANGE gestalts in the blended space). Seen in this light, outer death produces inner life, which similarly produces outer life. The reciprocal nature of the relationship remains in that transformational affectivity moves from OUT to IN and IN to OUT.

Regarding the OUT to IN affect, external suffering and/or death produces risen life in one's interior (καρδία or ὁ ἔσω ἄνθρωπος, 4:6, 16–18). Suffering is the means by which risen life is produced in the somatic interior. Death and life are interdependent for Paul, and they are mapped onto his body such that the death of the exterior produces life in the interior. That this resurrection process is currently at work in Paul's body underscores the participationist nature of the experience. The life through/in death pattern is not just a motif but an intrasomatic dynamic. Paul locates himself within an ongoing process of dying (externally) and rising (internally) with Christ: "if our outer person is being destroyed, our inner person is being renewed day by day" (4:16).

Regarding the IN to OUT affect, an important structure has emerged in the blended space that was not found in any of the inputs. On account of the temporal dimension of I_2 and the focus on inner life in I_1, this IN to OUT affectivity is bifurcated. This is because resurrection is understood to have both present and future referents. On the one hand, risen life is externally manifested in the present in two distinct ways:[56] (1) it is seen in the individual's body that is undergoing transformation, and on which glory is seen as in a mirror (3:18; 4:10–11); and (2) it is seen in the ecclesial body wherein the sufferings of the apostles impart life to the Corinthians (4:12).[57]

---

a human body (BODY IS CONTAINER). For ease of viewing, it has been visually represented as a CONTAINER.

56. Both of these external manifestations of risen life should be understood to complement the findings of §§4.1–2, where I demonstrated that the RESURRECTION IS CONSCIOUSNESS metaphor frames life in Christ with respect to notions of ethics.

57. That such experiences of suffering belong to the apostle(s) and not to the whole community does not preclude Paul's fundamental communal orientation. Indeed, Paul insists that what one member of the body experiences, all members experience (1 Cor 4:8; 12:26; 2 Cor 1:3–7; 7:2–3; Phil 1:7; 2:17–18; 4:14). As I demonstrated above, the CHURCH IS BODY (OF CHRIST) metaphor provides Paul a way of organizing individuals within the whole. By virtue of his insistence on intrasomatic polarity, it is

In both cases we are dealing with an intrasomatic polarity (either individuals' bodies or the ecclesial body), and the death of the one component is understood as imparting life to the other.[58] In addition to this present dimension, the external manifestation of risen life is also oriented toward the future, when the somatic exterior will be transformed and brought into pneumatic alignment with the interior (5:1–5; cf. 1 Cor 15:35–58). This is explicit in 2 Cor 4:16–18, where Paul's present experience of IN-OUT transformation anticipates the future "eternal weight of glory beyond measure" (4:17). If we take this bifurcation together, the process of transformation from IN to OUT correlates inward resurrection with both present and future outer resurrection; succinctly put, outer death results in inner life, which in turn results in outer life (partially now, fully later).[59]

As we can see, the full complexity of Paul's resurrection ideals are expressed in 4:7–18, as both present and future experiences of resurrection are integrated within a pattern of intrasomatic IN-OUT affectivity (i.e., OUT to IN via TRANSFORMATIVE PATH). In this way, Paul understands resurrection as a process that is currently happening to the body (both of the individual and of the ἐκκλησία) with a determinative orientation toward the anticipated goal of full somatic transformation.

5.2.3. Life in Death as a Pattern of Embodiment

To describe this process of life in death as a pattern of embodiment is to presume that Paul elsewhere utilizes the dynamic of IN-OUT affectivity as a way of framing life in Christ. While Rom 6–8 and 2 Cor 3–4 are the clearest expressions of this dynamic, related descriptions can be found

---

artificial to oppose individual and community, and it also is problematic to emphasize the community over the individual alone. Paul holds both in tension while at the same time insisting on their mutual interdependence.

58. It should be recognized that Paul has already mapped his relationship to the Corinthians according to the somatic interior and exterior: see 2 Cor 3:1–3, where the Corinthian believers are mapped to the hearts (IN) of the apostle and his companions. Seen in this light, the external sufferings of the apostolic body (OUT) produces risen life for the Corinthian community (IN).

59. This ongoing process of IN-OUT affectivity corresponds in many (though not all) ways to what Engberg-Pedersen (2009, 138) identifies as Paul's notion of "an initial transformation that is cognitive and complete ... [and that is] followed by a change of Christ followers which is physical and material and only gradual, but which may also imply a cognitive deepening."

throughout the undisputed epistles. In 1 Cor 9:25–27, for example, Paul insists that he "punishes" (ὑπωπιάζω) his "body" (σῶμα, OUT) so as not to be disqualified from future life.⁶⁰ Similarly, in 1 Thess 5:1–11 Paul exhorts the Thessalonians toward a present lifestyle that is framed by the RESURRECTION IS CONSCIOUSNESS metaphor and that is premised on a particular kind of anthropological composition: the trichotomous spirit-soul-body (= the enspirited earthly body [1 Thess 5:23]).⁶¹ The Epistle to Philemon lacks the language of dying and rising, though here we do find a consonant IN-OUT somatology whereby the interior—σπλάγχνον—is refreshed through a mutually affective dynamic between individual and community (Phlm 7, 12, 20). In Gal 2:19–20, Paul insists that his past crucifixion *with* Christ (συνεσταύρωμαι) results in Christ's present indwelling life (ζῇ δὲ ἐν ἐμοὶ Χριστός). Dunn (1998b, 485) has articulated the force of the perfect tense in 2:19 (συνεσταύρωμαι), suggesting that Paul perceives himself in an ongoing state of cocrucifixion.⁶² Past death with Christ has lasting effects in the present, which include ongoing life that is mapped to the somatic interior. Similarly, in Rom 12:1–3 Paul extends the logic of Rom 6–8 so as to insist that believers offer their "bodies" (σώματα) as a "living sacrifice" (θυσίαν ζῶσαν) to God so as to be "transformed by the renewal of the mind"

---

60. This passage foregrounds the external referents of present suffering/death and future life while backgrounding the interior referent of present life. As a result, the teleological focus of resurrection is explicit while the IN-OUT affective dimension is more muted.

61. Paul's paraenetical address in 1 Thess 5:1–11 distinguishes between two modes of existence that are organized by the CONSCIOUSNESS/UNCONSCIOUSNESS frame-structure:

CONSCIOUSNESS	UNCONSCIOUSNESS
awake (v. 6)	asleep (vv. 6–7)
day (vv. 6, 8)	night (vv. 5, 7)
light (v. 5)	darkness (v. 5)
sobriety (vv. 6–8)	drunkenness (v. 7)
clothed for action (v. 8)	—

The buttressing of these two paths (as it were) up against Paul's eschatological address in 1 Thess 4 creates a context in which resurrection is viewed as both a present (1 Thess 5:1–11) and a future (1 Thess 4:13–18) reality. Resurrection functions as the mode or pattern of existence here and now, and it is precisely the trichotomous composition of spirit-soul-body (1 Thess 5:23)—and the attendant dynamic of IN-OUT affectivity—that enables Christ-devotees to embody such resurrection life.

62. Thus Dunn (1998b, 485) summarizes Paul: "I have been nailed to the cross with Christ, and am in that state still; *I am still hanging with Christ on that cross.*"

(μεταμορφοῦσθε τῇ ἀνακαινώσει τοῦ νοός). The peculiarity of this image should not be missed. Paul describes a body that is at once living and yet continually being given over sacrificially to death. Here the transformative nature of the OUT to IN via PATH structure is obvious, as the external act of somatic sacrifice (death) results in a revitalization of the inner mind (life). Finally, perhaps the best example of this OUT to IN via transformation/change PATH pattern can be found in Phil 1:20–26, where Paul expresses his expectation that "Christ will be exalted in [his] body" (μεγαλυνθήσεται Χριστὸς ἐν τῷ σώματί μου, 1:20). In the midst of rhetorically contemplating suicide, the apostle insists that neither death nor life is of any consequence, for the former will result in postmortem propinquity with Christ while that latter in continued, fruitful labor (1:21–23). Paul here contrasts the bifurcated manifestations of outward-affected life. He is contemplating the merits of risen life in the present vis-à-vis risen life in the future. While Paul admits the latter is more preferable (1:23), in the end he opts for the former (1:24–26).[63]

The breadth of examples noted here indicates that the logic of IN-OUT affectivity permeates Paul's thought more generally. External experiences of suffering/death affect life on the interior, which in turn affects life on the exterior. The temporal referent is both present and future; death now affects life now and life then. It is to this end that Paul is working when he speaks in 2 Cor 4:11 of "always being given up to death for Jesus's sake, so that the life of Jesus may be made visible in our mortal flesh" (the present dimension), and later when he contrasts outer and inner persons with a teleological eye toward the invisible and the eternal (4:16–18):

> Therefore, we are not discouraged, because even though our outer person [ὁ ἔξω ἡμῶν ἄνθρωπος] is being destroyed, our inner person [ὁ ἔσω ἡμῶν] is being renewed day by day. For our slight momentary affliction is bringing about for us an eternal weight of glory beyond all measure, [because] we are looking not at what can be seen but [at] what cannot be seen; for what can be seen is temporary, but what cannot be seen is eternal.

---

63. This same bifurcation of present and future experiences of risen life is expressed also in Phil 3:10–11, where Paul contrasts a present knowledge of "the power of [Christ's] resurrection" with a future attaining of the "resurrection of the dead."

Where is the temporal referent in this text? It is both now and then, it is both already and not yet. The activity of "look[ing] ... [at] what cannot be seen" refers both to expectations for the eschaton *and* attention to the present, indwelling πνεῦμα. Death and life mutually interlace each other both now and then, and they are played out on the body. In articulating this view, Paul utilizes the logic of mutual affectivity so as to express both life *in* death (movement from OUT to IN) and life *through* death (movement from DOWN/FAR to UP/NEAR). The two notions are isomorphic, and they together constitute a system of metaphors by which Paul and his communities are able to organize or pattern their existence in Christ.

5.3. Patterns of Embodiment 2: Ecstasy, Ethnicity, and Resurrection

Though the participationist nuances of 2 Cor 3–4 are more implicit than explicit, we could conjecture that notions of dying and rising with Christ undergird much of Paul's address to the Corinthians. For Paul, the extraordinary divine power that raised Christ from the dead is now perceived to be working in Christ-devotees themselves (2 Cor 4:7). By correlating both life and divine presence with the somatic interior (i.e., UP/NEAR/IN), Paul's eschatology promotes his participationist ideals in that divine-human propinquity is grounded in the human σῶμα. Accordingly, this enables Paul to speak of resurrection as something that will happen with Christ in the future and yet is currently happening in believers in the present. In this final section, I return squarely to the topic of Paul's participationist ideals, exploring how participation and resurrection function as a pattern of embodiment that structures the identity of Christ-devotees.

As I demonstrated in chapter 1 (§1.3.3), scholarly treatments of Paul's participationist ideals tend to favor cognicentric solutions that fail to account for the full breadth of Paul's participationist language. Of the interpretive options briefly sketched in chapter 1, two come to the fore as hermeneutically illuminative: (1) apocalyptic notions of ecstatic heavenly ascents and (2) ideologies of patrilineal genetics.[64] When taken on their own, neither of these interpretive options is wholly satisfactory, as the

---

64. These interpretive options are preferable for two reasons: (1) they offer cross-cultural parallels and explanatory frameworks in which to make sense of Paul's language (in the apocalyptic case), and (2) they offer ancient descriptive contexts that make much sense of the rhetoric and literary forms in which Paul writes (in the patrilineal genetics case).

internal logic of each individual frame is not sufficiently robust to account for the full scope of Paul's participationist descriptions. In the discussion that follows, I offer an explanatory reading that seeks to account for the richness of Paul's participation language while also illuminating the congruence between Paul's apocalyptic and genealogical descriptions. As we will see, Paul's resurrection ideals exist at the creative intersection of these two domains of thought, thus creating a novel expression of Christ-devotee identity that structures patterns of resurrection embodiment.

5.3.1. Experience, Identity, and Ideals at the Nexus of Explanatory Pluralism

I want to open this discussion by bringing together the two treatments of 2 Cor 3–4 and 2 Cor 5 elaborated above. Though discussed independently (see §§5.2 and 3.2.3, respectively), these pericopes flow one into the other and thus should be read in tandem.[65] When viewed as a whole, the entire address of 2 Cor 2:14–5:10 presumes and elaborates on the trajectory of transformative embodiment that we have seen to be at work in Rom 6–8 and 1 Cor 15:35–57. In 2 Cor 2:14–4:15, Paul (and cowriters) engages in an apostolic self-defense where he speaks with an orientation toward the present: his concern is to (re)establish himself and his companions as apostolic authorities in relation to the Corinthians. With a certain degree of contrast, 2 Cor 5:1–5 concerns the temporal future: here, the expectation of risen life and the promise of a different and better CONTAINER (= body) comes to the fore.[66] Standing between these two addresses is 4:16–18, in which I have already demonstrated (§5.2.3) a certain ambiguity such that Paul's present and future referents interlace one another through conceptual correlations of UP/NEAR/IN and DOWN/FAR/OUT. This ambiguity is further carried forward into 5:6–10, where Paul again speaks of the σῶμα in a way that interlaces these conceptual juxtapositions.

Of particular note in 5:6–10 are Paul's three references to "being home" (ἐνδημέω) and "being abroad" (ἐκδημέω), which convey nuances of space and ethnogeographic identity.[67] Where "home" and "abroad" are, exactly,

---

65. This is true of both their canonical and fragmentary contexts; on the redactional character of 2 Corinthians, see ch. 1, n. 108.

66. Though the term σῶμα is not present in 2 Cor 5:1–5, it is used quite centrally in 5:6–10, which builds on and extends the logic of 3:1–5:5.

67. Of note, Paul contrasts ἐνδημέω with ἐκδημέω, which conveys the notion of

is not clear. Paul uses ἐνδημέω to speak both of the earthly body (DOWN/ FAR, 5:6) and of the heavenly presence of the Lord (UP/NEAR, 5:8), a qualitative description that conversely marks both the earthly body and the heavenly presence of the Lord as "abroad" (ἐκδημέω, 5:6 and 8). Accordingly, both the earthly and heavenly bodies are, in a sense, "home" and "abroad." Something of the heavenly is imbued in the earthly to such an extent that both have an element of familiarity and strangeness.[68] This spatial ambiguity is further nuanced by ethnogeographic overtones. Etymologically, ἐνδημέω (cognate of ἔνδημος, itself a compound from ἐν + δῆμος) conveys the sense not just of "liv[ing] at or in a place" (LSJ) but also of being a "native" (LSJ s.v. ἔνδημος) and even "[of] belonging to a ... people" (LS s.v. ἔνδημος). Conversely, ἐκδημέω conveys the notion of "leaving one's homeland" for a foreign land, and it can even imply overtones of exile (LSJ, BDAG). The senses of ἐνδημέω and ἐκδημέω go beyond notions of space to include overtones of identity and kinship. Accordingly, earthly and heavenly locales both have elements of being native and foreign places. This ambiguity points toward the transformative trajectory in which Paul locates Christ-devotees. What is in view is the ethnogeographic (perhaps even genetic) connection between Christ and believers. As we will see below, this blurring—better, blending—of somatic and kinship language is central to Paul's participationist ideals.

The ambiguities in 2 Cor 4:16–18 and 5:6–10 are somewhat akin, I think, to Paul's somatic uncertainty in 12:1–4. In this latter text, which comes from a different epistolary fragment (2 Cor 10–13) and is found in the rhetorically charged "fool's speech,"[69] Paul recounts his own experi-

---

leaving one's homeland for a foreign land (LSJ, BDAG); it can even imply overtones of *exile* (LSJ, BDAG). Both ἐνδημέω and ἐκδημέω occur only three times each in the New Testament, all within 2 Cor 5:6–10.

68. Again, much like Phil 1:20–26, the logic of the trajectory of transformative embodiment undergirds this passage.

69. The rhetorical aim of Paul's address in 2 Cor 11:16–12:10 should not be overlooked, and even here the logic of Paul's resurrection ideals finds creative articulation. On one level, Paul is engaging the Corinthians in a way that echoes the super-apostles, thus combating them on their own terms (as it were). At another level, however, Paul expresses a profound indifference toward heavenly ascents as an indicator of credibility and authority. Central to Paul's rhetoric, however, is the dynamic of IN-OUT affectivity, which Paul here applies to his body and the various revelations reported in 12:1–10. In a paradoxical way, Paul correlates weakness with the "thorn in the flesh" (σκόλοψ τῇ σαρκί, 12:7) and understands this exterior ailment as "the power of Christ

ence of heavenly ascent whereby he encountered God's Great Glory at the cosmic pinnacle. The ineffability of the vision's content (12:4), the somatic confusion of the adept (12:2–3), and the rhetorical aims to which these are put (12:5–10) all suggest that Paul here is recounting an ecstatic experience of heavenly ascent (see A. Segal 1990, 2004; Shantz 2009).[70] Modern scholarship has demonstrated both cross-cultural and ancient comparables for the apostle's description in 12:1–4, many of which are consistent with social-scientific explorations of Altered State of Consciousness (ASC).[71] The terminology Paul uses to describe this experience is ἀποκάλυψις (12:1, 7)—"revelation" or "apocalypse"—which belongs to the emic catalog of first-century ecstatic descriptors (DeConick 2006b, 1–2).[72] Of the eighteen occurrences of either ἀποκάλυψις or ἀποκαλύπτω in the undisputed epistles,[73] Paul's usage in Gal 1:12, 16 is also noteworthy. In Galatians we

---

rest[ing] upon me" (ἐπισκηνώσῃ ἐπ' ἐμέ, 12:9). Though Paul does not use ἐν ἐμοί here, the verb ἐπισκηνόω can carry the idea of being "quartered in" (LSJ) a dwelling (in this case, in Paul's body). More compelling are the string of container descriptions the apostle employs in 12:10, all of which suggest an IN-OUT distinction: "I am pleased in weakness [ἐν ἀσθενείαις], in insolence [ἐν ὕβρεσιν], in distress [ἐν ἀνάγκαις], in persecution [ἐν διωγμοῖς], and [in] difficulty [στενοχωρίαις]." Accordingly, if the Corinthians are to examine Paul's apostolic credentials, they are to do so based on his external sufferings and weaknesses, for these bear the signs of internal life and revelation. In this way, then, Paul employs the logic of the OUT to IN via transformative PATH pattern. He trades on the interplay of UP/NEAR/IN in such a way as to retain the value of such ecstatic encounters with the Lord—they are needed in order to have the transformed interior!—while also eschewing any sense of boasting therein.

70. Issues of the ineffable and somatic confusion point to an Altered State of Consciousness (ASC) context in that there are common comparative themes—both cross-textually and cross-culturally—that betray an ASC lurking behind 2 Cor 12:1–4.

71. See esp. Shantz 2009; A. Segal 1990, 2004. For an excellent primer on ASCs, see Craffert 2010.

72. Following DeConick (2006b), I use the terms *ecstatic*, *mystical*, or (the notoriously problematic) *religious experience* as etic categories that presume a catalog of cross-cultural comparatives by which to illuminate ancient religiosity. Consistent with the findings in ch. 3 above, the *ecstatic* or *mystical experiences* are understood best within the patterns of heavenly ascent and ἀποκάλυψις that permeate certain sectors of Jewish literature and praxis; such constitutes the emic catalog of early Jewish and Christian mysticism.

73. Of Paul's uses of ἀποκάλυψις (nine in total) and the cognate verb ἀποκαλύπτω (nine in total), as many as twelve refer to something that likely can be identified as ASC experiences (or the promotion thereof): 1 Cor 2:10; 14:6, 26, 30 (perhaps 1:7); 2 Cor 12:1, 7; Gal 1:12, 16; 2:2. Notably, since Paul patterns his understanding of resur-

again find Paul engaged in an act of defensive self-presentation so as to stylize his encounter with the risen Christ. Here, however, the encounter of the human with the divine is described not in the language of heavenly ascent (as in 2 Cor 12:1–4 or even 3:12–4:6) but rather in the language of somatic interiority and prophetic calling.[74] Christ is described as having been "revealed … in me" (ἀποκαλύψαι … ἐν ἐμοί, Gal 1:16; compare also 2:20). The interior in question is the somatic interior. It is to this location that the apostle maps his knowledge and "revelation" (ἀποκάλυψις) of Christ.

Even though the language of VERTICALITY is more at home in the heavenly ascent narratives that make up much of the apocalyptic genre, this sense of interiority is somewhat closer—conceptually speaking—to the philological roots of ἀποκάλυψις. Generally speaking, the term ἀποκάλυψις denotes not upward transposition to the heavens but rather the idea of "uncovering." It refers to the "uncovering of someone's head" or even the "unmasking" of someone's face (BDAG, LSJ). Conceptually speaking, the idea of ἀποκάλυψις is the notion of taking a container off of something so as to reveal the inside. This seems to be the schematic notions on which Paul is trading in Gal 1:11–17 and even 2:19–21, here intimating the unveiling of the inner heart so as to encounter Christ in one's somatic interior. The parallels with 2 Cor 3:12–4:6 are uncanny, even if they are implicit and based on conceptual schemata rather than shared terminology.

Though the persuasive and rhetorical aims of texts such as 2 Cor 12:1–10 and Gal 1:11–17; 2:19–21 constitute and color Paul's self-presentation,[75] this should not be seen as an insurmountable obstacle in

---

rection on his experience of heavenly ascent (as argued above and in the immediate section), it is perhaps not surprising that as many as five other occurrences refer to God's act of "revelation" at the eschaton (Rom 2:5; 8:18–19; 1 Cor 3:13 [perhaps 1:7]). (Note: I do not include Rom 16:25 in this count because it is not likely original to Paul [cf. NA[28]].)

74. On prophetic calling, Gal 1:11–17 shares intertextual parallels with Jer 1:4–5 and Isa 49:1. These parallels point to the extent that Paul's descriptions of ecstatic experiences are not presented as raw data. Rather, Paul's ecstasy is experienced within broader traditions and cultural frames—here the prophetic traditions of Israel.

75. Despite the fact that many of Paul's epistles were written by a group of cowriters, the issue of Paul's self-presentation is of key importance. On the one hand, A. Segal (1990) reminds us that Paul's autobiographical reflections always come in the midst of self-defense of his apostleship, a rhetorical feature that perhaps points to the centrality of his religious experience in formulating Christ-devotee identity. On the

speaking meaningfully of the apostle's religious experience.[76] Crucially, it is important to recognize that Paul seems quite comfortable deploying both VERTICALITY and CONTAINER schemata when stylizing his encounters with the risen Christ. For Paul, one ascends to the presence of Christ while Christ also is uncovered inside of believers. As we have already seen (§5.2), this correlation is explicit in 2 Cor 3:12–4:6, where Paul maps—better, blends—notions of heavenly ascent (UP-DOWN) onto the human body (IN-OUT) in such a way that one ascends inside one's body so as to encounter Christ, the Great Glory of God. This convergence of VERTICALITY and CONTAINER schemata exists as a conceptual indicator that hints at and helps us tease out the somatic foundations of Paul's ecstatic experiences. Shantz (2008, 2009) has done the most acute work to this end, specifically exploring the neurobiological foundations of ASCs and relating such findings to Paul's writings. She helpfully illuminates differences in somatic perception between ASCs and normal states of consciousness (see esp. Shantz 2009, 67–109; 2008, 200–204). In the midst of ecstatic

---

other hand, it is important to recognize that, in many respects, our sources speak not of Paul's actual experiences but rather of the experiential dimensions presumed in Paul's thought and world. The undisputed letters convey not raw experiential facts but rather Paul's own self-presentation to the Galatians, the Philippians, the Corinthians, or whomever. Rather than viewing Paul's rhetoric purely through a strong constructivist lens whereby nothing experiential can be found in Paul's address, we do better to see language and experience as spectrally interlacing each other in ways that allow the rhetorical to presume such experiential self-presentation.

76. There are, of course, many attendant problems that come with speaking of experience. In addition to issues of historical distance and cultural otherness, our primary window into Paul's experience is a textual window, which is to say that any discussion of Paul's ecstatic experience must contend with the attendant literary dimensions inherent therein (King 1988, 258; DeConick 2006b, 5–8; Flannery et al. 2008, esp. 6). Accordingly, I take it as axiomatic that religious experiences are, on the one hand, culturally mediated and thus inseparable from such mediation and, on the other, fundamentally embodied and thus constituted by certain somatic and neurobiological functions (see Shantz 2009). Methodologically speaking, the real challenge is to chart a course between essentialist positions that would limit explanation either to cultural or to neurobiological levels alone. Rather than pitting universals and particulars against one another, we do better to explore the dynamic and integrative ways in which culture and biology interlace and are mutually formative within the human subject (see Flannery, Shantz, and Werline 2008; esp. Flannery et al. 2008). In line with our paradigm of vertical integration, this study's focus on recurrent patterns of human embodiment offers one such way forward.

5. PARTICIPATING IN RESURRECTION 213

trance, though the body continues to be perceived, subjects loose conscious awareness of their weight, boundaries, pain, and even the ability to move and act.[77] Such euphoric experiences are particularly marked by two recurrent phenomena that Shantz summarizes. The first relates to perceptions of verticality:

> During intense phases of religious ecstasy, ... the body is perceived as present, but its sensations—its weight, boundaries, pain, or voluntary motion—are all absent from consciousness. In an attempt to interpret these phenomena as coherently as possible, ecstatics frequently report the sensation of floating or flying without physical boundaries between themselves and the people and objects in their awareness. Not surprisingly, descriptions of ascent are also common. (2009, 98)

The second relates to perceptions of boundedness:

> At the peak of neuropsychological tuning, this change in bodily perceptions extends to "a decreased sense or awareness of the boundaries between the subject and other individuals, between the subject and external inanimate objects, between the subject and putative supernatural beings, and indeed, at the extreme, the diminution and abolition of all boundaries of discrete being." This state results in a profound sense of unity that is nuanced by the enculturation of the mystic. The ecstatic experiences a certainty of oneness with a particular divine being or with all being, a certainty that endures long after the trance ends. (100–101, citing d'Aquili and Newberg 1993, 3)

Not all ASCs produce the same somatic effects (see Craffert 2010; Shantz 2009). While Paul may well have had ecstatic experiences that conflated perceptions of verticality and boundedness, he likely also had experiences of one kind or the other. The key point to stress is the phenomenology of the body in such experiences. In the above passages, Shantz is driving at the shared neurobiological happenings that accompany various instances of ecstasy in any human subject, regardless of their cultural context. For Paul, as for ecstatics cross-culturally, conceptions of VERTICALITY and CONTAINMENT prove particularly apt for describing such experiences. Indeed, it is concepts such as these that most intuitively reflect the adept's

---

77. Thus Shantz (2008, 202): "The body ... is stripped away and yet subjects continue to know themselves as embodied."

somatic perception in the midst of trance. These neurobiological happenings suggest somatic anchor points for Paul's blending of VERTICALITY and CONTAINMENT schemata. The apostle is able to describe his encounters with Christ in the ways he does precisely because such encounters were phenomenologically rooted in perceptions of upwardness and boundlessness.

We must recognize, however, that transcultural embodiment is never acultural embodiment. In an important respect, Paul's experience was a *Judean* experience.[78] It is not as though Paul had a raw experience for which he went looking for a ready-made language with which to express its contents.[79] Rather, from the start Paul's neurobiology was culturally and linguistically conditioned as a heavenly ascent to the throne of the Great Glory. The traditions of Jewish apocalyptic, which date to at least the mid-third century BCE,[80] are employed not because they provide a ready-made language for Paul but rather because they constitute the content and substance of Paul's experiences.[81]

---

78. A word of methodological nuance is in order here. Though all experience is constructed within linguistic and cultural contexts, constructions are never devoid of experience. Rather than opposing language and experience, we do better to think in spectral terms whereby the literary and the experiential are not set in an either/or binary. The literary provides the adept not only with a language by which to express the experience, but also—and this point is crucial—the conceptual and narratological substance of the experience itself. While such an assertion has led many to the stronger thesis of categorical pluralism—that is, to speak of mysticism*s* rather than mysticism (e.g., Katz 1978; Scholem 1961, 5–6)—such affirmations need not be taken in a strong constructivist sense so as to bracket out phenomenological, comparative, and/or scientific dimensions. Rather, in light of this study's commitment to the vertical integration of cognition and culture, we do better to look for ways in which language and experience—or narrative and ecstasy—can be seen within a reciprocally affective spectrum of mutuality.

79. For a helpful overview that explores various interpretations of Paul's religious/ecstatic experiences, see Brady 2006.

80. The principal early evidence that anchors this date is the Enochic Book of Watchers (ca. mid-late third century BCE; Nickelsburg and VanderKam 2004, 3). In several studies, Morray-Jones (1992, 1993a, 1993b) has traced the development of these literary and experiential trajectories in (what he calls) the apocalyptic-*merkabah* tradition.

81. For this reason, contra those who view Jewish apocalyptic texts as imaginative fictions (e.g., Himmelfarb 1993, 98), it seems more appropriate to recognize the interdependence of narratives with experiences such that certain narratives come to

Yet constitution does not limit description, and by no means is Paul confined to Jewish apocalyptic as the only frame through which to describe Christ-believer union. As we have seen above, the conviction of somatic oneness and togetherness is central to Paul's participationist ideals. On this point, perhaps Paul felt certain descriptive limitations of the apocalyptic framework, that it did not provide adequate tools with which to explore either the ineffable impact or the communal implications of his ecstatic experience (see also Shantz 2009, 95–101 and 107). While Jewish apocalyptic certainly provides ample resources for speaking of VERTICALITY (e.g., heavenly ascent), the tools with which to explore notions of CONTAINMENT seem more limited.[82] Accordingly, the language of apocalyptic does not provide Paul with enough conceptual content by which to explore what Shantz (2008, 203) refers to as the apostle's "somatic memory of union." While such a memory was apocalyptic in nature, individual epistolary addresses occasioned alternative frame-structures into which Paul could reflect and (re)cast—even remake—this memory of oneness/togetherness.

Quite independent of any focus on ecstatic or mystical experiences, Johnson Hodge (2007) argues convincingly that ideologies of patrilineal genetics function as a key frame-structure in enabling Paul's participationist ideals to find resonance among ancient readers.[83] (This is particularly evinced in Romans and Galatians, where Paul most explicitly constructs

---

find lasting appeal precisely because they cohere with recurrent experiences of ecstasy and ASC.

82. Even though the philological roots of ἀποκάλυψις denote a meaning premised on the CONTAINER schema—namely, "uncovering"—the recurrent themes in this genre stress notions of VERTICALITY (e.g., heavenly ascent) much more readily. There are of course thematic exceptions to this, though such are at best intimated in the Second Temple literature (see, e.g., Alexander 2011; Morray-Jones 2006).

83. Unfortunately, Johnson Hodge (2007, 93) quickly dismisses interpretive contexts of mysticism and/or religious experience as "modernist theological reflection … [that would not likely] have been meaningful to Paul's addressees." Similarly, Stowers (2008, 357) also rejects explanations that pivot to categories of experience, largely on the grounds that "Paul does not use our modern language of experience." In as much as such modern language is concerned primarily with an "individual's inner feel" (357), Stowers is absolutely correct. In the present study, I have sought to avoid such anachronistic pitfalls by taking the common space of the body as the primary ground for shared human experiences. In this view, experiences need not be seen as deterministically inextricable with the language that is used to meaningfully construct such experiences.

a myth of origins for gentile Christ-devotees.) Patrilineal genetics refers to ancient understandings of procreation and progeny.[84] Central here is the conviction that ancestors contain in themselves the "stuff" of those born in their line: "descendants are contained in their ancestors, whether in their seed or womb or in some other way" (Johnson Hodge 2007, 94). This "containment theory of descent" (95), as Johnson Hodge calls it, posits a reciprocal logic whereby "the notion of 'coming out of' (*ek*) your ancestors also shapes the concept of being 'in' your ancestors" (94). For Paul, the ancestral dimension is principally elaborated in Rom 4 and 9 and (especially) Gal 3–4, where Abraham is cast as the father of "those who come out of faith [or faithfulness]" (οἱ ἐκ πίστεως, Gal 3:7, 9). This includes both Judeans and gentiles, who now share a common ancestor. The ἐν/ἐκ language is both patrilineal and teleological, because it is traced from the male ancestor—Abraham—through the proper lineage of heirs—Isaac, and now Christ. Yet the ἐν/ἐκ language is reciprocal in that Paul constructs an inclusive and fictive kinship whereby all those who are ἐκ πίστεως are genealogically in Abraham. So Johnson Hodge (2007, 98), in speaking of Gen 12:1–3:

> The concept of Abraham becoming an *ethnos*, a whole people, illustrates the normative assumptions of patrilineal descent in which descendants are considered a united, corporate group and also understand themselves as elaborations of their ancestors. In this logic, there is a reciprocal relationship in which the ancestor represents all his descendants and the descendants collectively represent the ancestor. In the final verse of this passage [Gen 12:3], the scope broadens from the greatness of Abraham and the *ethnos* of Israel to a global claim: "all the tribes of the earth" are blessed "in" Abraham.

The ἐν/ἐκ language, then, marks several different planes of meaning: union with the progenitor, the lineage of inheritance, and in the context of the Hebrew Scriptures, inclusion in God's covenantal people. All of these elements are present in Paul's address in Gal 3–4, where the apostle "is not distinguishing between an ethnic group and a non-ethnic group [i.e., an ethnic vis-à-vis "true" Israel], but a privileged lineage within a larger ethnic

---

84. Johnson Hodge (2007, 94–97) draws on a range of Greek, Roman, and Judean texts, all of which span medical, philosophical, and political discussions of procreation and lineage; her primary witnesses are Aristotle (selections from *Generatione anamalium*), Philo (*Legat.* 54–56), Seneca (*Nat.* 3.29.2–3), and Gen 25:23.

group. It is this privileged lineage that gentiles-in-Christ join (not replace) when they are baptized" (Johnson Hodge 2007, 102). This all relates to Paul's conception of Christ as a container in that "the 'in' language signals the person through whom blessings and promises are transmitted" (103). Gentiles are brought into a new family, as it were; they have been included in the σπέρμα of Abraham (Gal 3:16) such that they are "one in Christ Jesus,... [they are] Abraham's descendants, heirs according to the promise" (εἷς ... ἐν Χριστῷ Ιησοῦ, ... Ἀβραὰμ σπέρμα,... κατ' ἐπαγγελίαν κληρονόμοι, Gal 3:29).

There is a definite materiality at work in this description of patrilineal genetics—ancestors and descendants are united with one another, because they share the same "stuff." Stowers (2008) has extended Johnson Hodge's work, arguing that Paul's new myth of origins posits a material lineage between ancestor and descendant. Though Paul's language of "promise" and "faith" may seem to denote immaterial notions of social solidarity or noetic affirmation, it is the apostle's material presumptions that give rhetorical teeth to his argument in Galatians.[85] Gentiles in Christ are part of Abraham's seed precisely because they physically possess the material πνεῦμα and therefore are of the same kind as Abraham and (importantly) Christ too:

> Gentiles who come to share the pneuma of Christ in baptism share in this contiguity back to Abraham and are thus seed of Abraham and coheirs as they participate in the stuff of Christ.... [There is] an ontological unity. Those in Christ are literally of the same stuff. All share the very same pneuma—Christ's. (Stowers 2008, 360)

A key feature of the treatments of Stowers and Johnson Hodge is the assertion that human subjects relate to and identify with one another according to the substances they share. Gentile Christ-devotees are in Christ because they share a concrete, physical connection with Christ, namely, the πνεῦμα imbued into the σῶμα at baptism. Because gentiles have been granted the πνεῦμα, their physical selves are changed: they "are materially improved people, who not only have past sins forgiven but more importantly are empowered and filled with a holy stuff that actively enables obedience to God" (Stowers 2008, 365).

---

85. On Paul's use of οἱ ἐκ πίστεως as viewed within the context of patrilineal genetics, see Johnson Hodge 2007, 79–91.

At the heart of Paul's elaboration of Christ-believer union (UNION) are the very presumptions at work in Paul's resurrection ideals: the somatic alteration effected in baptism, convictions of pneumatic transformation in the present, and the telos of transformative embodiment—these are all components that we have seen to be central in Paul's resurrection ideals. But they also are components that find resonance with Paul's self-presentation of ecstasy/heavenly ascent. Accordingly, these three aspects of Paul's life and thought—resurrection, patrilineal genetics, and ecstasy/heavenly ascent—mutually interlace and inform one another in the construction of meaning. This suggests that the transformation of the human σῶμα from enspirited earthly body to enspirited risen body—a transformation that is prefigured in ecstatic heavenly ascent—is directly connected to the participatory work of πνεῦμα. To speak of participation in/with Christ (in the genetic sense) is also to uncover Paul's resurrection ideals and, by implication, his self-presentation of ecstatic experience.

The intertwining of resurrection, patrilineal genetics, and ecstasy/heavenly ascent in Paul's life and thought can helpfully be demonstrated through a blending analysis (see fig. 5.4). Again, three input spaces are in play. The first input (I_1) is framed by the RESURRECTION gestalt and its constituent metaphors, which provide Paul with a certain set of stative notions (being dead, being alive, particular types of bodies, ethnogeographic kin relations, etc.) as well as various rationales (transitions from death to life, the process of transformation, reversal). Accordingly, I_1 contains all the frame-structure that goes with the RESURRECTION gestalt, the most pertinent of which (for this blend) are the following: the idea of passing from death to life, Judean notions of resurrection as a restoration of the ethnogeographical group, and the idea of transformed pneumatic or angelomorphic glory-bodies.

The second input (I_2) is that of ECSTATIC EXPERIENCE AS HEAVENLY ASCENT.[86] This input contains information that relates to traditions of both heavenly ascents (e.g., the correlation of divine/human proximity with somatic transformation) and euphoric ecstatic experiences (e.g., the correlation of VERTICALITY and CONTAINMENT in the somatic self-perception of the ecstatic). In the blend, I_1 and I_2 are cross-mapped with one another

---

86. I have titled this space ECSTATIC EXPERIENCE AS HEAVENLY ASCENT so as to underscore the deep cultural framing at work in Paul's ecstatic experiences.

5. PARTICIPATING IN RESURRECTION   219

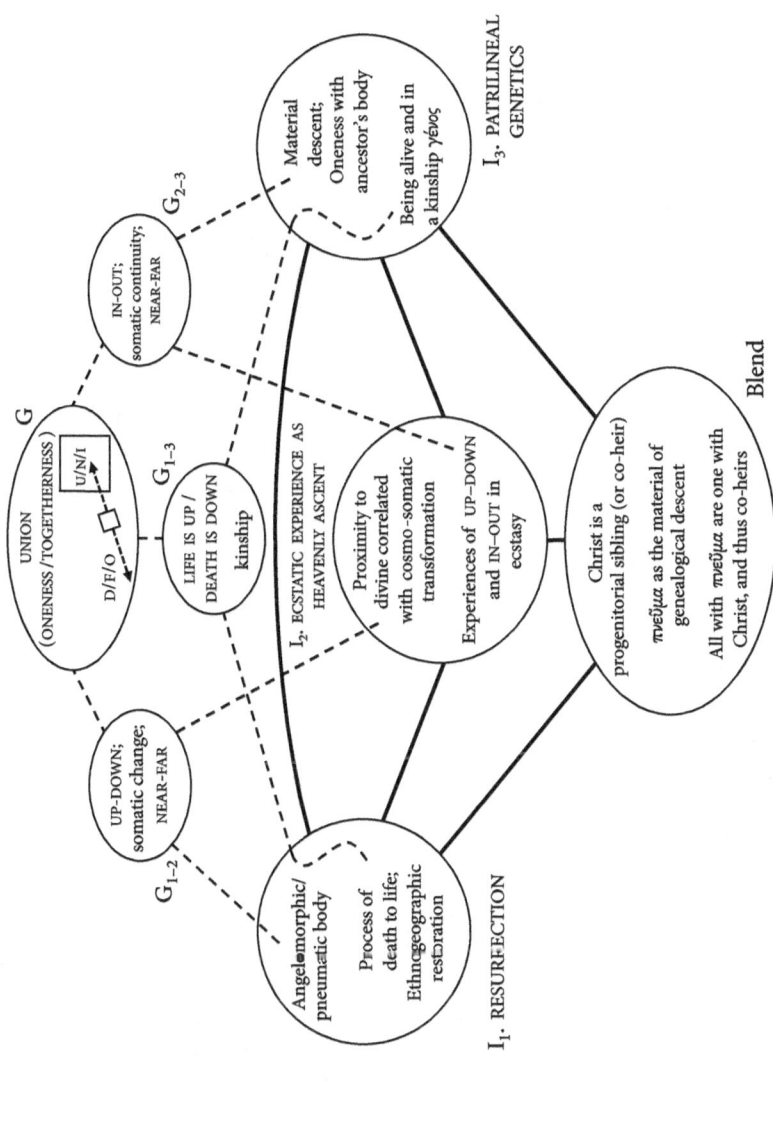

Figure 5.4. Participation in/with Christ

(G_{1-2}) in ways that are familiar.[87] The subgeneric space G_{1-2} correlates ideas of divine/human proximity and cosmo-somatic transformation, thus exploiting the notions of VERTICALITY, PROXIMITY, and crucially, the notion of somatic transformation.

The third input (I_3) concerns notions of patrilineal genetics, the other frame-structure in which Paul's participationist ideals are elaborated. This space contains two main elements: (1) the experience of being alive and within a kinship lineage (or γένος) that traces itself back to an ancestor, and (2) the material connection between ancestor and descendants.[88] As I have already demonstrated, these ideas are central to Paul's participationist ideals. Within the blending network, I_1 and I_3 are cross-mapped in G_{1-3} on account of kinship in-group identity (e.g., the ethnogeographic expectation that the descendants of Abraham will be resurrected) as well as qualitative notions that link life and death (UP and DOWN) to kinship health and well-being (recall: LAND IS LIFE/EXILE IS DEATH). At the same time, I_2 and I_3 are cross-mapped in G_{2-3} through related conceptions of PROXIMITY and CONTAINMENT (e.g., notions of ecstatic union [IN/NEAR] in I_2 and contiguity [IN/NEAR] with the progenitor in I_3), and crucially by the idea of somatic continuity between individuated subjects (e.g., between ancestor and descendant, or Christ-devotees and Christ).

The generic space (G) that ties these various elements together consists of the UNION gestalt (§5.1), which is adapted here so as to contain an UP-DOWN spatial element. The gestalt's correlation of UP/NEAR/IN vis-à-vis DOWN/FAR/OUT creates conceptual mappings wherein differing notions can come to relate to and blend with one another. Accordingly, being UP simultaneously means that one is both IN and NEAR and not DOWN, FAR, or OUT. While the generality of these correlations carry very little meaning in and of themselves, at human scale they enable notions of resurrection, patrilineal genetics, and heavenly ascent to meaningfully cohere with one another in Paul's construction of his participationist ideals. For Paul, resurrection, ascent, and inclusive kinship all correlate with one another through creative elaborations of the UNION gestalt.

What emerges in the blended space is a good deal of novel structure, all of which draws on the various inputs in creative ways. Perhaps the most

---

87. See esp. §3.1.1; both resurrection and heavenly ascent share much schematic structure, which thus enables these two ideas to commonly intersect with one another.

88. In addition to Johnson Hodge (2007), my use of terms such as *ethnicity*, γένος, and *kinship* are influenced by the work of Dennis Duling (2008).

significant emergent element is the identification of Christ as a progenitorial sibling (or coheir). Though this identification draws largely on the content of I_3, the notion of a progenitorial sibling is a contradiction in terms (as Johnson Hodge correctly notes) and is only made possible because of the constituent elements of the blend's input spaces.[89] On the one hand, the ethnogeographic element of I_1 includes presumptions of Abraham's kin line and the restorative place of resurrection therein—this casts Christ as Abraham's seed, an heir in Abraham. At the same time, in I_2 Christ is also the Great Glory encountered in heavenly ascent, a divine figure whose body is euphorically contiguous with the ecstatic's body and whose πνεῦμα indwells and imparts life to Christ-devotees—this casts Christ as a progenitor, a πνεῦμα ζῳοποιοῦν (1 Cor 15:45). In the blended space, the two images exist together so as to cast Christ as both progenitor and coheir of those who are in him (i.e., those who share his πνεῦμα).

In an important respect, πνεῦμα is a key thread that runs through all three inputs. I have already shown the central role πνεῦμα takes in Paul's resurrection and heavenly ascent ideals (§§3.2.2–3 and 4.2–3): it is through transformation into the pneumatically aligned angelomorphic body that one both rises in the eschaton (I_1) and ascends to heaven (I_2). In a related manner, Paul now posits πνεῦμα as the genetic substance that links ancestors and descendants (I_3), including Christ and Christ-devotees. It is hard to say from where Paul's notion of pneumatic descent emerged, though it is entirely possible that he found in I_1 and I_2 a blended understanding of πνεῦμα that also served his purposes in I_3.[90] Accordingly, the euphoric one-

---

89. One limitation of Johnson Hodge's approach—of which she herself is aware (2007, 103–6 and 115)—is that, while the logic of patrilineal descent illuminates Paul's *in Abraham* and *in Isaac* descriptions (Gal 3:8; Rom 9:7), Paul understands Christ not as an ancestral progenitor but rather as a coheir or sibling of those who are now located in him (Rom 8:14–17, 29). Succinctly put, it is not entirely clear how or why siblings can be seen to exist in one another or emerge out of one another. While Johnson Hodge suggests that Paul "creatively adapts" (103) the idea of descendants being located in their ancestors, she offers little by way explicating what spurs this creative adaptation. In light of the blend elaborated here, such creative adaptation results from Paul's (ecstatic) memory of somatic union, which blends with both the resurrection and patrilineal genetic inputs so as to create notions of somatic-morphing-together-with and material lineage. Accordingly, in the blended space, Christ is perceived as both progenitor and sibling.

90. Though Stowers (2008, 359) may be correct in asserting, "the 'in Christ' language derives from this logic of descent and genetic participation," we must recognize

ness that Paul experienced with Christ in ecstatic ascent is cross-mapped with notions of kinship—to be in Christ is to share Christ's πνεῦμα, both as an ecstatic ascender to heaven and as a pneumatic descendant of Abraham. To recall 2 Cor 5:6–10, "being home" (ἐνδημέω) with Christ is to be in a native place, among one's native kin. This is reflected in the blended space by the assertion that believers share the same kind of stuff—the same πνεῦμα—as Christ.

5.3.2. Ecstasy, Ethnicity, and Resurrection as a Pattern of Embodiment

In the foregoing, I have departed from my standard methodological procedure. Rather than beginning with a specific text and then exploring the blending structure reflected therein, I have instead sought to propose a blending structure that seems to be operative in Paul's writings more generally. On the whole, this structure undergirds much of the logic in Galatians, where Paul maps Christ's death and (resurrection-)life to the apostolic body (Gal 1:11–17; 2:19–21) and further develops this mystico-ecstatic understanding along the lines of patrilineal genetics (esp. 3:6–4:7).[91] Though the whole blending structure is present in Galatians, individual elements are not equally represented. Notions of patrilineal genetics are

---

that explanations of derivation do not necessarily connote explanations of genesis. On the reading presented here, because ecstatic experiences foster notions of somatic oneness and togetherness, it is Paul's self-perception of euphoric blurring between his body and Christ's glory-body (I_2) that prompts the blending of πνεῦμα with the logic of patrilineal genetics. Accordingly, this generative impulse leads Paul to speak of being in/with Christ both in the language of heavenly ascent and to elaborate these convictions further through the logical strictures of patrilineal genetics. For Paul, the ecstatic experience generates and enables description, though it does not exhaust description. Where the ascent traditions are limited, the patrilineal genetic traditions provide an alternative network of ideas within which to work.

91. Though many note the conspicuous lack of resurrection references in Galatians, the image-schematic approach taken in this study provides a way of identifying the contours of resurrection logic at work in the epistle. Central here is Paul's mapping of life to the somatic interior throughout Gal 1–3, as well as the insistence that faith causes one to "live" (3:11) vis-à-vis the law, which by contrast cannot "make alive" (ζωοποιέω, 3:21). Accordingly, life and death—specifically the resurrection process of moving from death to life—is very much part of Paul's logic in Galatians. More generally, the interconnections of (resurrection-)life with heavenly ascent and patrilineal genetics provides a way of seeing Paul's resurrection ideals at work in Galatians, even if resurrection terminology is not used in the epistle.

foregrounded throughout Gal 3–4, while ecstatic/heavenly ascent elements are backgrounded and thus less emphatic.[92] The uses to which Paul puts this blend are as much didactic as identity forming. In Gal 5:16–26, Paul insists that the death of the external (τὴν σάρκα) results in the proper subjection of the inner desires (τοῖς παθήμασιν καὶ ταῖς ἐπιθυμίαις, 5:24) to πνεῦμα. Conversely, this inner life results in the bearing of external, pneumatic fruit (5:22–23). As in Rom 6–8 and 12:1–3, the intrasomatic polarity of LIFE ⇄ DEATH forms the basis of didactic exhortation, thus constituting a pattern of embodiment through which Christ-devotees are to locate themselves within the unfolding process of resurrection.

A similar logic is at work in Rom 4, where selective fore-/backgrounding of the participation blend (fig. 5.4) is also evident. Paul here engages in the construction of a founding narrative for gentile Christ-devotees, and in the process of doing so he foregrounds patrilineal genetics and the death-to-life process while muting notions of ecstasy/heavenly ascent. Accordingly, Paul casts Abraham as the "ancestor of all who believe" and "the father of all of us" (4:11, 16). Though patrilineal genetics are explicit here, they find ideological expression through the taking on of certain resurrection ideals. Paul goes on to recount the scriptural story of Abraham (see LXX Gen 15, 17–18) in which the aged and childless patriarch is praised for his hope/faith in the God "who gives life to the dead" (Rom 4:17). The deceased subject, however, is not a corpse but rather Abraham and Sarah's procreative physiology. The apostle describes Abraham as one whose body already was "dead" (νενεκρωμένον) and Sarah as having a "dead womb" (τὴν νέκρωσιν τῆς μήτρας, 4:19). In Paul's framing of the scriptural narrative, resurrection is a process at work in the progenitors themselves. Like Abraham, righteousness is given to those who have faith in the God who brings life from death (4:17). For Christ-devotees, this means both recognition of Jesus's resurrection (4:24) and an ongoing participation in the death and resurrection pattern (Rom 6–8). Importantly, however, notions of heavenly ascent are entirely muted in 4:16–25, a feature that underscores the strength of the participation blend described above; that is, the connection

---

92. Mystico-ecstatic elements are contained largely to Gal 1:11–17 and 2:19–21, though images of Paul as an apocalyptist can be found at various points throughout the letter (1:12, 16; 2:2; see also 3:23). While notions of heavenly ascent are not explicitly developed in Galatians, when 1:11–17 and 2:19–21 are viewed in relation to 2 Cor 3–4, the language of "inward life" and "revelation" suggests heavenly ascent as a relevant category in Paul's address.

between patrilineal genetics and resurrection/life is strong enough that Paul is able to exploit the logic of this conceptual blend without having to give recourse to the primary impetus that first established this connection (namely, the ecstatic experience of somatic blurring between the apostle and Christ). Through the construction of this founding narrative, Paul establishes an ideological framework in which Christ-devotees are to view their lives and actions. For Abraham, as for believers, resurrection functions as a pattern of embodiment that characterizes and alters their bodies.

Within the undisputed Paulines, perhaps the fullest expression of the participation blend (fig. 5.4) is found in Phil 3:1b–4:1, an epistolary fragment that likely stems from a correspondence concerning the topic of gentile circumcision (3:2–3; see also Gal 5:2, 7–12).[93] Within the contours of the pericope, all three elements of the participation blend are, to varying degrees, foregrounded. Central here are two emphases: in-group identification through ethno-kinship reconfiguration (3:4–9), and Paul's participation through suffering in Christ's death and resurrection (3:10–16). The former is drawn directly from the Patrilineal Genetics input space (I_3), the latter from the Resurrection input space (I_1). The former concerns the redrawing of in-group boundary lines and the establishment of (fictive) kinship relations based on UNION with Christ (3:7–11) rather than similarity of σάρξ (3:2–6). The latter concerns the pattern of transformation that characterizes Paul's present and future self (3:10–16). Subtler, though no less present, are the mystico-ecstatic overtones of heavenly ascent (I_2), which find expression in Paul's overt use of συμμορφίζω (3:10) and σύμμορφος (3:21). As noted at the outset of this chapter, A. Segal (2004, 419) suggests that these terms are similar to our *metamorphosis* "but with a more intimate and transformative meaning.... [they suggest] the reformation will explicitly take place 'together with' (*syn-*) [Christ's] glorious body." In view here are the somatic underpinnings of Paul's mystico-ecstatic experiences of heavenly ascent (I_2). Because Paul fashions his understanding of resurrection on his experience of ascent, his resurrection ideals are premised on his "somatic memory of union" (Shantz 2008, 203). But such somatic absorption also has an important cosmological correlate, which is as much at home for Paul in the Patrilineal Genetics input (I_3) as in the Ecstatic Experience (I_2) and Resurrection (I_1) inputs, namely, the continuity of substance, which Paul understands variously as a pneu-

---

93. On source-critical matters, see §1.5 and n. 108 there.

matic continuity of ancestor and descendant (patrilineal genetics), earthly and heavenly bodies (resurrection), and/or the individuated earthly subject and the contiguously inclusive Great Glory (heavenly ascent). All of these ideas come together and are foregrounded in Phil 3:1b–4:1. Beyond the central rhetorical focus of this fragment—namely, UNION with Christ (3:7–11)—the apostle also bifurcates resurrection into present (3:10) and future (3:11–16) expressions, thus setting forth a vision of life in Christ that is in keeping with the findings of 2 Cor 3–5 (see §5.2, esp. fig. 5.3). In the end, Paul sets out a pattern of embodiment for gentiles whereby pneumatic kinship in Abraham necessarily implies UNION with Christ and ongoing participation in Christ's suffering, death, and resurrection.

5.4. Conclusions

The preceding discussion has covered an immense amount of ground in an effort to probe the conceptual correlations between Paul's participationist and resurrection ideals. We have explored the grammatical foundations of Paul's *in/with Christ* language, the dynamic of IN-OUT affectivity, the literary presentation and neurobiological underpinnings of religious experiences, and Paul's ideological and rhetorical construction of in-group identity. Running throughout these seemingly disparate elements, however, is the thread of the human body as the nexus of divine-human interaction.

As demonstrated in §5.1, Paul's participationist ideals are premised on the UNION gestalt, an embodied concept that enables the apostle to speak of both oneness and togetherness such that Christ and believers are in and with one another (i.e., the so-called hyperproximity of IN/NEAR). The findings of §5.1, which are necessarily abstract and more conceptual in nature, were then tested in §§5.2–3 in relation to two different patterns of resurrection embodiment in Paul's letters. In §5.2, we explored the life in/through death pattern that permeates much of Paul's writings. Here we concluded that the dynamic of IN-OUT mutual affectivity governs Paul's resurrection ideals such that the process of death and resurrection is understood as working itself out on the (apostolic) body. For Paul, Christ-devotees find themselves in an ongoing somatic trajectory of dying (OUT) and rising (IN) with Christ. In §5.3, we explored the experiential and rhetorical dimensions of Paul's self-presentation of identity construction. We found that, though the full breadth of Paul's participationist ideals are premised on the UNION gestalt, such ideals reflect a robust blending network that brings together the domains of resurrection, heavenly ascent, and patrilineal genetics. At the heart of this blend is the cosmo-somatic category of πνεῦμα, which functions as the material grounding of Paul's participationist, resurrection, and ascent ideals. Taking the findings of §§5.1–3 together, Paul is seen to presume and/or point to kinship, resurrection, and ascent as present, somatic experiences of oneness/togetherness that are premised on the hyperproximity (IN/NEAR) of the UNION gestalt. For Paul, resurrection is an ongoing event whereby both Christ's death and Christ's life are continually manifested in the Christ-believing body. In these ways, resurrection is an *embodied* experience.

Returning to the scholarly literature examined in chapter 1, we can see that the analysis in this chapter has advanced our understanding of Paul's resurrection ideals in three specific ways. First, I have further underscored the dubious distinction between future literal and present metaphorical resurrection(s). As we have seen, Paul envisions a single process of resurrection that has both present and future manifestations and that is worked out via the process of IN-OUT intrasomatic affectivity (IN ⇌ OUT). Asserting the metaphorical nature of resurrection does not render Paul's descriptions impotent, as though he must be read "literally" to be taken seriously. Rather, recognizing the metaphorical patterns in Paul's writings enables us to see how differing concepts relate to one another (e.g., life through death and life in death; or the interrelation of resurrection, ascent, and kinship). For Paul, RESURRECTION is the structure by which life in Christ is organized. In this way, resurrection is a metaphor that he and his communities live by.

Second, the nature of the enspirited earthly body's present experience of resurrection has now come into clearer focus: it is characterized by a process of ongoing outer death and inner life (LIFE ⇌ DEATH). Recognizing this process is only possible, however, once we dispense with dualistic oppositions and idealized monisms and instead recognize the experiential dimension of intrasomatic polarity. The process of continually sharing Christ's death and resurrection is somatically grounded by mutual IN-OUT affectivity and manifested in experiences of ecstasy and ideologies of patrilineal genetics. It is important to recognize, however, that Paul's understanding of the "body" is plastic enough that Christ-devotees participate in several different embodied existences at once—participation in the ecclesial body, in their own individuated bodies, and in Christ's risen glory-body.[94] This means that, for Paul, Christ-devotees need not engage

---

94. This point was stressed in §§5.2.1–2, where we saw that death and life are

in flights of ecstasy so as to exist as enspirited earthly body. Rather, by virtue of their participation in Christ/πνεῦμα, the ongoing process of death (OUT) affecting life (IN) is extend communally. This is indicated in 2 Cor 12:1–10 and especially 4:12, 15, where the communio-somatic dimension creates a caveat for the apostle whereby experiences of ecstatic ascent need not be prescriptively advocated. Accordingly, Pauline notions of intrasomatic polarity are quite elaborate, finding expression within several different somatic frame-structures.

Finally, by recognizing the plurality of Paul's participationist descriptions, in this chapter we have uncovered an elaborate blending network in which several different expressions of participation in/with Christ interlace one another. As we have seen, Paul's in/with Christ language fosters an understanding of resurrection as a pattern of embodiment. This was demonstrated not only with respect to the eschatological body, wherein IN-OUT somatic affectivity functions as the nexus of divine/human interrelation, but also with respect to the ethnic body, wherein πνεῦμα functions as the material stuff that binds together members of Paul's (fictive) kin group. In these ways, Paul's participationist ideals are not concerned with passive aeonic engagement, or noetic acts of faith, or even interpersonal solidarity (per se). Rather, Paul is concerned with pneumosomatic UNION (oneness and togetherness) whereby the death and life of Christ are continually enacted in Christ-devotees' bodies.

---

enacted in one or many bodies all at once—in Paul's body, in the risen Christ's body, and/or in the ecclesial body. All of these bodies interlace one another in Paul's descriptions such that the affectivity of resurrection is not bound to the single, individuated subject. On the diversity of "bodies" in Paul's resurrection and cultic ideals, see Tappenden 2012.

6
Embodying Resurrection:
Conclusions and Prospects

Paul's ideals are bodily ideals. His expectations are somatically oriented. His thinking is corporally grounded. While the bodily nature of resurrection in Paul's writings has not been lost in modern scholarship, too often it is taken up into dubious constructions of literal (or real) resurrection that are contrasted with metaphorical applications of resurrection. For many, Paul's resurrection ideals are concerned chiefly with postmortem modes of existence and only secondarily with assertions of somatic transformation on this side of death. Such tendencies disembody Paul's understanding of resurrection. They stress the body's function as the *mode* of resurrection, but not the body's function as the *location* of resurrection. In this study, I have sought to redress this imbalance.

I have argued in the preceding chapters that Paul's resurrection ideals are grounded in recurrent patterns of human embodiment. Drawing on methods developed in cognitive linguistics, I have shown that Paul's thought and writings are embodied in two important respects. On the one hand, the concept of RESURRECTION is somatically grounded in recurrent and familiar human experiences (e.g., verticality, proximity, containment). On the other hand, Paul understands the process of dying and rising as dynamics at work within the human σῶμα. The former is a more general thesis that reflects contemporary research exploring the nature of human cognition. The latter is a Paul-specific thesis that makes strong claims concerning the apostle's perception and engagement with his world. For Paul, the body functions not only as the mode of postmortem existence but also as the location of premortem transformation. I have argued these points in various ways throughout the preceding chapters. Here I offer a synthesis of this study's major conclusions and scholarly contributions.

6.1. Major Conclusions

In chapter 1 (§1.3), I examined three ways in which scholarly treatments of Paul's resurrection ideals suffer from the problem of cognicentrism: (1) the problem of identifying resurrection, (2) the nature of dualism and monism in Paul's thought and writings, and (3) the relationship between Paul's participationist and resurrection ideals. In response to these issues, five major conclusions emerged from the succeeding chapters.

First, I delineated more clearly a framework within which to identify and interpret resurrection texts. This was the chief aim of chapter 2, where I applied cognitive linguistic notions of image schemata and conceptual metaphor to a selection of Second Temple Jewish texts. In the process of identifying the RESURRECTION gestalt, it proved theoretically problematic and hermeneutically unhelpful to distinguish between literal and metaphorical expressions of resurrection. Instead, resurrection emerges as a thoroughly metaphorical concept. It is an abstract and creative domain of human thought that always is elaborated in relation to other, more concrete domains of experience. To stress the metaphorical nature of resurrection is not to suggest the concept lacks a concrete referent or foundation. Quite the opposite, as the RESURRECTION gestalt presumes a constellation of image-schematic concepts that emerge from recurrent patterns of human embodiment: concrete experiences such as standing, sleeping, walking on a path, being close to someone, and the like. In these ways, resurrection is an embodied rather than a propositional category.

Second, I demonstrated that Paul constructs his world as a unified whole wherein opposing forces exist interdependently with one another. This was principally explored in chapters 3 and 4, where I examined Paul's cosmology and anthropology with respect to issues of dualism and monism. Seeking to understand better the categories of reality with which Paul works, I found that the apostle holds to a dualistic framework that is characterized by tensive interrelation rather than opposition. I described this integrative dualism as a polarity. Paul's resurrection ideals are premised on the assertion that earthly and heavenly bodies are uniquely fashioned for their respective cosmological locales such that the current enspirited earthly body exists in a state of intrasomatic tension (see ch. 3). Building on this, my findings in chapter 4 demonstrate that earthly embodiment is characterized by intrasomatic polarity (*in* vis-à-vis *out*) and by intratemporal polarity (*already* vis-à-vis *not yet*), both of which intersect at the IN-OUT nexus of the human σῶμα. While much modern scholarship has stressed Paul as either an aeonic dualist or an anthropological monist, the recognition of integrative polarity in Paul's thought provides a more holistic understanding whereby cosmology and anthropology are brought into coordination.

Third, much of my analysis focuses on the wide variety of transformation metaphors in Paul's letters (chs. 3–5). To a large extent, expressions of CHANGE exist at the intersection of dualism/monism (on the one hand) and Paul's participationist ideals (on the other). This is expressly clear in Rom 6–8, where baptismal death with Christ produces a resurrection with Christ that is somatically inward, thus resulting in the material transformation of the (external) body. For Paul, Christ-devotees exist as enspirited earthly bodies that are in the process of transformation from ensouled earthly bodies to enspirited risen bodies. Importantly, resurrection is not only a future reality but also a present one. Paul envisions a single, ongoing process of transformation that begins with the infusion of divine πνεῦμα (thus resurrecting the somatic interior) and culminates with the transformation of the body (thus resurrecting the somatic exterior). Resurrection, then, is embodied in that the earthly bodies of Christ-devotees have already been raised inwardly and set into an ongoing transformative trajectory toward external transformation in(to) Christ.

Fourth, by stressing the present dimension of Paul's eschatology, I have clarified the relationship between participation and resurrection. As we saw in chapter 5, the blending of the UNION gestalt with Paul's eschatological somatology fosters perceptions that the bodies of Christ-devotees function as the location of divine-human propinquity. Paul does not abstract participation with Christ's death/resurrection as passive engagement in aeonic spheres, nor does he understand participation as a noetic act of faith and/or interpersonal solidarity. Rather, he understands resurrection as a transformative process that is happening already to the body and thus constitutes several different patterns of embodiment by which Christ-devotees perceive their existence. For Paul, metaphors of RESURRECTION organize life in Christ. They function as performative scripts that Christ-devotees live by. Transformation is not only an eschatological expectation but also an immediate program that orders somatic activities.

Finally, what did it mean, concretely and pragmatically, for Christ-devotees to embody resurrection? Did they engage in certain practices? Were there certain patterns of daily living that actualized this notion of ongoing transformation? In chapters 4 and 5, I argued that baptism seems to be one such realization of the life in/through death pattern (§4.1) and further that Paul's exhortations toward self-mastery are premised on the notion that ethical aptitude is enabled through the ongoing death and resurrection of the bodies of Christ-devotees (§§4.2–3 and 5.2). To these we could perhaps add the practice of the Lord's Supper (though here Paul focuses more on Christ's death and offers only minimal inclination toward resurrection ideals; see Tappenden 2012) and even Paul's exhortations toward (1) somatic sacrifice in the face of suffering (Phil 1:29–30; 1 Thess 3:14) and (2) sacrifice of individuals toward the community (Phil 2:3–4; Gal 6:2). Practices such as these function as sites where the logic of the RESURRECTION gestalt acquires concrete expressions in bodily activities.

Admittedly, however, the examples just elaborated tend toward prescription rather than description. At one level, this reflects the nature of our sources. It is very difficult to assess the degree to which Christ-devotees connected their own collectively individuated selves with the vision of resurrection-embodiment that emerges from Paul's writings. At another level, though, the prescriptive nature of these ideals indicates the globalizing tendency that is at work in Paul's epistles. Notions of RESURRECTION interlace several different aspects of Paul's writings and help give structure and order to domains of thought that often are treated disparately (as explored in §§2.2, 4.2, 5.1–3). To this end, RESURRECTION is a concept that proves useful and powerful in Paul's articulation of the identity of Christ-devotees. For Paul, this globalizing tendency is found in exhortations such as Rom 12:2–3, where believers are to offer their "bodies" (σώματα) as a "living sacrifice" (θυσίαν ζῶσαν), or 1 Thess 5:1–11, where Christ-devotees are to view their present embodied existence as an experience of resurrected life; or 2 Cor 3–4, where Christ-devotees participate in several different embodied existences at once (namely, the ecclesial body, their own individuated bodies, Christ's risen glory-body), thus expanding the life in/through death pattern across boundaries individual/communal, ἔσω/ἔξω ἄνθρωπος, and terrestrial/heavenly. All of this is premised on the realness of the resurrection process in Paul's perception: the bodies of Christ-devotees have been somatically altered through the granting of πνεῦμα; such bodies are in the midst of transformation toward the σῶμα πνευματικόν; and the entire process is characterized by ecstatic and genetic oneness/togetherness with Christ/πνεῦμα. In step with my affirmation of ontological pluralism in historical methodology (Craffert 2008; see §1.2 above), these perceptions point toward the embodied nature of Paul's resurrection ideals.

6.2. Scholarly Contribution and Areas of Further Research

Building upon these conclusions, in this study I advance scholarship and open new avenues of research in several ways. First, by putting aside the problematic divide between literal and metaphorical, I provide a theoretically sound and hermeneutically helpful framework in which to identify and interpret resurrection traditions. This is an advancement that promises to rescue notions of resurrection from narrowly configured temporal and/or thematic constraints while at the same time enabling meaningful scholarly discussion regarding the identification and understanding of resurrection within the period literature. In chapter 2 (§2.1.4), I briefly explored the implications of the RESURRECTION gestalt with respect to nonresurrection texts (Wisdom of Solomon) and to contested resurrection texts (Jubilees and the Enochic Book of Watchers). Beyond these cursory remarks, this analysis should be extended not only to other contested traditions (such as the sectarian literature from Qumran) but also to the variety of ancient Judean afterlife beliefs. To the latter, the RESURRECTION gestalt may prove helpful in mapping the diversity and intersections that exist between differing ideals.

Building on the findings of chapter 2, there is more work to be done on the concept of RESURRECTION on at least three fronts. First, one should pay attention to texts that envision resurrection as giving back rather than rising up (e.g., 1 En. 51:1; see Bauckham 1998, 269–89). Such descriptions may be premised on the PROXIMITY schema, thus cohering with the findings in chapter 2 while still representing novel expressions of resurrection belief. Second, further reflection should press Lakoff's (1987) theoretical discussion of categorization, particularly with respect to the idea of radial categories. Within cognitive linguistics, radial categorization provides an explanation for the presence of polysemy. Working from the principle of metaphorical elaboration, various and even divergent word usages relate to one another through chains of meaning. As an extension of the analysis in §2.1, radial categorization may provide a more robust way of linking various notions of resurrection that moves beyond this study's unidirectional procedure of somatic ground. A third line of research is the reception of resurrection traditions within the broader Western tradition. Thick historical description has aided my attempt to engage Paul on the terms of his own world, and in doing so I have identified notions of resurrection that are at home within the ancient Mediterranean. Building on these findings, we still have to see how the concept of resurrection changed and morphed in the centuries that followed. As a nonpropositional concept, RESURRECTION is not absolutely fixed but rather constructed within the cultural contexts in which it is used. Already in Paul's epistles, we have seen novel innovations in the meaning of resurrection, supplementing the conventional RESURRECTION IS UP and RESURRECTION IS NEAR metaphors with the related though distinct RESURRECTION IS IN metaphor. As the concept of resurrection continues to find cultural resonance in the centuries—even millennia—that follow Paul, in what ways is the concept changed or morphed? Into what new frame-structures are these metaphors elaborated, and with what new concepts is resurrection blended? A history of resurrection metaphors has yet to be written, and such an exploration would lie at the interdisciplinary intersection of cognitive historiography, cultural studies, hermeneutics, and theology.

Second, this study provides a way of engaging the complexity of Paul's thought and writings without recourse either to idealized systematicity or to overly drawn fragmentation. By focusing on human-scale blends and their underlying conceptual networks, I have demonstrated coherence amid diversity. With respect to Paul's resurrection ideals, we saw this in the dynamic oscillation between up/then and in/now expressions and also in the complementary but different ideas of life through death and life in death. Such fluidity reflects two distinct conceptual metaphors—RESURRECTION IS UP and RESURRECTION IS IN—both of which produce markedly different understandings of resurrection at human scale. By reading Paul in terms of underlying conceptual structures, we are able to find coherence in the apostle's thought even though systematicity is impossible.

Within Pauline studies more generally, this methodological approach could be applied to aspects of Paul's writings that evince similar—even greater—diversity of expression (e.g., Paul's attitude toward the law). Beyond the undisputed epistles, this study opens new interpretive avenues for exploring and assessing the Pauline pseudepigrapha. Much New Testament scholarship has axiomatically denied any sense of a realized resurrection in the undisputed letters, specifically objectifying and contrasting such assertions with the deutero-Paulines (esp. Col 2:12; 3:1–4; Eph 2:1–10). Since the present study has dislodged this entrenchment, there is a renewed need to assess the Pauline tradition more broadly, specifically with respect to the interrelations and intersections of the undisputed and disputed letters. On the one hand, there still are good reasons to distinguish between the undisputed and disputed letters: whereas the deutero-Paulines tend to speak of resurrection as a participatory event that already has happened (esp. Ephesians), the undisputed letters speak of resurrection as a participatory event that is in the process of happening. On the other hand, in this study I offer fresh ways of assessing and examining trajectories of resurrection belief within early Pauline interpretation, specifically with regard to issues of temporality. The undisputed epistles, for instance, contain indications that Paul's resurrection ideals evince (real or potential) misunderstanding with regard to temporality (1 Cor 4:8; 15:12; Phil 3:12; 1 Thess 4:13–5:11). The scholarly penchant for speaking of some form of realized eschatology at Corinth suggests conceptual imbalance between the already and the not yet among the Corinthian Christ-devotees. Beyond this, the deutero-Pauline tendency to bring resurrection squarely into the past/present (Col 2:12; 3:1–4; Eph 2:1–10) vis-à-vis the Pastor's insistence that Paul relegates resurrection to the eschaton (2 Tim 2:16–18; cf. also 2 Thess 2:1–12) indicates that even in the late first/early second century Paul's vision of resurrection was polarized along temporal lines. All of this suggests that the apostle's interpreters were not willing—perhaps not able—to hold together the already and the not yet in the same kind of tensive interrelation that we find evinced in the undisputed epistles. In light of the present study, such divisions perhaps reflect difficulties in negotiating the conceptual complexity of Paul's ideals. That is, while Paul was able to hold the RESURRECTION IS UP and RESURRECTION IS IN metaphors in intrasomatic tension, these concepts were not easily systematized and thus resulted in divergent yet equally Pauline understandings of resurrection among later readers. In this way, the variegated nature of Pauline interpretation in the first through third centuries likely has its roots in Paul himself.

Third, throughout this study I have explored several different aspects of Paul's writings concerning continuity and discontinuity across somatic states. For the most part my focus has been material in nature, stressing the categories of σῶμα, σάρξ, and πνεῦμα. Since these are the categories Paul himself works with, I am justified in doing so. Interestingly, what seems clear in Paul's writings is that both continuity and discontinuity concern these material aspects of the human subject. On the one hand, Paul envisions a trajectory of transformative embodiment in which the whole person is altered (hence, discontinuity). On the other, already in the baptized σῶμα something of the resurrection is present—the πνεῦμα—which is to say that there is continuity between earthly and heavenly existences. While such conclusions are well grounded textually, they are perhaps unsatisfying for those interested more in the philosophical and theological explorations of the self or person in Paul's writings. Admittedly, such categories are foreign to Paul, making it difficult to assess the continuity of the subject or self or person within Paul's writings. Consistent with this study's vertical integration paradigm, the more lofty work of philosophical and theological reflection remains.

Finally, my theoretical commitment in this study to vertical integration has yielded much explanatory leverage when analyzing the experiential nature of Paul's resurrection ideals. By grounding Paul's participationist language in recurrent patterns of human embodiment, I have meaningfully employed the category of experience without recourse to overly subjective conclusions. The key focal point in all this has been the body itself, which has proved useful both heuristically (in that it grounds cognition) and topically (in that it substantiates Paul's resurrection ideals). Building on the recognition that culture is grounded in the body, the vertical integration paradigm provides a matrix in which to reenvisage the intersection of myth, memory, and ritual within early Christianity: How is myth grounded in ritual? How does ritual function as a communicative medium? What is the role of both social and individual memory within this myth/ritual matrix? Framed within the vertical integration paradigm, questions such as these could yield fresh insights into our understanding of how beliefs in the resurrection of Jesus were preserved, transmitted, and actualized within the early Christian cultus. One group of texts that may benefit from this kind of analysis are the appearance narratives of the Gospels. In comparison with other strands of gospel tradition, these narratives emerge relatively late (they are absent from both Mark and Q) and evince a curious set of intra-Gospel parallels (Luke and John are closer than Luke and his Synoptic counterparts). Rather than positing a historical core for such traditions, a better way forward is to examine resurrection as a piece of embodied culture, one that is transmitted through conceptual structures that are variously expressed in ritual dynamics (baptism, the Lord's Supper, early Christian worship), interpretive praxis (scriptural exegesis, performative readings), and rhetoric (proclamation, genre, narrative). What is in view here is the extent to which conceptual metaphors manifest themselves in various discursive contexts, how such metaphors are inscribed into narrative and ritual contexts, and further how ritual and discourse intersect one another. To these ends, an exploration of the embodied foundations of myth, memory, and ritual could shed new light on the transmission of early Christian resurrection beliefs.

6.3. Final Observations

In one way, my critique of cognicentrism in this study ends in a place different than where it began. It is one thing to criticize scholarly presuppositions and methods (as in ch. 1), but it is another to insist that Paul himself presumes a certain degree of resurrection embodiment (as in chs. 4 and 5). The former is an issue of theory and method, the latter an issue of interpretation and contextualization. When considering Paul's resurrection ideals, the evidence of the undisputed epistles suggests that we must make the latter jump. Paul understands resurrection as grounded in and happening to the body itself. To return to the language of this study's introduction (§1.1), the eschatological and locative dimensions of resurrection interlace to such an extent that they are separated only artificially; resurrection is something that will happen to the body in the future and is happening in the body in the present. For Paul, resurrection is embodied.

Bibliography

Primary Literature

The following section includes all original language and translation texts consulted.

Andersen, F. I. 1983. "2 (Slavonic Apocalypse of) Enoch." *OTP* 1:91–221.
Baillet, M. 1982. *Qumrân grotte 4.III (4Q482–4Q520)*. DJD 7. Oxford: Clarendon.
Beentjes, Pancratius C. 1997. *The Book of Ben Sira in Hebrew: A Text Edition of All Extant Hebrew Manuscripts and a Synopsis of All Parallel Hebrew Ben Sira Texts*. VTSup 68. Leiden: Brill.
Black, Matthew. 1995. *The Book of Enoch or 1 Enoch: A New English Edition with Commentary and Textual Notes*. SVTP 7. Leiden: Brill.
Black, Matthew, and Albert-Marie Denis, eds. 1970. *Apocalypsis Henochi Graece: Fragmenta Pseudepigraphorum quae supersunt Graeca; Una cum historicorum et auctorum Judaeorum Hellenistarum fragmentis*. PVTG 3. Leiden: Brill.
Bradshaw, Paul F., Maxwell E. Johnson, and L. Edward Phillips. 2002. *The Apostolic Tradition: A Commentary*. Hermeneia. Minneapolis: Fortress.
Broshi, Magen, et al. 1995. *Qumran Cave 4.XIV: Parabiblical Texts, Part 2*. DJD 19. Oxford: Clarendon.
Burchard, C. 1985. "Joseph and Aseneth." *OTP* 2:177–247.
———. 2003. *Joseph und Aseneth*. PVTG 5. Leiden: Brill.
Colson, F. H., G. H. Whitaker, and Ralph Marcus, trans. 1929–1962. *Philo*. 12 vols. LCL. London: Heinemann.
Elliger, K., and W. Rudolph, eds. 1983. *Biblia Hebraica Stuttgartensia*. Stuttgart: Deutsche Bibelgesellschaft.
Fowler, Harold N., et al., trans. 1914–1935. *Plato*. 12 vols. LCL. London: Heinemann.

Gaylord, H. E., Jr. 1983. "3 (Greek Apocalypse of) Baruch." *OTP* 1:653–79.
Hanhart, Robert, ed. 1976. *Maccabaeorum liber II*. SVTG 9.2. Göttingen: Vandenhoeck & Ruprecht.
Harrington, D. J. 1985. "Pseudo-Philo." *OTP* 2:297–377.
Holmes, Michael W. 2007. *The Apostolic Fathers: Greek Texts and English Translations*. 3rd ed. Grand Rapids: Baker Academic.
Johnson, M. D. 1985. "Life of Adam and Eve." *OTP* 2:249–95.
Jonge, M. de. 1978. *The Testaments of the Twelve Patriarchs: A Critical Edition of the Greek Text*. PVTG 1. Leiden: Brill.
Kappler, Werner, ed. 1967. *Maccabaeorum liber I*. SVTG 9.1. Göttingen: Vandenhoeck & Ruprecht.
Kee, H. C. 1983. "Testaments of the Twelve Patriarchs." *OTP* 1:775–828.
Klijn, A. F. J. 1983. "2 (Syriac Apocalypse of) Baruch." *OTP* 1:615–52.
Mason, Steve. 2008. *Judean War 2: Translation and Commentary*. CFJ 1B. Leiden: Brill.
Metzger, B. M. 1983. "The Fourth Book of Ezra." *OTP* 1:514–59.
Milik, J. T. 1976. *The Books of Enoch: Aramaic Fragments of Qumrân Cave 4*. Oxford: Clarendon.
Miller, Walter, et al., trans. 1914–1998. *Xenophon*. 7 vols. LCL. Cambridge: Harvard University Press.
Murray, A. T., trans. 1919–1925. *Homer*. 4 vols. LCL. London: Heinemann.
Nestle, E., and K. Aland, eds. 2012. *Novum Testamentum Graece*. 28th rev. ed. Stuttgart: Deutsche Bibelgesellschaft.
Nickelsburg, George W. E., and James C. VanderKam. 2004. *1 Enoch: A New Translation based on the Hermeneia Commentary*. Minneapolis: Fortress.
Picard, J.-C., ed. 1967. *Apocalypsis Baruchi Graece*. PVTG 2. Leiden: Brill.
Priest, J. 1983. "Testament of Moses." *OTP* 1:919–34.
Rahlfs, Alfred, ed. 1979. *Septuaginta*. Stuttgart: Deutsche Bibelgesellschaft.
Robertson, R. G. 1985. "Ezekiel the Tragedian." *OTP* 2:803–19.
Rubinkiewicz, R. 1983. "Apocalypse of Abraham." *OTP* 1:681–705.
Sanders, E. P. 1983. "Testament of Abraham." *OTP* 1:871–902.
Stone, Michael E. 1972. *The Testament of Abraham: The Greek Recensions*. SBLTT 2. Missoula, MT: Society of Biblical Literature.
Thackeray, H. St. J., et al., trans. 1926–1965. *Josephus*. 13 vols. LCL. Cambridge: Harvard University Press.
Tromp, Johannes. 2005. *The Life of Adam and Eve in Greek: A Critical Edition*. PVTG 6. Leiden: Brill.

Wevers, John William, ed. 1974. *Genesis.* SVTG 1. Göttingen: Vandenhoeck & Ruprecht.
———, ed. 1977. *Deuteronomium.* SVTG 3.2. Göttingen: Vandenhoeck & Ruprecht.
———, ed. 1982. *Numeri.* SVTG 3.1. Göttingen: Vandenhoeck & Ruprecht.
———, ed. 1986. *Leviticus.* SVTG 2.2. Göttingen: Vandenhoeck & Ruprecht.
———, ed. 1991. *Exodus.* SVTG 2.1. Göttingen: Vandenhoeck & Ruprecht.
Wintermute, O. S. 1983. "Apocalypse of Zephaniah." *OTP* 1:497–516.
———. 1985. "Jubilees." *OTP* 2:35–142.
Wise, Michael O., Martin G. Abegg, and Edward M. Cook. 2005. *The Dead Sea Scrolls: A New Translation.* Rev. and updated ed. New York: HarperSanFrancisco.
Wright, Robert B. 1985. "Psalms of Solomon." *OTP* 2:639–70.
———, ed. 2007. *The Psalms of Solomon: A Critical Edition of the Greek Text.* JCTCRS 1. London: T&T Clark.
Ziegler, Joseph, ed. 1952. *Ezechiel.* SVTG 16.1. Göttingen: Vandenhoeck & Ruprecht.
———, ed. 1957. *Ieremias, Baruch, Threni, Epistula Ieremiae.* SVTG 15. Göttingen: Vandenhoeck & Ruprecht.
———, ed. 1962. *Sapientia Salomonis.* SVTG 12.1. Göttingen: Vandenhoeck & Ruprecht.
———, ed. 1965. *Sapientia Iesu Filii Sirach.* SVTG 12.2. Göttingen: Vandenhoeck & Ruprecht.
———, ed. 1967a. *Duodecim Prophetae.* SVTG 13. Göttingen: Vandenhoeck & Ruprecht.
———, ed. 1967b. *Isaias.* SVTG 14. Göttingen: Vandenhoeck & Ruprecht.
———, ed. 1982. *Iob.* SVTG 11.4. Göttingen: Vandenhoeck & Ruprecht.
———, ed. 1999. *Susanna, Daniel, Bel et Draco.* SVTG 16.2. Göttingen: Vandenhoeck & Ruprecht.

Secondary Literature

Adams, Edward. 2000. *Constructing the World: A Study in Paul's Cosmological Language.* SNTW. Edinburgh: T&T Clark.
Alexander, Philip S. 2006. *The Mystical Texts: Songs of the Sabbath Sacrifice and Related Manuscripts.* LSTS 61. London: T&T Clark.

———. 2011. "The Dualism of Heaven and Earth in Early Jewish Literature and Its Implications." Pages 169–85 in *Light against Darkness: Dualism in Ancient Mediterranean Religion and the Contemporary World*. Edited by Armin Lange, Eric M. Meyers, Bennie H. Reynolds III, and Randall Styers. JAJSup 2. Göttingen: Vandenhoeck & Ruprecht.

Angel, Joseph. 2010. "The Liturgical-Eschatological Priest of the *Self-Glorification Hymn*." *RevQ* 24:585–605.

d'Aquili, Eugene G., and Andrew B. Newberg. 1993. "Liminality, Trance, and Unitary States in Ritual and Meditation." *StLit* 23:2–34.

Asher, Jeffrey R. 2000. *Polarity and Change in 1 Corinthians 15: A Study of Metaphysics, Rhetoric, and Resurrection*. HUT 42. Tübingen: Mohr Siebeck.

Ashton, John. 2000. *The Religion of Paul the Apostle*. New Haven: Yale University Press.

Aune, David E. 1995. "Human Nature and Ethics in Hellenistic Philosophical Traditions and Paul: Some Issues and Problems." Pages 291–312 in *Paul in His Hellenistic Context*. Edited by Troels Engberg-Pedersen. Minneapolis: Fortress.

Balz, Horst. 1993. "χοϊκός." *EDNT* 3:469–70.

Barrett, C. K. 1962. *From First Adam to Last: A Study in Pauline Theology*. New York: Scribner's Sons.

Barrett, Justin L. 2011. *Cognitive Science, Religion, and Theology: From Human Minds to Divine Minds*. West Conshohocken: Templeton.

Barstad, Hans M. 1999. "Sheol שאול." *DDD* 768–70.

Batten, Alicia J. 2010. "Clothing and Adornment." *BTB* 40:148–59.

Bauckham, Richard. 1998. *The Fate of the Dead: Studies on the Jewish and Christian Apocalypses*. NovTSup 93. Leiden: Brill.

Betz, Hans Dieter. 2000. "The Concept of the 'Inner Human Being' (ὁ ἔσω ἄνθρωπος) in the Anthropology of Paul." *NTS* 46:315–41.

Bloom, Paul. 2004. *Descartes' Baby: How the Science of Child Development Explains What Makes Us Human*. New York: Basic Books.

———. 2006. "My Brain Made Me Do It." *JCC* 6:209–14.

Boer, Martinus C. de. 1988. *The Defeat of Death: Apocalyptic Eschatology in 1 Corinthians 15 and Romans 5*. JSNTSup 22. Sheffield: JSOT Press.

Bortone, Pietro. 2010. *Greek Prepositions: From Antiquity to the Present*. Oxford: Oxford University Press.

Bousset, Wilhelm. 1901. "Die Himmelsreise der Seele." *AR* 4:136–69, 228–73.

———. 1970. *Kyrios Christos: A History of the Belief in Christ from the Beginnings of Christianity to Irenaeus*. Translated by J. E. Steely. Nashville: Abingdon.
Boyarin, Daniel. 1994. *A Radical Jew: Paul and the Politics of Identity*. Contr 1. Berkeley: University of California Press.
Brady, Dean. 2006. "Paul and Religious Experience." Pages 471–90 in *The Changing Face of Judaism, Christianity, and other Greco-Roman Religions in Antiquity*. Edited by Ian H. Henderson and Gerbern S. Oegema. SJSHRZ 2. Gütersloh: Gütersloher Verlagshaus.
Brooke, George J. 2005. "Men and Women as Angels in *Joseph and Aseneth*." *JSP* 14:159–77.
Brooten, Bernadette J. 1996. *Love between Women: Early Christian Responses to Female Homoeroticism*. Chicago: University of Chicago Press.
Bultmann, Rudolf. 1951–1955. *Theology of the New Testament*. Translated by Kendrick Grobel. 2 vols. New York: Scribner's Sons.
———. 1964. "ζωοποιέω." *TDNT* 2:874–75.
Burkert, Walter. 1998. "Towards Plato and Paul: The 'Inner' Human Being." Pages 59–82 in *Ancient and Modern Perspectives on the Bible and Culture: Essays in Honor of Hans Dieter Betz*. Edited by Adela Yarbro Collins. Atlanta: Scholars Press.
Bynum, Caroline Walker. 1995. *The Resurrection of the Body in Western Christianity, 200–1336*. LHR 15. New York: Columbia University Press.
Cavallin, H. C. C. 1974. *An Enquiry into the Jewish Background*. Vol. 1 of *Life after Death: Paul's Argument for the Resurrection of the Dead in I Cor 15*. ConBNT 7. Lund: Gleerup.
Charlesworth, James H. 1980. "The Portrayal of the Righteous as an Angel." Pages 135–51 in *Ideal Figures in Ancient Judaism: Profiles and Paradigms*. Edited by John J. Collins and George W. E. Nickelsburg. SCS 12. Chico, CA: Scholars Press.
———. 2006a. "Prolegomenous Reflections toward a Taxonomy of Resurrection Texts (1QH[a], *1En*, 4Q521, Paul, Luke, the Fourth Gospel, and Psalm 30)." Pages 237–64 in *The Changing Face of Judaism, Christianity, and Other Greco-Roman Religions in Antiquity*. Edited by Ian H. Henderson and Gerbern S. Oegema. SJSHRZ 2. Gütersloh: Gütersloher Verlagshaus.
———. 2006b. "Where Does the Concept of Resurrection Appear and How Do We Know That?" Pages 1–21 in *Resurrection: The Origin and*

Future of a Biblical Doctrine. Edited by James H. Charlesworth. New York: T&T Clark.

Chmiel, Jerzy. 1979. "Semantics of the Resurrection." Pages 59–64 in *Studia Biblica 1978*. Vol. 1: *Papers on Old Testament and Related Themes*. Edited by Elizabeth A. Livingstone. JSOTSup 11. Sheffield: University of Sheffield.

Cleland, Liza, Glenys Davies, and Lloyd Llewellyn-Jones, eds. 2007. *Greek and Roman Dress from A to Z*. London: Routledge.

Collins, Adela Yarbro. 1995. "The Seven Heavens in Jewish and Christian Apocalypses." Pages 59–93 in *Death, Ecstasy, and Other World Journeys*. Edited by John J. Collins and Michael Fishbane. Albany: State University of New York Press.

Collins, John J. 1979. "Introduction: Towards the Morphology of a Genre" in "Apocalypse: The Morphology of a Genre." *Semeia* 14:1–20.

———. 1993. *Daniel: A Commentary on the Book of Daniel*. Hermeneia. Minneapolis: Fortress.

———. 1994. Review of Émile Puech, *La croyance des Esséniens en la vie future: Immortalité, résurrection, vie éternelle? Histoire d'une croyance dans le Judaïsme ancien*. DSD 1:246–52.

———. 1998. *The Apocalyptic Imagination: An Introduction to Jewish Apocalyptic Literature*. 2nd ed. Grand Rapids: Eerdmans.

———. 2009. "The Angelic Life." Pages 291–310 in *Metamorphoses: Resurrection, Body, and Transformative Practices in Early Christianity*. Edited by Turid Karlsen Seim and Jorunn Økland. Ekstasis 1. Berlin: de Gruyter.

Craffert, Pieter F. 2008. *The Life of a Galilean Shaman: Jesus of Nazareth in Anthropological-Historical Perspective*. Eugene, OR: Cascade.

———. 2010. "Altered States of Consciousness: Visions, Spirit Possession, Sky Journeys." Pages 126–46 in *Understanding the Social World of the New Testament*. Edited by Dietmar Neufeld and Richard E. DeMaris. London: Routledge.

Croft, William, and D. Alan Cruse. 2004. *Cognitive Linguistics*. CTL. Cambridge: Cambridge University Press.

Cullmann, Oscar. 1962. *Christ and Time: The Primitive Christian Conception of Time and History*. Translated by F. V. Filson. Rev. ed. Philadelphia: Westminster.

Dahl, Murdoch E. 1962. *The Resurrection of the Body: A Study of 1 Corinthians 15*. SBT 36. London: SCM.

Damasio, Antonio R. 1994. *Descartes' Error: Emotion, Reason, and the Human Brain*. New York: Putnam.

Dana, H. E., and Julius R. Mantey. 1939. *A Manual Grammar of the Greek New Testament*. New York: Macmillan.

Davidsen, Ole. 1995. "The Structural Typology of Adam and Christ: Some Modal-Semiotic Comments on the Basic Narrative of the Letter to the Romans." Pages 244–62 in *The New Testament and Hellenistic Judaism*. Edited by Peder Borgen and Søren Giversen. Aarhus: Aarhus University Press.

Davies, W. D. 1962. *Paul and Rabbinic Judaism: Some Rabbinic Elements in Pauline Theology*. London: SPCK.

Davies, W. D., and Dale C. Allison. 2004. *Matthew: A Shorter Commentary*. Edited by Dale C. Allison. London: T&T Clark.

Davila, James R. 1999. "Heavenly Ascent in the Dead Sea Scrolls." Pages 460–85 in vol. 2 of *The Dead Sea Scrolls after Fifty Years: A Comprehensive Assessment*. Edited by Peter W. Flint and James C. VanderKam. 2 vols. Leiden: Brill.

Day, John. 1996. "The Development of Belief in Life after Death in Ancient Israel." Pages 231–57 in *After the Exile: Essays in Honour of Rex Mason*. Edited by John Barton and David J. Reimer. Macon, GA: Mercer University Press.

DeConick, April D., ed. 2006a. *Paradise Now: Essays on Early Jewish and Christian Mysticism*. SymS 11. Atlanta: Society of Biblical Literature.

———. 2006b. "What Is Early Jewish and Christian Mysticism?" Pages 1–24 in *Paradise Now: Essays on Early Jewish and Christian Mysticism*. Edited by April D. DeConick. SBLSymS 11. Atlanta: Society of Biblical Literature.

Deissmann, Adolf. 1957. *Paul: A Study in Social and Religious History*. Translated by William E. Wilson. 2nd rev. and enl. ed. New York: Harper & Brothers.

Dimant, Devorah. 1996. "Men as Angels: The Self-Image of the Qumran Community." Pages 93–103 in *Religion and Politics in the Ancient Near East*. Edited by Adele Berlin. Bethesda, MD: University Press of Maryland.

Dodd, C. H. 1963. *The Apostolic Preaching and Its Developments: Three Lectures with an Appendix on Eschatology and History*. London: Hodder & Stoughton.

Dolansky, Fanny. 2008. "*Togam virilem sumere*: Coming of Age in the Roman World." Pages 47–70 in *Roman Dress and the Fabrics of Roman*

Culture. Edited by Jonathan Edmondson and Alison Keith. PhoSup 1. Toronto: University of Toronto Press.

Doyle, Brian. 2000. *The Apocalypse of Isaiah Metaphorically Speaking: A Study of the Use, Function and Significance of Metaphors in Isaiah 24–27*. BETL 151. Leuven: Leuven University Press.

Duling, Dennis. 2008. "'Whatever Gain I Had …': Ethnicity and Paul's Self-Identification in Philippians 3:5–6." *HvTSt* 64:799–819.

Dunn, James D. G. 1988. *Romans*. 2 vols. WBC 38A–B. Dallas: Word.

———. 1998a. "Spirit and Holy Spirit in the New Testament." Pages 3–21 in *Pneumatology*. Vol. 2 of *The Christ and the Spirit: Collected Essays*. Grand Rapids: Eerdmans.

———. 1998b. *The Theology of Paul the Apostle*. Grand Rapids: Eerdmans.

———. 1999. "'Baptized' as Metaphor." Pages 294–310 in *Baptism, the New Testament, and the Church: Historical and Contemporary Studies in Honour of R. E. O. White*. Edited by Stanley E. Porter and Anthony R. Cross. JSNTSup 171. Sheffield: Sheffield Academic.

Ehrman, Bart D. 2008. *The New Testament: A Historical Introduction to the Early Christian Writings*. 4th ed. Oxford: Oxford University Press.

Eijk, P. J. van der. 2000. "Aristotle's Psycho-Physiological Account of the Soul-Body Relationship." Pages 57–77 in *Psyche and Soma: Physicians and Metaphysicians on the Mind-Body Problem from Antiquity to Enlightenment*. Edited by John P. Wright and Paul Potter. Oxford: Clarendon.

Engberg-Pedersen, Troels. 2000. *Paul and the Stoics*. Edinburgh: T&T Clark.

———. 2008. "The Construction of Religious Experience in Paul." Pages 147–57 in *Inquiry into Religious Experience in Early Judaism and Early Christianity*. Vol. 1 of *Experientia*. Edited by Frances Flannery, Colleen Shantz, and Rodney A. Werline. SymS 40. Atlanta: Society of Biblical Literature.

———. 2009. "Complete and Incomplete Transformation in Paul: A Philosophical Reading of Paul on Body and Spirit." Pages 123–46 in *Metamorphoses: Resurrection, Body and Transformative Practices in Early Christianity*. Edited by Turid Karlsen Seim and Jorunn Økland. Ekstasis 1. Berlin: de Gruyter.

———. 2010. *Cosmology and Self in the Apostle Paul: The Material Spirit*. Oxford: Oxford University Press.

Evans, Vyvyan, and Melanie Green. 2006. *Cognitive Linguistics: An Introduction*. Mahwah, NJ: Erlbaum.

Fauconnier, Gilles, and Mark Turner. 2002. *The Way We Think: Conceptual Blending and the Mind's Hidden Complexities*. New York: Basic Books.

Fitzmyer, Joseph A. 1989. *Paul and His Theology: A Brief Sketch*. Englewood Cliffs, NJ: Prentice Hall.

———. 1993. *Romans: A New Translation with Introduction and Commentary*. AB 33. New York: Doubleday.

———. 1998. *The Acts of the Apostles*. AB 31. New York: Doubleday.

———. 2008. *First Corinthians: A New Translation with Introduction and Commentary*. AB 32. New Haven: Yale University Press.

Flannery, Frances, with Nicolae Roddy, Colleen Shantz, and Rodney A. Werline. 2008. "Introduction: Religious Experience, Past and Present." Pages 1–10 in *Inquiry into Religious Experience in Early Judaism and Christianity*. Vol. 1 of *Experientia*. Edited by Frances Flannery, Colleen Shantz, and Rodney A. Werline. SymS 40. Atlanta: Society of Biblical Literature.

Flannery, Frances, Colleen Shantz, and Rodney A. Werline, eds. 2008. *Inquiry into Religious Experience in Early Judaism and Early Christianity*. Vol. 1 of *Experientia*. SymS 40. Atlanta: Society of Biblical Literature.

Fletcher-Louis, Crispin H. T. 1996. "4Q374—A Discourse on the Sinai Tradition: The Deification of Moses and Early Christology." *DSD* 3:236–52.

———. 1997. *Luke-Acts: Angels, Christology, and Soteriology*. WUNT 94. Tübingen: Mohr Siebeck.

———. 2002. *All the Glory of Adam: Liturgical Anthropology in the Dead Sea Scrolls*. STDJ 42. Leiden: Brill.

———. 2008. "Religious Experience and Apocalypses." Pages 125–44 in *Inquiry into Religious Experience in Early Judaism and Early Christianity*. Vol. 1 of *Experientia*. Edited by Frances Flannery, Colleen Shantz, and Rodney A. Werline. SymS 40. Atlanta: Society of Biblical Literature.

———. 2011. "Jewish Apocalyptic and Apocalypticism." Pages 1569–607 in vol. 2 of *Handbook for the Study of the Historical Jesus*. Edited by Tom Holmén and Stanley E. Porter. 4 vols. Leiden: Brill.

Fossum, Jarl E. 1999. "Glory, כבוד, δόξα." *DDD* 348–52.

Frennesson, Björn. 1999. *"In a Common Rejoicing": Liturgical Communion with Angels in Qumran*. SSU 14. Uppsala: Uppsala University.

Furnish, Victor Paul. 1984. *II Corinthians: Translation with Introduction, Notes, and Commentary*. AB 32A. Garden City, NY: Doubleday.

Gibbs, Raymond W. 1994. *The Poetics of Mind: Figurative Thought, Language, and Understanding.* Cambridge: Cambridge University Press.

———, ed. 2008. *The Cambridge Handbook of Metaphor and Thought.* Cambridge: Cambridge University Press.

Goff, Matthew. 2005. Review of Crispin H. T. Fletcher-Louis, *All the Glory of Adam: Liturgical Anthropology in the Dead Sea Scrolls.*" RBL. Online: http://www.bookreviews.org/pdf/4774_4931.pdf.

Goldman, Norma. 2001. "Reconstructing Roman Clothing." Pages 213–37 in *The World of Roman Costume.* Edited by Judith Lynn Sebesta and Larissa Bonfante. Madison: University of Wisconsin Press.

Grady, Joseph Edward. 1997. "Foundations of Meaning: Primary Metaphors and Primary Scenes." PhD diss., University of California, Berkeley.

Gundry, Robert H. 1976. *Sōma in Biblical Theology: With Emphasis on Pauline Anthropology.* SNTSMS 29. Cambridge: Cambridge University Press.

Harner, Michael. 1990. *The Way of the Shaman.* 3rd ed. New York: HarperSanFrancisco.

Harris, Murray J. 2005. *The Second Epistle to the Corinthians: A Commentary on the Greek Text.* NIGTC. Grand Rapids: Eerdmans.

Hays, Richard B. 2008. "What Is 'Real Partricipation in Christ'? A Dialogue with E. P. Sanders on Pauline Soteriology." Pages 336–51 in *Redefining First-Century Jewish and Christian Identities: Essays in Honor of Ed Parish Sanders.* Edited by Fabian E. Udoh. Notre Dame: University of Notre Dame Press.

Himmelfarb, Martha. 1993. *Ascent to Heaven in Jewish and Christian Apocalypses.* New York: Oxford University Press.

Holleman, Joost. 1996. *Resurrection and Parousia: A Traditio-Historical Study of Paul's Eschatology in I Corinthians 15.* NovTSup 84. Leiden: Brill.

Hooker, M. D. 1959–1960. "Adam in Romans 1." *NTS* 6:297–306.

Horrell, David. 2006. *An Introduction to the Study of Paul.* 2nd ed. New York: T&T Clark.

Horsley, Richard A. 1976. "Pneumatikos vs. Psychikos: Distinctions of Spiritual Status among the Corinthians." *HTR* 69:269–88.

Howe, Bonnie. 2006. *Because You Bear This Name: Conceptual Metaphor and the Moral Meaning of 1 Peter.* BibInt 81. Leiden: Brill.

Howe, Bonnie, and Joel B. Green, eds. 2014. *Cognitive Linguistic Explorations in Biblical Studies.* Berlin: de Gruyter.

Jewett, Robert. 1971. *Paul's Anthropological Terms: A Study of Their Use in Conflict Settings*. AGJU 10. Leiden: Brill.

———. 2007. *Romans: A Commentary*. Hermeneia. Minneapolis: Fortress.

Johnson, Mark. 1987. *The Body in the Mind: The Bodily Basis of Meaning, Imagination, and Reason*. Chicago: University of Chicago Press.

———. 2005. "The Philosophical Significance of Image Schemas." Pages 15–33 in *From Perception to Meaning: Image Schemas in Cognitive Linguistics*. Edited by Beate Hampe. CLR 29. Berlin: de Gruyter.

Johnson Hodge, Caroline. 2007. *If Sons, Then Heirs: A Study of Kinship and Ethnicity in the Letters of Paul*. Oxford: Oxford University Press.

Johnston, Philip S. 2002. *Shades of Sheol: Death and Afterlife in the Old Testament*. Downers Grove, IL: InterVarsity Press.

Käsemann, Ernst. 1964. "The Pauline Doctrine of the Lord's Supper." Pages 108–35 in *Essays on New Testament Themes*. Translated by W. J. Montague. London: SCM.

———. 1969. "On the Subject of Early Christian Apocalyptic." Pages 108–37 in *New Testament Questions of Today*. Translated by W. J. Montague. NTL. London: SCM.

———. 1971a. "Justification and Salvation History in the Epistle to the Romans." Pages 60–78 in *Perspectives on Paul*. Translated by Margaret Kohl. Philadelphia: Fortress.

———. 1971b. "The Faith of Abraham in Romans 4." Pages 79–101 in *Perspectives on Paul*. Translated by Margaret Kohl. Philadelphia: Fortress.

———. 1971c. "On Paul's Anthropology." Pages 1–31 in *Perspectives on Paul*. Translated by Margaret Kohl. Philadelphia: Fortress.

———. 1971d. "The Theological Problem Presented by the Motif of the Body of Christ." Pages 102–21 in *Perspectives on Paul*. Translated by Margaret Kohl. Philadelphia: Fortress.

———. 1980. *Commentary on Romans*. Translated by Geoffrey W. Bromiley. Grand Rapids: Eerdmans.

———. 2010. "Corporeality in Paul." Pages 38–51 in *On Being a Disciple of the Crucified Nazarene: Unpublished Lectures and Sermons*. Edited by Rudolf Landau and Wolfgang Kraus. Translated by Roy A. Harrisville. Grand Rapids: Eerdmans.

Katz, Steven T. 1978. "Language, Epistemology, and Mysticism." Pages 22–74 in *Mysticism and Philosophical Analysis*. Edited by Steven T. Katz. London: Sheldon.

Kim, Jung Hoon. 2004. *The Significance of Clothing Imagery in the Pauline Corpus*. JSNTSup 268. London: T&T Clark.

King, Sallie B. 1988. "Two Epistemological Models for the Interpretation of Mysticism." *JAAR* 56:257–79.

Kister, Menahem. 2007. "'In Adam': 1 Cor 15:21–22; 12:27 in Their Jewish Setting." Pages 685–90 in *Flores Florentino: Dead Sea Scrolls and Other Early Jewish Studies in Honour of Florentino García Martínez*. Edited by Anthony Hilhorst, Émile Puech, and Eibert J. C. Tigchelaar. JSJSup 122. Leiden: Brill.

Koester, Helmut. 2000. *Introduction to the New Testament*. 2nd ed. 2 vols. Berlin: de Gruyter.

Kooten, George H. van. 2008. *Paul's Anthropology in Context: The Image of God, Assimilation to God, and Tripartite Man in Ancient Judaism, Ancient Philosophy and Early Christianity*. WUNT 232. Tübingen: Mohr Siebeck.

Lakoff, George. 1987. *Women, Fire, and Dangerous Things: What Categories Reveal about the Mind*. Chicago: University of Chicago Press.

———. 1993. "The Contemporary Theory of Metaphor." Pages 202–51 in *Metaphor and Thought*. Edited by Andrew Ortony. Cambridge: Cambridge University Press.

———. 1996. *Moral Politics: What Conservatives Know That Liberals Don't*. Chicago: University of Chicago Press.

Lakoff, George, and Mark Johnson. 1980. *Metaphors We Live By*. Chicago: University of Chicago Press.

———. 1999. *Philosophy in the Flesh: The Embodied Mind and Its Challenge to Western Thought*. New York: Basic Books.

Lakoff, George, and Mark Turner. 1989. *More Than Cool Reason: A Field Guide to Poetic Metaphor*. Chicago: University of Chicago Press.

Lakoff, George, and Rafael E. Núñez. 2000. *Where Mathematics Comes From: How the Embodied Mind Brings Mathematics into Being*. New York: Basic Books.

Langacker, Ronald W. 1992. "Prepositions as Grammatical(izing) Elements." *LeuB* 81:287–309.

Law, Timothy Michael, and Charles Halton, eds. 2014. *Jew and Judean: A Forum on Politics and Historiography in the Translation of Ancient Texts*. The Marginalia Review of Books. http://marginalia.lareviewofbooks.org/jew-judean-forum.

Lehtipuu, Outi. 2009. "'Flesh and Blood Cannot Inherit the Kingdom of God': The Transformation of the Flesh in the Early Christian Debates Concerning Resurrection." Pages 147–68 in *Metamorphoses: Resurrec-*

tion, Body and Transformative Practices in Early Christianity. Edited by Turid Karlsen Seim and Jorunn Økland. Ekstasis 1. Berlin: de Gruyter.

Levison, John R. 1987. *Portraits of Adam in Early Judaism: From Sirach to 2 Baruch*. JSPSup 1. Sheffield: JSOT Press.

Lincoln, Andrew T. 1981. *Paradise Now and Not Yet: Studies in the Role of the Heavenly Dimension in Paul's Thought with Special Reference to his Eschatology*. SNTSMS 43. Cambridge: Cambridge University Press.

Lohse, Eduard. 1976. *The New Testament Environment*. Translated by J. E. Steely. Nashville: Abingdon.

Longenecker, Richard N. 1998. "Is There Development in Paul's Resurrection Thought?" Pages 171–202 in *Life in the Face of Death: The Resurrection Message of the New Testament*. Edited by Richard N. Longenecker. Grand Rapids: Eerdmans.

Lüdemann, Gerd. 1994. *The Resurrection of Jesus: History, Experience, Theology*. Translated by John Bowden. Minneapolis: Fortress.

Lundhaug, Hugo. 2007. "Conceptual Blending in the *Exegesis of the Soul*." Pages 141–60 in *Explaining Christian Origins and Early Judaism: Contributions from Cognitive and Social Science*. Edited by Petri Luomanen, Ilkka Pyysiäinen, and Risto Uro. BibInt 89. Leiden: Brill.

———. 2010. *Images of Rebirth: Cognitive Poetics and Transformational Soteriology in the Gospel of Philip and the Exegesis on the Soul*. NHMS 73. Leiden: Brill.

Martin, Dale B. 1995. *The Corinthian Body*. New Haven: Yale University Press.

Martyn, J. Louis. 1997. *Theological Issues in the Letters of Paul*. SNTW. Edinburgh: T&T Clark.

Mason, Steve. 1991. *Flavius Josephus on the Pharisees: A Composition-Critical Study*. Leiden: Brill.

———. 2003. *Josephus and the New Testament*. 2nd ed. Peabody, MA: Hendrickson.

Matera, Frank J. 2010. *Romans*. Paideia. Grand Rapids: Baker Academic.

McNeel, Jennifer Houston. 2014. *Paul as Infant and Nursing Mother: Metaphor, Rhetoric, and Identity in 1 Thessalonians 2:5–8*. ECL 12. Atlanta: SBL Press.

Meeks, Wayne A. 1967. *The Prophet-King: Moses Traditions and the Johannine Christology*. NovTSup 14. Leiden: Brill.

———. 2003. *The First Urban Christians: The Social World of the Apostle Paul*. 2nd ed. New Haven: Yale University Press.

Merleau-Ponty, Maurice. 1945. *Phénoménologie de la perception.* Paris: Gallimard.

Meyer, Ben F. 1986. "Did Paul's View of the Resurrection of the Dead Undergo Development?" *TS* 47:363–87.

Mitchell, Margaret M. 1991. *Paul and the Rhetoric of Reconciliation: An Exegetical Investigation of the Language and Composition of 1 Corinthians.* Louisville: Westminster John Knox.

———. 2005. "Paul's Letters to Corinth: The Interpretive Intertwining of Literary and Historical Reconstructions." Pages 307–38 in *Urban Religion in Roman Corinth: Interdisciplinary Approaches.* Edited by Daniel N. Schowalter and Steven J. Friesen. HTS 53. Cambridge: Harvard University Press.

Morray-Jones, Christopher R. A. 1992. "Transformational Mysticism in the Apocalyptic-Merkabah Tradition." *JJS* 43:1–31.

———. 1993a. "Paradise Revisited (2 Cor 12:1–12): The Jewish Mystical Background of Paul's Apostolate, Part 1: The Jewish Sources." *HTR* 86:177–217.

———. 1993b. "Paradise Revisited (2 Cor 12:1–12): The Jewish Mystical Background of Paul's Apostolate, Part 2: Paul's Heavenly Ascent and its Significance." *HTR* 86:265–92.

———. 2006. "The Temple Within." Pages 145–78 in *Paradise Now: Essays on Early Jewish and Christian Mysticism.* Edited by April D. DeConick. SymS 11. Atlanta: Society of Biblical Literature.

Moulton, James, Wilbert Francis Howard, and Nigel Turner. 1906. *A Grammar of New Testament Greek.* 4 vols. Edinburgh: T&T Clark.

Nagy, Gregory. 2002. "Can Myth Be Saved?" Pages 240–48 in *Myth: A New Symposium.* Edited by Gregory Schrempp and William Hansen. Bloomington: Indiana University Press.

Newman, Carey C. 1992. *Paul's Glory-Christology: Tradition and Rhetoric.* NovTSup 69. Leiden: Brill.

———. 1997. "Resurrection as Glory: Divine Presence and Christian Origins." Pages 59–89 in *The Resurrection: An Interdisciplinary Symposium on the Resurrection of Jesus.* Edited by Steven T. Davis, Daniel Kendall, S.J., and Gerald O'Collins, S.J. Oxford: Oxford University Press.

Nickelsburg, George W. E. 1999. "Son of Man, בר אנש, בן אדם, ὁ υἱὸς τοῦ ἀνθρώπου." *DDD* 800–804.

———. 2001. *1 Enoch: A Commentary on the Book of 1 Enoch, Chapters 1–36; 81–108.* Hermeneia. Minneapolis: Fortress.

———. 2006. *Resurrection, Immortality, and Eternal Life in Intertestamental Judaism and Early Christianity*. Expanded ed. HTS 56. Cambridge: Harvard University Press.

Niederwimmer, Kurt. 1998. *The Didache: A Commentary*. Hermeneia. Minneapolis: Fortress.

Oden, Robert A., Jr. 1992. "Cosmogony, Cosmology." *ABD* 1:1162-71.

Oepke, Albrecht. 1964. "βάπτω, βαπτίζω, βαπτισμός, βάπτισμα, βαπτιστής." *TDNT* 1:529-46.

Olson, Kelly. 2003. "Roman Underwear Revisited." *CW* 96:201-10.

Osiek, Carolyn, and Jennifer Pouya. 2010. "Constructions of Gender in the Roman Imperial World." Pages 44-56 in *Understanding the Social World of the New Testament*. Edited by Dietmar Neufeld and Richard E. DeMaris. London: Routledge.

Parsons, Mikeal C. 2008. *Acts*. Paideia. Grand Rapids: Baker Academic.

Pearson, Birger A. 1973. *The Pneumatikos-Psychikos Terminology in 1 Corinthians: A Study in the Theology of the Corinthian Opponents of Paul and Its Relation to Gnosticism*. SBLDS 12. Missoula, MT: Society of Biblical Literature.

Pervo, Richard. 2009. *Acts: A Commentary*. Hermeneia. Minneapolis: Fortress.

———. 2010. *The Making of Paul: Constructions of the Apostle in Early Christianity*. Minneapolis: Fortress.

Pinker, Steven. 2007. *The Stuff of Thought: Language as a Window into Human Nature*. New York: Viking.

Polaski, Donald C. 2001. *Authorizing an End: The Isaiah Apocalypse and Intertextuality*. BibInt 50. Leiden: Brill.

Porter, J. R. 1965. "The Legal Aspects of the Concept of 'Corporate Personality' in the Old Testament." *VT* 15:361-80.

Porter, Stanley E. 1999. *Idioms of the Greek New Testament*. 2nd ed. BLG 2. Sheffield: Sheffield Academic.

Puech, Émile. 1990. "Ben Sira 48.11 et la Résurrection." Pages 81-90 in *Of Scribes and Scrolls: Studies on the Hebrew Bible, Intertestamental Judaism, and Christian Origins, Presented to John Strugnell on the Occasion of His Sixtieth Birthday*. Edited by Harold W. Attridge, John J. Collins, and Thomas H. Tobin, S.J. CTSRR 5. Lanham, MD: University Press of America.

———. 1993. *La croyance des Esséniens en la vie future: Immortalité, résurrection, vie éternelle? Histoire d'une croyance dans le judaïsme ancient*. EBib 21-22. Paris: Gabalda.

———. 2006. "Resurrection: The Bible and Qumran." Pages 247–81 in *The Dead Sea Scrolls and the Qumran Community*. Vol. 2 of *The Bible and the Dead Sea Scrolls*. Edited by James H. Charlesworth. Waco, TX: Baylor University Press.

Robertson, A. T. 1919. *A Grammar of the Greek New Testament in the Light of Historical Research*. 3rd ed. London: Hodder & Stoughton.

Robinson, H. Wheeler. 1936. "The Hebrew Conception of Corporate Personality." Pages 49–62 in *Werden und Wesen des Altes Testaments*. Edited by Paul Volz, Friedrich Stummer, and Johannes Hempel. BZAW 66. Berlin: Töpelmann.

Robinson, John A. T. 1952. *The Body: A Study in Pauline Theology*. SBT 5. London: SCM.

Robinson, Thomas M. 2000. "The Defining Features of Mind-Body Dualism in the Writings of Plato." Pages 37–55 in *Psyche and Soma: Physicians and Metaphysicians on the Mind-Body Problem from Antiquity to Enlightenment*. Edited by John P. Wright and Paul Potter. Oxford: Clarendon.

Rogerson, John W. 1970. "The Hebrew Conception of Corporate Personality: A Re-examination." *JTS* 21:1–16.

Rowland, Christopher. 1982. *The Open Heaven: A Study of Apocalyptic in Judaism and Early Christianity*. London: SPCK.

Rowland, Christopher, and Christopher R. A. Morray-Jones. 2009. *The Mystery of God: Early Jewish Mysticism and the New Testament*. CRINT 12. Leiden: Brill.

Sanders, E. P. 1977. *Paul and Palestinian Judaism: A Comparison of Patterns of Religion*. Philadelphia: Fortress.

———. 1985. *Jesus and Judaism*. Philadelphia: Fortress.

Sawyer, John F. A. 1973. "Hebrew Words for the Resurrection of the Dead." *VT* 23:218–34.

Schnelle, Udo. 1996. *The Human Condition: Anthropology in the Teachings of Jesus, Paul, and John*. Translated by O. C. Dean Jr. Minneapolis: Fortress.

Scholem, Gershom. 1961. *Major Trends in Jewish Mysticism*. New York: Schocken Books.

Schweitzer, Albert. 1968. *The Mysticism of Paul the Apostle*. Translated by W. Montgomery. New York: Seabury.

Schweizer, Eduard, and Friedrich Baumgärtel. 1971. "σῶμα, σωματικός, σύσσωμος." *TDNT* 7:1024–94.

Segal, Alan F. 1980. "Heavenly Ascent in Hellenistic Judaism, Early Christianity and their Environment." *ANRW* 23.2:1333–94.

———. 1990. *Paul the Convert: The Apostolate and Apostasy of Saul the Pharisee.* New Haven: Yale University Press.

———. 1998. "Paul's Thinking about Resurrection in its Jewish Context." *NTS* 44:400–419.

———. 2004. *Life after Death: A History of the Afterlife in Western Religion.* New York: Doubleday.

———. 2006. "Religious Experience and the Construction of the Transcendent Self." Pages 27–40 in *Paradise Now: Essays on Early Jewish and Christian Mysticism.* Edited by April D. DeConick. SymS 11. Atlanta: Society of Biblical Literature.

———. 2008. "The Afterlife as Mirror of the Self." Pages 19–40 in *Inquiry into Religious Experience in Early Judaism and Early Christianity.* Vol. 1 of *Experientia.* Edited by Frances Flannery, Colleen Shantz, and Rodney A. Werline. SymS 40. Atlanta: Society of Biblical Literature.

Segal, Robert A. 2006–2007. "Myth and Ritual." Pages 101–21 in vol. 1 of *Theorizing Rituals.* Edited by Jens Kreinath, Jan Snoek, and Michael Stausberg. 2 vols. SHR 114. Leiden: Brill.

Shantz, Colleen. 2008. "The Confluence of Trauma and Transcendence in the Pauline Corpus." Pages 193–205 in *Inquiry into Religious Experience in Early Judaism and Early Christianity.* Vol. 1 of *Experientia.* Edited by Frances Flannery, Colleen Shantz, and Rodney A. Werline. SymS 40. Atlanta: Society of Biblical Literature.

———. 2009. *Paul in Ecstasy: The Neurobiology of the Apostle's Life and Thought.* Cambridge: Cambridge University Press.

Slingerland, Edward. 2004. "Conceptual Metaphor Theory as a Methodology for Comparative Religion." *JAAR* 72:1–31.

———. 2008a. *What Science Offers the Humanities: Integrating Body and Culture.* Cambridge: Cambridge University Press.

———. 2008b. "Who's Afraid of Reductionism? The Study of Religion in the Age of Cognitive Science." *JAAR* 76:375–411.

———. 2013. "Body and Mind in Early China: An Integrated Humanities-Science Approach." *JAAR* 81:6–55.

Slingerland, Edward, and Maciej Chudek. 2011. "The Prevalence of Mind-Body Dualism in Early China." *CogSci* 35:997–1007.

Smith, Jonathan Z. 1990. *Drudgery Divine: On the Comparison of Early Christianities and the Religions of Late Antiquity.* JLCRS 14. Chicago: University of Chicago Press.

Songe-Møller, Vigdis. 2009. "'With What Kind of Body Will They Come'? Metamorphosis and the Concept of Change: From Platonic Thinking to Paul's Notion of the Resurrection of the Dead." Pages 109–22 in *Metamorphoses: Resurrection, Body and Transformative Practices in Early Christianity*. Edited by Turid Karlsen Seim and Jorunn Økland. Ekstasis 1. Berlin: de Gruyter.

Staden, Heinrich von. 2000. "Body, Soul, and Nerves: Epicurious, Herophilus, Erasistratus, the Stoics, and Galen." Pages 79–116 in *Psyche and Soma: Physicians and Metaphysicians on the Mind–Body Problem from Antiquity to Enlightenment*. Edited by John P. Wright and Paul Potter. Oxford: Clarendon.

Stendahl, Krister. 1976. "The Apostle Paul and the Introspective Conscience of the West." Pages 78–96 in *Paul among Jews and Gentiles, and Other Essays*. Philadelphia: Fortress.

Sterling, Gregory E. 1995. "'Wisdom among the Perfect:' Creation Traditions in Alexandrian Judaism and Corinthian Christianity." *NovT* 37:355–84.

Stovell, Beth M. 2012. *Mapping Metaphorical Discourse in the Fourth Gospel: John's Eternal King*. LBS 5. Leiden: Brill.

Stowers, Stanley K. 1995. "Romans 7.7–25 as a Speech-in-Character (προσωποποιία)." Pages 180–202 in *Paul in His Hellenistic Context*. Edited by Troels Engberg-Pedersen. Minneapolis: Fortress.

———. 2003. "Paul and Self-Mastery." Pages 524–50 in *Paul in the Greco-Roman World: A Handbook*. Edited by J. Paul Sampley. Harrisburg, PA: Trinity Press International.

———. 2008. "What Is 'Pauline Participation in Christ'?" Pages 352–71 in *Redefining First-Century Jewish and Christian Identities: Essays in Honor of Ed Parish Sanders*. Edited by Fabian E. Udoh. Notre Dame: University of Notre Dame Press.

Stuckenbruck, Loren T. 2007. *1 Enoch 91–108*. CEJL. Berlin: de Gruyter.

Tannehill, Robert C. 1967. *Dying and Rising with Christ: A Study in Pauline Theology*. BZNW 32. Berlin: Töpelmann.

Tappenden, Frederick S. 2010. "Aural-Performance, Conceptual Blending, and Intertextuality: The (Non-)Use of Scripture in Luke 24.45–48." Pages 180–200 in *The Gospel of Luke*. Vol. 3 of *Biblical Interpretation in Early Christian Gospels*. Edited by Thomas R. Hatina. LNTS 376. London: T&T Clark.

———. 2012. "Luke and Paul in Dialogue: Ritual Meals and Risen Bodies as Instances of Conceptual Blending." Pages 203–28 in *Resurrection of*

the Dead: Biblical Traditions in Dialogue. Edited by Geert Van Oyen and Tom Shepherd. BETL 249. Leuven: Peeters.
Taylor, Charles. 1989. *Sources of the Self: The Making of the Modern Identity.* Cambridge: Harvard University Press.
Thaden, Robert H. von, Jr. 2012. *Sex, Christ, and Embodied Cognition: Paul's Wisdom for Corinth.* ESEC 16. Dorset, UK: Deo.
Thagard, Paul. 1996. *Mind: Introduction to Cognitive Science.* Cambridge: MIT Press.
Theissen, Gerd. 2007. *Erleben und Verhalten der ersten Christen: Ein Psychologie des Urchristentums.* Gütersloh: Gütersloher Verlagshaus.
Thiessen, Matthew. 2014. "Paul's Argument against Gentile Circumcision in Romans 2:17–29." *NovT* 56:373–91.
Thiselton, Anthony C. 2000. *The First Epistle to the Corinthians: A Commentary on the Greek Text.* NIGTC. Grand Rapids: Eerdmans.
Thrall, Margaret E. 1994. *A Critical and Exegetical Commentary on the Second Epistle to the Corinthians.* ICC. 2 vols. Edinburgh: T&T Clark.
Trilling, W. 1990. "ἁρπάζω." *EDNT* 1:156–57.
Tronier, Henrik. 2001. "The Corinthian Correspondence between Philosophical Idealism and Apocalypticism." Pages 165–96 in *Paul Beyond the Judaism/Hellenism Divide.* Edited by Troels Engberg-Pedersen. Louisville: Westminster John Knox.
Uro, Risto. 2010. "Ritual and Christian Origins." Pages 220–32 in *Understanding the Social World of the New Testament.* Edited by Dietmar Neufeld and Richard E. DeMaris. London: Routledge.
———. 2011. "Towards a Cognitive History of Early Christian Rituals." Pages 109–27 in *Changing Minds: Religion and Cognition through the Ages.* Edited by István Czachesz and Tamás Biró. GSCC 42. Leuven: Peeters.
Varela, Francisco J., Evan Thompson, and Eleanor Rosch. 1991. *The Embodied Mind: Cognitive Science and Human Experience.* Cambridge: MIT Press.
Vielhauer, Philipp, and Georg Strecker. 1991. "Apocalypses and Related Subjects: Introduction." Pages 542–68 in vol. 2 of *New Testament Apocrypha.* Edited by Wilhelm Schneemelcher and R. McL. Wilson. Rev. ed. 2 vols. Louisville: Westminster John Knox.
Vos, Geerhardus. 1961. *The Pauline Eschatology.* 2nd ed. Grand Rapids: Eerdmans.
Wallace, Daniel B. 1996. *Greek Grammar beyond the Basics: An Exegetical*

Syntax of the New Testament with Scripture, Subject, and Greek Word Indexes. Grand Rapids: Zondervan.

Waltke, Bruce K., and M. O'Connor. 1990. *An Introduction to Biblical Hebrew Syntax*. Winona Lake, IN: Eisenbrauns.

Wasserman, Emma. 2007. "The Death of the Soul in Romans 7: Revisiting Paul's Anthropology in Light of Hellenistic Moral Psychology." *JBL* 126:793–816.

———. 2008. *The Death of the Soul in Romans 7: Sin, Death, and the Law in Light of Hellenistic Moral Psychology*. WUNT 256. Tübingen: Mohr Siebeck.

———. 2013. "Paul beyond the Judaism/Hellenism Divide? The Case of Pauline Anthropology in Romans 7 and 2 Corinthians 4–5." Pages 259–79 in *Christian Origins and Hellenistic Judaism: Social and Literary Contexts for the New Testament*. Edited by Stanley E. Porter and Andrew W. Pitts. TENTS 10. Leiden: Brill.

Wedderburn, Alexander J. M. 1980. "Adam in Paul's Letter to the Romans." Pages 413–30 in *Studia Biblica 1978*. Vol. 3: *Papers on Paul and other New Testament Authors, Sixth International Congress on Biblical Studies, Oxford, 3–7 April, 1978*. Edited by E. A. Livingston. JSNTSup 3. Sheffield: Department of Biblical Studies, University of Sheffield.

———. 1985. "Some Observations on Paul's Use of the Phrases 'In Christ' and 'With Christ.'" *JSNT* 25:83–97.

———. 1987. *Baptism and Resurrection: Studies in Pauline Theology against Its Graeco-Roman Background*. WUNT 44. Tübingen: Mohr Siebeck.

Williams, Ronald J. 1976. *Hebrew Syntax: An Outline*. 2nd ed. Toronto: University of Toronto Press.

Williams, Sam K. 1988. "Promise in Galatians: A Reading of Paul's Reading of Scripture." *JBL* 107:709–20.

Wise, Michael O. 2000. "מי כמוני באלים: A Study of 4Q491c, 4Q471b, 4Q427 7, and 1QHa 25:35–26:10." *DSD* 7:173–219.

Wolf, Hans-Georg. 1994. *A Folk Model of the "Internal Self" in Light of the Contemporary View of Metaphor: The Self as Subject and Object*. ASLL 284. Berlin: Lang.

Wright, N. T. 1992. *The New Testament and the People of God*. Christian Origins and the Question of God 1. Minneapolis: Fortress.

———. 2003. *The Resurrection of the Son of God*. Christian Origins and the Question of God 3. Minneapolis: Fortress.

Zerwick, Maximilian. 1985. *Biblical Greek*. SPIB 114. Rome: Editrice Pontificio Istituto Biblico.

Ancient Sources Index

Hebrew Bible/Old Testament

Genesis
1–2	99, 108, 117
1:3	194
1:26	176
1:26–27	100
2:7	96, 97, 100
2:24	105
3:19	48
12:1–3	216
12:3	216
14:10	49
15	223
15:5	90
17–18	223
19:1–29	95
21:19	49
25:8	50
25:17	50
25:23	216
32:25–31	95
35:18	148
35:29	50
37:35	48, 49
41:5	49
47:30	50
49:33	50

Exodus
3:6	80
13:21–22	95
15:12	49
16:7	95
16:10	95
19	196
19:9b–25	194
19:12	196
19:12–13	196
19:17	196
19:20	196
19:21–25	196
19:23	196
20:21	196
24:1	196
24:1–2	196
24:9	196
24:9–18	195, 196
24:12	196
24:15	196
24:16	196
24:17	196
27:16	195
32:30	196
33:7–23	194
33:12–34:9	95
33:17–23	95
33:18	196
33:22	196
34	195
34:1–35	194
34:3	196
34:4	196
34:5–6	95
34:29–35	195
34:30	195
34:33–35	195
34:34	194, 197
40:34–38	95, 194

Leviticus		11:8	48
17:11	101, 148	11:8–9	48
		14:1–2	48
Numbers		14:10–12	48
4:8–14	195	14:12	49
16:29–33	49	17:14	49
16:30	48	19:25–27	48
16:33	48	26:5	49
20:24	50	26:6	48, 66
27:13	50	28:22	48
31:2	50	31:12	48
		33:24	48
Deuteronomy		34:15	48
30:11–20	53	38:7	60
30:16	53		
30:17–18	53	Psalms	
30:19	53	3:6	49
30:20	53	13:4	49
31:16	50	16:10	49, 66
32:50	50	22:30	47, 48, 49
		30:4	49
Judges		30:10	48
2:10	50	39:13	47
		40:3	49
2 Samuel		55:4	48
7:12	50	55:16	48, 49
14:14	48	55:24	49
		63:10	49
1 Kings		69:16	49
2:10	50	73:1	65
11:43	50	73:3	65
19:5	49	73:12	65
		73:17	65
2 Kings		73:23–24	65
22:20	50	73:23–25	65
		73:25–26	65
2 Chronicles		73:27	65
9:31	50	73:27–28	65
34:28	50	84	65
		88:5	49
Job		88:5–6	48
3:13	48, 49	88:5–7	66
3:21	47	88:6	49
7:9	48	88:7	49
7:21	47, 49	88:10	49

88:12	48	26:11	53
91:1	65	26:14	49
91:3–6	65	26:15	53
91:7–8	65	26:16–18	53
91:9	65	26:19	49, 53, 70
91:14–16	65	26:20–23	53
112:4	194	37:12	53
139:8	48, 66	38:17	49
139:8–9	48	38:18	48, 49, 66
139:15	49	40:4	105
		40:5	96
Proverbs		43:17	49
1:12	49	44:23	49
2:18	49	49:1	211
5:5	48	58:5	96
5:15	49	59:19	96
9:18	49	60:1–3	96
15:11	48, 66	66:24	70
21:16	49		
27:20	48, 49	Jeremiah	
30:16	49	1:4–5	211
		17:13	49
Song of Songs		31:31–33	194
4:15	49	51:39	49
		51:57	49
Isaiah			
5:14	49	Ezekiel	
5:27	49	1:26	96
7:11	48	1:26–28	96
9:1	194	8:2	96
14:1	56	9:3–4	96
14:1–20	56	10:4	96
14:2	56	18	66
14:8	49	26:20	49
14:9	49	31:14	49
14:11–12	56	31:15–17	48
14:15	49, 56	31:16	49
14:19	48	31:18	49
24	53	32:18	49
24–27	53	32:21	49
25:8	53	32:24	49
26	8, 9, 53	32:27	48
26:2	53	32:30	49
26:9	53	34:25	49
26:10	53	36:36–37	194

Ezekiel (cont.)		7:16	66
37	8, 9	7:19	57
37:1–14	53	7:26	56
37:10	53	7:33	66
37:12	53	7:36	57
39:13	96	12:43–45	57
39:21	96	12:44–45	50
		12:45	50
Daniel		14:43–46	51, 64
7	95		
9:21	95	Sirach	
10–12	57	49:14	84
10:5–6	95	49:16	84
10:16–18	95		
11:40	56	Wisdom of Solomon	
12	8, 45, 54	1:12	71
12:1–3	8, 43, 54, 56, 58, 70, 80	1:15	71
12:2	36, 50, 58, 70	1:16	71
12:2–3	70	3:1–3	71
12:3	52, 58, 60, 63, 67, 70, 80	3:4	71
		3:6–7	71
Hosea		3:13	71
6:2	9	3:18	71
		4:6	71
Amos		4:11	84
5	66	4:14	71
5:6	66	4:20–5:14	71
5:11	66	5:1–14	71
5:14	66	5:15	71
5:16–20	66	7:25–26	198
5:27	66		
9:2	48	Old Testament Pseudepigrapha	
Habakkuk		Apocalypse of Abraham	
2:5	49	12:10	90
		13:14	91
Deuterocanonical Works		15:4–7	90
1 Maccabees		Apocalypse of Zephaniah	
4:6	195	8:3–4	91
2 Maccabees		2 Baruch	
7	45	4:2–7	194
7:9	57, 81	59:3–11	194
7:10–11	51, 64		

ANCIENT SOURCES INDEX

3 Baruch		103:7–8	58
4:16	93	103:8	164
		104	58
1 Enoch		104:2	52, 58, 60, 63, 67
1–5	44	104:4	60
1:1	164	104:6	60, 63, 67
6–7	95		
9:1	95	2 Enoch	
14–16	84	1:8–3:1	84
14:8–9	89	22:8–10	91
14:18–21	96	30:11	93
19:1	95		
22	130	Ezekiel the Tragedian	
22:4	71	68–72	96, 194
22:9–14	71, 72		
22:11	71	Joseph and Aseneth	
22:13	44, 71, 72	12:8	84
39:3	84, 89	12:11	84
39:7	52	14:3(4)	95
39:12–13	95		
51	56	Jubilees	
51:1	233	5:13–16	43
51:5b	54	10:7	43
58:2–6	52	23:11	43
61:12	95	23:22–31	72
62	56	23:22–32	43
62:14	67	23:26–29	72
62:15–16	52, 91	23:27	72
62:16	67	23:29	72
69:11	93	23:29–31	43, 71, 72
70–71	84, 89	23:30	72
71:5	89	23:31	72
71:7	95		
71:11	90, 114	Liber antiquitatum biblicarum	
86:1	60	(Pseudo-Philo)	
86:3	60	12:1	194
90:20–27	56		
90:21	60	Life of Adam and Eve	
90:28–38	122	4:1–2	93
90:33	54	13–15	93
92:3	50	20:1–2	93
93:2	50	37:3	84
99:11–102:3	56, 58	39	93
100:5–6	50	47	93
100:7	164		

Psalms of Solomon		Josephus	
3	45, 50		
3:1–2	50	*Antiquitates judaicae*	
3:2	50	13.171–173	82
3:9–12	50	18.11	81
3:11–12	56	18.13	82
3:12	52, 67	18.14	81, 94
		Bellum judaicum	
Testament of Abraham		2.119	81
3:6	95	2.162–165	82
4:9	95	2.163	80, 94, 130
9:2	95	3.374	81, 94, 95
11:9	95	3.525–527	140
15:4	95	4.137	140
15:4–6	95		
16:2	95	*Contra Apionem*	
Testament of Levi		2.218	81
5:1–3	90	Philo	
Testament of Moses		*De opificio mundi*	
10	45, 56, 60	24–25	100
10:7–10	54	35–36	100
10:9	52, 60	134	100
10:9–10	58, 63–64	135	153
10:10	60	136–150	100
		De sacrificiis Abelis et Caini	
Dead Sea Scrolls		5	95
4Q204		*De virtutibus*	
1 VI, 21	89	72–79	194
4Q374		*De vita Mosis*	
2 II	194	1.155–158	194
4Q491		2.288–292	194
11 I	90	*Legatio ad Gaium*	
11 I, 12	90	54–56	216
11 I, 13–15	90, 112	*Legum*	
11 I, 14	90, 114	1.31	101
11 I, 14–15	90	1.31–32	100
11 I, 18	90, 112	1.42	101

1.105–107	151	20:27–40	82
1.105–108	150	20:35–36	60
3.18	140	20:36	80
		21:33	164

Quaestiones et solutiones in Exodum
2.40	194	John	
		5:24	105, 106

Quaestiones et solutiones in Genesin
1.86	84, 194	11:11–14	50
2.56	100	11:23–24	50
		12:1	50
		12:17	50

Quis rerum divinarum heres sit
55	153	Acts	
55–56	101	2:20	105
56	100, 101	7:16	105
56–57	100, 101	7:29	179
57	101	7:60	50
		8:39	84, 141

Quod Deus sit immutabilis
111–113	150	13:34	105
		18:1	104
		23:6	82
		23:6–10	82
		23:8	82, 94

New Testament

		26:24	105
Matthew			
3:16	141		
9:24–25	50	Romans	
19:5	105	1:4	153, 200
20:3	178	1:7	74
22:30	60, 80	1:8	182
22:32	80	1:16	74
27:52	50	1:18–32	153
		1:18–3:31	75
Mark		1:23	79
1:10	141	2:1–16	84
1:29	105	2:5	211
5:39–42	50	2:12–16	75
10:8	105	2:15	75
12:18–27	80	2:16	75, 182
12:25	60, 80, 94	2:25–39	75
		2:28	75
Luke		2:29	75
3:5	105	3:22	182
8:52–55	50	4	216, 223
10:7	105	4:11	223
13:19	104, 107	4:16	223

Romans (cont.)	
4:16–25	223
4:17	110, 223
4:19	223
4:24	223
5:5	119, 131, 154, 159, 182
5:6	74
5:11	182
5:12	76
5:12–21	75–76, 78, 79
5:17–19	76
5:19	74
5:20	137
5:21	182
6	30, 141, 142, 144, 146
6–7	155
6–8	19, 41, 136, 149, 152, 154, 156, 164, 167, 169, 172, 173, 190, 193, 204, 205, 208, 223, 231
6:1	137
6:1–2	143
6:1–4	143, 147
6:1–11	2, 8, 25, 44, 137–46, 152
6:1–14	158
6:2	137, 145, 152
6:3	140, 182
6:3–5	74
6:4	136, 137–39, 140, 142, 143, 145, 146, 154, 172
6:4–5	145
6:4–8	23, 25, 135
6:5	23, 135, 145, 175–76, 185, 192
6:6	139, 145, 146
6:7	152
6:8	23, 135, 145
6:11	135, 136, 139, 146, 152, 182
6:12	20, 147
6:12–13	147
6:12–14	150, 156
6:13	145, 146
6:14–23	151
6:16–23	185
6:17	146
6:18–19	147
6:19	147, 156
7	146, 150, 159
7:5–6	156
7:7–25	20, 149–50, 155, 156
7:8	149
7:9–13	151–52
7:14	149
7:14–25	16, 149
7:15–17	149
7:17	149
7:18	149, 156
7:19–20	149
7:20	149, 150
7:22	20, 146, 149
7:22–24	149
7:22–25	150
7:23	149, 151
7:24	20, 156
7:25	149
8	120, 155, 185
8:1	74, 153, 157, 159, 182
8:1–10	158
8:1–30	150
8:4–6	153
8:4–17	154
8:5–6	154
8:5–13	156
8:5–17	156
8:6–7	156
8:9	158, 159, 185
8:9–10	160
8:9–11	74, 119, 146, 153, 155–63
8:10	153, 159
8:11	158, 159, 200
8:12–17	190
8:13	156
8:14–17	221
8:14–23	74
8:15	154
8:15–17	119, 159
8:16	153, 154, 156
8:17	10, 23, 114
8:17–18	13, 96, 120
8:18	165
8:18–19	211
8:18–25	173

8:21	105	2:8	13, 96
8:22–23	157	2:10	210
8:23	1, 13, 153	2:11	153
8:26–27	153	2:14–3:3	117–18
8:29	13, 24, 74, 77, 87, 96, 97, 114, 153, 175, 176, 185, 221	2:16	119
		3:1	116
8:32	185	3:1–3	118, 119
8:34	153	3:13	211
8:38	164	3:16	119, 184
9	216	3:16–17	122
9:1	19	3:22	164
9:7	221	3:23	185
10:12–14	74	4:8	184, 203, 235
11:17–24	175	4:10	182
11:21	77	4:17	182
12:1–3	205, 223	6:4	183
12:2–3	232	6:11	142, 182
12:4–8	183	6:12–20	187
12:5	184	6:14	187, 200
13:11–14	165	6:15	184
13:12–14	131	6:15–20	184
14:14	182	6:16	105
15:13	200	6:16–17	187
15:17	182	6:17	184, 188
15:19	200	6:19	119, 122, 184
15:30	182	6:19–20	185
15:31	74	6:20	184
16:2	184	7:26	164
16:3	41, 182	7:26–31	164
16:5	41, 182	7:29–31	165
16:8	182	9:1	182
16:9–10	29	9:25–27	205
16:11–13	182	10:2	182
16:20	165	10:10	99
16:22	182	10:11	164
16:25	211	10:16–17	74
		11–14	74
1 Corinthians		11:7	97
1–4	19	11:11	182
1:2	182	11:32	185
1:5	182	12	183
1:7	165, 210, 211	12:3	182
1:17–2:5	190	12:7	184
1:18–2:16	74	12:8	182
2:4–5	200	12:9	182

1 Corinthians (cont.)	
12:12–13	184
12:12–27	74
12:13	131, 182, 188
12:26	184, 203
12:28	183
13:12	198
14:6	210
14:26	210
14:30	210
15	8, 17, 19, 43, 44, 76, 77, 78, 83, 103, 120, 132, 155, 157, 159, 173
15:1–11	169
15:3–4	34, 36–39
15:3–5	74
15:12	106, 235
15:20	153
15:20–28	18
15:21	78, 79
15:21–22	75
15:22	78, 79, 110, 159
15:23	153, 185
15:24	84
15:29	143
15:35	106, 108, 118
15:35–49	120
15:35–50	41, 88, 103, 106–21, 108, 117
15:35–54	87
15:35–57	1, 73, 77, 208
15:35–58	204
15:36	108, 110
15:36–38	108, 109, 110
15:37	108, 109, 110, 111, 126
15:37–38	108
15:38	109, 110, 111
15:39	112
15:39–41	112
15:39–44	113
15:40	112, 114
15:40–41	13, 96, 120
15:41	112
15:42–44	108
15:42b–43	113, 114, 116
15:43	200
15:44	20, 115–20, 131, 159
15:44a	115–16
15:45	93, 96, 100, 110, 120, 172, 186, 221
15:45–49	75, 78–79, 96, 117, 159
15:46	117
15:47	100
15:47–49	100
15:47–59	97
15:49	110, 117, 121, 122, 126
15:50	117, 125
15:51	87
15:51–52	110, 165
15:53–54	110, 117, 121, 122, 126
15:54	130
16:9	41

2 Corinthians	
1:1	185
1:1–2:13	40
1:3–7	203
1:3–9	192
1:5	182
1:19–20	73, 182
1:20	182
1:21	182
1:22	119, 154, 159
2:14–15	193
2:14–4:15	208
2:14–5:10	208
2:14–6:13	40, 193
3	195
3–4	177, 193, 204, 207, 208, 223, 232
3–5	121, 225
3:1–3	204
3:1–4:6	194
3:1–5:5	208
3:2	129, 193
3:2–3	193
3:3	119, 159
3:4	182
3:7	194, 195
3:7–4:6	29, 120
3:8	194
3:9–10	194

ANCIENT SOURCES INDEX 269

Reference	Pages
3:10	194
3:11	194
3:12	194, 197, 201
3:12–18	121
3:12–4:6	193–99, 211, 212
3:12–4:7	194
3:13	194, 195
3:13–15	197, 201
3:14	182, 195
3:15	196, 197
3:15–16	199
3:16	194, 197
3:16–18	194, 197
3:16–4:6	196
3:17	159, 194, 197
3:17–18	153, 197
3:17–4:6	153
3:18	2, 13, 87, 96, 97, 104, 120, 197, 198, 203
4:1	199
4:4	97, 199
4:4–6	13, 96, 120
4:6	121, 194, 197, 199, 203
4:7	121, 129, 199, 200, 201, 207
4:7–18	2, 44, 193, 199–204
4:8–12	200
4:10	2, 200
4:10–11	74, 192, 193, 200, 201, 203
4:10–12	201
4:11	200, 206
4:12	201, 203, 227
4:14	185
4:15	201, 227
4:16	10, 125, 146, 203
4:16–18	121, 193, 200, 201, 203, 204, 206, 208, 209
4:17	204
4:17–18	201
5	103, 121, 126, 131, 132, 171, 173, 208
5:1	131
5:1–2a	122, 124–25
5:1–5	1, 2, 41, 77, 87, 88, 103, 117, 121–32, 131, 194, 204, 208
5:1–10	73
5:2	13, 126, 130, 131, 157
5:2b	126–31
5:3	130, 132, 163
5:4	126–31, 157
5:4b	130
5:5	119, 131, 132, 154, 159
5:6	209
5:6–10	129, 194, 208–9, 222
5:8	209
5:10	84
5:11–17	194
5:12	194
5:13	194
5:16	194
5:16–17	198
5:17	182
5:18	182
5:21	182
6:11–13	193
6:14–7:1	40
7:2–3	203
7:2–4	40, 193
7:3	184
7:5–16	40
8	40
9	40
10–13	209
10:1–13:10	40
11:16–12:10	209
12	89
12:1	210
12:1–4	74, 209, 210, 211
12:1–10	29, 73, 90, 209, 211, 227
12:2	182
12:2 3	210
12:2–4	84, 92
12:4	210
12:5–10	210
12:7	209, 210
12:9	200, 210
12:9–10	190
12:10	210
13:4	185, 192, 200
13:11–13	40

Galatians		6:2	232
1–3	222	6:10	74
1:1	182		
1:2	74	Ephesians	
1:4	164	2:1–10	234–35
1:6	105	5:31	105
1:7	105		
1:11–16	74	Philippians	
1:11–17	211, 222, 123	1:1	29, 182
1:12	210, 223	1:1–3:1a	40
1:15–16	166	1:7	184, 203
1:16	210–11, 223	1:20	74, 206
1:22	29, 182	1:20–26	206, 209
2:2	210, 223	1:21–23	206
2:16	182	1:23	185, 206
2:19–20	190, 205	1:24–26	206
2:19–21	211, 222, 223	1:27	184
2:20	211	1:29	192
3	30	1:29–30	232
3–4	177, 216, 223	2:1–5	184
3:6–4:7	222	2:1–11	190
3:7	216	2:2	184
3:8	221	2:3–4	232
3:9	216	2:6	97
3:11	222	2:6–11	141
3:16	217	2:7	79
3:21	222	2:17–18	184, 203
3:23	223	3:1b–11	166
3:26	182	3:1b–4:1	40, 224–25
3:27	131, 143, 182	3:2–3	224
3:28–29	185	3:2–6	224
3:29	217	3:4–9	224
4:1–7	19	3:4–11	190
4:4	164	3:7	182
4:6	154	3:7–11	224, 225
5:2	224	3:9	182
5:6	182	3:10	24, 200, 224, 25
5:7–12	224	3:10–11	2, 176, 192, 206
5:13–15	184	3:10–14	44
5:16–26	119, 154, 159, 223	3:10–16	224
5:22–23	154, 223	3:11–16	225
5:22–26	184	3:12	235
5:24	152, 185, 223	3:14	182
6:1	119, 159	3:21	1, 13, 24, 77, 79, 87, 96, 114, 120, 153, 175–76, 185, 200, 224
6:1–5	184		

4:2–3	40	2 Timothy	
4:4–7	40	2:16–18	235
4:7	182		
4:8–9	40	Philemon	
4:10–20	40	6	182
4:11–13	190	7	205
4:14	184, 203	8	182
4:21–23	40	12	205
		20	182, 205

Colossians
1:13	104, 107	Hebrews	
2:12	234–35	11:5	105
3:1–4	234–35	13:2	95

1 Thessalonians
		James	
1:1	182	4:9	104, 107
1:5	182, 200		
1:10	84	1 Peter	
2:13–16	190	1:3	105
2:14	182	2:9	105
3:14	232		
4	83, 205	1 John	
4:13	83, 84	3:14	105, 106
4:13–15	84		
4:13–18	8, 43, 73, 77, 83–85, 89, 205	Jude	
4:13–5:11	19, 235	4	105
4:14	84, 85, 182, 185		
4:15	165	Revelation	
4:15–17	83	12:5	84
4:16	84, 85		
4:16–17	84		
4:17	77, 84, 85, 87, 92, 110, 165, 185		
4:18	84		

Apostolic Fathers and Ancient Christian Writings

5:1–3	165	Barnabas	
5:1–11	205, 232	11:11	141
5:2–4	84		
5:5	74, 205	Didache	
5:6	205	7:1–4	141
5:6–7	205	7:2–3	141
5:8	131, 205		
5:10	185	Shepherd of Hermas, Mandate(s)	
5:23	153, 205	4.3	141

2 Thessalonians
		Shephard of Hermas, Similitude(s)	
2:1–12	235	9.16	141

Hippolytus, *Traditio apostolica*
    21.14–19   141

Greco-Roman Literature

Homer, *Iliad*
    5.845   123
    6.340   123
    18.416   123

Plato, *Respublica*
    9.571–577   150

Plutarch, *De virtute et vitio*
    101A   150

Seneca, *Naturales quaestiones*
    3.29.2–3   216

Xenophon, *Symposium*
    2:25   110

Modern Authors Index

Adams, Edward	17, 98	Collins, Adela Yarbro	90
Alexander, Philip S.	90, 94, 215	Collins, John J.	9, 18, 43, 53, 54, 56, 57, 65, 70
Allison, Dale C.	80		
Angel, Joseph	90, 94	Craffert, Pieter F.	4, 210, 213, 232
d'Aquili, Eugene G.	213	Croft, William	34, 51
Asher, Jeffrey R.	77, 102, 103	Cruse, D. Alan	34, 51
Ashton, John	28	Cullmann, Oscar	136
Aune, David E.	21, 122, 148	Dahl, Murdoch E.	2, 20–21
Baillet, M.	90	Damasio, Antonio R.	5
Balz, Horst	97	Dana, H. E.	178, 180
Barrett, C. K.	76	Davidsen, Ole	76
Barrett, Justin L.	6	Davies, Glenys	195
Barstad, Hans M.	49	Davies, W. D.	24, 80, 165
Batten, Alicia J.	126	Davila, James R.	90
Bauckham, Richard	233	Day, John	9, 70
Baumgärtel, Friedrich	110	DeConick, April D.	28, 210, 212
Betz, Hans Dieter	21, 146	Deissmann, Adolf	28, 171
Bloom, Paul	14	Dimant, Devorah	93
Boer, Martinus C. de	17, 18	Dodd, C. H.	136
Bortone, Pietro	179–80	Dolansky, Fanny	123
Bousset, Wilhelm	25, 28, 91	Doyle, Brian	53
Boyarin, Daniel	73, 75	Duling, Dennis	220
Bradshaw, Paul F.	141	Dunn, James D. G.	20, 21, 23, 25, 28, 73, 99, 130, 136, 142, 144, 153, 158, 167, 168, 175, 182, 185, 205
Brady, Dean	214		
Brooke, George J.	93		
Brooten, Bernadette J.	187	Ehrman, Bart D.	25
Bultmann, Rudolf	16, 19–20, 26–27, 31, 32, 99, 110, 150, 173	Eijk, P. J. van der	118
		Engberg-Pedersen, Troels	1, 4, 10–11, 12, 98, 99, 117, 120, 149, 150, 154, 155, 176, 192, 200, 204
Burkert, Walter	146, 147, 148		
Bynum, Caroline Walker	2		
Cavallin, H. C. C.	9, 43, 44, 53, 70	Evans, Vyvyan	34
Charlesworth, James H.	8, 12, 94	Fauconnier, Gilles	33, 35, 36, 37, 39, 53, 160
Chmiel, Jerzy	8		
Chudek, Maciej	14–15	Fitzmyer, Joseph A.	82, 110, 165, 175, 189
Cleland, Liza	195		

Flannery, Frances 212
Fletcher-Louis, Crispin H. T. 17, 18, 93, 194
Fossum, Jarl E. 96
Frennesson, Björn 93
Furnish, Victor Paul 198
Gibbs, Raymond W. 35, 86, 140
Goff, Matthew 93
Goldman, Norma 123
Grady, Joseph Edward 66
Green, Joel B. 35
Green, Melanie 34
Gundry, Robert H. 99
Halton, Charles 13
Harner, Michael 3–4
Harris, Murray J. 195
Hays, Richard B. 31, 183
Himmelfarb, Martha 89, 90, 92, 214
Holleman, Joost 8, 9, 27, 31, 83
Hooker, M. D. 96
Horrell, David 167
Horsley, Richard A. 100, 101
Howard, Wilbert Francis 178
Howe, Bonnie 35, 36, 178–79
Jewett, Robert 40, 41, 142, 148, 149, 156, 158, 176
Johnson, Mark 5, 6, 11–12, 33, 34–35, 36–37, 39, 46–47, 55, 56, 57, 61, 62, 76, 88, 121, 140, 195
Johnson, Maxwell E. 141
Johnson Hodge, Caroline 30–31, 76–77, 78, 176, 215–17, 220, 221
Johnston, Philip S. 47–48, 49
Käsemann, Ernst 15–17, 19, 25, 28, 31, 32, 150, 158, 173, 183
Katz, Steven T. 214
Kim, Jung Hoon 126
King, Sallie B. 212
Kister, Menahem 30, 76, 78
Koester, Helmut 40, 41
Kooten, George H. van 23, 97, 100, 101, 119, 151, 153, 154
Lakoff, George 5, 11–12, 33, 34, 35, 36–37, 39, 46–47, 55, 56, 57, 61, 62, 76, 140, 179, 195, 233

Langacker, Ronald W. 180
Law, Timothy Michael 13
Lehtipuu, Outi 2
Levison, John R. 94, 100
Lincoln, Andrew T. 136, 165, 171
Llewellyn-Jones, Lloyd 195
Lohse, Eduard 24, 25
Longenecker, Richard N. 77
Lüdemann, Gerd 29
Lundhaug, Hugo 35, 36
Mantey, Julius R. 178, 180
Martin, Dale B. 98–99, 114, 116–17, 148, 151, 153, 183
Martyn, J. Louis 17–18
Mason, Steve 80, 81–82, 94–95
Matera, Frank J. 25, 158
McNeel, Jennifer Houston 35
Meeks, Wayne A. 1, 141, 194
Merleau-Ponty, Maurice 5–6, 33
Meyer, Ben F. 77
Mitchell, Margaret M. 40, 183
Morray-Jones, Christopher R. A. 29, 91, 214, 215
Moulton, James 178
Nagy, Gregory 144
Newberg, Andrew B. 213
Newman, Carey C. 95–96
Nickelsburg, George W. E. 44, 50, 53, 56, 60, 70, 71, 83, 95, 214
Niederwimmer, Kurt 141
Núñez, Rafael E. 35
O'Connor, M. 60
Oden, Robert A., Jr. 48
Oepke, Albrecht 140
Olson, Kelly 131
Osiek, Carolyn 187
Parsons, Mikeal C. 82
Pearson, Birger A. 100–101
Pervo, Richard 82, 190
Phillips, L. Edward 141
Pinker, Steven 11
Polaski, Donald C. 53
Porter, J. R. 30
Porter, Stanley E. 178, 180
Pouya, Jennifer 187

MODERN AUTHORS INDEX

Puech, Émile 43, 45, 54
Robertson, A. T. 178, 180
Robinson, H. Wheeler 29–30, 31
Robinson, John A. T. 1, 19, 21
Robinson, Thomas M. 99
Rogerson, John W. 30
Rosch, Eleanor 33
Rowland, Christopher 18, 29, 84
Sanders, E. P. 31–32, 40, 73–74, 80, 81, 88, 95, 183, 185, 188, 189
Sawyer, John F. A. 8
Schnelle, Udo 21
Scholem, Gershom 214
Schweitzer, Albert 24, 27–28, 31, 165, 166, 189, 190
Schweizer, Eduard 110
Segal, Alan F. 21, 29, 31, 43, 44, 79, 91, 92, 95, 96, 116, 176, 210, 211, 224
Segal, Robert A. 144
Shantz, Colleen 3–4, 28, 29, 210, 212–14, 215, 224
Slingerland, Edward 5–6, 7, 11, 14–15, 33, 34, 35
Smith, Johnathan Z. 24
Songe-Møller, Vigdis 61, 103, 162
Staden, Heinrich von 98, 117
Stendahl, Krister 20
Sterling, Gregory E. 100
Stovell, Beth M. 35
Stowers, Stanley K. 98, 119, 149, 150, 215, 217, 221
Strecker, Georg 17
Stuckenbruck, Loren T. 50, 60
Tannehill, Robert C. 17, 26, 28, 31, 141–42, 144, 192
Tappenden, Frederick S. 36, 37, 39, 227, 232
Taylor, Charles 147, 156–57
Thaden, Robert H. von, Jr. 36
Thagard, Paul 6
Theissen, Gerd 22, 152, 157
Thiessen, Matthew 75
Thiselton, Anthony C. 20–21, 115–16, 165
Thompson, Evan 33
Thrall, Margaret E. 197, 198, 199
Trilling, W. 84
Tronier, Henrik 108
Turner, Mark 11, 33, 35–36, 37, 39, 46–47, 53, 160
Turner, Nigel 178
Uro, Risto 140
VanderKam, James C. 60, 214
Varela, Francisco J. 33
Vielhauer, Philipp 17
Vos, Geerhardus 136, 167, 168
Wallace, Daniel B. 178, 182
Waltke, Bruce K. 60
Wasserman, Emma 19, 20, 23, 150–51, 156
Wedderburn, Alexander J. M. 8, 9, 24, 25, 30, 31, 76, 96, 144, 145, 146, 192
Werline, Rodney A. 212
Williams, Roland J. 60
Williams, Sam K. 31
Wise, Michael O. 94
Wolf, Hans-Georg 33
Wright, N. T. 8–10, 12, 14, 21, 43, 44, 48, 51, 53, 57, 65, 70, 73, 77, 82, 97, 115, 136, 165–66
Zerwick, Maximilian 181

Subject Index

Abraham
  as ancestor, 75
  as ancestral progenitor, 78, 185, 216–17, 220, 221, 223
  as heavenly ascender, 90, 91
  as representational figure, 29, 30
  and resurrection, 223–24
Adam
  ADAM FOR UNBELIEVERS (metonymy), 76
  ADAM IS DEATH [DOWN] (metaphor), 76
  ADAM IS DOWN (metaphor), 78–79, 112
  and Christ typology, 75–77, 78–79, 96–97, 112, 152, 180. *See also* Christ
  death of Adam and Eve, 151
  as metonymic value for antagonists, 76–77
  and prelapsarian glory, 92–94, 153
affective. *See also* IN-OUT affectivity
  definition, 193
already/not yet, 145–46, 164–65, 169–71, 206–7. *See also* eschatology, eschatological somatology *and* time.
  and baptism, 25–26, 145–46
  as cosmological dynamic, 208–9, 230–31
  in early Pauline interpretation, 234–35
  and glory, 194
  and resurrection, 25–26, 135–36, 145–46, 155, 206–7
  as somatic dynamic, 136–37, 155, 164–71, 172, 194–95, 197–98, 206–7, 230–31
  as temporal dynamic, 25–26, 198
Altered States of Consciousness (ASC). *See* ecstatic experience
angelomorphism
  angels as asomatic, 95
  and heavenly ascent, 90–92
  as luminous, 60
  as postmortem ideal, 60, 80, 82, 159
  and Qumran worship, 93–94
  as somatic ideal, 92–95, 112–14, 120, 159
anthropology
  ancient views on, 21–22, 80–81, 94, 99–101, 147–48, 150–52, 153, 205
  and body. *See* body
  and cosmology, 13–23, 87–89, 119, 230–31. *See also* cosmology
  and eschatology, 163, 169–71. *See also* eschatological somatology
  and ethics, 119, 146–55
  Greek dualism, 13, 21–22, 87, 132–33
  holism, 19–23, 102.
  as holistic and partitive, 22, 88, 102, 132–33, 155–56, 230–31
  in-out somatic mappings, 75, 116–21, 121–22, 131, 146–48, 149, 155–56, 163, 169–71, 194–99, 200–202, 205, 211, 230–31
  Jewish monism, 13, 21–22, 87, 132–33
  Paul's view of, 22, 88, 115–21, 121–32, 146–55, 163, 196, 200–201, 205, 230–31

SUBJECT INDEX

Philonic views of, 99–101, 117
Platonic views of, 99
πνεῦμα. See πνεῦμα
problems with anthropological dualisms, 5–7, 88–89
problems with anthropological holisms, 21–23
and resurrection, 13–14, 87, 154, 205
soul. See soul
trichotomous, 99–101, 150–52, 153
anthropomorphism, 95–97
  of angels, 95
  of the Great Glory, 95–96
  of Yahweh, 95–96
apocalyptic/apcalypticism
  and anthropology, 26, 158–59, 180
  as context for Paul's writings, 89–92
  and cosmology, 15–19
  and ecstatic experience, 29, 207–8, 210–11
  and eschatology, 15–19
  and heavenly ascent, 89–92, 207–8, 211, 215. See also heavenly ascent
  as multivalent with other frame structures, 19, 88–102, 108, 215, 218–22
apocalyptic dualism, 15–19, 87, 171
  and participation, 26, 31, 32, 158–59, 180
  problems with, 17–19, 171
backgrounding, 105–7, 205, 223
baptism, 137–46
  and apocalypticism, 25–26
  as asymmetrical metaphor, 25, 144–45
  ΒΑΠΤΙΖΩ IS DOWN (metaphor), 140
  and clothing, 131, 143, 183
  and death. See baptism, baptismal death
  as downward movement, 140–41
  in early Christian description, 140–41
  as embodied practice, 137, 139–45
  EMERGENCE FROM WATER IS LIFE, 143
  EMERGENCE FROM WATER IS UP, 141
  ENTRY INTO WATER IS DEATH, 143
  ENTRY INTO WATER IS DOWN, 141
  as literary metaphor or trope, 9–10, 137, 141–42, 144–45
  and participation, 24–26, 142–45, 176, 182, 185
  and patrilineal genetics, 176, 217
  and resurrection, 142–46, 151–52, 154, 155, 162, 169, 182–83, 231
  and the RESURRECTION gestalt, 138, 139, 142–44, 169
  and transformation, 143, 144–45, 152, 154, 156, 162, 169, 217–18
  and VERTICALITY schema, 140–42
being awake. See consciousness
BEING SUBJECT TO CONTROL IS DOWN (metaphor), 56
blended space. See conceptual blending theory
blending of PATH and CONTAINER schemata, 62–63, 103, 186–88
  and Adam-Christ typology, 78–79
  and change. See CHANGE (gestalt)
  and UNION. See UNION (gestalt)
blending of PROXIMITY and CONTAINER schemata, 186–87, 188, 190, 197, 220
  as UNION. See UNION (gestalt)
blending of VERTICALITY and CONTAINER schemata, 153–54, 156, 192–93, 206–7, 210–14
  and ecstatic experience, 209–14, 215
blending of VERTICALITY and PATH schemata, 55–56, 209
  and Adam-Christ typology, 76–77
blending of VERTICALITY, PATH, and PROXIMITY schemata, 66, 67, 68–69
  as resurrection. See RESURRECTION (gestalt)
blending of VERTICALITY, PROXIMITY, and CONTAINER schemata, 196–97, 207, 208, 210, 218–20
blending theory. See conceptual blending theory

body
  Adamic body, 79, 97, 112, 114. *See also* σῶμα, σῶμα ψυχικόν *and* ensouled earthly body
  angelomorphic. *See* angelomorphism
  celestial, 52, 112–14. *See also* angelomorphism *and* glory, as heavenly body
  as central in Paul's theology, 1–2, 170–71, 229
  Christic body, 79, 112, 114, 159, 176. *See also* σῶμα, σῶμα πνευματικόν *and* ensouled earthly body
  as cosmologically suited, 90–91, 92–97, 118–20, 230–31
  ecstatic perceptions of, 213
  enspirited earthly body. *See* enspirited earthly body
  as eschatological hope, 1–3, 79, 94–95, 106–21, 121–32
  and flesh, 2, 22, 90, 112–14, 118–19, 125, 152, 154, 156, 187–88, 194, 206
  and glory. *See* glory, as heavenly body
  as hierarchical, 98, 118, 150–52
  as holistic and partitive, 22, 88, 102, 132–33, 155–56, 230–31
  as improperly ordered. *See* passion-ruled self
  in-out mapping. *See* anthropology, in-out somatic mapping
  as integrative polarities. *See* polarity, intrasomatic
  as location of eschatology, 137, 154, 159–63, 164–71, 189–90, 231
  as location of resurrection, 1–3, 142–45, 146–47, 152–55, 155–63, 167–71, 172–73, 189–90, 192–93, 204–7, 218–22, 222–25, 226–27, 229, 231–32
  as location of revelation, 194–99, 210, 211, 223
  as luminous, 52, 60, 96
  as partitive, 22–23, 88, 98, 102, 147–48, 149, 155–56, 160, 200–204
  problems in systematizing, 156
  as properly ordered, 99–101, 118
  and self-mastery, 150–52, 154, 156–57, 172
  and society, 98, 183
  σῶμα πνευματικόν. *See* σῶμα, σῶμα πνευματικόν *and* ensouled earthly body
  σῶμα ψυχικόν. *See* σῶμα, σῶμα ψυχικόν *and* ensouled earthly body
  as trichotomy, 99–101, 150–52, 153
  and universe, 98
  variety of bodies in Paul's writings, 200–201, 226, 227
body, metaphors for
  BODY IS CLOTHING (metaphor), 126–27, 129, 131
  BODY IS CONTAINER, 121–22, 126, 130, 131, 132, 147–48, 154, 158, 160, 163, 183, 184, 189, 199, 203
  BODY IS HOUSE, 122–23, 124–25, 129
  BODY IS TENT, 124–25
BUILDING IS CONTAINER (metaphor), 122
CHANGE (gestalt), 60–63, 103–6
  embodied grounding, 61. *See also* PATH (image schema) *and* CONTAINER (image schema)
  and postmorten transformation, 63–64, 68, 77–79, 80, 81–82, 85, 110, 114–15, 126–32, 169, 188–89, 200–204, 231
  STATES ARE LOCATIONS (metaphor), 62
  and this-worldly transformation, 144–45, 155–63, 169, 198–99, 201–4, 205–6, 231
  and trajectory of transformative embodiment. *See* patterns of resurrection embodiment
change, metaphors for,
  CHANGE IS MOVEMENT, 61, 62, 63, 103–6, 121
  other metaphors for CHANGE, 61

SUBJECT INDEX

Christ
  and Adam typology, 75–77, 78–79, 96–97, 112, 152, 180. *See also* Adam
  CHRIST FOR BELIEVERS (metonymy), 76
  CHRIST (frame). *See* frame structures
  CHRIST IS CONTAINER (metaphor), 181, 182, 183, 188
  CHRIST IS LIFE [UP] (metaphor), 76
  CHRIST IS UP (metaphor), 78–79, 112
  as Great Glory, 96–97, 120, 197, 199, 212, 221
  as metonymic value for protagonists, 76–77
  and πνεῦμα, 120, 131, 194, 222
church
  as body of Christ, 183–85
  CHURCH IS BODY (OF CHRIST) (metaphor), 183, 184–85, 203
  ecclesial body in the resurrection process, 200–201, 203–4, 226–27
clothing, 123–27, 130–31
  and baptism, 131, 143, 183
  CLOTHING IS CONTAINER (metaphor), 123–26, 195
  Greek and Roman, 123–26, 130–31
  as metaphor for resurrection, 122, 123–32
  as metaphor for somatic transformation, 90–91, 110, 121–32
  undergarments, 130–31, 163
  veils, 195
cognicentrism, 3–7, 32–33, 230, 237
  and disembodiment, 7
  and epistemology, 4–5
  and eschatology, 165–66
  and participation, 24, 27, 30, 31–32, 32–33, 158, 207
  and resurrection, 9, 10, 12, 32–33, 230, 237
cognitive linguistics,
  analysis of ἐν, 177–81
  as corrective to cognicentrism, 33–34
  and embodied grounding. *See* image schema
  intellectual roots, 33
  as methodological apparatus, 33–39, 233
  and vertical integration, 7, 33–39
cognitive sciences, 6–7, 14–15, 33
  and dualism, 14–15
  and ritual studies, 140
  and vertical integration, 6–7
collectivism
  and soteriology, 139
  individual and community, 16, 30, 74, 139, 184–85, 200–201, 203–4, 205, 220, 226, 227, 232
  and intrasomatic polarity, 184–85, 200–201, 203–4, 205, 220
  and resurrection process, 162, 200–201, 203–4, 232
conceptual blending theory, 35–36
  blended space, 36
  generic space, 36
  human scale, 36
  input spaces, 36
  kinds of conceptual networks, 36
  mental spaces, 37
  vital relations, 36, 37
conceptual metaphor, 11–12, 34–35
  embodied grounding, 47
  as multimodal, 35, 139–40
  use of small caps, 35
consciousness
  and being awake, 36–39
  CONSCIOUSNESS IS UP (metaphor), 46 50
  definition of, 47
CONTAINER (image schema), 61–62
  and ἀποκάλυψις, 211, 215
  embodied grounding, 61, 121–22
  integration with PATH (image schema). *See* CHANGE (gestalt)
  relation to PROXIMITY (image schema), 65, 186–88
continuity
  and patrilineal genetics, 220, 224–25

continuity (cont.)
  across somatic states, 95, 108, 110, 115, 121, 131, 132–33, 162–63, 173, 224–25, 235–36
  of identity, 72, 81–82, 235–36
  in the midst of change, 103, 131, 162–63
corporate figures. *See* patrilineal genetics and congnicentrism, 30
cosmology
  and apocalyptic, 15–19, 89–92
  and anthropology, 13–23, 87–89, 119, 230–31. *See also* anthropology
  and eschatology, 165, 171
  as integrative polarities, 102, 132, 230–31. *See also* polarity
  nonvertical conceptions of, 90, 215
  as one-world model, 88, 89–92, 97–98, 101, 102, 112, 115, 130–31, 133
  vertical conceptions of, 48, 89–90, 215
culture
  as formative in meaning creation, 88–89, 214. *See also* vertical integration
death
  and Adam, 76–77, 152
  baptismal death, 24–26, 30, 135–36, 137–46, 152, 154, 169, 185, 231, 232
  as embodied, 144–45, 190–93. *See also* patterns of resurrection embodiment
  embodied experience of, 47
  as enslaving power, 17
  in the Hebrew scriptures, 47–58, 64–67
  mapped to somatic exterior, 149, 156, 199–204, 204–7, 223
  mapped to the somatic interior, 151–52, 199–204
  not necessary for resurrection, 84–85, 87, 110
  in Platonic discourses, 151–52
  as present experience, 44. *See also* death, baptismal death
death, metaphors for
  DEATH IS DISTANCE FROM YAHWAH, 65
  DEATH IS DOWN, 46–54, 84, 141
  DEATH IS DOWN/FAR/SOURCE, 66
  DEATH IS DOWN/OUT, 192
  DEATH IS FAR, 64–65
  DEATH IS OUT, 201
  DEATH IS SLEEP, 36–39, 50, 51, 52, 70
  DEATH IS UNCONSCIOUSNESS, 51
  diversity of metaphors, 46
discontinuity
  across somatic states, 16, 95, 115, 121, 132–33, 162–63, 235–36
dualism(s), 3–7, 13–23
  anthropological, 22–23, 87–88, 99–101, 102, 117–19, 147–48, 171, 230–31
  apocalyptic, 15–19, 87. *See also* apocalyptic dualism
  body-soul, 19, 20, 21, 99–101, 118–19, 151, 155, 163
  Cartesian, 4–5, 6, 20, 33, 98, 99
  cosmological, 13, 15–19, 87–88, 92, 99, 102, 230–31
  cultural, 21–22
  definition of, 14–15
  and duality, 14–15
  and embodiment, 6–7, 15, 147–48
  folk dualism, 14–15, 21, 147–48
  Form-Image, 100–101
  as integrative polarities, 102, 118–19, 132, 143, 150–52, 155, 163, 226, 230–31. *See also* polarity
  matter versus nonmatter, 98, 99
  mind-body, 4–5, 6–7, 14–15, 102, 148
  and monism in Paul, 13–23
  as oppositions, 17
  permeability of, 89, 90, 92–93, 94, 97, 102
  and Philo, 99–101
  and Plato, 21, 99–100
  sense-thought, 99, 102

SUBJECT INDEX

of subject and object, 20
ecstatic experience. *See also* religious experience
and Altered States of Consciousness (ASC), 3-4, 47, 210, 212-14
definition of, 210
ECSTATIC EXPERIENCE IS HEAVENLY ASCENT, 218-20
embodied grounding of, 213-14
emic terminology for, 210-11
as pattern of embodiment, 222-25
EMOTIONAL INTIMACY IS PROXIMITY (metaphor), 66
ἐν, 177-81, 216-17. *See also* participation, being in Christ
ἐν Χριστῷ, 158, 177-90
embodied foundations of, 177-81
ἐν πνεύματι, 157-63, 175
ἐν σαρκί, 157-63, 175
ensouled earthly body, 115-16, 117-18, 119, 121, 132, 155-56, 159-63, 172, 231. *See also* σῶμα, σῶμα ψυχικόν *and* body, Adamic body
enspirited earthly body, 118, 119, 132, 155, 156-57, 159-63, 172, 200, 205, 218, 226, 230, 231
as presently embodying resurrection, 155-63, 226
enspirited heavenly/risen body, 115-16, 117-18, 119, 121, 132, 155, 157, 159-63, 172, 186, 218, 231. *See also* σῶμα, σῶμα πνευματικόν *and* glory, as heavenly body
eschatology, 164-71, 188-90
as cognicentric, 165-66
in early Pauline interpretation, 25, 234-35
emphasis on divine-human proximity, 189-90
eschatological reservation, 25-26, 135-36, 145-46, 189-90
eschatological somatology, 137, 159-63, 164-71, 206-7, 231
mapped to the body, 154, 155, 163, 189-90, 198, 206-7

modification of Jewish eschatology, 77, 136, 164-71, 172
ethnicity. *See also* kinship *and* patrilineal genetics
and space, 208-9
and identity, 208-9
and participation, 215-18, 218-22
and resurrection, 52-54, 56, 58, 218-22, 222-25
ethnicity, related metaphors
EXILE IS DEATH, 52, 220
LAND IS LIFE, 52-54, 220
LAND IS UP, 56
RESTORATION TO THE LAND IS GOAL, 58
RESURRECTION IS RESTORATION TO THE LAND, 54
experience
as difficult analytical category, 28, 211-12, 236
as disconnect from language, 4-6, 141-42, 144, 214
as foundations of language and meaning, 33-39. *See also* image schema
and social constructivism, 5, 166, 214
flesh. *See also* σῶμα, σῶμα ψυχικόν
correlated with Adam, 112, 114
as cosmic, enslaving power, 16, 158
as existential disposition, 20
FLESH IS DOWN, 112
as part of the somatic composition, 10, 22-23, 118-20, 125, 156
and self-mastery, 152, 154, 156
as somatic exterior, 154, 156, 206
as substance suited for earthly body, 90, 101, 112-14, 118-20, 125, 157, 188
foregrounding, 105-6, 107, 115, 145, 205, 223, 224, 225
frame structures, 51
(CELESTIAL) LUMINOSITY, 52, 58-61, 63-64, 73, 114
CHRIST (frame), 73-74, 190-92
CLOTHING (frame), 126, 130

frame structures (cont.)
    CONSCIOUSNESS (frame), 46–47, 64, 205
    ETHNOGEOGRAPHIC RESTORATION (frame), 52–54, 73
    PERSECUTION (frame), 51
    PLANT GROWTH (frame), 108–9
    protagonists and antagonists, 51
    role values, 50–51, 57
    SELF-MASTERY (frame), 150, 154, 172
    SOCIAL INJUSTICE (frame), 51
generic space. *See* conceptual blending theory
glory
    Adamic glory, 92–94, 96–97
    correlated with Christ, 13, 96–97, 112, 114, 197, 199, 212, 221, 226, 232
    and covenant(s), 194
    and flesh, 108, 112–14
    GLORY IS UP, 112
    glory of Yahweh, 95–96, 196
    and heavenly ascent, 90–91, 194–99, 209–10, 212, 214, 221
    as heavenly body, 13, 80, 90–91, 92–97, 108, 112–14, 115, 117, 120, 153, 159, 218, 222. *See also* enspirited heavenly/risen body
    as the human appearance of God, 95–96
    mapped to the somatic interior, 194–99, 200, 203–4, 206–7
    and Moses, 195–96
    and πνεῦμα, 119–20, 153–54, 159, 194
    and transformation, 13, 67, 80, 90–91, 92–95, 96–97, 108, 112–14, 115, 120, 159, 194–99, 203–4, 206–7
Great Glory
    Christ as, 96–97, 120, 197, 199, 212, 221
    in Jewish tradition, 90, 93, 95–96, 196, 210, 214
HAVING CONTROL IS UP (metaphor), 56
heavenly ascent, 89–92, 194–99, 209–14, 218–22
    and angelomorphism, 90–92
    and ἁρπάζω, 84–85, 92
    discursive limits of, 29, 215
    as ecstatic experience, 29, 209–14, 218–22
    ECSTATIC EXPERIENCE IS HEAVENLY ASCENT, 218–22
    and Enoch, 84
    mapped to the in-out coordinates of the body, 194–99, 212
    and neurobiology, 29, 212–14
    as pattern of embodiment, 218–22, 222–25
    and patrilineal genetics, 29, 207–9, 215, 218–22, 222–25
    and Paul, 29, 74, 92, 209–14, 227
    and priestly nuances, 110
    and resurrection, 29, 64, 69–70, 83, 84–85, 91–92, 218–22, 222–25
    terminology for, 84–85, 210–11
    and transformation, 63–64, 69–70, 89–92
house metaphor, 121–32. *See also* CONTAINER (metaphors)
human scale. *See* conceptual blending theory
ideals, definition of, 1. *See also* perception
image schema, 34
    CONTAINER. *See* CONTAINER (image schema)
    embodied grounding, 34
    PATH. *See* PATH (image schema)
    PROXIMITY. *See* PROXIMITY (image schema)
    VERTICALITY. *See* VERTICALITY (image schema)
    use of small caps, 34
IN ⇌ OUT. *See* IN-OUT affectivity
IN-OUT affectivity, 149, 154, 156, 159–63, 189–90, 193–99, 200–204, 204–7, 209–10, 225

SUBJECT INDEX

as communio-somatic dynamic, 195–96, 200–201, 203–4, 223–24, 226–27. *See also* polarity
intrasomatic affectivity, 149, 159–63, 189–90, 193–99, 200–204, 223, 226–27. *See also* polarity
and resurrection, 149, 154, 156, 159–63, 169–71, 189–90, 199–204, 204–7, 223, 225, 226–27
and self-mastery, 149, 154, 156, 172, 193
IN-OUT (image schema). *See* CONTAINER (image schema)
input spaces. *See* conceptual blending theory
intrasomatic polarity. *See* polarity, intrasomatic
Judean/Jewish (terminology), 13
JUST RECOMPENSE IS GOAL, 52–53, 58
kinship, 30–31, 78, 208–9, 215–17, 220, 222, 223–24, 224–25, 226
life
  and Christ, 76–77, 152
  in/through death, 190–93. *See* patterns of resurrection embodiment
  as embodied, 144–45, 190–93. *See also* patterns of resurrection embodiment
  embodied experience of, 47
  in the Hebrew scriptures, 47–58, 64–67
  mapped to the somatic exterior, 199–204, 204–7
  mapped to the somatic interior, 151–52, 153, 154, 157, 159–63, 169, 199–204, 204–7
  semantic range, 145–46
LIFE ⇌ DEATH. *See* IN-OUT affectivity
life, metaphors for,
  diversity of metaphors, 46
  LIFE IS BEING AWAKE, 36–39, 50, 51, 52, 53
  LIFE IS BEING NEAR TO YAHWEH, 65, 66
  LIFE IS CONSCIOUSNESS, 70, 145

LIFE IS GOAL, 66
LIFE IS IN, 201
LIFE IS NEAR, 64–65
LIFE IS NEAR/GOAL, 66
LIFE IS UP, 46–54, 84, 141–42
LIFE IS UP/IN, 192
LIFE IS UP/NEAR/GOAL, 66
RESTORED LIFE IS GOAL, 58
light/darkness
  as embodied experiences, 52
  as interpretive context, 52, 54, 68
literal
  as dubious category, 5, 8–13, 86, 145–46, 226, 230, 233
  and metaphorical, 8–13, 32, 86, 146, 173, 226, 229, 230, 233
  postmortem resurrection as, 2, 8–13, 25, 32, 85–86, 135, 145–46, 226, 229, 230, 233
macro-PATH. *See* PATH (image schema)
mental spaces. *See* conceptual blending theory
metaphor
  conceptual metaphor. *See* conceptual metaphor
  conventional metaphors, 36–37
  dead metaphors, 36–37
  and literal, 1–3, 5, 8–13, 86, 145–46, 173, 226, 229, 230, 233
  as pervasive aspect of human thought and meaning, 11–12, 24–35, 229
  resurrection as, 1–3, 8–13, 32, 36–39, 46–72, 85–86, 106–21, 121–32, 142–45, 145–46, 190, 226, 229, 230, 231, 233. *See also* patterns of resurrection embodiment
metonymy, 76
micro-PATH. *See* PATH (image schema)
monism, 13–23, 87–88, 102, 132–33
  and anthropology, 13–14, 87–88, 230–31
  cosmological holism, 89–92, 97–98, 101, 102, 132–33, 230–31
  and dualism in Paul, 13–23, 87–88, 102, 132–33

monism (cont.)
  Jewish anthropology, 21–22, 132–33
  mind-body holism, 5–7, 101, 102.
    See also cognitive linguistics *and* image schema
Moses
  as ascender to heaven, 194, 199
  as ascender of Sinai, 194–197, 199
  and angelomorphic transformation, 94
  and the law, 194
  MOSES FOR SCRIPTURE (metonymy), 196
  as representational figure, 200–201
  and veiling, 195–96
mutual affectivity. *See* IN-OUT affectivity *and* polarity
mysticism. *See also* religious experience
  definition of, 210
  and theology, 27–28
  and participation, 27–29
NEAR-FAR (image schema). *See* PROXIMITY (image schema)
Objectivism, 5, 11
  problems with, 5–6
ontological pluralism, 4, 232
PATH (image schema), 55
  macro-PATH, 55–58, 75–77
  micro-PATH (CHANGE) gestalt, 58–64, 77–79, 103–6. *See also* CHANGE (gestalt)
  as structure of hope, 57, 84
  as structure of purposes, 57
  as structure of time, 56–57
parousia, 83, 87, 125, 165, 169–70
participation, 23–32
  and baptism, 24–26, 142–45, 182–83
  being in Christ (ἐν Χριστῷ), 175, 177–90
  being with Christ (σὺν Χριστῷ), 177, 185–86, 189–90
  and congnicentrism, 24, 26, 27, 30, 31–32, 32–33, 158, 207
  and death, 23–24, 142–45, 192, 193, 199–204, 204–7

  as embodied, 24, 144–45, 188–90, 193, 199–204, 204–7
  as experiential, 176
  interpretive understandings, 31–32, 207–8
  as mysticism, 27–29. *See also* religious experience
  as ongoing process, 189–90, 204–7, 222–25, 226–27
  as oneness (CONTAINER schema), 182–85
  and patrilineal genetics, 29–31, 176, 215–17, 218–22, 223–27
  as pattern of embodiment, 199–204, 204–7, 218–22, 222–25, 225–26
  and resurrection, 23–32, 81, 137–46, 153, 175–77, 188–90, 192, 193, 199–204, 204–7, 218–22, 231–32
  and suffering, 190–92, 199–204, 204–7, 224–25
  as theological proposition, 26–28, 30
  as togetherness (PROXIMITY schema), 185–86
  and UNION. *See* UNION
patterns of embodiment
  as foundation of language and thought, 33–34. *See also* image schema
patterns of resurrection embodiment, 155–63, 199–204, 204–7, 218–22, 222–25, 231–32
  life in/through death, 199–204, 204–7, 225
  participation in ethnicity, ecstasy, and resurrection, 218–22, 222–25, 225–26
  self-mastery, 145, 150–55, 163, 172, 231–32
  trajectory of transformative embodiment, 149, 155–63, 190, 208, 225, 231, 235–36
patrilineal genetics, 29–31, 76–77, 77–79, 176, 215–17, 218–22, 223–27
  and the Adam-Christ typology, 76–77, 78–79

SUBJECT INDEX   285

and corporate figures, 29–30
and genetic connection, 176, 215–17
and participation, 29–31, 176, 215–17, 218–22, 223–27
as pattern of embodiment, 218–22, 222–27
and religious experience, 31, 207–8, 215, 218–22, 223–27
and representational figures, 29–30
and resurrection, 31, 176, 218–22, 222–25
passion-ruled self, 150–52
Paul
    and the Pharisees, 79–83
    coherence of thought, 79, 183, 192, 234–35
    as heavenly ascender, 29, 74, 92, 209–14, 227
    as thinker, 27–28
Pauline Epistles
    compositional integrity, 40–41
    disputed, 25, 40, 190, 234–35
    undisputed, 25, 40, 190, 234–35
perception, 34, 167. *See also* ideals
performance,
    and linguistic embodiment, 35, 137, 139–40, 144. *See also* conceptual metaphor, as multimodal
    resurrection as performative scripts, 231. *See also* patterns of resurrection embodiment
    and theological embodiment, 142, 143, 144–45
permeability
    of earthly and heavenly locales, 89, 90, 92, 102
    of earthly and heavenly somatic states, 92–93, 94, 97, 102
    of trajector PATHS, 77, 142–43
Pharisees, 79–83
    and angelomorphism, 81–83, 94–95
    and Jesus, 80
    and Paul, 79–83
    as a philosophical school, 81
    on reincarnation, 81–82

phenomenology, 5–6, 33, 214
Philo
    on ethical behaviour, 101
    on human composition, 99–101
    interpretation of Gen 1–2, 100–101, 117–18
    plant metaphor, 106–21
Plato, 21, 99–101
πνεῦμα, 153–54
    as aeonic-ruling power, 16
    blurring of human and divine, 120, 153
    continuity of, 131–32, 162–63, 173, 235–36
    and the earthly body, 101, 117–20, 131–32, 153–54, 158–63, 207, 223, 231–32
    and glory, 119–20, 159
    as granted to Christ-devotees, 119, 131, 132, 152, 153–54, 158–63, 172, 184, 232
    and heavenly ascent, 207, 218–22
    as immaterial, 99, 116
    as material, 98–99, 116, 118–19, 154, 217, 226, 232
    and patrilineal genetics, 176, 217, 218–22
    and power, 200
    and resurrection, 82–83, 118–20, 131, 132, 152–56, 163, 172, 173, 200, 207, 218–22, 226, 231–32
    and the risen body, 20, 116–17, 119–20, 155, 157, 158–63, 207, 231–32
    and self-mastery, 101, 152–54, 156, 162–63, 172, 223
    and sexual intercourse, 187–88
    and somatic tension, 118–21, 155–56, 157, 160
    as soma-ruling power, 20, 118–19
    spatial configuration, 115–16, 118–20, 131–32, 153–54, 156, 158–63, 197, 207, 231–32
    and trichotomous anthropology, 100–101, 117–19, 120, 153–54, 159, 160, 162, 223

polarity, 102, 119
  as communio-somatic dynamic, 184–85, 195–96, 200–204, 226–27
  definition, 102
  future suspension of, 119–20, 157, 186, 204
  as IN-OUT affectivity, 193–204
  intracosmic, 119, 132–33
  intrasomatic, 118–19, 132–33, 150–52, 155–56, 160, 163, 169, 172, 184–85, 193, 201, 203–4, 223, 226–27, 230–31
  temporal, 163
prepositions, 177–81
profile-frame relationship, 50–51
PROXIMITY (image schema), 64–66
  relation to CONTAINER (image schema), 65
  and UNION. See UNION (gestalt)
PURPOSES ARE DESTINATIONS (metaphor), 57
rationality
  Cartesian, 1, 4–5.
  Paul as thinker, 27–28
religious experience, 27–29, 210–14. See also ecstatic experience
  and Altered States of Consciousness (ASC). See ecstatic experience
  and apocalypticism, 29, 210–11
  definition of, 210
  as difficult analytical category, 166, 212, 215
  embodied grounding of ecstatic experiences, 213–14
  and heavenly ascent, 29, 194, 207–8, 210–12, 218–22
  and participation in/with Christ, 27–29, 207–8, 218–22
  and Paul, 209–14
  and resurrection, 28–29. See also resurrection, and/as heavenly ascent
  as visionary experiences, 28–29, 166
representational figures. See patrilineal genetics
  and congnicentrism, 30

resurrection
  and baptism. See baptism
  as contested theme in ancient texts, 43–44, 70–72, 233
  and developments in Paul's thought, 77
  as disembodied concept, 2–3, 10, 12, 24, 26, 32–33, 229, 230. See also cognicentrism
  as embodied concept, 1–3, 39, 40, 67, 85–86, 142–45, 163, 192–93, 229, 231. See also RESURRECTION (gestalt)
  and ethical uprightness, 81, 119, 145, 151–53, 154–55, 163, 173, 203, 232. See also self-mastery
  as future experience, 1–3, 8–13, 106–21, 121–32, 136–37, 145–46, 153–54, 155–63, 203–4, 225, 231
  as gestalt structure. See RESURRECTION (gestalt)
  and glory. See glory
  and/as heavenly ascent, 84–85, 91–92, 218–22. See also heavenly ascent
  identification of, 43–45, 68–72, 85–86
  and immortality of the soul, 43
  and intermediary state, 44, 82, 130
  and interpretive flexibility, 12–13, 44–45, 69–72, 85
  linguistic description of, 8, 25–26, 85–86, 135–36, 145–46, 171–72
  as literal, 8–13, 85–86, 145–46. See also literal, postmortem resurrection as
  as metaphor, 8–13, 85–86, 145–46. See also metaphor, resurrection as
  and participation. See participation
  as pattern of embodiment. See patterns of resurrection embodiment
  and Pharisees, 79–83, 94–95
  and πνεῦμα. See πνεῦμα
  as present experience, 2–3, 29, 135–37, 142–45, 160–62, 200–207, 224–25, 229, 231–32. See also resurrection, as somatic process

SUBJECT INDEX

problem of identifying, 8–13
as restoration of creation, 56–57, 153
as self-mastery. *See* self-mastery
of the somatic interior, 41, 130–31, 146–47, 152–55, 162–63, 169–71, 172–73, 197, 200, 201, 203, 205, 206, 231
as somatic process, 3, 142–45, 155–63, 167–71, 172, 189–90, 200–204, 204–7, 218–22, 222–25, 226–27, 229, 231–32
terms for, 8, 85–86, 145–46, 171–72. *See also* resurrection, linguistic description of
as theological proposition, 2, 7, 10, 27, 33, 40, 86, 230, 234
and Two Ways theology, 56
resurrection, metaphors for
RESURRECTION IS BEING AWAKE, 35, 36–39
RESURRECTION IS CELESTIAL LUMINOSITY, 60, 63–64, 69, 70, 115, 120, 173
RESURRECTION IS CONSCIOUSNESS, 52, 60, 64, 69, 145, 154, 155, 172, 173, 203, 205
RESURRECTION IS GOAL, 54–64, 83
RESURRECTION IS IN, 154, 172, 177, 234, 235
RESURRECTION IS NEAR, 64–67, 176, 234
RESURRECTION IS NEARNESS TO YAHWEH, 66
RESURRECTION IS RESTORATION TO THE LAND, 54
RESURRECTION IS REVERSAL, 58, 190–92
RESURRECTION IS UP, 46–54, 69–70, 154, 176, 234, 235
RESURRECTION (gestalt), 68–85, 167–71, 230, 233
and baptism. *See* baptism
as consistent with broader Jewish eschatology, 167–71

and contested resurrection texts, 70–72
description of, 68–69
and Josephus, 81–82
and other afterlife beliefs, 70–72, 233
and PATH. *See* PATH (image schema)
and Paul's writings, 72–85
and PROXIMITY. *See* PROXIMITY (image schema)
and VERTICALITY. *See* VERTICALITY (image schema)
REVERSAL (concept), 57–58, 190–92
ritual
as communicative medium, 139–44, 236
and myth, 144
role values. *See* frame structures
scriptures, definition, 45
self-mastery, 150–53, 154–55, 156, 172, 193, 232
and resurrection, 145, 152–53, 154–55, 156, 163, 172, 232
and speech-in-character, 149–50
sexual intercourse, 186–88
Sinai, 194–97. *See also* heavenly ascent
sleep
as metaphor for death, 35–39, 49–52, 70, 84, 230
as metaphor for present living, 205
small caps, use of, 34, 35
SOCIETY IS BODY (metaphor), 183
somatic interior
and glory. *See* glory, mapped to the somatic interior
inner person (ὁ ἔσω ἄνθρωπος), 20, 125, 146, 149, 150, 152, 156–57, 162–63, 172, 198, 200–204, 206–7, 232
inner revelation, 194–99, 210, 211, 223
inner veil, 195–96
history of interpretation, 147–48, 156–57
and resurrection. *See* resurrection, of the somatic interior.

soul
  ancient views on, 14, 21–22, 80–81, 94, 99–101, 147–48, 150–52. *See also* anthropology
  in analytical description, 14, 20, 21
  as embodied, 22, 99, 100–101, 102, 118–19, 150–52
  immortality of, 43
  in Paul's writings, 117–19, 151, 205
  and πνεῦμα, 153–54
  reembodiment of, 80–81, 94, 130
  and resurrection, 21, 117–19, 151–53, 156, 162–63
  and self-mastery, 150–52, 155–56, 162–63
  and trichotomous anthropology, 99–101, 102, 117–18, 150–52, 155–56, 205
SOURCE-PATH-GOAL (image schema). *See* PATH (image schema)
speech-in-character, 149–50
spheres of existence,
  aeonic/cosmic, 16, 17, 31, 158–59, 163, 173, 183, 231
  and intrasomatic polarity, 163
  regarding Adam and Christ, 76–77, 78
Stoicism, 98
Subjectivism, 5, 11
  problems with, 5–6
σὺν Χριστῷ. *See* participation, being with Christ
σῶμα. *See also* body.
  σῶμα πνευματικόν, 20–21, 108, 115–21, 132, 157, 159, 232. *See also* enspirited heavenly/risen body
  σῶμα ψυχικόν, 78, 108, 115–21, 132. *See also* ensouled earthly body
theology
  as disembodied, 1–3, 4, 10, 24, 26
  as embodied, 3, 144–45, 163, 164–71, 229, 237. *See also* metaphor, resurrection as *and* patterns of resurrection embodiment
  as propositional, 1, 2, 4, 24, 26, 27–28

time, 56–57, 154
  in early Pauline interpretation, 234–35
  as linear, 56–57, 169
  as nonlinear and mapped to the human body, 154, 169–71. *See also* already/not yet *and* eschatology
trajectors, 55, 62–63, 74–75, 103–4
  and Adam-Christ typology, 75–77
  determined by IN-OUT concepts, 75
  determined by UP-DOWN concepts, 57–58, 68. *See also* frame structures, protagonists and antagonists
trajectory of transformative embodiment. *See* patterns of resurrection embodiment
transformation, 58–64, 68–70, 77–79, 106–21, 121–32, 142–46, 149–55, 155–63, 188–90, 199–204, 204–7, 218–22, 222–25, 229, 231–32. *See also* CHANGE (gestalt)
  and Adam-Christ typology, 77–79, 96–97, 112
  and baptism. *See* baptism, and transformation
  and clothing metaphor, 90–91, 123–32
  conceptual structures for, 60–63, 103–6
  embodied grounding of, 61–63
  as embodied process, 144–45, 155–63, 169, 172, 188–90, 199–204, 204–7, 218–22, 222–25, 229, 231–32. *See also* patterns of resurrection embodiment
  and heavenly ascent, 90–92, 212–14
  and housing metaphor, 122–23, 126–32
  as part of resurrection process, 58–64, 68–70, 77–79
  and plant metaphor, 106–15
  self-mastery enabled by, 145, 149–55, 156, 163, 172, 232
  of somatic interior, 149–55, 197, 199–204, 231. *See also* resurrection, of the somatic interior.

transformative trajectory, 155–63.
See also patterns of resurrection embodiment
transformative PATH. *See* CHANGE (gestalt) *and* PATH, micro-PATH
unconsciousness,
    definition of, 47
    UNCONSCIOUSNESS IS DOWN (metaphor), 46–50
union, between Christ and believer, 23–24, 175–77, 218–22, 225–26
    as articulation of identity, 29
    as ecstatic experience, 29, 213, 215, 218–22
    and patrilineal genetics, 216–17, 218–22
    and resurrection, 65, 188–90, 218–22, 225–26
    and sexual intercourse, 187–88
UNION (gestalt), 182, 186–88, 231
    embodied grounding, 186–87
    reflected in Paul's participationist ideals, 187–88, 218–22, 225–26
    as togetherness (PROXIMITY), 185–86
    as oneness (CONTAINER), 182–85
UP-DOWN (image schema). *See* VERTICALITY (image schema)
vertical integration, 6–7
    and formative role of culture, 88–89, 213–14
    as methodological apparatus, 7, 177, 212, 214, 236
    and reductionism, 7
VERTICALITY (image schema), 34, 37–39, 46–47
vital relations. *See* conceptual blending theory

www.ingramcontent.com/pod-product-compliance
Lightning Source LLC
Chambersburg PA
CBHW021820300426
44114CB00009BA/249